Hinton Rowan Helper

Oddments of Andean Diplomacy And Other Oddments

Hinton Rowan Helper

Oddments of Andean Diplomacy And Other Oddments

ISBN/EAN: 9783744695343

Printed in Europe, USA, Canada, Australia, Japan

Cover: Foto ©Thomas Meinert / pixelio.de

More available books at **www.hansebooks.com**

ODDMENTS

OF

ANDEAN DIPLOMACY.

ODDMENTS

OF

ANDEAN DIPLOMACY;

AND

OTHER ODDMENTS;

Including a proposition for a Double-Track Steel Railway from the westerly shores of Hudson Bay to the midway margin of the Strait of Magellan; the two terminal points, measured along the line contemplated, being nearly, if not quite, eight thousand miles apart;

Together with an inquiry whether, in view of certain facts of grave international and intercontinental polity and proceedings herein portrayed, the proposed road should not, in all justice and fairness, and in conformity with the highest attributes of republican foresight and vigilance, be deflected so far away from Brazil as to cut her off entirely from its boundless benefits, so long as her antiquated and antagonistic system of government remains imperial or otherwise monarchical.

BY

HINTON ROWAN HELPER;

FORMERLY OF THE BLUE RIDGE REGION;
NOW OF THE MISSISSIPPI VALLEY;

Who has voluntarily and irrevocably emitted from himself, and deposited in the Bank of Commerce, of St. Louis, Missouri, five thousand dollars for five of the best attainable Essays, three in Prose and two in Poetry, in promotion of the immensely needed and matchlessly grand North and Central and South American Longitudinal Railway thus projected.

ST. LOUIS:

W. S. BRYAN, *PUBLISHER*,
602 North Fourth Street.
NEW YORK: CHAS. T. DILLINGHAM, 678 Broadway.
SAN FRANCISCO: A L. BANCROFT & CO., 721 Market Street.
CHICAGO: J. S. GOODMAN, 142 LaSalle Street.
NEW ORLEANS: GEORGE ELLIS, 7 Decatur Street.
1879.

Copyright, 1879, by H. R. HELPER,
ST. LOUIS, MISSOURI.

Rights of translation reserved.

RYAN, JACKS & CO., Printers,
ST. LOUIS.

STRASSBURGER & DRACH, Stereotypers,　　BECKTOLD & Co., Bookbinders,
ST. LOUIS.　　　　　　　　　　　　　　　　ST. LOUIS.

DEDICATION.

NOT at all to the somnolent, short-sighted and shallow-souled subjects of Monarchical Portuguese Brazil,—a country notoriously and disreputably characterized by preternatural retardation and stagnation, because, sadly and strangely enough, even at this late day, it is not yet in accord with the whiter and freer and better ideas and institutions of the New World;

Nor in the least to the bigoted and fanatical adherents of the absurd, befooling and baneful religion of Rome, to which the repeated revolutions and wreck and ruin of so many of the Commonwealths of South and Central America, and the illiteracy and poverty and decadence of Italy, Spain, Portugal, Ireland, Poland, and other Catholic countries of Europe, are in the main attributable; than which body-degrading, mind-debasing and state-destroying system of theology,—an aggregation of odiously false and misleading doctrines, a creed of most insidious and pernicious idolatry, hypocrisy, superstition and knavery,—no formulated or dogmatic religion at all would, as he firmly believes, be far preferable; but

To the more liberal, enlightened and progressive citizens of Republican Spanish America, among whom he has had the good fortune to find the best friend he ever had,— his WIFE,—this book is most respectfully dedicated, with even warmer wishes and purer purposes than he can here adequately express.

H. R. H.

A SINGLE REMARK.

IF by any possibility it be true, as, with a slight tinge of credibility, it was once reported, that there are certain people in this world,—people not generally reckoned in the category of idiots,—who sometimes read the body of a book before perusing even the title-page, the preface, or any other pertinent prefixture, I have to request that no one of them, nor any one else, will ever presume to take such an unwarrantable liberty with this volume; as a perfect knowledge of its preliminaries, as indeed of the preliminaries of every publication, is absolutely essential to a proper understanding of the subsequent portions.

H. R. H.

PREFACE.

This book is put before the public as a special contribution to the general stock of ideas which, auspiciously for the future of the whole western hemisphere, are now beginning to actuate the whiter and higher and better portions of the people of the three Americas, North, Central, and South, who have already come to be affected by a yearning and unyielding desire for an early and everlasting establishment of closer commercial and companionable relations with each other. During more than a dozen years,—counting back from to-day,—while constantly and successfully exercising the utmost care never to say anything in positive explanation of the subject until now, I have been deeply and anxiously impressed with the conviction that the one thing most needed to secure in perpetuity an uncommonly high degree of wellbeing for the inhabitants of all the countries of the New World, is a longitudinal midland double-track steel railway from a point far north in North America to a point far south in South America; it being important, as I think, though not superlatively important, that the line of the road should, in most latitudes, be as nearly as possible equidistant between the Atlantic and Pacific oceans. This is a consideration, however, which may very rightly be influenced and modified by the physical features and characteristics of particular tracts of country through which able engineers will make all necessary surveys and examinations, preparatory to the final selection and location of the route.

Since November, 1866, scarcely one of my wakeful hours has been free from thoughts on the subject of this road; and yet, to a mind of mere mediocrity like my own, the unmeasured dimensions, the curious complications, and the diverse difficulties of the problem, are so formidable and overwhelming, that I am still involved in serious doubt as to the steps which might perhaps be most prudently taken in certain directions. In this dilemma, before attempting to proceed any further with the enterprise on my own account, I have deemed it proper to call to my aid, as will more specifically appear on subsequent pages, the superior wisdom of five of my probably unknown fellow-men, no matter in what part of the universal Republic of Letters they may reside, for whose written facts, arguments, suggestions and sentiments at large, prosaic and poetic, in support and improvement of the plans of the project here presented, I have already had the pleasure of making provision to pay in cash an aggregate of five thousand dollars; a much too meagre sum, which I should most willingly increase twofold at least, so it might be more in harmony with the unequaled greatness and grandeur of the undertaking, but for my financial inability to act herein commensurately with my desires. It is believed, though, that the friendly competitors,—and more especially the successful ones, respectively,—in this literary contest, controlled by a courteous and freehearted spirit of emulation, will be influenced quite as much by the impulses of patriotism, and by the honorable ambition to achieve an intellectual triumph, as by any mere pecuniary consideration.

In addition, however, to the five thousand dollars thus given in lump, I have, with an eye and purpose principally devoted to the prosecution of this design, already expended considerably more than a like sum in the long courses of my two crossings and other trying and tiresome traversings of the continent of South America. As a mere matter of fact, therefore, I may here very properly speak of an actual expenditure, by myself alone, thus far, of from eleven to twelve thousand dollars, as representing to that extent the illimitable degree of hope and confidence which I repose in this grand scheme. Moreover, in this connection, it may not be amiss for me to state, that, down to the present time, I have finished no less than five trips to and from South America since the spring of 1851, when I first went there. That was a trifle more than twenty-eight years ago, and was only a few months after I had attained my majority.

The multifarious and ever-enduring benefits which this road will bring about, on a scale almost inconceivably extensive, will themselves but constantly increase and expand the vast sphere of their own inherent usefulness, and, whether as active or passive sources for good, will forever foster and develop the very weightiest and loftiest interests of mankind, material, mental and moral, sanitary, sacred and sublime. For the perfect unfoldment and preservation of these transcendent interests, there will be a wide and always widening and invariable demand for a much higher order of intelligence than one may ever find emanating from the peurile understanding of little boys, or from the feminine intellectuality of underteen girls; the proper performance of these mighty tasks, alike noble and ennobling, will require nothing less than the virile thought and mature judgment, the robust and rectifying wisdom, of full-grown men.

Every State in South and Central America and Mexico is now sorely afflicted with at least half a dozen overpowering evils, separate or in combination, and yet another, even more sweepingly and perniciously overpowering, afflicts Brazil. These various deadly drawbacks may be grouped and catalogued in the following order:

1. A largely preponderating, idle, vicious and worthless population of negroes, Indians and bi-colored hybrids.

2. The complete, intolerant and fanatical sway of Roman Catholicism, which, when seen and felt and known, as I have seen and felt and known it, on no less than four continents and divers islands of the oceans, but more particularly in South America, where its maleficent mastery is as yet unopposed and undisputed, and where, on the right hand and on the left, before and behind, it brazenly unvails itself in all its naked deformity and dishonor and shamelessness, may very justly be regarded as the meanest and most irrational religion ever recognized by any race of white men, Mormonism and Mohammedanism only excepted.

3. General apathy and improgressiveness, and the very common and calamitous neglect of agricultural, mechanical, manufacturing, and other highly important industrial pursuits, coupled with an almost universal contempt and disdain of every sort of manual labor.

4. Among the masses of the people, unlettered stupidity, excessive thrumming and twanging on the guitar, attuning and tinkletankling on the tambourine, maudlin singing, senseless

and vulgar dancing, fortune-telling, lotteries, gambling, bullfighting, intemperance, licentiousness, social and political depravity, brutal violence, and cruelties and crimes of every class.

5. On the part of a very small but extraordinarily influential minority of the inhabitants, arrogant and aristocratic absolutism, in conjunction with oligarchal and military despotism; and also the outbreak of such frequent, unnecessary and sanguinary revolutions as bring deep and indelible reproach on the true principles of republican institutions.

6. Disregard of the sacredness of individual and official engagements, both verbal and written, and the most scandalous incompetence and malfeasance in public office.

7. Throughout the vast valley of the Amazon, a glamour-glazed, hollow-hearted, meretricious and obstructive monarchy, which, despite all imperial and splenetic denials of the truth, is still banefully black and brown and beggarly with Africans, Indians, mulattoes and other menial and monstrous mongrels; and balefully base and besotted and barbarous with chattel slavery, rigidly and brutally enforced under the thin gauze of delusive laws ostensibly framed for emancipation.

In the direct and indirect influences which will be gradually exerted by the New World longitudinal railway herein proposed, every one of the ponderous and portentious evils thus listed and held up to public reprobation, will be mitigated and lessened; and at least a few of them, it is confidently believed, will be eventually and utterly destroyed. It is true, unfortunately true, that our own country is not entirely free from all the evils thus inveighed against in Spanish and Portuguese America. On the contrary, it must be admitted that many of these evils are indisputably of more than sufficient rifeness and enormity in certain localities not far from us, as, for instance, in such Catholic-cursed cities as New York and Cincinnati, where, with the plottings and prayers and other peculiar practices of the priests, and with the apparent approbation of the prelates and the primates and the popes, power is deliberately placed in the hands of such detestable miscreants as Tweed, Purcell, Sweeney, Barnard, Walsh, Morrissey, and Reilly, and in such wretched and despicable negro or semi-negro States as Mississippi, South Carolina, and Louisiana, as also in portions of Tennessee, where that high and saving degree of moral sense which is always inseparable from honor-affecting rights and obligations, is only half perfect, because the population is only half white. But with us as a nation, such gross immoralities are only spasmodic and exceptional; whereas in all South and Central America and Mexico, as indeed in all Catholic countries, as also in all non-Caucasian countries, they are both regular and general.

But why, if the standard of integrity among the people of this vast southerly region of the Western World is no higher than I have here depicted it, why do I advocate the construction of the longest and the costliest and best railway ever yet devised, expressly as a means and for the purpose of cultivating more amicable and intimate relations with them? Because without the road it is not likely that there will ever be much amendment; and even the little that may be reasonably expected, will be at best only one-sided and slow; but with the road, the opportunities and prospects for mutual improvement will soon become absolutely boundless and interminable. The dwellers in those countries have millions of square miles of fertile lands and precious metals and tropical forests and fruits, and other sources of inexhaustible wealth, the true values of all of which we shall help them to develop, in a cheerful spirit of ready amenability to the great commercial law of demand and supply; and, on the other hand, we shall sell to them, at handsomely remunerative profits to ourselves, tens of thousands of carloads of our surplus manufactures and other merchantable products, which, while fitly affording them all promised gratification, will constantly create within them a craving for still newer and better things, and will thereby, for the first time in their lives, awaken within them the exquisite delights of self-regulated and rightful unrest, activity and achievement.

Journeys of both vocation and recreation southward will be made by countless numbers of our own people at particular seasons; and similar journeys by corresponding numbers of their people will be made northward at certain other seasons; whilst at all times there will be a merry stir and noisy bustle of regular and abundant business. A continuous rush of trade and travel each way, occupying both tracks day and night throughout the year, may be taken into account with quite as much certainty as we may depend on the rising and setting of the sun, or the ebbing and flowing of the tide. At first, as happy results of our uninterrupted and general intercourse with each other, they will be rendered richer in mind and morals, and we shall be rendered richer in money and manners; for it is but frank to state the fact, that the genteel and educated classes of the Spanish Americans,—of course I mean those of them only who are purely white,—are the peers, if not the paragons, of the politest and highest-toned people in the world. They are, besides, possessed of the cardinal virtues in as full degree and practice as the most moral-reputed portion of mankind. By association with this superior class, whose comparative smallness of number is almost the only bad thing about them,—a class, by the way, which, as I have often noticed, one never finds at church, for the very good reason that there is no church among them in any respect worthy of their devotional presence or attention,—we, as well as they, shall be gainers from the very start; and so, each will soon become and forever remain toward the other a respectful and sincere and equal friend, a well-wishing and reciprocal and perfect helper.

This is the class of eminently able and good men in South and Central America and Mexico, which, though numerically weak, yet, being intellectually and morally strong, will most earnestly and efficiently coöperate with us in building the road, and also in effecting every necessary change and reform in other matters. Even now it is possible for them to be of very great service to us; and it may, as I doubt not it will, soon be possible for us to be of corresponding service to them. With much manly and patriotic solicitude for the future welfare of their respective countries, they are now crying aloud to us for help in the strenuous efforts they are making to attain for themselves and for their posterity a civilization less akin to the twelfth century, and more in harmony with the nineteenth. If we do not help them in the sagacious manner suggested by the exigencies of the situation, which ultimately will cost us nothing, but in the end prove of profuse and perpetual advantage to us as well as to themselves, we shall, by such refusal of expedient and friendly assistance, deserve to be roundly censured and execrated by the enlightened judgment of all mankind. Helping them, in conformity with their very reasonable and right request, we shall thereby but simply do our duties to our neighbors and to ourselves; not helping them, we shall be recreant to one of the plainest and brightest duties that ever devolved on a mighty people; a remarkably peculiar and attractive duty, fragrant with dignity and honor for all who engage in it, and dazzlingly lustrous with the fascinating qualities of legitimate self-interest.

In view, however, of a new and very general condition of things hitherto quite uncommon among us, which may possibly come into existence as one of the fortunate results of the leading proposition contained in this book, I here feel it incumbent on myself to place our people vigilantly on their guard against the habitual unfairness and artifice and faithlessness of most of the *governments*, as contradistinguished from the *individuals*, of South and Central America; and I know not how I can more fully or effectually perform this delicate but important task than by submitting for their perusal the two following cases of gross wrong and injury officially perpetrated by Bolivia, on the one hand, against Joseph H. Colton, of Brooklyn, New York, and by Brazil, on the other hand, against Ernest Fiedler, formerly of St. Louis. Missouri, but at the time of Brazil's tortious treatment of him, a resident of the city of New York. Though these cases, as here reported and presented to the Congress of the United States for final redress, are only compendiums or briefs of the cases *in extenso*, yet ample details are given in each suit to show exactly what my readers may expect if they should ever, by any strange misfortune, become creditors of such honorless and blushless and shameless governments as either that of the so-called Republic of Bolivia, or that of the real Empire of Brazil.

The germ, and a very considerable part of the growth of the project of the Three Americas Longitudinal Double-Track Steel Railway, will be found explained,—in so far as explanation was possible and prudent under the circumstances,—in the course of the Fiedler claim against Brazil. It has been more than once intimated, if not positively asserted, that it is an exceedingly difficult task for even the blandest and best-intentioned philanthropist to bless certain needy but idiosyncratic individuals. How much more difficult it has been for me, not being a philanthrophist of any sort, but only an average sort of man, of common sense and common justice, to bless Brazil by well-meant correspondence and interviews with her Emperor Dom Pedro II and the head of his Home Ministry, many of the following pages will plainly attest. My own judgment, whatever may be believed of any other man's, is fallible, and my thoughts may be unusually awry in this case; but it is my candid opinion, nevertheless, that Brazil, as an Empire, has irretrievably lost the opportunity of earning and securing the choicest blessing ever yet placed within her reach; and it may now behoove her, amid the confusion of her great guilt, to avoid, if she can, a blessing's antithesis. It may be, though, and it is by no means improbable, that, as a sort of final issue of this affair, the loss of the Empire will prove the gain of the Republic,—the Republic of Brazil; and if so, both happenings will ultimately afford occasion for the most profound and prolonged rejoicing among all right-thinking and well-acting Americans, whether of South America, of Central America, or of North America. Meanwhile, let the railway of railways be built with such wholesome deflection to the west of the western boundaries of the Empire of Brazil, that all the Spanish-speaking Republics of America, following the example of the United States, shall respectively and speedily become rich, populous and powerful; and then, if not before, the broad valley of the Amazon, and other misgoverned lands adjoining, may be easily reclaimed from the rakish and rickety and rascally and ruinous rule of royalty. Placidly, contentedly, confidently is the Fiedler claim held in abeyance. If not paid in one way, it being just and legal, it must be paid in another. Twice, thrice, ever so many times, has this valid and equitable reclamation been rejected by the Brazilian Empire; it is now preparing to await, if necessary, the action of the Brazilian Republic.

Notwithstanding the astounding prevalence of wrong-doing and wickedness in high and low places throughout all the States of South and Central America, yet in every one of those commonwealths there are tens of thousands of well-informed and upright men,—white men in fact and anti-Catholics at heart,—with whom it will be just as safe to do business as with the very best men in our own or any other country. The more generally and intimately we become acquainted with this conspicuously honorable and excellent class of Spanish Americans, the better we shall like them, and, in all things, the better will it be for both them and us. It is this class whose numbers and powers we must, by extending to them the right hand of good-fellowship, help to increase to such an extent that, in due course of time, they will be enabled to supplant entirely the cumbersomely and worthlessly base and black and brown elements in the vile-visaged and deleterious forms of human rubbish around them. Moreover, it is this very class to whom we must now look for several of the necessary charters and franchises, for the requisite guarantees of interest on capital, and for other proper pledges of practical coöperation, which will make it possible for us soon to evolve into one of the grandest realities of the nineteenth century the idea of a New World Longitudinal Double-Track Steel Railway. So soon as we shall be favored with the vital and indispensable assistance which it is believed the intelligent and enterprising Spanish Americans will promptly render in the premises, let us all go to work at once, and build the road without permitting any one of ourselves to indulge too leisurely a day's absence from labor, until we shall have consummated an undertaking so indubitably essential to the high and perfect civilization of three Americas. H. R. H.

ST. LOUIS, Mo., September 23, 1879.

THE COLTON CLAIM AGAINST BOLIVIA.

ANOTHER MEMORIAL

FROM

JOSEPH H. COLTON, OF NEW YORK, TO THE CONGRESS OF THE UNITED STATES, AGAINST THE GOVERNMENT OF BOLIVIA.

To the Honorable the Senators and Representatives of the United States of America, in Congress Assembled:

GENTLEMEN: Your petitioner, Joseph H. Colton, of New York, through his attorney, Hinton R. Helper, recently of North Carolina, but now of Missouri, had the honor, informally, to submit for your perusal, on the third day of January, 1874, a printed pamphlet, wherein, down to that date, he briefly presented the principal facts relating to a case of most grievous injustice, which the Government of Bolivia has perversely and persistently perpetrated against him during the last twenty-one years. An unusual feature of the pamphlet thus referred to appears in the fact of its having been so guarded and protected by copyright as to prevent the general publicity of any such proceeding or transaction on the part of Bolivia as might prove lastingly humiliating or discreditable to her. To that unique feature of the publication your petitioner respectfully appeals as an undeniable evidence of the fact that no intention has ever been cherished by either himself or his attorney to act toward Bolivia otherwise than in such manner as is compatible with real and considerate friendship, where no sacrifice of justice is required as a condition of good-will. How the delicate regard which thus actuated your petitioner in his always well-meant relations with Bolivia, has been met by her with contumely, and with yet fresher and further manifestations of injustice and injury against both himself and his attorney, will be but too plainly apparent in many of the following pages of this new memorial.

Bolivia does not seem to recognize the principle that the high and exact rules of morality which ought invariably to govern the intercourse of individuals with each other, are also binding upon States; nor does she accept the idea that those same rules are fitly applicable to international relations. Although she herself has been fully recognized by us as a nation in diplomacy, yet she appears to know very little indeed of any code of diplomatic morality. She certainly deserves to be very severely reprimanded and punished for her almost numberless acts of violated faith in this affair. Your petitioner dispassionately challenges her to refute or deny the damnatory accusations and evidences which a long-accumulating and long-urging sense of duty has thus at last impelled him to file against her.

By an honorable and admirable system of arbitration,—though somewhat constrained and extraordinary, yet far less so than war,—the Government of the United States, in 1872, compelled the Government of Great Britain to pay $15,000,000 due by the latter to American citizens. Four years previously, that is to say in 1868, our Government compelled the Fiji Islands to pay $45,000 to citizens of the United States, whose rights of property the unruly and vicious inhabitants of those Islands had grossly outraged. These two nationalities or communities represent respectively the very extremes of aggregated human puissance on the one hand, and impotence on the other. As may be very readily perceived, however, your petitioner's still unsettled claim against Bolivia is not an affair of Strength, nor of Weakness, but simply an affair of Right. It is an affair which very intimately concerns individual truth, national honor, and universal probity.

Justice only is what your petitioner craves ; nor would he ever contend for anything that is not demonstrably due to him in both law and equity. Most respectfully and earnestly does he entreat your honorable body to constrain Bolivia to make just and speedy reparation for the repeated and ruinous wrongs which she has inflicted upon him, and which will be cited somewhat in detail in subsequent portions of this record of her iniquitous conduct. On the sixth day of May, 1874, your petitioner, sorely chafed and oppressed under the burden of increased provocations from Bolivia, formally submitted to your honorable body a protest, a memorial, of which he here feels it alike incumbent on himself and a duty to others, to present to you, at this time and in this form, the following reprint:

Private and Confidential until May 5, 1874.

BOLIVIA,

AS THE

INSIDIOUS AUTHOR

AND

PERSISTENT PERPETRATOR

OF

A New International Crime.

"Ni malas palabras,
Ni buenas acciones."
Extract from an Epigram against Bolivia, by an offended Spanish-speaking German.
(Neither bad words,
Nor good actions.)

For fifteen years, now going on sixteen, Bolivia owes for her National Maps, and always promises to pay for them, but seems secretly determined never to do it.
WILL SHE PAY FOR THEM NOW?

An Appeal to the Congress of the United States for Justice in Behalf of the Claimant, Joseph H. Colton, *by his Attorney,* Hinton Rowan Helper.

———•••———

WASHINGTON,
January 3, 1874.

Not with the intention of selling—for not even so much as a single copy is to be sold at any price whatever—but, on the contrary, as a means of effectually preventing publicity, in exact accordance with the assurances herein given to the Hon. Secretary of State of Bolivia, under date of January 3, 1874, this pamphlet is

Entered according to act of Congress, in the year 1874 (January 3), by HINTON ROWAN HELPER, in the office of the Librarian of Congress at Washington.

A MEMORIAL

FROM

JOSEPH H. COLTON, OF NEW YORK, TO THE CONGRESS OF THE UNITED STATES, AGAINST THE GOVERNMENT OF BOLIVIA.

To the Honorable the Senators and Representatives of the United States of America in Congress Assembled:

GENTLEMEN: At more than seventy-three years of age, baffled and perplexed up to a point of complete discomfiture in a matter of officially-admitted justice due to me, for the last fifteen years, by a foreign government, with which the Government of the United States has long been in amicable diplomatic relations, I respectfully come before you with details and complaints of a series of audacious wrongs, to which I have been again and again subjected under the operations of a new species of international crime, which, in this auspicious era of progressive family-ship and fair-dealing among civilized individuals and nations, could hardly have had its inception or perpetration outside of Bolivia.

During the summer of 1858, two of Bolivia's most able and distinguished military engineers, Colonel Juan Ondarza and Commandant Juan Mariano Mujia, under commission from their government, came and introduced themselves to me, at my place of business, in the city of New York, proposing terms for the engraving and publishing of a large map of the Republic of Bolivia, of which map, in rough outline, they themselves, as army and topographical engineers, of the nation, were the authors. On the 21st of September of the same year, 1858, I acceded to the final terms which they proposed, and, under that date, entered into a written contract with them accordingly.

Under the conditions of that contract, I was to engrave the map artistically and in the best manner, on copper-plate, and was then to print neatly, paste on good canvas, and fit up with mouldings, rollers and rings, ready for suspension against walls, ten thousand copies of the work—a map six feet in length by five feet in height—for the round sum of twenty-five thousand dollars in gold. This was at the rate of only two dollars and fifty cents for each of the said maps; a price, even at that notable time of plenty and cheapness, which was, indeed, but very little above the actual cost of the first rate materials and labor employed by me. The engraving, printing, and publishing of such maps now, maps of the same dimensions, and of equal quality in all respects, would cost very nearly, or quite, one hundred per cent. more.

At one time the Bolivian Government itself, as will be conclusively proved in the course of the following pages, sold two thousand copies of these same maps at twelve dollars per copy, and, at another time, three thousand copies at five dollars per copy; thereby realizing, as proceeds of the sale of only one-half of the edition of the said map, a sum total of thirty-nine thousand dollars, which, as public funds, went into the national treasury. I am also informed, on unquestionable authority, that certain of these said maps of Bolivia, which were taken thence to the Argentine Republic, have been sold in Buenos Ayres, and elsewhere in that Confederation, at the uniform price of twenty dollars in gold per copy.

Accompanying this memorial is a copy of the map in question. Please examine it carefully, and dispose of it in whatever manner you may deem most proper. First the Bolivian Commissioners in New York, and afterward the

Bolivian Government itself, at La Paz, not only approved my work most entirely and heartily, but expressed themselves as highly delighted with the map, and even went so far as to tender me an ostentatious and formal compliment on the skill and success which, as they were pleased to say, I had displayed as an American artisan and map-maker. Those compliments, like many other stupendous monuments in my possession of Bolivian verbosity, have proved to be of the value of a very small fraction of the paper on which they are written.

A part of the foregoing statement of facts is here made in evidence of the additional fact (a fact fit to be held in constant remembrance,) that I did not, either in person or by agent, go to Bolivia soliciting business, but that Bolivia came to me, seeking my skill as an engraver, requesting my services as a publisher, and, by means of false pretenses and fraudulent promises, betraying me into the expenditure of a large portion of my patiently and justly acquired earnings, the accumulations of long years of industry and economy on my part, for the gratification and advantage of herself alone.

Of the twenty-five thousand dollars which the Bolivian Commissioners, acting for their government, were to pay me in this transaction, the sum of two thousand dollars was to be paid on the commencement of the work, and the larger sum, twenty-three thousand dollars, was to be paid on the completion and delivery of the maps, or very soon afterward. The smaller sum here mentioned was paid at the time agreed upon; but the larger sum, being the bulk of the amount due me, has never been paid, not even so much as one cent of it, to this day; notwithstanding the fact that the Bolivian Government has, meanwhile, repeated.y passed acts, resolutions, and decrees, issued orders in council, given scores of presidential assurances, indulged in hundreds of ministerial promises, and dealt out consular and diplomatic pledges without number, and of the most solemn and binding character, all acknowledging the sacredness of Bolivia's purpose and duty to pay the debt, and (in words only, words inflated and befouled with the falsehoods of fifteen years, words, words, words,) defining the ways and means, and declaring the times and places, for a final adjustment of the obligation.

These ever-ready, endless and unfulfilled promises of a nation to pay an eminently just and frequently acknowledged debt—promises which have gradually taken on, since 1858, every phase of official and extra-official solemnity that the vilest stretch of disengenuous diplomacy can possibly apply to any case of debt or credit existing between a government on the one hand and an alien individual on the other—constitute the new crime upon which I thus especially arraign before the highest bar of American justice, and, more generally, before the enlightened public judgment of all mankind, Bolivia, one of the sovereign and independent powers of the earth, a so-called republic, destitute of truth, destitute of honor, destitute of shame, and most conspicuously and painfully destitute of the modicum of merit necessary to entitle her to even the lowest and meanest place among the august family of nations. And for this new species of crime, of which it would appear that Bolivia is alone the execrable author—a crime which she has wilfully and wickedly perpetrated against me times and ways without number, I now, and in this manner, respectfully petition your honorable body for speedy and equitable reparation to myself, and for adequate and condign punishment of the criminal. Other high crimes and misdemeanors frequently and flagrantly committed by Bolivia, to the galling shame of the friends of enlightened self-government, and to the deep disgrace of true republican institutions, and upon which glaringly nefarious acts she ought, in a supreme international court of honor and equity, to be at once indicted and denationalized, will be briefly recorded against her toward the close of this memorial.

The precise measures of redress which I seek, will be found fully and clearly indicated in the following pages, in which the whole case at issue is amply elucidated in the correspondence of my last and present attorney, Mr. Hinton Rowan Helper, who holds full, exclusive and irrevocable powers from me, in this case, and with whom your honorable body, or the Honorable Secretary of State, or other officer or officers of the United States, will please adjust and finally settle and close this matter at the earliest convenient day.

It would be unbecoming and cruel, on my part, to burden the Congress of my country, or any other body of beings, mortal or immortal, with all the letters, notes, memorandums, dispatches, decrees, resolutions, orders and acts, which have had their origin in this case; and of which Bolivia, on her own part especially, has been prolific to a most marvelous and reprehensible extent For the last three years and more, my attorney aforesaid has given close and constant attention, both in Bolivia and out of Bolivia, to my interests in the premises; and from his own voluminous correspondence and papers in this regard (saving myself the labor of going back to cull from the musty archives of a whole decade of antecedent writings,) I have selected the following documents, which constitute a fair *resume* of the entire case; and these documents I thus most repectfully submit for the careful perusal, and for the equitable action, of your honorable body. On the slightest intimation of your desire to examine them, all the papers in the case, from first to last, from 1858 to 1873, inclusive, will at once be laid before you.

SECRETARY FISH TO MR HELPER.

DEPARTMENT OF STATE,
WASHINGTON, *December* 21, 1870.

HINTON ROWAN HELPER, *Esq.*

SIR: I have received your letter of the 19th instant, referring to one from you of the 28th ultimo, soliciting information in regard to the condition of the claim of Mr. Joseph H. Colton against the government of Bolivia, and asking the friendly interposition of this Department in behalf of the claimant.

In reply, I have to state, that the latest information upon the subject is contained in a note from the Minister of Foreign Affairs of Bolivia, under date of the 29th of May, 1869, to Mr. Caldwell, then United States Minister at La Paz, promising that his government will take into serious consideration the claim made by Mr. Colton, and adopt such action as justice shall require.

Pursuant to your request, instructions will be addressed to Mr. Markbreit, the present United States Minister in Bolivia, to renew the friendly offices which have been heretofore exercised with that government in regard to the claim adverted to.

I am, sir, your obedient servant,

HAMILTON FISH.

MR. HELPER TO SECRETARY CORRAL.

SUCRE, BOLIVIA, *November* 1, 1871.

HON. CASIMIRO CORRAL, *Secretary of State for Bolivia.*

SIR: As a citizen of the United States of America, I have the honor to inform you, that I have just arrived within the capital of Bolivia, under full and perfect power of attorney to settle, with the Government of Bolivia, a certain matter of business of long standing, which I will now briefly explain.

In the summer of 1858, there arrived in the city of New York, two experienced and distinguished engineers of Bolivia, Colonel Juan Ondarza and Commandant Juan Mariano Mujia, duly commissioned by the Bolivian Government to procure the engraving and the publishing of ten thousand large maps of the Republic of Bolivia, from rough but careful and correct sketches in manuscript by those gentlemen themselves. On the 21st of September, 1858, more than thirteen years ago, Colonel Ondarza and Commandant Mujia entered into an agreement with Mr. Joseph H. Colton, of New York, one of the most celebrated map-publishers in the world, by which agreement Mr. Colton was to engrave the map faithfully and artistically on a copper-plate, and to publish therefrom (he furnishing all the materials and labor) ten thousand well-finished copies of the same, for the sum of twenty-five thousand dollars of the United States,—a sum equivalent to thirty thousand dollars, more or less, of the Republic of Bolivia. In all respects the work was well executed by Mr. Colton,—the map itself having been one of the finest and best labors of his life,—and not an iota of his part of the contract was left unfulfilled. Of the whole amount stipulated to be paid, the sum of two thousand dollars was advanced; but since then Mr. Colton, greatly to his disappointment and injury, has not received one cent.

It is to the honor of Bolivia that she has always acknowledged her obligation to pay this debt; but mere acknowledgments of obligation, and idle promises to pay, can never compensate Mr. Colton for his very large outlay of money and labor in behalf of Bolivia, thirteen years ago. Indeed, he has assured me that the actual cost to himself of the materials and labor he used, in the publication of the ten thousand maps, without charging anything whatever for his own personal services, was twenty-one thousand dollars in gold. The two thousand dollars paid, deducted from the twenty-one thousand dollars of real, unavoidable expenses, leaves nineteen thousand dollars as the sum in money, in addition to his own personal and valuable services, which Mr. Colton, in that way, advanced to Bolivia so long ago as 1858 ; and, as already remarked in substance, on this large amount, so manifestly due upon the commonest principles of justice and equity, nothing whatever, in the way of interest or otherwise, has ever been paid. Moreover, in addition to the regular and heavy expenses thus incurred, Mr. Colton also paid all the incidental charges for boxing and shipping the maps, and for the marine insurance and freight on them, from New York to Arica, amounting in the aggregate, to something over thirteen hundred dollars ; which, added to the $21,000 already mentioned, makes the sum total of $22,300 as the whole first cost to himself of the various issues of this very unfortunate transaction ; leaving a dead loss, thus far, of $20,300 in gold, as principal, actually paid out for Bolivia, thirteen years ago.

It may, I think, be seriously doubted whether Bolivia may reasonably or rightly expect that an altogether favorable impression will ever be produced on the minds of those who examine her maps—the maps which exhibit her as a part of the world—so long as those maps remain unpaid for. This I say because, having full faith in an invisibly active and augmentative moral influence throughout the universe, I believe that an avenging spirit of justice will, soon or late, and with unerring exactitude and propriety, punish and correct every wrongful act.

On the 20th of September, 1864, President Acha addressed to the Congress of Bolivia a special and patriotic message upon the subject of this debt, eloquently asking for the passage of an act authorizing its speedy payment ; and Congress, responsive to his just and prudent pleadings touching the honor and dignity of Bolivia, passed an act instructing the Secretary of the Treasury to pay the amount then due, including the interest and difference of exchange, which, with the principal, amounted, at that time, to $38,242 in Bolivian money. Yet, as twice remarked already, not one cent has Mr. Colton ever received since the first and only payment—a payment in advance—of only two thousand dollars.

Here follows an extract translated from the well conceived message of President Acha, September 20, 1864, recommending, but recommending in vain, that payment be made:

"The history of this business, the engraving and publishing of the valuable map of Bolivia, by Mr. J. H. Colton, a citizen of the United States, most clearly shows how just the claim is, and how loudly the dignity of the nation calls for its payment. * * * I reiterate my preceding recommendation, and trust that the subject will receive the serious attention of Congress, since, although the Minister of the United States has not given an official character to his request for the satisfaction of this claim, it is none the less the duty of the Republic to preserve its honor, which is now so deeply committed for the payment."

Having thus briefly stated to your Excellency the facts in this case, I beg that you will, in conference with President Morales, seriously consider the sacredness of the obligation involved, and, in recognition of the duty of Bolivia to discharge the debt without further delay, name to me an early day and hour when I may have the honor of calling on you with the view of arriving at a good understanding as to the time and place of full and final payment.

A letter which I have in hand from the Hon. Hamilton Fish, Secretary of State of the United States, referring to another letter from the Department of State at Washington, addressed to the Hon. Leopold Markbreit, United States Minister to Bolivia, bearing upon this same subject, will be submitted to you, when I shall have the honor of calling on you according to your appointment; Mr. Markbreit himself not being in Sucre at this time.

I am, sir, with great respect, your obedient servant,

H. R. HELPER.

SECRETARY CORRAL TO MR. HELPER.

[Translation.]

DEPARTMENT OF GOVERNMENT AND FOREIGN AFFAIRS,
SUCRE, BOLIVIA, *November* 4, 1871.
HINTON ROWAN HELPER, *Esq*.

SIR: I have received your highly esteemed communication of the 1st instant, advising me of your arrival in this city with full powers for prosecuting against this government the claim of Mr. Joseph H. Colton, of New York, for the maps of Bolivia, which were published under the contract with Messrs. Juan Ondarza and Juan Mariano Mujia.

The government finds itself animated by the best desires to satisfy all just demands, and hopes you will adduce the necessary vouchers and accounts, to the end that such equitable action may be taken as will contribute to the interest and credit of the nation.

With this motive, I am much pleased to offer you assurances of the respect and consideration with which

I am your attentive and faithful servant,

CASIMIRO CORRAL.

AFFIDAVIT OF GEN. JUAN MARIANO MUJIA.

[Translation.]

Sucre, Bolivia, *November* 9, 1871.

The citizen Juan Mariano Mujia, of Bolivia, at the suggestion in person of Mr. Hinton Rowan Helper, a citizen of the United States of America, declares and certifies as follows: That on the 8th of March, 1858, a Cabinet Council of the Republic of Bolivia, passed a Supreme Resolution, authorizing the publication of the National Map of Bolivia, then only in rough outline, for account of the nation. In consideration and virtue of that Supreme Resolution, the National Congress, assembled in Cochabamba, passed a law, on the 27th of October, 1864, ordering that payment be made to Mr. Joseph H. Colton, of New York, of the whole amount of his account for the edition of the said map.

The law thus mentioned, in Mr. Colton's favor, was enacted by the Congress of Bolivia, having in full view all the previous papers in the case, including the record of the fact that two thousand copies of the map had already been sold, for account of the Government, at *twelve dollars* per copy, amounting in the aggregate to $24,000, which was then almost sufficient to pay the debt for the whole edition. Afterward, of the eight thousand copies still stored in the Custom-house at Arica, three thousand copies were brought forward, and also sold for account of the Government, at *five dollars* per copy, yielding a gross sum of $15,000, which, added to the other gross sum of $24,000, made a sum total of $39,000, which has been actually paid into the National Treasury of Bolivia, from the sale of only one-half of the said maps; and all this without taking into account other copies since ordered by the Government, and sold at different prices.

By the brief statement I have thus made, the truth of

which statement is in the conscience of all around me, it will be seen that the edition of the Map of Bolivia, because of the money already received for copies sold, can never occasion burden or loss to the National Treasury.

Delay, in the matter of payment, has been caused solely by our political dissensions and civil wars, to which must be attributed the increase, by way of interest, in the amount now due to Mr. Colton, who, on his part, faithfully fulfilled all the conditions of the contract that we, as the representatives of Bolivia, entered into with him, and which said contract has been solemnly recognized and sanctioned by various acts of our National Congress.

Finally, let it suffice to say, that the payment of the claim now made by Mr. Colton's attorney, Mr. Hinton Rowan Helper, than which claim nothing can be more just, will only be complying with the laws of the Republic, and, at the same time, be in harmony with our public faith and our national honor.

JUAN MARIANO MUJIA.

Conformably to the laws of Bolivia, the foregoing affidavit of Gen. Mujia was, on the 14th of November, 1871, duly acknowledged, and sworn to, before Jose Feliz Ona, a Notary Public, and Celedonio Avila, the Prefect of Sucre, otherwise sometimes called Chuquisaca.

H. R. H.

AFFIDAVIT OF COL. JUAN ONDARZA.

[Translation.]

LA PAZ, BOLIVIA, *December* 23, 1871.

The undersigned, Juan Ondarza, Engineer in Chief of the Republic of Bolivia, declares and certifies as follows:

1. That I was one of the original public contractors for

the engraving, publishing and transmission of ten thousand copies of the map of the Republic of Bolivia, which was ordered by the National Government, in Cabinet Council, by decree of March 8, 1858, which commissioned for that purpose the authors themselves of the said map, Juan Mariano Mujia and myself—who were provided with authority, instructions and recommendations the most convenient and ample.

2. That, in virtue of the said decree, authority and instructions, we proceeded to New York, in the United States of America, and there became parties to a solemn agreement in writing with Joseph H. Colton, a citizen of that Republic, who was the proprietor of one of the largest and most reputable map-publishing establishments in that country for the engraving on copper of the said map, and for the publishing and shipping of ten thousand complete copies of the same, (most of them mounted on rollers, but some with flexible seams for folding) for the round sum of twenty-five thousand dollars in gold, which sum the Government of Bolivia was to pay to the said Colton soon after the publication of the map.

3. That the said agreement was approved and accepted by the Government of Bolivia, which obligated itself to pay Mr. Colton the amount stipulated, and to do so within a brief period, as expressed in the peremptory decree of April 21, 1860.

4. That the debt for the maps was again recognized by an Act of the Bolivian Congress in May, 1861, which ordered payment of the money, from that time forward, by installments.

5. That, acting on the last-mentioned law, the administration of President Jose Maria Acha, fixed the sum of eight hundred dollars to be paid monthly out of the public treasury of La Paz, into the hands of the Minister Resident of the United States near the Government of Bolivia.

6. That none of the aforementioned laws or provisions having been carried out, it devolved on the National Congress, assembled in Cochabamba, in October, 1864, to make, and it made accordingly, a new and solemn recognition of the debt; fully guaranteeing the amount due, and ordering it to be paid to the new ministerial representative from the United States, the Hon. Allen A. Hall, who was also the representative of Mr. Colton.

7. That, sad to relate, the law last mentioned was not complied with, because, almost immediately after its enactment, the successful rebellion of Melgarejo caused the trampling out and ignoring of all the preéminent rights and duties of the nation.

8. That, as Chief of the Commission named and delegated to have the Map of Bolivia published, and as a principal author of the said map, I have always endeavored to have our part of the contract made good, having frequently appeared before the Congress and Government of my country, soliciting such effective resolutions and decrees as would lead to the fulfillment in good faith of the sacred obligations resting upon us in this regard, and with which obligations the honor and credit of Bolivia are now so intimately connected.

9. That, with his part of the contract, Mr. Colton observed the most scrupulous and punctual compliance, engraving and publishing, at his place of business, in New York, the ten thousand copies of the map of Bolivia ; and then, as per request and instructions, shipping the same, in boxes, at his own cost, to the port of Arica, subject to the order and disposition of the Bolivian Government ; that, for a long while, most of the said maps were kept in the Customhouse at the said port of Arica ; and that, in conformity with the decree of March 8, 1858, two thousand copies of the said map were delivered to the Government, at La Paz,

by Mr. Mujia, from the proceeds of the sale of which our own account was to have been paid. These two thousand copies of the map were sold at *twelve dollars* per copy, and the money deposited in the National Treasury.

10. That subsequently, in accordance with the law of October, 1864, three thousand other copies of the said map were disposed of by the Government at *five dollars* per copy. The aggregate of the two sums thus actually realized by the Government of Bolivia, from the sale of only five thousand copies of the map, was in excess of the sum total of Mr. Colton's account at that time.

11. That the late Minister Resident of the United States in Bolivia, the Hon. John W. Caldwell, at the instance of his own Government, addressed to our Bolivian Secretary of State, during Melgarejo's administration, an official communication, of the nature of an international question, looking to reclamation in this matter. The communication in question was forwarded to me at Copacabana, where I was then confined in feeble health, asking me for exact information touching all the points of this case; and, on the 19th day of September, 1869, I replied thereto at length, substantially in accordance with these present declarations.

12. In conclusion, having positive and correct knowledge of all the facts of this case from its very incipiency, having been a witness in my own person of the praiseworthy labors and sacrifices of Mr. Colton, who so ably and successfully fulfilled his part of the contract, and who gave his faith and credit to the Government of Bolivia, in the manner here explained, I further declare and certify, that I am aware that the unjustifiable disappointments and delays to which the said Mr. Colton has been subjected from time to time by the said Government of Bolivia, have, more than once, nearly caused his financial ruin, and seriously crippled and retarded him in his business. Wherefore, I now venture to entreat

the exalted sense of equity and duty of the Patriotic President, Gen. Augustine Morales, and of the Illustrious Secretary of State, Dr. Casimiro Corral, in favor of this preëminently just claim, which is now again presented for final settlement by Mr. Colton's new and special attorney, the Hon. Hinton Rowan Helper, a distinguished citizen of the United States, in whose hands I have the honor to place this present synopsis of information and declaration, to the entire truth of which I here give my name in autograph and my word of honor.

JUAN ONDARZA.

On the 27th of December, 1871, the foregoing affidavit of Col. Ondarza was duly acknowledged, and sworn to, in conformity with Bolivian law, before Lorenzo Vargas, a Notary Public, and Uladislao Silva, the Prefect, of La Paz.

H. R. H.

SECRETARY CORRAL TO MR. HELPER.

[Translation.]

DEPARTMENT OF GOVERNMENT AND FOREIGN AFFAIRS,
    LA PAZ, BOLIVIA, *January* 4, 1872.
HINTON ROWAN HELPER, *Esq*.

SIR: I have received, and have submitted to His Excellency, the President of the Republic, your very agreeable communication of yesterday, relative to the claim of Mr. Joseph H. Colton, for the Maps of Bolivia, which were engraved and published in New York.

For the taking of this matter into full and just consideration, nothing else is now necessary than the arrival in this city of the Hon. Leopold Markbreit, Minister Resident of the United States.

So soon as the arrival in question shall have taken place,

the business you have in hand with this Government will be acted upon in conformity with the principles of strict justice.

With this motive, I offer to you the assurances, and especial consideration, with which,

I am your attentive servant,
CASIMIRO CORRAL.

MR. HELPER TO SECRETARY CORRAL.

La Paz, Bolivia, *January* 16, 1872.
Hon. Casimiro Corral, *Secretary of State of Bolivia.*

Sir: In the United States, where, for the last ninety-six years, we have been making steady and auspicious progress toward the true principles of republican government, and toward such condition of things generally as should characterize mankind in the highest and best estate attainable in this life, an Act or a Resolution of Congress is regarded as a proceeding so solemn and binding as to be held sacred. I am somewhat familiar with our Federal Laws (our Statutes at Large), and am not aware that it has ever been necessary for our national legislators to pass more than one Act, or one Resolution, to accomplish a single object.

In Sucre, more than ten weeks ago, just before President Morales and yourself set out on the way from that city to this, I had the honor to acquaint or re-acquaint you fully with the old-standing, long-unsettled business, in connection with your Government, that has brought me to Bolivia, and to solicit your aid in its early and equitable settlement. I am now in La Paz for the same purpose; for the purpose of obtaining payment of the money due Joseph H. Colton, of New York, for ten thousand large maps which he engraved and published of and for the Republic of Bolivia in the year

1858; and considering the extraordinary and important fact that the Bolivian Government has already, by Acts and Resolutions of Congress, and by Presidential Decrees, on no less than five different occasions, ordered payment of the amount due the claimant, I trust that your Excellency will perceive the justice and propriety of closing the case accordingly, without further delay.

In connection with the three letters besides this, which I have already had the honor to address you, the first under date of November 1, 1871, the second dated November 4, 1871, and the third bearing date of January 2, 1872, I now most respectfully submit to you, for your examination, the twelve additional papers herewith inclosed, numbered and described as follows:

No. 1. Memorandum and substance of the Presidential Decree of March 8, 1858, under which decree authority was given to contract for the engraving and publishing of the map.

No. 2. Original agreement between the Bolivian agents and Joseph H. Colton, for the engraving and publishing of ten thousand copies of the map.

No. 3. Printed Solicitation made by Colonel Juan Ondarza and Commandant Juan Mariano Mujia, to the Government of Bolivia, in behalf of Joseph H. Colton, May 23, 1861.

No. 4. Resolution of the Government, May 7, 1860, ordering payment of the amount due the claimant; not paid.

No. 5. Legislative Resolution, August 12, 1861, ordering payment of the amount due the claimant; not paid.

No. 6. Legislative Resolution of July 22, 1863, ordering payment of the amount due the claimant; not paid.

No. 7. Act of Congress, October 27, 1864, ordering payment of the amount due the claimant; not paid.

No. 8. Financial Law and Budget of Bolivia, published

at Cochabamha, in 1865, under Government authority, recognizing (on the last page but one) the obligation of the Republic to pay the debt; not paid. In plain truth, this paper may be said to constitute the sixth (as yet) unfulfilled deliberative promise of the Nation to pay its long-waiting, long-suffering creditor.

No. 9. Statement and Declaration of Col. Juan Ondarza, in favor of Joseph H. Colton, dated at La Paz, December 23, 1871; the same being a concise, terse, and truthful history of the whole case.

No. 10. Statement and Declaration of Commandant Juan Mariano Mujia, in favor of Joseph H. Colton, dated at Sucre, November 9, 1871. This paper, like Col. Ondarza's paper, is historically and statistically valuable, and shows, as Col. Ondarza's paper also shows, that the Government has already received $39,000 from the sale of only one-half of the maps, besides having unsold maps suspended, for general reference, in most of its public offices throughout the Republic. Interest fairly calculated on the amount thus actually received from the sale of only one-half of the maps, and added to the principal, would probably amount to considerably more than the sum total of the claimant's account now awaiting payment.

No. 11. The semi-official newspaper, *La Reforma*, of La Paz, No. 25, June 28, 1871, first page, sixth column, in the course of an article on the finances and liabilities of the nation, mentioning the debt due to Mr. Colton, and twice stating the amount at $56,000, which is considerably more than Mr. Colton claims under the six per cent. agreement. It is understood that this article was written by a gentleman to whom the Bolivian Ministry itself had, two years previously, referred the papers in this case, requesting him to make up the account.

12. Original power of attorney given by Joseph H. Col-

ton, claimant, to Hinton Rowan Helper, to collect from the Government cf Bolivia the money due the said claimant, and to give the said Government a final receipt and acquittance therefor.

I beg that your Excellency will bestow upon these papers the earliest attention that you can conveniently give them, so that I may not be unnecessarily detained here on expenses and loss of time, which would cause an aggravation of a case already too aggravated in certain of its features. My client, Mr. Colton, is now getting to be an old man, at least three score years and ten, and expects soon to be gathered to his fathers. He has more than once feelingly and sadly assured me that, up to the present time, his business relations with Bolivia have caused him more disappointment, vexation and trouble than all the other business relations of his life put together. A timely application of the genuine principles of law and equity in this case, may redeem Bolivia in the estimation of this long-indulgent creditor, this good old man (and of many other right-minded men,) before the final summons shall be received to pass from earth; and that this may be so, I confidently rely on the generally conceded superior morality, prudence and power of your present government.

I remain, sir, most respectfully,
Your Excellency's obedient servant,
H. R. HELPER.

CERTIFICATE OF MINISTER MARKBREIT.

Legation of the United States,
La Paz, *January* 22, 1872.

I hereby certify that, on the 18th instant, I placed in the hands of the Hon. Casimiro Corral, Secretary of State of Bolivia, the original of the foregoing copy, together with the twelve inclosures therein specified.

[L. S.]
L. MARKBREIT,
United States Minister Resident.

DECREE OF THE BOLIVIAN GOVERNMENT.

[Translation.]

MINISTRY OF FINANCE AND INDUSTRY,
LA PAZ, BOLIVIA, *February* 1, 1872.

In view of the contract made in New York, on the 21st of September, 1858, between Joseph H. Colton, of the one part, and Juan Ondarza and Juan Mariano Mujia, of the other part, for the engraving and publishing of ten thousand maps of Bolivia, for the sum of twenty-five thousand dollars in gold; in view also of the decree of March 8, 1858, authorizing the making of the said contract; also the laws of August 12, 1861, and October 27, 1864, which order payment of the sum due the claimant; also the financial law of the Republic for the year 1865, which recognizes the debt, including interest, at the rate of six per cent. per annum, and difference of exchange, in the sum total, at that time, of thirty-eight thousand dollars: It is hereby acknowledged and declared, that the claim now made by Joseph H. Colton, through his attorney, Hinton Rowan Helper, is just, and entitled to preference in payment: In virtue whereof, the Government of Bolivia, desiring to maintain the national credit, recognizes as now due the claimant, by way of principal, interest and difference in exchange, the full sum of fifty-one thousand nine hundred and eighty-five dollars in Bolivian currency, or, as otherwise expressible, the sum of forty-one thousand five hundred and eighty-eight dollars and fifty-four cents in gold, to be paid religiously out of the first funds that are obtained from the loan authorized by the Congress of 1871.

Take notice of this, and pass it to the Director General of Accounts, for the registry of the sum of forty-one thousand five hundred and eighty-eight dollars and fifty-four

cents in gold ($41,588.54,) to be paid to Joseph H. Colton,
Sign-manual of His Excellency,
PRESIDENT MORALES.
By order of His Excellency,
GARCIA,
Secretary of the Treasury.

CERTIFICATE OF MINISTER MARKBREIT.

LEGATION OF THE UNITED STATES,
LA PAZ. BOLIVIA, *February* 6, 1872.

I, the undersigned, United States Minister Resident in Bolivia, do hereby certify, that the foregoing is a true and correct copy of the original decree; which said original decree is deposited in this Legation.

In testimony whereof, I have hereunto set my hand and affixed the seal of this Legation.

[L. S.]
L. MARKBREIT,
United States Minister Resident.

MR. COLTON TO MINISTER MARKBREIT.

NEW YORK, *March* 27, 1872.
HON. L. MARKBREIT,
United States Minister, La Paz, Bolivia.

DEAR SIR: Mr. Helper has returned to this city, and has laid before me numerous papers in relation to my claim against Bolivia, which, after the long period of fourteen years, is, I regret to have to say, still unpaid. However, the Decree passed by the Bolivian Government, on the first day of last month, again recognizing the debt, and promising to pay it, will, I trust, soon be fulfilled, in both letter and spirit, and so bring the case, even though at this late date, to an amicable and satisfactory conclusion.

Among the papers, or copies of papers, submitted to me

by Mr. Helper, is one in the form of an explanatory and defensory supplement to the account rendered by him to the Government of Bolivia in my behalf. In this paper, he shows plainly that, while the legal rate of interest here, where the debt was incurred, and is due, is seven per cent. per annum, he has, with the understanding that the whole amount is to be paid a few months hence, charged Bolivia only six per cent., and that this lower rate of interest, for so long a time, considering the amount of the principal, is much in favor of Bolivia, and against me.

As you are doubtless well aware, it is a universal custom here with the banks and other financial houses, whenever a note or other obligation falls due, and is not paid, to have it renewed in the sum of both the principal and the accrued interest; and thenceforward the obligation draws interest on the whole amount so consolidated. Why, then, should Bolivia, to the detriment of myself, be an exception to this rule? Are nations to be more favored than individuals, and accounted at the same time as less responsible and less honorable? On various occasions, in years past, Bolivia has solemnly promised to pay me a specified sum, as the full amount due me. Suppose she had done so, as, in good faith, she ought to have done, and I had put the money out at simple interest in New York, I would, meanwhile, have been receiving here seven per cent.; whereas, in Bolivia, I am now receiving (if, indeed, I am receiving anything at all, other than plentiful promises) only six per cent. on the original sum of indebtedness.

It would have been both right and proper for Mr. Helper, as my attorney, to have charged seven per cent.; for I myself have had to pay seven per cent., and in some cases considerably more than seven per cent., for money to sustain me in the very business wherein Bolivia, in consequence of having failed to fulfill her equitable obligations, greatly embarrassed and crippled me fourteen years ago. And why, if I may ask, why should I be forced to pay seven per cent., to accommodate Bolivia at six per cent.? I do not say these things in condemnation of Mr. Helper, and certainly not, in any respect, as reflecting upon yourself; for I feel under sincere obligations to both you and him, and am quite disposed to accept, as a final closing up of the whole case, the sum twice mentioned in the last decree, namely, forty-one thousand five hundred and eighty-eight dollars and fifty-four cents, in gold, or its equivalent; and all the more so, as I am informed by Mr. Helper that President Morales and Secretary Corral both assured you that the whole amount should be paid within "about four months" from the date of the said decree.

When I tell you, as I may with all candor and truth, and with no small degree of unavoidable vexation and sadness on my own part, that the high rates of interest which I have had to pay for money, the execution and verification of legal papers, the salaries and fees of agents and attorneys, and other expenses attending my fourteen years' unavailing efforts to obtain justice from Bolivia, have amounted, and will amount, by the time I get through with the case, even if at once closed up in accordance with the last decree, to considerably more than one-half of the whole amount mentioned therein, you will readily understand with what grace and justice, (or rather with what lack of grace and justice,) Bolivia can still withhold from me the money so long and so manifestly overdue. Thus, as you will perceive, no matter how soon I may receive the amount, the whole amount mentioned in the last decree, I shall, in fact, as for myself, be the recipient of less than fifty per cent. of the entire sum. Transactions of this kind, where, in reality, the extraordinary delays, inconveniences and costs of the collection of just debts are so great as to practically reduce the amount to less than one-half the sum due in equity, may or may not, require comment as against the delinquent party, but I am deeply impressed with the conviction that it is impossible for the injured party to forget them.

In conclusion, permit me to request that you will be so kind as to state to President Morales and Minister Corral the substance of this letter, and solicit from them, without further delay, an order on the bankers in London, who hold the funds out of which my long-deferred claim is to be paid, an order in form and substance similar to the one herewith inclosed, and which is, for the most part, a copy of a proposed order which I have found among the several papers submitted to me by Mr. Helper. The debt paid in this manner will at least save me from still further loss by way of exchange, or otherwise; and, in view of the foregoing statement of facts, I am sure that your own quick and correct sense of honorable dealings as between man and man, or as between men and governments, will recognize the perfect reasonableness of my request.

I am, dear sir, yours, very truly,
JOSEPH H. COLTON.

MINISTER MARKBREIT TO MR. HELPER.

LA PAZ, BOLIVIA, *March* 31, 1872.
HON. HINTON ROWAN HELPER.

MY DEAR SIR: I have the pleasure to acknowledge receipt of your favors written from Arequipa, Lima and Panama, and was glad to know that, on the 5th instant, you had arrived safely at the latter place. Mr. Colton's prospects are *good*. The Church loan seems to be almost certain of success. Just so soon as I learn that the loan has been realized, I shall insist upon this government giving me

a draft for the entire amount of the claim, upon Messrs. Lumb, Wanklyn & Co., or rather, upon General Campero, the Bolivian Minister. I shall know in less than one month. Excuse haste.. With kindest regards,
I am, your friend,
L. MARKBREIT.

SECRETARY CORRAL TO MINISTER MARBREIT.

[Translation.]

DEPARTMENT OF GOVERNMENT AND FOREIGN AFFAIRS,
LA PAZ, BOLIVIA, *June* 1, 1872.
HON. LEOPOLD MARKBREIT, *United States Minister Resident.*

SIR: With your pleasing communication of yesterday, I have received Mr. Colton's letter to you, from New York in which he expresses his thanks to the National Government for the decree of the 1st of February, which ordered payment of the amount due him for ten thousand maps of this republic; asking at the same time, payment by draft in his favor, against Messrs Lumb, Wanklyn & Co., negotiators of the Bolivian Loan in London.

So soon as we shall have received a full statement in regard to the said loan, the draft asked for will be given, as the National Government is interested that payment of Mr. Colton's claim be made, with preference, as soon as possible.
With this motive, I have the honor to subscribe myself,
Your most attentive and faithful servant,
CASIMIRO CORRAL.

MINISTER MARKBREIT TO MR. HELPER.

LA PAZ, BOLIVIA, *June* 4, 1872.
MY DEAR MR. HELPER: I wrote you last on the 28th

ultimo. I now transmit to you a note from Dr. Corral, in answer to one from me, relative to the Colton claim. I think it will prove satisfactory, for in it they promise to give a draft for the amount due, on Messrs. Lumb, Wanklyn & Co., as soon as they can ascertain the amount of their credit. You may believe me when I tell you that I shall not rest till they pay up. What if they decline to pay interest from the date of the decree? Should I, in that case, refuse to receive the draft? Send me instructions on this point. Congress will meet here. I don't send copy of my note to Mr. Colton, for want of time.

Your Friend,
L. MARKBREIT.

MR. HELPER (FOR MR. COLTON) TO MINISTER MARKBREIT.

NEW YORK, June 14, 1872

HON. LEOPOLD MARKBREIT,
    U. S. Minister, La Paz, Bolivia.

SIR: One of the ablest writers of antiquity, well known and deservedly honored in Hebrew literature, has assured us that there is a time for everything; and if that assurance be true, then there is a time when nations, like individuals, should pay for their maps. At any rate, there is a time, now near at hand, when I, as an individual, am either to receive from the Republic of Bolivia, pay for the maps which I engraved and published for her, fourteen years ago, or shall have to relinquish, at once and forever, all faith in the integrity of her purposes and promises.

You are aware that both President Morales and Secretary Corral assured you that the last decree of the Bolivian Government issued in my favor, under date of February 1, 1872, should certainly be made good, in all its provisions, within about four months from that time; but the four months mentioned, and half a month more, are now up and gone, and I am still suffering the injustice of the inconvenience and burdens of the interminable delays of a faithless debtor. Under these circumstances, I will be as brief and pointed as possible in stating the final determination to which I have come. It is as follows:

1. If the whole amount of $41,588.54, in gold, due me according to the terms of the decree of the first of last February, be not paid by or before the last day of next September, I shall, on the day following, submit all the papers in the case to our Department of State at Washington, and will solicit the Honorable Secretary of State to collect the money for me, including the large additional costs and charges, which are just and legal, but of which I shall never make any account whatever, provided the amount mentioned in the said decree, and now overdue, be paid by or before the 30th day of next September.

2. Immediately after the meeting of our Congress, early in December of the present year, I shall, if my claim be still unsettled, submit to that honorable body, copies of all the correspondence and papers in the case, earnestly petitioning that a war vessel, or two or more such vessels, if necessary, be dispatched to Cobija, or to Mejillones, for the collection of the money, and that Bolivia be required to pay, besides the increased amount that will be found to be justly due me, all expenses of the naval expedition. I am well aware of the great gravity of these words, and of the peculiar positiveness of their import in this connection; having calmly deliberated with myself, and dispassionately advised with others, before determining on this outline of proceeding as a course of action to be followed. No other recourse is left me. I must do this or do nothing. My own sense of equity, linked with a

sense of duty, tells me, that, in the contingency alluded to, it will be eminently right and proper for me to make the petition thus contemplated; and if it does, indeed, become right and dutiful on my part to make the petition, then, as a moral sequence, it will be but right and dutiful on the part of Congress to grant it.

3. In the event that, in a last effort to obtain my rights in this case, it shall become necessary for me to pursue the course here foreshadowed, I shall take occasion to urge upon our Government the very serious consideration of the question, whether a nationality that is either too dishonest or too poor to pay for its maps, is, in any respect, worthy of a place among the family of nations? Taking the negative of this question, I shall, with such humble ability as I possess, endeavor to prove that Bolivia, having, for the full period of fourteen years, been either too dishonest or too poor to pay for her maps, is no longer worthy of recognition as a distinct nationality.

4. Well justified and strongly fortified as I feel I shall be in the position thus assumed, I shall argue further, that it is derogatory to the dignity of the United States to maintain a Minister or even a Consul, within the limits of such a self-exhausted and disreputable community as Bolivia; and will further give it as my opinion, with reasons in detail, that all honorable nationalities should at once withdraw from that unworthy country every system and grade of international intercourse, and not only permit, but effectually encourage, the speedy and complete absorption of Bolivia by one or more of the contiguous Commonwealths; in other words, that Bolivia must immediately conform her conduct to a higher standard of honesty and truth and dignity, or be forever ignored and blotted out from the family of nations, and her territory and obligations allowed to lapse to one or more of the abler and better conterminous States,—to Peru,

to Chili, or to the Argentine Republic; or to any two or to all, of those neighboring nationalities.

Inclosed herewith you will find a copy of this communication, which, in the event that the money so long overdue is still withheld, and in the further event that you deem it right and proper that the Government to which you are accredited should be advised, in ample time, of this determination on my part, you will please transmit to the Honorable Secretary of State of Bolivia.

I have the honor to be,
    Very respectfully, your obedient servant,
            JOSEPH H. COLTON.
        By his Attorney:
            HINTON R. HELPER.

MINISTER MARKBREIT TO MR. HELPER.

LA PAZ, BOLIVIA, *July* 3, 1872.

MY DEAR MR. HELPER: I am in receipt of your letter dated June 14, and, in reply, beg to say that *if you and Mr. Colton will only have a little more patience, I will insure you the full payment of the latter's claim before the next meeting of our Congress.* You will gain nothing by threats; while I have the firm conviction that I can collect every cent of your claim, if you will only leave the management of the matter to me. Excuse the brevity of this note, but I am exceedingly occupied to-day in making preparations for a grand dinner, which I intend to give to-morrow. Keep cool, my dear Mr. Helper, and I give you my word that I shall see that justice is done Mr. Colton.

    Truly yours,
            L. MARKBREIT.

MR. HELPER TO MINISTER MARKBREIT.

NEW YORK, *August* 7, 1872.

HON. LEOPOLD MARKBREIT,

United States Minister, La Paz, Bolivia.

DEAR SIR: Your letter of the 3d of July is before me. Let us reason together. After Mr. Colton, with the faith of an Abraham and the patience of a Job, had waited nearly fourteen long years for Bolivia to keep just one of the numerous official promises in the form of decrees, resolutions and orders, which at various intervals during that period, she has issued in his behalf, as so many tokens of her intention to pay him for ten thousand large maps, which he engraved and published for her in 1858, it became but too evident that she was only trifling with him. Congressional acts, legislative orders, government decrees, presidential promises, ministerial pledges, diplomatic guarantees, and consular assurances, have again and again been given with a readiness and redundance that might have been honorable, but for their uniform disingenuity and non-fulfillment.

Meanwhile, as stated in his letter to you, under date of the 27th of March, Mr. Colton, in his long series of efforts to obtain at least an approximation to justice in this case, has already been put to the enormous expense of more than one-half of the whole amount mentioned in the last Bolivian decree. Are these proceedings on the part of Bolivia to be taken as examples of the honor and justice of certain newly-organized nationalities in the nineteenth century? and are these the inklings and rules of morality that those nationalities would teach their citizens? If so, the sooner such nationalities cease to exist as sovereign states, the better will it be for mankind, and for the world at large.

When, at great disadvantage to Mr. Colton, and no little peril and expense to myself, I went personally to Bolivia, last year, it was to make a *final* effort to obtain the money due on this eminently just and long-pending claim. President Morales and Secretary Corral both said yes, and proposed another decree, as if, forsooth, the claimant had not already, for nearly half a generation, been gorged and surfeited and nauseated on such worthless papers. Bolivia's previous and frequent disregard of the sacredness of such obligations had naturally filled me with distrust; yet, in deference to your opinion and advice, I accepted the proffered document; with the distinct understanding, however, that the money should be forthcoming in the matter of about four months from the first of February, which would bring the time of maturity down to about the first of June.

It is now August, 1872; the money, due since 1858, has not been paid; a youthful nation still owes an elderly individual an old debt for its maps; it is a debt of fourteen years' standing; the creditor, an aged man, now in his 73d year, has waited and waited, respectfully and patiently, almost to the end of his days; and yet the debtor, one of the distinct governing powers of the earth, has the hardihood, not to say shamelessness, to ask for a longer indulgence of time. I will not here protest that this request comes accompanied by circumstances which would warrant the inference that, in the estimation of Bolivia, Mr. Colton is now in his dotage, or that he has become wholly oblivious to those priceless sentiments of self-respect and manhood which are so peculiarly characteristic of almost every American citizen; but this I will say, that it is the direct cause of a provocation that would seem to justify the use of words far more forcible and scathing than complimentary; but I will forbear.

In the plenitude of your faith in Bolivia's integrity, as I learn from your note of the 3d of July, you kindly speak for her as follows: "If you and Mr. Colton will only have a little more patience, I will insure you the full amount of the latter's claim before the next meeting of our Congress." To which, in addition to what I have already said above, I have simply to reply, that Mr. Colton and I, again deferring to your wishes and advice (and on your account alone,) have concluded to hold everything in suspense, and will wait, if necessary, until the next meeting of our Congress; but under no consideration whatever will we wait one day or one hour longer, except as formal and public petitioners to the government of the United States for the righting of this gross, musty, and cruel wrong; a wrong with which we, as mere individuals, endowed with but a single life-time, and not gifted with the strength of a Samson or the longevity of a Methuselah, feel we have no power to cope.

I am, dear sir, very respectfully, your friend and servant,

H. R. HELPER.

MR. HELPER TO MINISTER MARKBREIT.

NEW YORK, *August* 19, 1872.

HON. LEOPOLD MARKBREIT,

United States Minister, La Paz, Bolivia.

DEAR SIR: With all our Ministers to Bolivia, except yourself, since the Colton claim fell due, fourteen years ago, Bolivia has played fast and loose, and has adroitly succeeded in making them, each in his term, believe fib after fib, and falsehood after falsehood, until from some cause or other, their terms of office were respectively up, when the spell would be broken, and they would at last awaken to the sorry fact that they had, all the while, allowed themselves to be most craftily and egregiously duped. That Bolivia is now boldly presuming to play this same low and dishonest trick upon you also, is, to me, as unwelcomely apparent as is the most brazen-faced embodiment of vice that struts the streets. But I have great confidence that you will not suffer yourself to be so ungraciously and pitiably deceived by her; albeit the false promise she gave you that she would pay the Colton money in "the matter of about four months" from the first of February last, is still unfulfilled, after the lapse of more than half a year. Indeed, I shall not, for one moment, permit myself to doubt that you will find a way to vindicate your dignity, both as a man and as a minister, and, of course, you are much better qualified than I am to judge how far, if at all, you should consider, as entailed upon yourself, the many indignities of chicanery and untruth which have been so long and so often manifested by Bolivia toward at least three or four of your most immediate predecessors at La Paz.

There are some cases of shortcomings, and failures, and forfeitures of word, of such frequent and indefensible repetition, that, as it seems to me, there should be given, from a specified date to a specified date, but one further extension of credence; and, in my judgment, Bolivia was clearly a case of this kind, when, after fourteen years' practice of the most unblushing Machiavelism, she promised, on the first of February last, as she had similarly promised for the thousandth time, more or less, that she would pay the Colton money in "the matter of about four months."

What can be fairer than that this particular act of bad faith on the part of Bolivia, should be charged against her, not as a single act, but as an act in addition to numerous others, equally bad, which she has artfully and meanly perpetrated during the last fourteen years? And what possible fitness or propriety is there in our maintaining, at a high salary, a Minister at the capital of a nation possessed of so little sense of justice, truth, or honor? Or rather, what rational excuse can be given for thus belittling and degrading the improved and elevated system of American diplomacy which has its fountain-head at Washington?

You will remember with what reluctance I accepted Bolivia's last Colton decree, hardly believing it of more value than its weight in chaff, so far as it represented any honest purpose on the part of its authors. But on your assurance that you thought they really did mean to pay, and would do so, as they promised, in " the matter of about four months," I deferred to your views and wishes, and left the case in your hands, formally requesting you, in the power of attorney which I executed to you, on the 7th of February, to collect the money and transmit it here to Mr. Colton. According to the written and verbal provisions and conditions of this last decree, the money should have been paid about the first of June. In a mood of excessive liberality, under the circumstances, I only insisted that payment should be made not later than the 30th of September. You now ask for Bolivia, that the time be extended to the first of December. Be it so. Herewith, under date of the 7th instant, you have my letter, signed both by Mr. Colton and myself, comp., ing with your request.

Mr. Colton earnestly hopes that he may not be wearied nor worried in this matter with any more despicable devices, flagrant insincerities, nor unconscionable postponements. For such limitless stratagems and circumventions on the part of a nation, he feels that the life of an individual is too short, especially when, as in his own case, more than seventy-two years have already passed. He wants justice from Bolivia; he wants it now; he has been waiting for it fourteen years; he wants the money due him since 1858. Henceforth any and every letter from Bolivia that fails to bring the money will prove unsatisfactory. What reassurance can you give that this claim will be certainly and finally settled by the time you mention, or that in fact, without an appeal to force of some sort against

Bolivia, it is now any nearer adjustment than it was fourteen years ago? Please give me full and explicit information in this regard, so that I may know, in good time, whether or not it will be necessary for me to prepare a memorial on the subject for the action of our Congress in December.

I am, dear sir, very respectfully, your friend and servant,

H. R. HELPER.

MINISTER MARKBREIT TO SECRETARY CORRAL.

[Unofficial and Private.]

LA PAZ, BOLIVIA, *October* 17, 1872.

To His Excellency, Casimiro Corral, &c., &c.

ESTEEMED SIR AND FRIEND: By this mail I have received letters from Mr. Joseph H. Colton, of New York, in which he says that, not having received payment of his claim against Bolivia, he has determined to present to the Congress of the United States, which will assemble on the second of December, a memorial petitioning for the active intervention of that government in his favor. I permit myself to communicate to you the intentions of Mr. Colton, because to me it would be extremely disagreeable if he should, indeed, carry out those intentions; believing as I do that it would operate much to the discredit of Bolivia to have the case taken up before our Congress; and with these views, I submit whether it may not be better to adopt measures to satisfy the just claim of Mr. Colton. If this gentleman is now impatient, he is hardly to be wondered at, or blamed, seeing that fourteen years have passed since he has been waiting to be paid. Up to this date, the total amount of the claim is $42,648.39 in gold.

Of good disposition toward your Excellency,

I am your attentive friend,

L. MARKBREIT.

SECRETARY CORRAL TO MINISTER MARKBREIT.

[Translation.]

LA PAZ, BOLIVIA, *October* 17, 1872.
TO MR. LEOPOLD MARKBREIT, *Etc.*

DISTINGUISHED AND ESTIMABLE FRIEND: At this very moment I have received your valued letter of to-day, in which you acknowledge receipt of communications from Mr. Joseph H. Colton.

I am very sorry that the gentleman intends to present a memorial to the Congress of the United States.

Be you persuaded and assured that the Government of Bolivia knows how to regard its obligations touching this just and legal claim, after having acknowledged the debt, and pledged its honor to pay it with preference. Consequently the time is not distant when the sum of the indebtedness can be raised; and for this reason I do not think it necessary that Mr. Colton should resort to the extreme measures which he seems to contemplate.

Having thus answered your esteemed favor of to-day, I have the pleasure to subscribe myself,
   Your attentive friend and faithful servant,
                                        C. CORRAL.

MR. HELPER TO MINISTER CROXTON.

NEW YORK, *February* 13, 1873.
HON. JOHN T. CROXTON,
   United States Minister to Bolivia.

SIR: After an unaccountable detention of nearly two weeks in Washington, your note of the 30th ultimo has been forwarded to me at New York. I went to Washington, some weeks ago, with the intention of laying before Congress a memorial, publicly petitioning that honorable and supreme body, for the abolition of our mission to Bolivia, and for the forcible collection, by the Navy of the United States, of a somewhat ancient but eminently just debt, due for the last fourteen years and more, from the Government of Bolivia to Mr. Joseph H. Colton, of this city. But having promised our present minister at La Paz, Mr. Markbreit, that I would take no positive step in that direction before about the 15th of January, I found, after consultation with several Senators and Representatives, that no final action could be had on the case during the few weeks that then remained of the present short session of Congress.

Meanwhile, I conferred with Secretary Fish also, who kindly assured me, that, if I desired and requested it, he would, in the event of my not laying the case before Congress at this session, urge the matter a little stronger with our Minister to Bolivia. Under these circumstances, I concluded to withhold the case entirely from Congress, for the present, and to make one more earnest effort to obtain justice privately and peaceably. That effort, in connection with my own individual and independent efforts, I am now making through the Hon. Secretary of State, Mr. Fish, whose predecessors in the State Department, for many years past, also gave, from time to time, more or less attention to the case.

In accordance with the suggestions of some of my friends in Congress, it is my intention, as attorney for the claimant, soon to communicate directly with the Bolivian Secretary of State on this subject, copies of which communication will be duly transmitted to both Secretary Fish and yourself; and after I shall have so communicated, there will probably remain very little, if anything, for you to do; and, perhaps, little or nothing for you to do before then. About this, however, I shall know better after I shall have had the pleasure of an interview with you. When will you arrive in New York, on your way to Bolivia, and at what hotel will you stop in this city? Any information that I may be able to give you in regard to your necessary outfits for sea and land (for you will need one particular outfit for your ocean passage, and another for your mountain journey,) will be given most cheerfully.

Yours, very respectfully,

H. R. HELPER.

MR. HELPER (FOR MR. COLTON) TO THE HON. SECRETARY OF STATE OF BOLIVIA.

NEW YORK, *February* 15, 1873.

To the Honorable the Secretary of State
of the Republic of Bolivia.

SIR: Of equal significance with this letter itself, is the inclosure herewith, to which your attention is respectfully invited. This inclosure is substantially a copy of a communication which I addressed to Minister Markbreit, under date of the 14th of June last, stating to him, that the money so long overdue from the Government of Bolivia to Joseph H. Colton, of this city, must be paid by the 30th of September following, or, in the event of non-payment, specific complaint of Bolivia's many acts of bad faith in the matter would then be made by me to my own Government, at Washington, and an earnest petition presented thereto, for an early redress of the gross and multitudinous wrongs to which I have herein been subjected during the last fourteen years. In reply to my particular communication to Mr. Markbreit, of which the inclosed paper of the 14th of last June is a copy, he said he could not, consistently with his diplomatic duties and responsibilities, lay that communication before the Bolivian Government; but, instead of serving me and furthering the ends of justice in the manner I suggested, he took it upon himself, in effect, if not in purpose, to serve Bolivia, and perpetuate and augment an already overgrown iniquity by using to me, in July last, these suasive and delusive words:

"If you and Mr. Colton will only have a little more patience, I will insure you the full payment of his claim against Bolivia before the next meeting of our Congress."

Deceived by the foregoing false promise, as I had already been deceived time and again, year in and year out, by other false promises, I waited until the first of last December, and even then, considering it possible that Minister Markbreit meant to assure me that it was at La Paz, and not in New York, that the money was to be paid "before the next meeting of our Congress," I advised him of the quandary that had arisen in my mind on the subject of the particular time and place of payment promised, and informed him that I would, as an additional proof of my patience and forbearance, give Bolivia the benefit of the doubt, and not take any decisive action against her until he could be heard from in reply, or until sufficient time had elapsed for me to hear from him in. that regard. As yet he has made no reply whatever, and, strange enough, too strange, indeed, I have not received a line from him since the 20th of October, a blank interval as from him to me of nearly four months. Nevertheless, that engagement on my part restrained me in honor from any earnest effort to induce Congressional intervention in my behalf until about the 15th of January, a month past, when, on consultation with a number of our Senators and Representatives at Washington, I was informed that the present short session of Congress was then already too far spent to admit of a careful consideration of the case, and final action upon it, before the 4th of next month, March, when the session will expire.

Cheated thus out of one-half of the present session of Congress, and assured that the period of the other half was, notwithstanding the justice of my cause, too limited for me to obtain the important legislation I desired, I concluded, on further consultation with Senators and Representatives, not to press the matter any further in that way for the present, but to afford Bolivia, as I now do by this writing, one more generous opportunity to liquidate the debt in graceful compliance with the behests of amity and equity. If, as is but too true, there have been a thousand such opportunities afforded heretofore, not one of which has ever been honored with just recognition, please consider the number now a thousand and one, and this one the last.

Having submitted to you the foregoing paragraphs of information and explanation, I now deem it proper to lay before you the most essential part of this communication; and I do so, respectfully, by giving you the additional information that, unless the whole amount of the money so long overdue to me from Bolivia shall be paid to me here in New York by or before the 15th of next August, I shall immediately thereafter publish all the principal facts of the case in pamphlet form, and will send the same to every one of our own Senators and Representatives, to our President, and to each of the members of his Cabinet; and also to all the Governments of Europe and South America; and to the leading newspapers of the world. I shall also, in the event of not receiving payment within the period of the six months thus given, take, or cause to be taken, so far as I can, all the compulsory measures against Bolivia which I have mentioned in the inclosure herewith.

It is true that our Congress will not meet again until the

first Monday in next December, but I will not wait till then; for, having already been beguiled into waiting nearly half a generation, it now behooves me to be more mindful of my own rights, and of the solemn duties I owe to my creditors, to my family, and to myself. Hence my desire and purpose to impart to our Senators and Representatives a full and true knowledge of the facts of the case in advance of their assembling in Washington, so that intelligent and warrantable action may be taken by them early in the ensuing session.

You will observe that, in the foregoing remarks, which are already more copious than I intended to make when I began this letter, I have said nothing in detail of the numerous deceptions and chicaneries that have been practised by Bolivia since 1858 to reduce and belittle (by allowing only unusually low, less than legal, rates of interest and otherwise,) the amount lawfully due me, nor of the innumerable hollow promises and heartless delays that have caused me so much labor and loss of time, and an expense, up to this present moment, of more than twenty-six thousand dollars in gold, in unavailing efforts to collect the sum which Bolivia so justly owes me, and which should have been paid to me many, many years ago, without subjecting me to any expense whatever; but, the facts here alluded to will form a part of my printed complaint to our Congress at Washington—if indeed I am eventually forced to make such complaint—and I shall then and there ask to be indemnified accordingly.

Yet I hope you will not, by inflicting upon me the glaring injustice of still further delays and disappointments, render it necessary for me to take the decisive step here foreshadowed. By or about or before the 1st of July, send to me in duplicate (the first by one mail and the second by another, payable to the order of Joseph H. Colton, No. 80 Broadway, New York,) a draft for the full amount due me according to the last Bolivian decree, dated February 1, 1872, and all will be well. Such a draft shall itself be your voucher of complete and final discharge from all indebtedness in the premises; but, if you desire it, the Minister of the United States to Bolivia is hereby authorized and requested to execute to you any additional release of the obligation that you may require, and his writing of release so executed shall be as absolutely good and binding against me as if the same were executed by myself in person. Let it be distinctly understood, however, that the functions and privileges of the said Minister are hereby limited in time, in this case, to the 15th of July at furthest, as that is the very latest date from which a letter posted at La Paz can reach New York by the 15th of August, after which particular time I am firmly resolved not to wait on Bolivia one day longer, save only as I may have to do so in awaiting equitable action against her in my favor by the Congress of the United States.

Both the Government and the people of the United States are devotedly wedded to the principles of peace and good will toward others; they are also strongly attached to the principles of honor and justice toward themselves; but it is possible to offend them by subjecting them, for the full period of fourteen years on a stretch, to the endurance of a series of chafing and conspicuous wrongs; and, once offended in that way, they are apt to seek, and not unapt to obtain, redress for all the outrages so perpetrated against them.

There is now on file, in the American Legation at La Paz a large number of elaborate documents bearing on this case, and although it may not now be necessary for you to examine any one of them (it being only necessary for Bolivia to pay the money so many years overdue to me,) yet I should be glad if our Minister there would, on your request, lay before you for your perusal my letters to him under these several dates in 1872: March 27, March 29, June 14, July 29, August 7, August 19, September 9, and October 19; also my last communication immediately preceding the issue of the last Bolivian decree to Secretary Corral, January 16, 1872, and the affidavits of Colonel Juan Ondarza, December 23, 1871, and General Juan Mariano Mujia, November 14, 1871; also my letter to our new Minister, General Croxton, February 13, 1873. (General Croxton, still here, will soon take the place of Mr. Markbreit, who has been recalled.)

These several papers are fair samples of those which, with the Bolivia-Colton decrees themselves, will constitute my indictment against the Government and nationality of your country, and it is for you and the other gentlemen associated with you in the guardianship of your Republic to decide whether or not Bolivia — faithless Bolivia, long-delinquent Bolivia — can afford to provoke into action the grave proceedings thus contemplated.

Herein my work is done; my word is spoken; I have nothing more to say. Nor will I again suffer myself to be drawn into further barren correspondence with Bolivia, or with any one in Bolivia, on this subject. If any new attempts be made in this case to kill more time by useless inquiries, ambiguous statements, disingenuous promises, or Machiavelian propositions—such as have already occasioned me so much sad and ruinous expense in years and years gone by—I shall meet those attempts only by sending in reply a copy of this communication with its inclosure; copies of both of which papers I shall, within a fortnight from to-day, transmit to the honorable Secretary of State at Washington, and to the United States Minister to Bolivia, respectively. Duplicates of the same papers will also be forwarded to you in due time.

I am, sir, very respectfully, your obedient servant,

JOSEPH H. COLTON.
By his Attorney:
HINTON R. HELPER.

MR. HELPER TO PRESIDENT FRIAS.

[Private Note.]

NEW YORK, *February* 15, 1873.
To His Excellency, the HON. THOMAS FRIAS,
President of Bolivia.

MY DEAR SIR: It grieves me exceedingly that duty and justice to my much-worried and much-wronged client, Mr. Colton (now nearly seventy-three years of age,) have at last constrained me to adopt the most specific and stringent measures for bringing this very just and officially recognized claim against Bolivia, before the Government of the United States, at the earliest possible day and in the strongest possible manner, provided the matter be not amicably and equitably settled by the time mentioned in the long communication which I have this day dispatched to the honorable Secretary of State of Bolivia. Your Excellency may remember that when I was in Chuquisaca, in 1871, I there had the honor to deliver to you a letter of introduction from Governor Frias, of Tucuman, in the Argentine Republic, and I myself have a very pleasing remembrance of the honor you did me in that city when you called on me at the residence of our amiable and worthy friend, Senor Don Mariano Ypina. Do induce your people to pay at once the money so long and so justly due—so many years overdue—to Mr. Colton, and let us all, as Americans, and as men of reason and honor, be friends and not enemies.

With many sincere wishes for the success of your administration and for your health and happiness and long life,

I am, dear sir, very truly, your friend and servant,

H. R. HELPER.

MR. HELPER TO SECRETARY CORRAL.

[Private Note.]

NEW YORK, *February* 15, 1873.
HON. CASIMIRO CORRAL, *Secretary of State for Bolivia.*

MY DEAR SIR: The accompanying letter and its inclosure are so long and exhaustive, that, in strict propriety, this note ought to be brief. The conclusion and determination of Mr. Colton and myself, as explained in the papers referred to, are final. In extending the time for payment six months more from the present date, in addition to the fourteen years and upward already taken by Bolivia, we trust that our patience and our liberality of disposition will be conceded, and that we may not be eventually compelled, under greatly aggravated convictions of unjust usage, to resort for relief to the harsh and disruptive measures which I have foreshadowed. Simple justice, which we have so often—in so many years of the past—respectfully solicited, and which Bolivia has so frequently promised, is all we desire; let us have that, even at this late day, peaceably and in honor, and we will, by your consent, remain mutual friends and well-wishers.

Even in a mere pecuniary and worldly point of view, leaving out entirely the moral aspect of the question, (if indeed one may *ever* dare to disregard that sublime and transcendent consideration,) it is for the interest of Bolivia to pay this debt, and to pay it, at the very furthest, within the ultimate time mentioned in my more elaborate communication of this same date. Without taking against Bolivia the general action which I contemplate in the contingency alluded to, I could, I think, have had our mission to La Paz abolished before now. So that, of one thing at least, I can now very confidently assure you: unless the Colton claim be soon paid, you will, as I believe, have, in the person of Gen. Croxton, if he lives to arrive at your Capital, the last United States Minister to Bolivia; and even him you will probably have for a period of only about twelve months, perhaps less.

I sincerely hope and trust that your action in this matter will be such as to contribute to the maintenance and promotion of harmony and justice and all worthy and honorable relations, international and personal. It is said here that President Frias is to Bolivia what Thiers is to France; and this saying is highly complimentary to both of the distinguished statesmen whose names are thus mentioned in juxtaposition. I remember His Excellency, Senor Frias, very well, and very favorably, having had a letter of introduction to him, (delivered in Chuquisaca, in 1871,) from Governor Frias, of the Province of Tucuman, in the Argentine Republic. Pray be good enough to hand to His Excellency the inclosed note.

I am, dear sir, very respectfully,
Your friend and servant,
H. R. HELPER.

MR. HELPER TO MINISTER CROXTON.

NEW YORK, *February* 28, 1873.
HON. JOHN T. CROXTON,
United States Minister to Bolivia.

SIR: I respectfully solicit your attention to the somewhat elaborate communication herewith, and also to the inclosures which accompany it, addressed by Mr. Joseph H. Colton and myself, on the 15th instant, to the Hon. Secretary of State of Bolivia. These papers are all in relation to an eminently just and fully and frequently admitted debt, due since 1858, from the Government of Bolivia to the said Mr. Colton, and he and I are all the more desirous of rightly and honorably inducing you to give them special attention, because they are framed with certain last conditions, looking to an equitable and amicable settlement (in this fifteenth year of the delinquency,) which the authorities of the country to which you are accredited may do well to consider and act upon without further delay.

Trusting that your diplomatic services in this case, and in all other cases, may be promotive of justice, peace and good will,

I have the honor to be, very respectfully,
Your obedient servant,
H. R. HELPER.

MR. HELPER TO SECRETARY FISH.

NEW YORK, *February* 28, 1873.
HON. HAMILTON FISH, *Secretary of State, Washington.*

SIR: There must be some inherent defect in the system of diplomacy itself, which, when respectfully appealed to, and implicitly relied on, by a citizen of one Republic seriously damaged in his property by the Government of another Republic, leaves the aggrieved and despoiled party, after a period of more than fourteen years, just where it found him, —if not in a worse condition. This predicate is certainly true, incontrovertibly and conspicuously true, of the Colton case against Bolivia. During all the many years of the pendency of this case, there has been no time when Bolivia did not (because of documentary vouchers that could not be questioned,) unreservedly admit the justice of the claim, and promise to pay the money.

Last summer Bolivia raised successfully in London, a loan of ten millions of dollars, less the stipulated discounts and commissions. In February previously she gave me a decree, solemnly pledging her honor and her "religious" faith to the payment to me, out of the first proceeds of that loan, of the forty odd thousand dollars due to Mr. Colton; but, notwithstanding the formality and solemnity of that national obligation, she has not paid one dime of the amount; and I am now very apprehensive that her real purpose is never to pay a dime, more or less, so long as she can avoid payment by false promises, by cunning delays, or by other measures of duplicity, such as have, all the while, been peculiarly characteristic of her conduct. From first to last, since 1858, when the debt was contracted, the creditor and his attorneys have spent over twenty-six thousand dollars, and a vast amount of time and labor,—to say nothing of the countless number of vexatious disappointments incurred,—in fruitless efforts to obtain at least an approximation to justice in this matter; to save something, even though that something be less than a moiety, from the unfortunate transaction with Bolivia. Yet, distressing to relate, no appeal, no argument, no pleading, however just and earnest, seems adequate to the task of arousing in Bolivia either an honest impulse or a sense of shame. It is less fitting that such a country should be recognized and honored as a Republic, than that Buncombe County, in North Carolina, should be set up and flattered as an Empire.

I mpst respectfully solicit your careful attention to the six inclosures herewith, all of which bear immediately and pressingly on the Colton case against Bolivia; and I beg to assure you that Mr. Colton and I will feel both honored and favored by your action in the premises, if you, through our minister at La Paz as a medium of communication, can and will at last so manage the case as that even the mere semblance of justice, which is now only possible to the claimant, may be had fairly and peaceably within the time mentioned in the inclosures. Only by some such settlement as this, made by or before the 15th of next August, can be obviated the necessity for a memorial on the subject to our Congress at Washington. Should you, at any time, be requested by Congress or by the President, to furnish more or less of the correspondence on file in the State Department, in this case,—as you may possibly be sometime next winter,—please let this letter and its six inclosures appear among the papers which you will transmit in response to such request. Promising not to trouble you again in Mr. Colton's behalf during the next six months, unless it be in reply, or in regard, to some important communication or information which I may receive meanwhile,

I have the honor to be, with great respect,
Your obedient servant,
H. R. HELPER.

SECRETARY TERRAZA TO MR. COLTON.

[Translation.]

DEPARTMENT OF GOVERNMENT AND FOREIGN AFFAIRS.
LA PAZ, BOLIVIA, *April* 3, 1873.
JOSEPH H. COLTON, *Esq*.

SIR: This department has received your communication of the 15th of February last, and inclosed in it a copy of the one you addressed, under date of the 14th of June, last year, to Mr. Leopold Markbreit, then United States Minister to the Government of this Republic. Having brought the contents of both to the notice of the President of the Republic, he charges me to say, in reply, that very soon the debt you claim, for the publication of the map of Bolivia, shall be satisfactorily and completely determined; since, with a view of bringing to an end the involuntary delay

which this business has caused, to the grave detriment of the interests of the State, the Government will obtain from Congress, to meet during the latter part of the present month, the necessary authority for a payment to be made with the funds actually in hand arising from the 17 per cent. which has been deducted from the loan of £10,000* destined for the railroad of the Madeira and Mamoré.
Respectfully,
MELCHOR TERRAZA.

PRESIDENT FRIAS TO MR. HELPER.

[Translation.]

LA PAZ, BOLIVIA, *April*, 17, 1873.

HINTON ROWAN HELPER, *Esq*.

MY DEAR SIR: In reply to your letter of February 15, I have the honor to assure you of the earnest desire of the Bolivian Government to satisfy the recognized debt in favor of Mr. Colton; in virtue of which, I dare announce to you that payment will certainly commence to be made during the present year, 1873. In case there should not be at La Paz any direct representative of the creditor, the matter might be placed in the hands of the Legation of the United States.

With this motive, I offer to you my sentiments of gratitude for your amiable congratulation upon my official investiture.

Your affectionate and sincere servant,
TOMAS FRIAS.

*This is a mistake,—a very great mistake; the discrepancy between the real truth and the written error in the premises, amounting to no less than $9,950,000. The gross amount of the loan, successfully raised in London, in the summer of 1872, was $10,000,000.
H. R. H.

EXTRACT FROM THE MESSAGE OF PRESIDENT FRIAS TO THE CONGRESS OF BOLIVIA, APRIL 28, 1873.

[Translation.]

"Having already spoken of national obligations, which may be regarded as results of the personal acts of the late President Morales, I must not omit to speak also of the absolute preference given to Mr. Colton's claim, which comes of compromises strictly national; in virtue of which, I have not hesitated to assure him and his attorney, that satisfaction of the debt shall be commenced during the present year; considering this as one of our first duties toward the liquidation of our national obligations."

MR. COLTON TO THE SENATE AND HOUSE COMMITTEES ON FOREIGN AFFAIRS.

NEW YORK, *January* 1, 1874.
*To the Honorable the Senate and House Committees
on Foreign Affairs, Washington.*

GENTLEMEN: You will receive herewith my petition to the Congress of the United States for justice to myself from the Government of Bolivia, which, in a most extraordinary and aggravating manner, has persistently injured me in my property for the last fifteen years. My age, (I being now in my seventy-fourth year,) and my feebleness of health, prevent me from going to Washington, in person, to seek redress for the gross wrongs which I have so often suffered through the many acts of bad faith of the Bolivian Government; but Hinton Rowan Helper, Esquire, who holds from me complete and permanent powers of attorney in this regard, and who is familiar with all the facts of the case, from first to last, will deliver to you this and the accompanying papers, and will, I doubt not, be able to give whatever additional information you may require. I have the honor to request, therefore, that you, as upright American Senators and Representatives, having official cognizance of the conduct of nations, as that conduct affects the citizens of our own country, will, with a swiftness of dispatch commensurate with Bolivia's interminable, wilful and wicked delays, adjust this matter·with Mr. Helper, my only, absolute and irremovable attorney, with full powers herein. Any settlement made with him will be as valid and final, in all respects, as if made with myself personally.

I have the honor to be,
Very respectfully, your obedient servant,
JOSEPH H. COLTON.

MR. HELPER (FOR MR. COLTON) TO THE HON. SECRETARY OF STATE OF BOLIVIA.

[Private and Confidential until May 5, 1874.]

WASHINGTON, *January* 3, 1874.

To the Honorable the Secretary of State of Bolivia.

SIR: Acting on advice. which I am unwilling to disregard, I have the honor to address you as follows: Under the two connected dates of January 3, 1874, and May 5, 1874, you will receive herewith a printed copy of my Memorial to the Congress of the United States, against the Government of Bolivia. Till the latter date no public proceedings in the case will be taken, and none even then, provided the whole amount of the money so long overdue to me from Bolivia, be, by that time, received; otherwise the case, as printed, will, immediately thereafter, be submitted for the serious consideration and action of my own government. I am informed that the present (long) session of our Congress will probably not close until about the middle of July. By the amount thus claimed as overdue, I mean only the amount so often admitted by Bolivia herself to be due; as appears in her last decree, of February 1, 1872. Yet, as I have heretofore explained, that amount is, in reality, much less than the amount due in equity; nor does this include one cent of the enormous expenses thus far incurred by me, in fruitlessly seeking justice in the case, namely, twenty-six thousand eight hundred and forty dollars in gold, up to the 1st instant; together with the accruing expenses of my attorney, now in Washington, and the cost of printing the accompanying pamphlet, still to be added. I am willing to forgive (but can never forget,) the great injustice apparent in these ponderous expenses, provided full payment of the amount due by the said last decree, of February 1, 1872, together with the interest which shall have legally accrued thereon up to the date of the receipt here of the money, be made, in good faith, not later than the 5th of May, of the present year. The money, in the form of a draft, may be either sent directly to me or to the State Department at Washington, subject to my order. If complete satisfaction of the said last decree be not given by the time mentioned above, I shall most earnestly, (and I am sure most rightfully,) publicly petition the Congress of the United States, as by the inclosed printed pamphlet, to make good to me, to the uttermost farthing, all original dues and actual expenses in the premises. By three different steamers, sailing on different days, you will, if there be no miscarriage of the mails, receive this letter and the inclosed pamphlet, in triplicate.

I am, sir, respectfully, your obedient servant,
       JOSEPH H. COLTON.
  By his attorney:
       HINTON R. HELPER.

THUS, honored Senators and Representatives of the American Congress, have I had the honor to submit to you, both by way of making complaint and by way of seeking redress, an epitome of the many acts of gross injustice and insult which, for half a generation, I, as a citizen of the United States, have been forced to endure, and am still forced to endure, at the hands of dishonorable Bolivia, with whose Government you are (no doubt but imperfectly acquainted with the real character of that despicable country) yet pleased to maintain relations of international friendship and comity.

The main facts of the case in point may be summarized as follows:

Of her own volition and overture, whether wily or worthy, Bolivia became largely indebted to me in the year 1858 for ten thousand large maps of herself as one of the governing powers of the earth.

Two years afterward, in 1860, having already time and again proved false to her solemn word with me, and I having meanwhile appealed to the honorable Secretary of State at Washington for aid in the effort to recover the amount due me, she promised our then Minister Resident at La Paz that she would soon pay off the debt. Her failure to keep that promise constituted her first flat indignity and insult, or at least what should have been regarded as an indignity and insult, to a diplomatic representative of the United States.

In still later years, from 1860 to 1873, she has repeatedly given the most positive assurances to me and to each and every Minister Resident whom we have sent to her capital, that she would pay the money "very soon;" but, up to this present day, not once has she been veracious enough to keep her word, or honest enough to pay one cent. For the exact truth of all these statements I would respectfully refer you to the six following named Ministers and ex-Ministers of the United States, whose field of diplomacy is, or has been, Bolivia; or, if not to those gentlemen themselves in person, to the archives of our State Department in Washington, where dispatches from them respectively on this subject will be found on file:

Hon. John Cotton Smith, Sharon, Connecticut.
Hon. David K. Cartter, Washington, D. C.
Hon. Allen A. Hall, Nashville, Tennessee.
Hon. John W. Caldwell, Cincinnati, Ohio.
Hon. Leopold Markbreit, Cincinnati, Ohio.
Hon. John T. Croxton, Paris, Kentucky.

Not merely has Bolivia, by profuse and ordinary promises, written and verbal, misled me and my special agents, and hood-winked every Minister whom our Government has sent to her between the years 1858 and 1873, but she has also, during the same time, by numerous public and official declarations and extraordinary messages, issued under the signatures and seals of her nationality, audaciously trifled with all our illustrious Secretaries of State, from the days of the Hon. Lewis Cass to the Hon. Hamilton Fish, inclusive.

Up to this present time, no dispute—no misunderstanding —has ever existed between Bolivia and myself as to the amount due, and her many admissions of strict justice of the debt have, as is clearly shown in the preceding pages, always been accompanied by the most solemn and formal assurances of early payment. "Yes," is the ever ready but deceitful word upon her lips. "Yes, the obligation is one of honor and equity; the principal is correctly stated; you have charged the minimum rate of interest; the amount is right, and the money shall be paid very soon;" but just there everything is allowed to rest quietly until, whether months or years afterward, she is again addressed on the subject, when, with an air of augmented ardor and virtue, she reiterates, privately and publicly, all previous promises, and pledges herself anew. In this way there is indeed great danger that from the new crime of Bolivia here described—unless that crime be speedily repressed and punished—a progeny of countless and direful evils may soon issue.

Bolivia's most shameful conduct in this matter is a fact notorious all over Bolivia itself; and, to my certain knowledge, the comparatively few good men in that country mourn over it as they would mourn over any other distinct national disgrace. It is an example of barefaced fraud and falsehood on the part of the State, inevitably corrupting the private character of her own citizens, and giving a sort of public license for the plotting and practice of rascality throughout the world. Therefore, both in consideration of my own admitted rights, and as a moral and necessary lesson to the great majority of the Bolivians themselves, Bolivia should now, at last, be required to do her obvious duty just once, as that duty has been so often and so exactly defined by herself; and thereby furnish to the world at least one instance of a forced (in the absence of a voluntary) observance of the commonest principles of truth and justice.

Even to hint at all the high crimes and misdemeanors of Bolivia, other than the one now under particular consideration, and all of which should be matters of the deepest concern with those numerous and right-minded people who are so earnestly struggling for better conditions of individual and national life, would require much more time and space than I now have at my disposal.

The forty-seven revolutions with which Bolivia has so fatally afflicted herself and her neighbors during the brief period that she has been an independent power, since 1825; her impermanence and precariousness of political metropolis, she having, in the course of years past, held her sessions of Congress at no less than five different places, namely, Chuquisaca, La Paz, Tapacari, Oruro, and Cochabamba; her perverse alienation from herself, many years ago, of all the diplomatic representatives from Europe; her barbarous assassinations of most of her Presidents; her practical denial to her citizens of the rights of personal liberty and private judgment; her contempt of the elevating and ennobling pursuits of peace; her inattention to the civilizing inventions and industries of the age; her disregard of the refining influences which result from a proper application of labor to the useful arts; her apathy in all matters of enlightened comfort, convenience, and progress, even within her own borders; she being a country without roads, without bridges, without hotels, and without manufactures; having no art, no science, no literature, little agriculture, and less commerce; and her shocking indecencies of daily and hourly and incessantly eating lice in the public streets, as unblushingly as in the private houses, of all her cities and towns; — these are some of the subjects which, under other circumstances, might be more elaborately discussed in evidence of Bolivia's unfitness to be any longer recognized as a civilized nation.

But for the very positive assurances given me by both President Frias and Secretary Terraza, in April last, in reply to my letters of final conditions under date of February 15, 1873,—all of which assurances and letters you will have found herewith,—I should have had the honor of presenting this petition to your honorable body before now; for I presumed that you would expect me to believe the holographic and explicit words of an Illimanian President, and his Secretary of State. Yet you see now, as I have long seen to my sorrow, what such words are worth; what, in fact, they have been worth for these last fifteen years; just nothing at all; especially when the President and Secretary of State in question are born of Bolivia.

A strikingly strange and suspicious feature of the assurances of President Frias and Secretary Terraza, is apparent in these words: " Payment will certainly commence to be made during the present year, 1873." This is an *ex parte* provision or arrangement, and I here openly protest against it. It is only another piece of sheer artifice on the part of Bolivia; it bodes more mischief; it is rank with the sinister designs of double-dealing; it means a gradual and indefinite lengthening out, into oblivion, of a comparatively insignificant debt of a country for its maps, already overdue for the full period of fifteen years; it smacks of delay till the crack of doom. Only contemplate for a moment this youngest offspring of the New Crime of Bolivia. What a matchless and monstrous spectacle of perfidious baseness!

Here is a regularly recognized Republic, a Republic in name at least, passing all manner of official acts and resolutions, year after year, always frankly admitting its undeniable duty to pay for its maps published in 1858, frequently authorizing the payment to be made in full, and then, in 1873, promising to " commence " payment sometime during the fifteenth year of the delinquency; and yet, even after so many extraordinary exhibitions of pitiable shabbiness, as if no depth of dishonor was low enough for Bolivia, failing to pay one cent! I have some little knowledge of the language in which I am writing this Memorial, and it may be that, if put to the test, I might succeed in applying a few appropriate terms to a so-called gentleman who would seek to evade his just obligations to a washerwoman; but never yet have I seen or heard any words of ordinary usage at all adequate to the description of such varied and unending acts of ineffable meanness as Bolivia is guilty of in this map matter.

I respectfully entreat your honorable body to cut short the barefaced and baleful career of Bolivia in this New Crime. Not only do I ask that, as the very least that can be done with any sort of propriety, you will at once suspend diplomatic relations with Bolivia until she learns something of the good faith due to her national promises and pays me for her maps ; but I also earnestly beseech you, as the superior functionaries of my own Government, and as the highest and best representatives of American republican nationality, to grant me the more exact and certain measures of justice which are adverted to in my letters of final conditions under dates respectively of June 14, 1872, and February 15, 1873.

In addition to the sum of $41,588.54 in gold, due to me by the decree of February 1, 1872, and which should be so much the more as interest at the rate of seven per cent. over six per cent. per annum would make it, Bolivia ought, in equity, to be required to pay me the heavy expenses to which I have been subjected during the last fifteen years, in vain efforts to obtain from her what she so justly owes me. All told, the expenses alone amount to $26,840 in gold; and with this additional amount (having given her at least eighteen months of fair admonition and warning,) I now charge her; requesting that, henceforth, on this sum of expenses, thus far, as also on the sum mentioned in the last decree, seven per cent. per annum be allowed.

It has thus been my painful duty to acquaint your honorable body with the bad character of one of the nations of the new world, with which you, on your own part, are in regular diplomatic and friendly alliance ; although that nation herself, at this time, has neither a Minister nor a Consul—if, indeed, she *ever* had a Minister—within the United States. Her Consul under commission at New York, a gentleman engaged in mercantile pursuits, is not a Bolivian, has never been in Bolivia, has been in Europe for the last seven months, and will, I hear, probably remain absent from the United States at least twelve months longer. Is there not lacking here both a principle and a practice of true international courtesy and reciprocity? Is it not, in truth, a very one-sided business? The United States are not unrepresented in Bolivia; but Bolivia is unrepresented in the United States.

Lord Clarendon bluntly blotted Bolivia from the Diplomatic map of Great Britain in 1853. France, Germany, Russia, and all the other governing powers of Europe, have likewise long since ceased to regard Bolivia as worthy of notice as a nation. Out of South America, it is our own country alone that maintains a minister in Bolivia.

Honorable Senators and Representatives of the American Congress: The intelligent and well-meaning world has already, more than once, had occasion to applaud the reasonable measures of protection and indemnification which you, as national legislators, as republican statesmen, have accorded to those of your less fortunate fellow-citizens who for a time have been despoiled of either their rights or their property by inconsiderate foreign Governments. I now ask that you will, with your usual moderation and fairness toward all concerned, afford to the better portion of mankind another proof of the fact that citizenship of the United States is indeed a great and glorious privilege—a high prerogative—carrying with it the amplest guarantees of rightful consideration at home and of due respect abroad.

Only the plain truth about Bolivia have I told your honorable body. She came to me. I did not go to her. Scores of times has she grossly deceived me. In both spirit and purse has she greatly injured me. Truth finds no welcome with her. From justice she hides her face. Honor she never knew. She knows no shame. Absolutely incapable has she proved herself of performing one little straightforward act of honesty. As a nation she is abject to the last degree. Not only does she not pay the amount originally due to me, but, in the fruitless efforts which I have made during fifteen years to collect the money, she has thus far caused me an additional loss, in actual expenditures and binding compromises, of nearly twenty-seven thousand dollars in gold! Is this justice? Is it not a gross outrage against all the principles of honorable dealings? Is it not a species of national swindling and robbery, and should not the nation so manifestly guilty of such criminal conduct be either compelled herself to pay the aggregate amount of principal, interest and costs, or unceremoniously dislodged from the eminence of sovereign power, and her territory and obligations allowed to lapse to an honest and solvent neighboring nationality? For an equitable and affirmative reply to this last inquiry, and for action accordingly, I confidently appeal to the enlightened and just judgment of my own great Government, as that Government is now supremely and preëminently represented in the Congress of the United States.

JOSEPH H. COLTON, *Claimant.*
By his Attorney:
HINTON R. HELPER.
Correct,—APPROVED:
JOSEPH H. COLTON.

AFFIDAVIT OF JOSEPH H. COLTON.

NEW YORK, *May* 6, 1874.

I, the undersigned, Joseph H. Colton, do hereby, in truth and honor, solemnly declare and swear, that all the documents and other papers printed on the foregoing pages of this pamphlet are genuine and true, as they purport to be, and what the Government of Bolivia owes me, in justice and equity, the two sums respectively of forty-one thousand five hundred and eighty-eight dollars and fifty-four cents in gold, ($41,588.54,) with interest due thereon from February 1, 1872, and twenty-seven thousand three hundred and sixteen dollars in gold ($27,316,) as expenses actually paid and to be paid by me and by my attorney, Mr. Helper, in this long-pending case, up to the present date, May 6, 1874. And herein I most earnestly entreat the sovereign and influential Congress of my country to do me at last, whilst yet surviving in my old age, that long-deferred justice which I can now no longer look for from the interminably false-promising Government of Bolivia, which, for the full period of fifteen years, has trifled with me, in this grave matter, far more recklessly and viciously than any wanton ever yet did trifle with a toy.

JOSEPH H. COLTON.

Witnesses.
M. RANDOLPH.
O. C WOOLSON.

Subscribed and sworn to before me, this the eleventh day of May, 1874, in the City and County of New York.

WALTON P. BELL,
[L. S.] *Notary Public.*

Such, then, honored Senators and Representatives of the Congress of the United States of America, such, then, is the antecedent memorial which, informally on the 3d of January, 1874, and formally on the 6th of May of the same year, your petitioner had the honor to submit for your consideration and action against Bolivia. Moreover, during the progress of your patient and enlightened deliberations on the subject, your petitioner took occasion, from time to time, between the 6th of May, 1874, and the 3d of March, 1875, to lay before you, through the mediumship of your learned and able Committee of the Senate on Foreign Affairs, the various additional briefs, letters and opinions which here follow:

MINISTER HALL TO MR. COLTON.

LEGATION OF THE UNITED STATES,
COCHABAMBA, BOLIVIA, *September* 8, 1864.
JOSEPH H. COLTON, *Esq., New York.*

DEAR SIR: A fortnight ago I transmitted to the State Department, at Washington, a copy of a very elaborate statement which I have laid before the Bolivian Government, and in which is carefully reviewed the whole course of wrong and injustice which they have pursued toward you. My object in drawing up that statement, which is upward of seventy cap-paper pages in length, was two-fold: First, to satisfy our own Government that there existed abundant grounds for their intervention, if I could not otherwise induce this government to pay your just claim in full; and, second, to reach the sensibilities and awaken the apprehensions of the Bolivian government, by showing how bad the case was, and leaving them to infer that they would be compelled to pay, if they did not do so voluntarily and speedily. For, when I came to examine all the papers in the case, I saw, in the acts of the government of Bolivia, good grounds for the intervention of the United States; and I confidently expect permission from Washington, after my full statement shall have been read there, to notify this government officially, that the claim must be adjusted without further delay.

Yours truly,

ALLEN A. HALL.

EX-MINISTER CALDWELL TO MR. HELPER.

CINCINNATI, *November* 29, 1870.
H. R. HELPER, *Esq.*
DEAR SIR: * * * I presented Mr. Colton's claim

orally and in writing to the government of Bolivia, through the Bolivian Secretary of State, in 1868 and 1869, elaborately. The Secretary replied that his government desired a report on the subject from Messrs. Ondarza and Mujia, the engineers and commissioners on the part of Bolivia, in reference to the execution of the work, and that, on the reception of such report, I should be informed of the action his government would take. Both of the gentlemen named were distant from La Paz, living in separate, interior places; and some time would necessarily have to elapse before their answers could be received. Meanwhile I was myself relieved from office, and retired from La Paz. I presented the claim in very strong terms. In my intercourse with the Bolivian government in regard to the matter, I invariably stated that I considered the validity of the claim as completely established and settled by the government of Bolivia itself; and that now nothing further was necessary, or in order, but payment by that government of the amount due to Mr. Colton. Copies of my correspondence with the government of Bolivia, and with the government of the United States, on this subject, may be found in the Department of State at Washington; and they are also on record as a part of the archives of the United States Legation at La Paz, in Bolivia.

Respectfully yours,
JOHN W. CALDWELL.

The action of the Bolivian Government, as explained in the last foregoing letter, in postponing a reply to Minister Caldwell, under the plea that it desired first to correspond with its absent engineers and commissioners, who had, more than ten years previously, bargained in New York for the engraving and publishing of the map, and whose regular proceedings in the premises had always been matters of governmental record and approbation, was only another stratagem,—one of a thousand, more or less, on the part of an atrociously untruthful and dishonest nation. Many times already had Colonel Ondarza and Commandant Mujia patiently and carefully reported all the facts in this case to the new and ever-changing governments of Bolivia; sometimes verbally, sometimes in writing, and at other times in print; and, although they promptly prepared and presented still another full and correct statement at the particular time here mentioned, clearly demonstrating, as they had so often demonstrated before, that Bolivia was entirely in the wrong and Mr. Colton entirely in the right, yet their faithless government took no notice of it whatever, and until questioned about it, nearly three years afterward, never even so much as intimated its existence to the new Minister of the United States. In the graphic affidavits respectively of Colonel Ondarza and Commandant Mujia, as given personally to Mr. Helper, one at Chuquisaca, and the other at La Paz, toward the close of the year 1871, and as embodied in his published appeal to Congress, under date of January 3, 1874, the Colton case against Bolivia is, simply in those two Bolivian documents themselves, so ably and admirably condensed as to be singularly perspicuous and complete.

H. R. H.

ASSISTANT SECRETARY HALE TO MR. HELPER.

DEPARTMENT OF STATE,
WASHINGTON, *April* 10, 1872.
H. R. HELPER, *Esq., New York.*

SIR: Your letter of the 4th instant, on the subject of Mr. Joseph H. Colton's claim against the Government of Bolivia, has been received, and the suggestions therein contained will receive attention.

I am, sir, your obedient servant,

CHARLES HALE.

MR. COLTON TO SECRETARY FISH.

NEW YORK, *April* 9, 1872.

HON. HAMILTON FISH,
Secretary of State, Washington.

SIR: On application at the Bolivian Consulate in this city, a few days since, for a certified copy in English of the Decree in Spanish, which was issued by the Bolivian Government, on the first day of last February, in my favor, the Consul, or rather Mr. J. J. Ribon, who, in the absence of Mr. Munoz, in Jamaica, is now acting here in the capacity of Bolivian Consul, refused to give me a certificate for the true and full amount due. I beg leave to request, therefore, that you will be kind enough to favor me with a free and correct translation into English of the said Decree, as you may have received it officially from Bolivia; so that, although I am not myself familiar with the Castilian language, I may yet be satisfied, and be able to satisfy others with whom I have business relations, of the exact amount for which the Decree was issued, and also of the true sense, in all respects, if not the precise wording, of the same.

Feeling that I have no right to request the Government of the United States to incur the expense of having the translation made for my benefit, I having already, from time to time, asked and received so many favors from your Department, without any charge whatever, I shall expect to be informed of the amount of fees and other charges, if any, that are usual and equitable in cases of this kind; and all such fees and charges will at once be paid. Indeed, in this particular case of Bolivian delinquency, during the last fourteen years, I have had so much burdensome experience in paying for the execution and verification of legal documents before lawyers, notaries public, consuls and other functionaries, and for the more extended and laborious services of agents, correspondents and attorneys, that I have now become quite accustomed, though by no means reconciled to it ; my total disbursements and liabilities in the case, as stipulated by agreements, having already considerably exceeded fifty per cent. of the whole amount mentioned in the Decree! Still I trust that Bolivia may soon be brought to a full and anxious knowledge of the fact that it is neither just to me, nor honorable to herself, to subject me indefinitely, year after year, for so long a period, to such ruinously disadvantageous experience.

I have the honor to be, very respectfully,
Your obedient servant,
JOSEPH H. COLTON.
By his Attorney:
HINTON R. HELPER.

ASSISTANT SECRETARY HALE TO MR. HELPER.

'DEPARTMENT OF STATE,
WASHINGTON, *April* 12, 1872.
HINTON R. HELPER, *Esq.*, *New York.*

SIR: Your letter of the 9th instant has been received. In compliance with the request which it contains, a copy of a translation of the recent Decree of the Bolivian Government, providing for the claim in the Colton case, is herewith

transmitted. This translation is the one which accompained a dispatch from Mr. Markbriet on the subject.
I am, sir, your obedient servant,
CHARLES HALE.
Enclosure: Translation of Decree, relative to the claim of J. H. Colton.

MR. HELPER TO SECRETARY FISH.

NEW YORK, *December* 10, 1872.
HON. HAMILTON FISH, *Secretary of State, Washington.*
SIR: It is with profound disappointment and regret, mingled with no small degree of disgust toward the delinquent, that the duty is again imposed upon me of soliciting your attention to the apparently endless series of insincere and treacherous promises of Bolivia, in the matter of her indebtedness to Mr. Joseph H. Colton, of this city, for ten thousand large maps which he engraved and published for her, in the year 1858. Time and again has the debt been fully and frankly acknowledged by the Government of Bolivia, and time and again has Bolivia, by Congressional Acts, by Presidential Decrees, by Diplomatic Assurances, and otherwise solemnly promised to pay the money; but all her promises have proved worse than simply worthless; and sorely aggrieved by the magnitude, variety and duration of the provocations to which she has so cunningly subjected Mr. Colton and myself, I feel that it is but just to denounce her, to yourself and to all the world, as a shameless trifler, a delusion and a snare.

On the first day of last February, when Bolivia issued to me in person, as Mr. Colton's attorney, at La Paz, her sixth governmental act in his behalf, I was "religiously" assured, by both President Morales and Secretary Corral, that the money should be paid " in the matter of about four months." According to that pious promise, payment of the money should have been made about the first of June; but it distresses me to know that that promise, like a thousand and one other similar promises given by Bolivia, within the last fourteen years, turned out to be an exceedingly false and misleading promise. In the early part of July, our Minister at La Paz, Mr. Markbreit, in reply to an ultimatum from Mr. Colton and myself, gave me this unqualified assurance: " If you and Mr. Colton will only have a little more patience, I will insure you the full payment of the latter's claim against Bolivia before the next meeting of our Congress." Though nettled by the remembrance of so many years of Illimanian perfidy, yet Mr. Colton and I did "have a little more patience." We informed Mr. Markbreit that, while it was impossible for us to exercise any further faith in the Punic promises of Bolivia, yet we could believe him, and would wait. We waited accordingly, and are waiting still; but still the money has not been paid; and I am now clearly of the opinion that Bolivia never meant to pay, and never will pay, one dollar of the debt, if she can possibly avoid it. Nor do I doubt in the least that she will artfully and trickishly avoid her duties in the premises until doomsday, unless, meanwhile, some measure of compulsion can be successfully brought to bear against her.

I now have it in contemplation to publish, very soon, in pamphlet form, a brief but perspicuous history of the whole case, purposing to submit a copy of the same to every member of our Senate and House of Representatives, respectfully petitioning them for such redress as simple justice may demand; but, before doing so, I have thought it best to lay before you this restatement of the facts, and to ascertain definitely whether, under all the circumstances, it may not be right and proper for you, as the American Secretary of State, and as both a national and international conservator of equity and honor and peace, to insist that Bolivia shall at once cease her deceitfulness and general meanness of conduct toward our worthy citizen, Mr. Colton, and pay him the money she has owed him so long, and in regard to which you yourself, and several of your predecessors in the State Department, have been so frequently annoyed. Pray be good enough to favor me with a reply to this last paragraph, and I shall then be able to determine whether or not to go to Washington, and there publicly lay the case before our Congress.

I have the honor to be, most respectfully,
Your obedient servant,
H. R. HELPER.

SECRETARY FISH TO MR. HELPER.

DEPARTMENT OF STATE,
WASHINGTON, *December* 11, 1872.
HINTON ROWAN HELPER, *Esq., New York.*

SIR: This Department has received your letter of yesterday, relative to the debt of the Bolivian Government to Mr. Joseph H. Colton, for copies of a map of that Republic. The delay in the payment of that debt is a matter of regret. The Department in this case, however, has done all it can properly do, or which it is usual to do, in the case of a contract between a citizen of the United States and a foreign Government. Hitherto no Secretary of State, so far as I am aware, has deemed himself authorized to regard any such contract as guaranteed by this Government. The good offices, therefore, only, and not the official interposition of the Ministers of the United States in Foreign countries, have been sanctioned. I am not aware of any circumstances in the case of Mr. Colton, which would warrant or require a deviation from the policy adverted to. It must be presumed that, in making his bargain, he took into consideration both the ability and the disposition of the Bolivian Government to fulfill its share of the agreement, and charged accordingly.

I am, sir, your obedient servant,
HAMILTON FISH.

NOTE FROM MR. COLTON: New York, *December* 14, 1872: —If, by the two or three closing words of the foregoing letter from Secretary Fish, he means to intimate or suggest that I charged Bolivia one cent more than I would have charged the United States or any other body politic, corporation, or company, or himself, or any other individual, he is entirely mistaken, and raises against me a new and strange question, which Bolivia herself, with all her glaring faults and faithlessness, has never once urged, or even hinted at, in the slightest degree. On the contrary, at the time of the contract, in 1858, feeling myself preferred and honored by the commission to execute so large an order for a far-distant government, I undertook and did the work at such low rates, that, even if Bolivia had paid me fully and promptly, as I expected she would do, in accordance with the conditions of the agreement, I should have realized only a very small profit. Then, too, everything was at the very lowest price; now, that is to say, at this very time, the engraving and publishing and finishing of the same maps would cost about twice as much, or one hundred per cent. more. Making no charge whatever for my own time and assiduous services as contractor and supervisor, my actual expenses for the materials and labor employed in the execution of the order, and for boxing, shipping and insurance, amounted to over twenty-two thousand dollars in gold; and, in addition thereto, my attorneys and myself, in the numerous fruitless efforts which we have since made to obtain my just dues in the premises, have spent, up to the present time, by actual outlays of money, and by binding contingencies, in the form of fees and commissions payable on the final satisfaction of the debt, upward of twenty-six thousand dollars!

JOSEPH H. COLTON.

CORROBORATIVE NOTE FROM MR. HELPER: New York, *December* 14, 1872:—It is but the simple and incontestable truth to say, that Mr. Colton published the maps for Bolivia at an extraordinarily low figure. The dimensions of the map are five feet by six; it is very artistically engraved, and is beautifully finished in every respect, with rollers, mouldings and rings, ready for convenient suspension against walls. The ten thousand copies, all on canvas of the best quality, were furnished at the rate of two dollars and fifty cents each. When I was at Buenos Ayres, in 1871, I found, in a book store there, two of the maps in question, they having been taken there from Bolivia. I desired to purchase one of them, and would have done so, but for the fact that the owner would not sell them, nor either of them, for anything less than twenty dollars in gold per copy. A member of the Cabinet of the Argentine Republic bought one of those copies, at that very price, whilst I was there.

H. R. HELPER.

CONGRESSMAN MYERS TO MR. HELPER.

WASHINGTON, *December* 20, 1872.
H. R. HELPER, *Esq.*

DEAR SIR: I return herewith the copy of your letter to the Secretary of State, and also his reply, in reference to the debt due by Bolivia to Mr. J. H. Colton, of New York. I do not like to advise what you shall do in this matter. It is, as you are aware, very difficult to obtain intervention by authority of Congress in such a case. Where the claims against a foreign government are made by a number of our citizens, we have, in a number of instances, as in the case of Venezuela, interposed, and endeavored to obtain satisfaction of them. There have also been some instances, where our authorities have asserted the claim of even a single one of our citizens; but these latter are few; and where the claim is old, the chances of success are not strong. You must therefore use your own judgment in the matter.

Very truly, yours,

LEONARD MYERS.

SECRETARY FISH TO MR. HELPER.

DEPARTMENT OF STATE,
WASHINGTON, *March* 1, 1873.
HINTON R. HELPER, *Esquire, New York.*

SIR: Your communication of yesterday, relative to the claim of Mr. Joseph H. Colton against the Bolivian government, has been received and placed on file.

I am, sir, your obedient servant,

HAMILTON FISH.

MR. HELPER TO MINISTER CAMPERO.

HAVRE, FRANCE, *April* 18, 1873.
HON. NARCISO CAMPERO, *Bolivian Ambassador to Europe.*
DISTINGUISHED SIR: While in London last week, I made

inquiry for your Excellency, intending to submit to you, orally at least, the firmly fixed determination of Mr. Joseph H. Colton, of New York, in the matter of Bolivia's long-standing obligation to him for the maps which he engraved and published for her in the year 1858. But having been informed, by Col. Church and others, that you had left England for the Continent, I have now concluded to lay before you the inclosed copy of a communication, in the form of an ultimatum, which Mr. Colton and I, as his attorney, addressed to the Hon. Secretary of State for Bolivia, on the 15th of February of the present year. So far, however, as your Excellency is individually concerned, I have no particular request nor suggestion to make in this regard; only deeming it proper thus to acquaint you, as Bolivia's highest and ablest representative in Europe, of the unalterable purpose to which Mr. Colton and I have been finally provoked by the frequent and flagrant delinquencies of Bolivia. Yet I sincerely hope that, for her own sake, as well as for the sake of her shamelessly deceived creditor, Bolivia may at last act with at least a passable degree of prudence and honesty in this time-worn and temper-trying affair.

I am, sir, very respectfully,
Your Excellency's obedient servant,
H. R. HELPER.

MINISTER CROXTON TO MR. COLTON.

LEGATION OF THE UNITED STATES,
LA PAZ, BOLIVIA, *June* 7, 1873.
MR. JOSEPH H. COLTON.

DEAR SIR: * * * Soon after my arrival at La Paz, I proceeded to examine into the status of your claim against the Bolivian government, and discovered that President Frias, and those by whom he was surrounded in the administration of the government, recognized the justice of the claim, and were anxious to see it paid. * * * Since the incoming of President Ballivian's administration, I have again presented the matter and find the disposition to pay you quite as strong now as it was under Frias. I am sure Senor Baptista, the Secretary of State, has a strong feeling in your favor, and, indeed, appreciates very fully the damage to his own government by the long delay you have suffered. * * *

Yours, very respectfully,
JOHN T. CROXTON.

MR. HELPER TO SECRETARY FISH.

NEW YORK, *September* 1, 1873.
HON. HAMILTON FISH, *Secretary of State, Washington.*

SIR: In the course of the long letter which I had the honor of addressing to you, under date of the 28th of last February, in relation to Mr. Joseph H. Colton's claim, of nearly fifteen years' standing, against the Government of Bolivia, I took occasion to assure you that I would probably not trouble you again in that regard for the full period of six months. That time is now up; and it is with very sincere regret that I feel called upon to renew to you my well-founded complaint of the prolonged and unparalleled duplicity of the Bolivian Government in this case. It is now a deep-settled conviction with both Mr. Colton and myself, that Bolivia is immeasurably untruthful and dishonest, and that she does not mean to pay, and never will pay, one cent of the amount so long and so justly due, save only under stress of the most positive compulsion. In the absence, therefore, of any offsetting or satisfactory information or assurance from yourself, as Secretary of State of the United States, it is the intention of the creditor and his attorney to proceed at once against Bolivia, as earnestly and effectively as possible, in exact accordance with the plan detailed in my communication addressed directly to the Bolivian Secretary of State under date of the 15th of last February; a copy of which communication was transmitted to you on the 28th of the same month. If, then, you know of any good reason, based on considerations of amity or equity or prudence, why I should pursue any other course of action than the one mentioned above, pray be kind enough to favor me with it, and I shall be governed accordingly.

I have the honor to be, most respectfully,
Your obedient servant,
H. R. HELPER.

MR. COLTON TO SECRETARY FISH.

NEW YORK, *December* 4, 1873.
HON. HAMILTON FISH, *Secretary of State, Washington*.

SIR: This letter will be handed to you by Hinton R. Helper, Esquire, who again goes to Washington, with full and permanent powers from me, to renew his endeavors to effect a fair and honorable settlement of my very just claim, of fifteen years' standing, against the Government of Bolivia; and to this end, I thus again most respectfully solicit for him your valuable advice and coöperation. Mr. Helper will have the honor to submit to you several late and important papers from Bolivia, which I presume you have not yet seen. Any letter or letters which may be received at the State Department, for me, from Bolivia, will be on this business; and may be delivered to Mr. Helper, with whom, as my attorney, any settlement of my said claim may be made as validly and finally as if made with myself personally.

I have the honor to be, with all respect,
Your obedient servant
JOSEPH H. COLTON.

MR. HELPER TO SENATOR CAMERON.

WASHINGTON, *December* 15, 1873.
HON. SIMON CAMERON, *United States Senator.*

DEAR SIR: Accompanying this note you will find a somewhat lengthy Memorial from Mr. Joseph H. Colton, of New York, to the Congress of the United States, against the Government of Bolivia, to which I, as the claimant's attorney, respectfully solicit the attention of yourself as Chairman of the Senate Committee on Foreign Affairs. You may remember that I had the honor of speaking with you briefly, on this same subject, last winter. I shall not ask you to read the whole of the Memorial just now, unless it be quite agreeable to you to do so, as I shall not want any public action on the case until the New Year shall have come; but I trust that you may be pleased to peruse at least a portion of it, so as to be able to advise me on a single point of it, when I shall have the honor of calling on you a few days hence.

I have the honor to be, very respectfully,
Your obedient servant,
H. R. HELPER.

MR. HELPER TO SENATOR CAMERON.

WASHINGTON, *January* 7, 1874.
HON. SIMON CAMERON,
Chairman of the Senate Committee on Foreign Affairs.
SIR : Your attention is most respectfully solicited to the inclosed copy of my printed protest against the Government of Bolivia, touching the fifteen years' recognized indebtedness of that Government to my aged client, Mr. Joseph H. Colton, of New York, in whose behalf I had the honor of speaking with you here, last winter. Yet, as you will perceive, I do not desire any Congressional proceedings in the case until after the 5th of May, of the present year; nor shall I desire any such proceedings even then, provided payment of the whole amount so long overdue be made by that time. You will be duly advised of any action which, within the next four months, the Bolivian Government may be pleased to take in the premises. Meanwhile, however, if the general Diplomatic and Consular Bill be brought up for the action of the Senate, I trust that you will cause a consideration of the usual appropriation for the support of our mission to Bolivia to be postponed until after the expiration of the date above mentioned, the 5th of May, as, in the event of the continued non-payment thus apprehended, I shall submit to your Committee other documents, proving still more conclusively, as I think, that our mission to that unworthy country ought to be abolished altogether.

I am, sir, very respectfully,
Your obedient servant,
H. R. HELPER.

PROFESSOR DAVIDSON TO MR. HELPER.

NEW YORK, *January* 12, 1874.

H. R. HELPER, *Esq*.

DEAR SIR : * * * The Colton-Bolivia memorial is spicy reading ; and I have enjoyed it accordingly, in its literary aspect. I am amazed that any government pretending to even a merely respectable position among the civilized nations of the earth, should dare even once, as, in this case, Bolivia has dared time and again, to treat with contempt and neglect the plainest and most fundamental principles of international justice. In my opinion, Bolivia's repeated and extraordinary acts of bad faith toward Mr. Colton clearly demand the immediate, vigorous and decisive intervention of our own government in behalf of one of its seriously injured and outraged citizens.

Respectfully and sincerely yours,
JAMES WOOD DAVIDSON.

MR. HELPER TO BOLIVIA'S SECRETARY OF STATE.

NEW YORK, *February* 5, 1874.

To the Honorable the Secretary of State for Bolivia.

SIR : If this be not my last word with Bolivia, on the subject of the Colton claim, the fault, as always in the past, will be Bolivia's, and not mine. As is very plainly intimated in my printed letter to your Excellency, under date of the 3d ultimo, which, as therein promised, has already been forwarded to you in triplicate, Bolivia's extraordinary prevarications and shortcomings toward Mr. Colton during the last fifteen years, have, with both himself and his attorney, now reached a point of personal honor, which no amount of money, however large, can ever possibly control. Two years ago, when your Government gave to me in person, at La Paz, the last decree issued in this case (as if there should ever have been any occasion or necessity for issuing more than one such document, the first of five or six similar documents having been issued as far back as 1860!) I was solemnly promised full payment, "with preference," out of the "first proceeds" of the London loan, which it was then thought would be raised, and was raised, about four months thereafter.

As the decree itself shows, to this positive promise of full payment " with preference " out of the " first proceeds " of the London loan, President Morales and his Cabinet, with pious hypocrisy, pledged the "religious" faith of Bolivia. The entire loan, representing a gross sum of ten millions of dollars in gold, was, as already stated, successfully raised in London about four months after the said last decree was given; and yet, so far from the whole amount having been " religiously " paid " with preference " out of the " first proceeds " of the said loan, Bolivia, during the last two years, as during the previous thirteen, has given nothing but an apparently limitless series of plausible and delusive assurances. Even to this day she has never paid one cent! Fit condemnation by pen or speech of such untruthful and dishonest conduct on the part of a government is simply impossible; language itself, even in its strongest forms and most ingenious combinations, is utterly inadequate to the task. In effect, if not by way of example, such a government gives to its own people, and to all other peoples, a license to practice the grossest falsehood and fraud, and is, therefore, in reality, the impious enemy and corrupter of mankind at large.

Down to the present time, the total expenses which, during the last fifteen years, have been incurred in unavailing efforts to obtain from Bolivia even the elements of equity in this affair, amount to over twenty-seven thousand dollars in gold. I have already assured your Excellency that Mr. Colton and I are now disposed to overlook and abate (though we may never be able to forget,) these ruinous expenses, provided the whole amount of the principal and interest due according to the last decree of the Bolivian Government be paid here, in good faith, not later than the 5th of May, of the present year. This assurance I now repeat; and Mr. Colton and I will, in the future, as in the past, always be true to Bolivia, notwithstanding the fact that she has never yet even once been true to us. Weightily impressed, however, with a sense of the point of honor to which I have referred above, this I must say, besides, that although I am, on the condition mentioned, willing to omit and renounce the whole of the large sum of twenty-seven thousand dollars in gold thus manifestly due in law and in equity, yet if the tenth part of one dime of the special amount so long overdue according to the last Bolivian decree, dated February 1, 1872, remain unpaid here on the 6th of May, of the present year, I shall then lay solemn and tenacious claim to all my rights in the premises, including the principal, interest and expenses, and will thenceforth never be content to receive the smallest fraction of a cent less. Nor, until Bolivia shall have reclaimed herself somewhat from the loathsome baseness and barbarity of bloody bigotry, from social and civil and military villainy, and from other demoralizing and atrocious issues of Catholicism and negroism and Indianism and bi-colored hybridism, will I ever consent to give credence for one moment to any word or promise which she may proffer, or hold myself bound to regard her as entitled to any more kindly consideration than that which should invariably be exercised toward a highway-robber, or a notorious outlaw.

I am perfectly aware that this letter is not couched in smooth and mystical and misleading phrases, such as but too commonly encumber the records of mediaeval and modern diplomacy. It was not intended to be a letter of that sort; but it is something better; it is a letter of truth, aiming at justice. Unmixed with device, and free from ambiguity, it is unvarnished verity, simply expressed; and, so help me Heaven, I shall stand by it and defend it to the last, come what may. Considering the number, the duration and the circumstances of the provocations in this case, the farther use of ephemisms in reasonings and expostulations with Bolivia, would, in a more than ordinary sense, be beneath the dignity of true manhood; on the one hand, it would be rank with the turpitude of treachery to truth itself, and on the other, it would be repulsively foul and offensive with the most perfidious betrayal of justice.

I am, sir, very respectively,
Your obedient servant,
H. R. HELPER.

MR. HELPER TO SECRETARY FISH.

NEW YORK, *February* 5, 1874.
HON. HAMILTON FISH,
Secretary of State, Washington.

SIR: A few weeks before I left Buenos Ayres, toward the close of last summer, the Hon. Adolfo Carranza, the Bolivian Consul-General at the capital of the Argentine Republic,—himself an Argentine citizen,—exhibited to me, at his office, (whither I had repaired for any open information of interest from Bolivia,) a copy of the First Quarterly Report, for 1873, from the Department of Finance and Industry, by the Hon. Casimiro Corral, the then Secretary of State for Bolivia; on the 19th page of which I saw a new acknowledgment of the Colton claim against Bolivia, with interest allowable thereon, as stated, at *twelve* per cent. per annum, which is, I believe, the regular commercial and general business rate of interest in that country. This new proceeding on the part of Bolivia, on which she has never consulted either Mr. Colton or myself, and of which neither of us had ever received any notification whatever, forms another link in the long and complicated chain of her inexplicable freaks and follies in this affair. Only *six* per cent. per annum was the rate of interest which, by way of compromise, Bolivia herself stipulated to pay me for Mr. Colton.

Particularly desirious of obtaining a copy of the report above mentioned, I wrote on two different occasions, by different mails, to our present Minister Resident at La Paz, the Hon. John T. Croxton, respectfully requesting him to send me a copy of the same; but, thus far, I have not received from him either the report itself, or any other reply whatever. Neither have I ever received from him any reply to any of my other three letters, which I had previously written to him, more than eleven months ago. Nor yet have I, nor has Mr. Colton, ever received from him anything whatever in the shape of any Bolivian document, of any sort, bearing on this subject; although in a letter to Mr. Colton, dated June 7, 1873, he says he incloses therein an extract from the favorable message of President Frias to the Bolivian Congress, on the 28th of last May. His letter contained no inclosure whatever. Fortunately for Mr. Colton, however, and thanks to the consideration and politeness of Mr. Carranza, one of Bolivia's own Consuls,— in this case more considerate and more polite than the American Minister in Bolivia,—I myself, in July last, obtained the whole of that message at Buenos Ayres.

I may not now understand perfectly well the reciprocal rights and duties which exist, or should exist, between tax-paying American citizens at home, and salaried American Ministers abroad, whose salaries are paid out of their fellow-citizens' money; but I am hopeful of being able to learn something more in this regard during the present session of Congress. Because of the facts herein stated, I deem it proper, both on my own account and on account of my client, Mr. Colton, to complain to you, Mr. Secretary of State, as I thus do complain, of Gen. Croxton's remissness and neglect of duty in the Ministerial position which he now occupies.

I also feel it incumbent on myself to protest to you, that Gen. Croxton, even after having received from me full information of the fact that this case against Bolivia has already cost Mr. Colton, up to the present time, not only the amount of the principal originally due, but also the interest thereon, and worse still, more than twenty-seven thousand dollars in expenses, incurred in fruitlessly prosecuting his just claim, during the last fifteen years, he himself, as Minister, now has the hardihood to ask Mr. Colton to allow him ten per cent. of the whole amount of the claim, for an anonymous agent whom he proposes to employ; as if, forsooth, there could possibly be any necessary or legitimate use for the employment of more agents, and the consequent incurring of more expenses, in a case which has already, for the thousandth time, more or less, been formally recognized and admitted by the nation-debtor, the very nation to which he is accredited, as eminently just, and entitled to preference in payment! Nor is this the first instance that has come to my knowledge of our national misfortune in having under commission, and in full function, certain ministers who selfishly care more for themselves abroad, than for the rights of their fellow-citizens at home, or for the honor or the interests of their country. Would it not be well for our diplomatic service generally, and for our Republic in every other respect, if all such ministers were at once recalled from foreign lands? A proper regard for the growth and maintenance of our fair fame and influence in far-distant domains, would seem to require that our Presidents should henceforth invariably exercise more patriotic solicitude and discretion in the designation of our diplomatists.

Yet this ten per cent. proposition of Gen. Croxton, in the Legation of the United States at La Paz, is even surpassed in rapacity and audacity by one from Ex-Minister Markbreit, at Cincinnati, who, in a letter to Mr. Colton, under date of May 7, 1873, proposes, after all that has been done, and in full view of his past personal and official connection with the case, to return to Bolivia, and there undertake the collection of the money due, for twenty-two per cent. of the amount which that unparagoned national debtor may be graciously pleased to pay, provided Mr. Colton will, in any event, defray his expenses hence to Arica, in Peru, and back to New York! This indeed, under the aggravated circumstances of the case, is a proposition too stupendous to admit of mild or measured comment. Looking with my mind's eye at Minister Markbreit at La Paz, in 1872, when, on his own false assumptions, he gave the most positive assurances that the money due to Mr. Colton should be paid before the meeting of our Congress in December of that year, and at Ex-Minister Markbreit at Cincinnati, in 1873, when deprived of office, and with so much ironical disinterestedness, he proposes to go back to Bolivia, at Mr. Colton's expense, and collect the money for twenty-two per cent. of whatever amount he may obtain, I am absolutely confused and dumbfounded in amazement.

I have been reliably informed, however, that, during the single year of 1872, Bolivia gave Minister Markbreit at least *thirty* separate and distinct promises to pay the Colton money "very soon;" yet that over-credulous and cajoled Minister, without ever receiving even so much as a half-dime of the amount due, remained, of his own accord, meekly and submissively at La Paz, until, from certain exigencies arising from the ups and downs of party politics in our own country, he was, not a day too soon, suddenly recalled from the scene of his sunny sinecure. How any American Minister, gifted with a grain of true manhood, and already in full possession of a knowledge of Bolivia's unparalleled perfidy in the premises, could, under so many inexcusable and dignity-dispelling circumstances, accept and cherish even one-half the number of thirty such hypocritical promises, without asking for his passports and returning home, is a mystery in international statecraft, which I have neither the ability to explain nor the desire to comprehend.

As Americans of self-respect and honor, let us send no more unfledged Ministers to Bolivia, to be there deceived and corrupted by her; no more diplomatic officials of any sort, in any event, until she shall have paid her fifteen years' debt for her national maps, and thereby removed at least one great source of evil to herself and of injury to others. The very atmosphere of such a country is defiled and infected with the noxious vapors of depravity.

I should still be glad to receive the *ex parte* and high-interest-assigned Bolivian document above mentioned,— Secretary Corral's Financial and Industrial Report for the First Three Months of 1873,—or the semi-annual republication of the same; but as self-respect imperatively forbids my ever again addressing Gen. Croxton on any subject whatever, I would sincerely thank you yourself for such simple action in the State Department as may be necessary to secure a copy for me. The postal expenses and other charges which may attend the procuring of the document will be cheerfully borne by me. With many thanks for the many favors which you have already kindly rendered me in this protracted case against Bolivia, the guilty cause of so much misdemeanor, ill-feeling and accusation,

I have the honor to be, most respectfully,
Your obedient servant,
H. R. HELPER.

MR. BLYTH TO MR. HELPER.

NEW YORK, *February* 23, 1874.

H. R. HELPER, *Esq*.

DEAR SIR. I have perused with much interest your pamphlet exposing the iniquity of the Government of Boivia in its relation as debtor to Mr. Joseph H. Colton. Evidently there are not two sides to this case; and there can, as it seems to me, be but one opinion concerning it. It is plain that the conduct of that Government, and of some of the diplomatic officials of our own Government, who have pretended to aid in the matter, is, as regards bad faith and gross injustice, almost without parallel. It appears to me, however, that the greatest hindrance to your success in the case, thus far, might be traced to the fact that you have endeavored to collect a just claim by just and honorable means only. Had you figured your claim at $99,855.62, and expended all above $50,000 in carefully oiling the machinery of the Bolivian Government, you would probably, years ago, have obtained in clean cash the latter amount.

Yours sincerely,
HENRY A. BLYTH.

MR. FIELD TO MR. HELPER.

NEW YORK, *February* 25, 1874.

H. R. HELPER, *Esq.*

DEAR SIR: I have read with great interest your pamphlet in regard to the claim of Mr. Colton against the Government of Bolivia. If there had been any dispute about the contract made, or the amount due under it, the conduct of the Government of that country might, in part at least, be excusable; but, under the circumstances set forth, there appears to be no excuse nor palliation whatever. It is no new thing in history for a nation to compel another nation to pay claims due to a private citizen; and there can hardly be found an instance where the intervention of the Government of our own country would be more justifiable than in this. It is to be hoped, however, that a proper representation from Washington to Bolivia, will bring about a settlement as amicable and complete as that attained upon the Alabama Claims between the United States and Great Britain.

Very truly yours,
DUDLEY FIELD.

MR. OLMSTED TO MR. HELPER.

NEW YORK, *March* 14, 1874.

H. R. HELPER, *Esq.*

DEAR SIR: * * * There is one penalty to which any people must submit who have not attained the habits of patience, providence and honesty necessary for the maintenance of a strong and stable government,—that of doing without the fruits of civilization; and when those answering

for a government once acknowledge by their acts that their
people are in such a condition, the penalty named is sure to
follow; and the sooner and more widely the acknowledgment
is published to the world, the less will there be of such crue
injustice as Mr. Colton has suffered.
>
Yours respectfully,
FREDERICK LAW OLMSTED.

JUDGE ONDERDONK TO MR. HELPER.

MANHASSET, NEW YORK, *March* 19, 1874.
H. R. HELPER, *Esq*.

DEAR SIR: I have just arisen from a perusal of the pamphlet you sent me, relating to the mean and belittling conduct of the Republic of Bolivia in its dealings with Mr. Joseph H. Colton; and the feelings it excites are those of shame and indignation; shame that the name of Republic should be so profaned by such paltering, in a double sense, respecting a concededly just debt due to a private individual; and indignation that the representatives of our government should evince such culpable indifference to the interests of a defenseless citizen, so basely trifled with. An appropriate function of government is to see that its citizens are not maltreated with impunity, in matters weighty or otherwise, by any foreign power. Were Mr. Colton a British subject, I doubt not that a frigate would, long ago, have appeared off the coast of Bolivia, and there enforced payment of this just claim at the cannon's mouth. Yet in this case, a very few earnest words from our Minister Resident at La Paz, or from our Secretary of State at Washington, would doubtless be efficacious, and secure the measure of justice so long withheld from our fellow-citizen. Other governments would certainly interfere in such a case, and you may very properly urge ours to do so. It is obvious that Bolivia really never intends to pay Mr. Colton; but having so often admitted the justice of his claim, she is, as yet, ashamed to avow her dishonest intentions. It would not be beneath the dignity of our government (and would have a salutary effect,) to announce to the government of Bolivia, that if it is not ashamed to resort to the duplicity and the baser artifices of diplomacy for postponing indefinitely the payment of a just debt, then it is incompatible with our honor to longer maintain a Minister at her capital. Nor should we grieve to see some adjacent commonwealth extend over Bolivia the dignity and power of such honorable and efficient government as would entitle her people to hold up their heads among the civilized and respected peoples of the earth. I discover that, in the management of this matter, you have encountered certain diplomatic jugglers, who "keep the word of promise to the ear, but break it to the hope," and that you have penetrated their designs; for it is manifest that you have presented your ultimatum with rare judgment, and I trust that it may soon prove fitly effective.

Sincerely, your friend,
H. G. ONDERDONK.

EX-MINISTER SMITH TO MR. HELPER.

SHARON, CONNECTICUT, *March* 27, 1874.
H. R. HELPER, *Esq*.

DEAR SIR: I have carefully read your printed case against the government of Bolivia, in relation to the claim of Mr. Colton. I supposed this just debt had been settled long before now, and am sorry for Mr. Colton's losses and disappointments. The case as made out in your pamphlet is a strong one. * * * During the time I was in Bolivia, as Minister Resident, (I having arrived in La Paz in 1858, and left there in 1861,) several efforts were made to obtain from the government of that country payment for the maps published by Mr. Colton. The arrangement for the maps had been effected during the ministership of my immediate predecessor, the Hon. John W. Dana, Ex-Governor of Maine, who, before leaving Bolivia, pressed the claim upon the attention of President Linares, who, some time previously, had come into power by a revolution which ousted Jorge Cordova, the son-in-law and successor of Belzu. * * * President Linares was convinced of the justice of Mr. Colton's claim, and promised me it should be paid; and I believe he would have kept his word, if he had only been favored with a somewhat longer term of office; but, unfortunately, in March, 1861, shortly before I left the country, he was deposed by an intrigue of his own Cabinet, and exiled to Chili, where he soon died. Linares was a lawyer by profession, of good family, and of pure Caucasian descent. The mixture of races is the greatest curse of Bolivia, and Cholo and other hybrid Presidents there, have no regard either for personal character or public reputation. * * *

Very truly yours,
JOHN COTTON SMITH.

MR. FRISBIE TO MR. HELPER.

NEW YORK, *April* 23, 1874.

H. R. HELPER, *Esq.*

DEAR SIR: Your Colton-Bolivia memorial has been received and perused. Although pride in general has never been charged against me as an item in the long list of my demerits, yet I willingly confess that I am very proud indeed of one particular thing ; namely, my citizenship of the United States. It is true, however, that the high degree of pride which I have always cherished in my nationality was several times severely threatened, and occasionally weakened, during the progress of our proceedings under the Treaty of Washington, in the Alabama Claims question, but the final result of those proceedings at Geneva has sufficiently sustained my feelings of high satisfaction, which are still buoyant. Similar emotions and sentiments now affect me in regard to the Colton Claim against Bolivia, for the National Maps of that Republic, published as far back as 1858, and obtained from the creditor under a series of artful misrepresentations and delinquencies by the debtor.

Our government at Washington can expect to retain the sympathy and devotion of its best citizens, only by affording them, with vigilant exactness, the amplest protection and indemnification due from foreign aggression ; and the action of Bolivia in sending here for her maps, which, strange to say, she has never yet paid for, and seems determined not to pay for, was plainly an aggression against the rights and property of an American citizen ; an aggression, too, which has been greatly aggravated in its culpability by the extraordinary instances of double-dealing which she has constantly practiced toward the claimant, and toward the officials of our own government acting for the claimant, ever since she first disregarded her solemn stipulations and pledges in the premises. Holding in view all of Bolivia's dishonored decrees and other assurances to Mr. Colton and his agents, and her innumerable broken promises to our Ministers Resident and Secretaries of State, covering intervals of more than fifteen years, our dignity as a nation, and our duty to the sacred principles of both individual and international justice, are unequivocally compromised. Whether the unbounded respect and admiration which I have always entertained toward the government of my country will be retained in full force, or very materially diminished, will depend in great measure on the action of Congress in this remarkable case, than which, as it affects the Government of Bolivia, I know of nothing more despicable or disgraceful in all the archives of diplomacy.

Yours, very respectfully,
OSCAR FRISBIE.

MR. NEWCOMB TO MR. HELPER.

NEW YORK, *April* 25, 1874.

H. R. HELPER, *Esq*.

DEAR SIR: Your pamphlet on the subject of Bolivia's indebtedness to Mr. Joseph H. Colton, of this city, has been received. Our government has frequently interposed its power to enforce justice to American citizens, whose rights of property had been outraged by foreign nations; but never, as it seems to me, has any such case called more loudly, or with better reason, for such interposition than the one laid bare in your vigorous pamphlet against Bolivia. Calmly and correctly viewed in all its bearings, the action of Bolivia toward our fellow-citizen, Colton, is not merely violative of the spirit of our treaty of amity and commerce with that country, but, worse still, it is certainly tantamount to a very positive spoliation. According to my understanding of the case, it is clearly the duty of our government, scarcely less in the vindication of its own dignity, than in the enforcement of the rights of a despoiled citizen, to demand and compel the immediate payment of the amount so long admitted to be due; the satisfaction of which debt Bolivia has so many times, in so many years of the past, solemnly and formally promised to our Ministers Resident at La Paz, and, through them, to our Secretaries of State at Washington. Hoping that our government will not fail to take a like view of the matter, and that their prompt action will result in the immediate payment by Bolivia of the debt due to Mr. Colton,

    I am, very truly, yours,
        CHARLES S. NEWCOMB.

EX-MINISTER CARTTER TO MR. HELPER.

      WASHINGTON, *May* 13, 1874.
H. R. HELPER, *Esq.*

DEAR SIR: In all my intercourse with the public men of Bolivia, during the period of my ministership there, in the years 1861 and 1862, Mr. Colton's claim against the government of that country was invariably recognized, and payment promised. It is an eminently just claim, and is due under circumstances which should have led to its final settlement many years ago.

    Yours, very respectfully,
        D. K. CARTTER.

MR. HELPER TO A COMMITTEE OF SENATORS.
     WASHINGTON, *May* 18, 1874.
To the Honorable the Committee
    of the Senate on Foreign Affairs.
GENTLEMEN: Herewith you will receive one hundred

papers, numbered in regular order from 1 to 100, in relation to the very just and long-pending claim of Mr. Joseph H. Colton, of New York, against the Government of Bolivia; which Government, for more than fifteen years, besides practicing every sort of deception and subterfuge upon the claimant and his attorneys, has been dallying most scandalously with all our Secretaries of State at Washington, and all our Ministers Resident in Bolivia, since 1858. The papers from No. 1 to No. 5, inclusive, contain and present the case in ample completeness; the ninety-five other papers are merely collateral, corroborative and confirmatory. I have in hand, and shall have the honor of laying before you, if you desire to examine them, at least one hundred other papers, additionally elucidative of this same subject.

Most respectfully and earnestly do I entreat you, gentlemen of the Committee, to cause full and speedy justice to be done to our worthy and aged and outraged fellow-citizen, the claimant. By so doing, you will give to the world another wholesome proof of the fact, now especially needed in this very case, that our uniformly veracious and upright international dealings are to be maintained in all their wonted dignity and distinctness, and that, in no country, and on no account, must any American embassy ever be degraded to the demoralizing diplomacy of duplicity and dishonesty.

I have the honor to be, most respectfully,
   Your obedient servant,
         H. R. HELPER.

INCLOSURES: That is to say, a memorandum of a series of accompanying vouchers, comprised in six separate bundles of documents numbered respectively from 1 to 100:
First bundle—The Case Condensed - - - - - 1 to 5.
Second bundle—Dispatches from Sec'y Fish - - 6 to 18.
Third bundle—Bolivian Documents - - - - 19 to 37.
Fourth bundle—Diplomatic Correspondence - - 38 to 60.
Fifth bundle—Communications to Mr. Helper - 61 to 75.
Sixth bundle—More Bolivian Documents - - 75 to 100.

SECRETARY FISH TO SENATOR CAMERON.

DEPARTMENT OF STATE,
WASHINGTON, *May* 27, 1874.

THE HON. SIMON CAMERON,
Chairman of the Senate Committee on Foreign Relations.

SIR: I have the honor to acknowledge the receipt of your note of the 26th instant, in relation to the claim of Mr. Joseph H. Colton against the Government of Bolivia. The claim in question was presented to this Department, on behalf of Mr. Colton, many years ago, and has several times been brought to its attention by the Attorney of the Claimant. This Department has considered the claim as a meritorious and just one against the Government of that Republic, and instructions were accordingly given by the Department to the Diplomatic representative of this Government near that of Bolivia, to use his good offices with the Bolivian authorities in the claimant's behalf, with a view of facilitating its adjustment and payment. The claim, however, being one originating in a contract voluntarily entered into by a citizen of the United States with the Government of Bolivia, belongs to a class of claims in regard to which it is not the usage of this Government to put forth diplomatic interposition otherwise than by the exercise of its good offices.

I have the honor to be, sir,
Your obedient servant,
HAMILTON FISH.

SECRETARY FISH TO MR. HELPER.

DEPARTMENT OF STATE,
WASHINGTON, *June* 3, 1874.

HINTON. R HELPER, *Esq., Washington.*

SIR: Your letter of the 30th ultimo, concerning the claim

of Mr. J. H. Colton against the Government of Bolivia, has been received. In reply I have to state that a letter, under date of the 27th ultimo, upon the subject of his claim, was sent by the Department to the Committee on Foreign Relations of the Senate, on the 27th ultimo.

I am, sir, your obedient servant,
HAMILTON FISH.

DR. WOOLSEY TO MR. HELPER.

CORNWALL, CONNECTICUT, *August* 8, 1874.
H. R. HELPER, *Esq*.

DEAR SIR: I am in the country, away from home, and from my books, which are in New Haven; but the principle in the case of Colton against Bolivia, is so clear that it hardly needs to be fortified by the opinions of others. You will find in my work on International Law, in the first pages relating to the legitimate grounds of war, the remark that private claims on foreign powers, as well as public injuries, demand intervention on the part of the Government to which the wronged individual owes allegiance.

Yours, very truly,
THEODORE D. WOOLSEY.

OPINION OF DR. THEODORE D. WOOLSEY.

CORNWALL, CONNECTICUT, *August* 8, 1874.

From an examination of the papers relating to the claim of Joseph H. Colton, of New York, against the Republic of Bolivia, it appears:

1. That the work done by him, for the said Republic, in engraving a Map of Bolivia and printing ten thousand copies thereof, was done on contract made between him and authorized agents of Bolivia, and that no complaint appears ever to have been made that he did not faithfully fulfill his part of the contract.

2. That the Government and the Congress of Bolivia have repeatedly acknowledged the debt to Mr. Colton, and that there have been several Congressional acts in Bolivia, authorizing payment of the amount due to him.

3. That he has been put off for many years, and that ten years have expired since the passage of the final act of the Bolivian Congress authorizing such payment for the last time.

In despair of otherwise recovering the money, Mr. Colton now appeals to the Congress of the United States for justice in his behalf. I am asked, as a person supposed to be acquainted with the principles of International Law applicable to this case, what my opinion is in regard to the rights and duties of the Uuited States Government as the authorized and only protector of citizens who have been wronged by foreign powers.

The law applicable to the case is simple enough. If there were a clear intention to evade the payment of a just claim, the United States would be authorized to make the demand with a threat of resort to force in case the payment should not be made within a certain time; or possibly reprisals might be resorted to on the property of Bolivians within the territory of the United States, if any such could be found. If there is a mere inability to pay a just debt, owing to the poverty of the Government, that is an alledged inability,—the United States must judge whether such inability really exists, and must act accordingly.

In many cases of debt due to a private person from a

foreign power, the original contract, or some subsequent transaction, may be open to suspicion, so as to afford a pretext at least for delay, or even for an absolute denial of payment. In this case, there appears to be no room for any such plea. It is admitted by all publicists that the obligations of States are not affected by any political changes or revolutions of any kind. Nothing that has happened, or can happen, in Bolivia, can destroy the force of an obligation once entered into like the one in question.

These opinions are expressed in reply to a letter from Mr. Helper, and are given without fee or reward.

THEODORE D. WOOLSEY.

OPINION OF WILLIAM M. EVARTS.

NEW YORK, *September* 28, 1874.

H. R. HELPER, *Esq.*

DEAR SIR: I have examined Mr. Colton's claim against the Republic of Bolivia, as presented in his memorial to the Congress of the United States, and have read Dr. Woolsey's opinion under date of August 8, 1874; and I entirely concur in the opinion given you by that eminent publicist. In the absence of any plea of inability to pay this admitted debt of the Republic of Bolivia, made in good faith, and accepted as true by our own Government, it seems the manifest duty of the latter to compel the payment of the money due Mr. Colton, by the ordinary coercive processes known among nations and justified by International Law.

I am yours, very truly,

WM. M. EVARTS.

OPINION OF GEORGE TICKNOR CURTIS.

NEW YORK, *September* 8, 1874.

H. R. HELPER, *Esq*.

DEAR SIR: It appears, from the papers which you have laid before me, that the Republic of Bolivia is, and has been for fifteen years, indebted to Mr. Joseph H. Colton, a citizen of the United States, in a sum now exceeding forty thousand dollars in gold, principal and interest; that this debt, originally accrued on contract, has been repeatedly acknowledged by the Bolivian Government in various forms, and repeated promises to pay it have been made, none of which have been fulfilled as to any part of it; and that, especially on the first day of February, 1872, the President of the Republic, Senor Morales, issued a decree which was countersigned by the Secretary of the Treasury, again admitting this debt, and promising " religiously " to pay it " out of the first funds that are obtained from the loan authorized by the Congress of 1871 ;" and ordering the Director-General of Accounts to register the obligation to Mr. Colton; which last promise of payment has been neglected, like the preceding ones; although in June and July, 1872, the Republic negotiated in London a loan of $10,000,000. Under these circumstances, you ask me, What is Mr. Colton's remedy?

It is an undoubted principle of international law, that a State cannot be sued in its own or in any other court, unless it has expressly agreed to be subject to that form of redress. For this reason, the law of nations has long admitted that the State whose citizens or subjects have suffered any wrong at the hands of another State, may demand for them full redress and satisfaction, and may enforce that demand by reprisals or by war. The government whose citizen is injured has only to be satisfied of the justice of his demand, and that justice has been denied; and in Mr. Colton's case the debt has been so often and so solemnly admitted by the Government of Bolivia, that the United States can have no occasion to make further inquiry. The repeated failures to pay what has been so repeatedly promised, amount to a denial of justice, as flagrant and palpable as if the Government of Bolivia had refused to admit the debt. Under these circumstances, principle and practice alike require that the Government of the United States demand from the Government of Bolivia immediate payment of this claim.

We are most familiar with the exercise of this national right to enforce the claims of individuals, in cases of tortious injury to person or property, inflicted by a foreign State. But the public law makes no distinction between cases of tort and cases of contract. The text-writers, from Grotius to Wheaton and to Phillimore, rest the practice on the principle that, as there is no other mode of redress by which justice can be obtained, it is the right of the president or sovereign, whose fellow-citizen or subject has suffered any wrong at the hands of a foreign State, to compel justice to be done. If the law of nations were to make any distinction between debts arising upon contract and claims for compensation for tort,—if it were to admit that the promise of a State to pay a sum of money to an individual foreigner is not within the principle that authorizes a State to compel justice to be done to its citizens or subjects by other States, —one of the chief supports of the public credit of governments would be swept away. Governments are enabled to bind the nations which they rule, in contracts with individuals, and so to secure what they could not otherwise command, because the public law treats the government as the agent of the nation, and regards a national pecuniary obligation, when it is once clearly incurred, as a claim which the State to which the holder of that obligation belongs may, if need be, enforce upon the property of the State that owes the debt, or upon the property of its citizens or subjects, wherever it can be found. Of all the countries in the world, it concerns the United States not to allow any relaxation of this principle, for we are a great debtor nation; our public debts are largely held by foreigners; and while no one has yet had occasion to impugn our national honor, our Government cannot afford to deny that the foreign holder of our national promises to pay, has the ultimate security of a collection of his debt by his president or sovereign, if he shall ever need that remedy. I hold it to be just as clear that the United States can enforce payment of a simple contract debt, admitted to be due by a foreign State to a citizen of the United States, as that they can compel a foreign State to make compensation for any tortious injury or trespass on my property or person, committed by the direct authority, or through the culpable negligence of a foreign power. To say nothing of the other and former promises, the decree of February 1, 1872, signed by President Morales, belongs to the highest class of pecuniary obligations, being of as solemn and special a nature as a bond would be, executed under all the forms and sanctions of law.

The diplomatic department of the Government of the United States is the department to which it belongs to demand payment of this claim. I do not well see how the State Department can refuse to act in this case; and if it has not already given instructions to our Minister in Bolivia to make a peremptory demand in behalf of Mr. Colton, I cannot doubt that it will do so, when fully informed of the facts.

If, after such demand, it should become necessary to resort to reprisals, it would be proper for Congress to pass a joint resolution giving authority to the President to apply that remedy. Neither the fact that this claim is the claim of a single individual, nor the amount of the demand, can vary the principle which determines the power and the duty of the United States to act in the manner I have suggested. The public law does not require that a claim of this nature should rise to a certain specific dignity before it can become a subject of international action. All the dignity that is requisite is reached when it appears that there is a palpable denial of justice; and when this is the case, a government that does its duty to its citizens is just as much bound to act upon a case of forty thousand as it could be to act upon a case of forty millions of money.

I am, sir, yours, very respectfully,
GEORGE TICKNOR CURTIS.

OPINION OF DAVID DUDLEY FIELD.

NEW YORK, *November* 19, 1874.

Mr. Hinton Rowan Helper has asked my opinion upon the right and duty of the United States to intervene, either by persuasion or force, for the purpose of obtaining from the Government of Bolivia the payment of a certain debt due to Mr. Joseph H. Colton, of the city of New York. The debt, amounting to forty thousand dollars and upwards, including interest, is for maps of Bolivia ordered by the Government, and engraved and printed by Mr. Colton. The Government of that country admits the debt to be due, has often, in the most solemn manner, through both the executive and legislative departments, engaged to pay it, and is and has for years been able to fulfill the engagement. I am of opinion that it is not only the right, but also the duty, of the United States to intervene, and for the following reasons, among others:

First: Every nation owes to its members the maintenance of their rights. So long as it exacts allegiance and obedience, so long is it bound, by the corresponding obligation, to protect. This results from the relations between the citizen and the State.

Second: Commerce, in its double signification of intercourse and traffic, may lawfully be carried on between one nation and its members, and the other nations and their members. From this arises an obligation on the part of every nation to protect the members of other nations coming to it in their lawful commerce, and to enforce engagements made with them.

Third: The obligation of a nation can be enforced only by other nations. This results from the fact, that a member of a nation cannot do it, both because he is forbidden, and because he is too weak. He is forbidden by his own nation to assert his rights by violence, or to do anything for himself in respect to a foreign nation, except to resort to its tribunals, and to ask of its government.

Hence arise two obligations, that of Bolivia to Mr. Colton, a foreigner, to pay him the debt contracted, and that of the Uni e 1 States to Mr. Colton, their citizen, to enforce the obligation of Bolivia. In other words, the claim of Mr. Colton upon Bolivia, should be taken up and enforced by the nation to which he belongs, the claim being admitted, he himself being powerless to enforce it, and his nation being bound to maintain his rights. I am here stating a doctrine of international law, as applicable to a particular case. It is not a new doctrine. We have enforced it against France, and against Mexico. England is committed to it. So long ago as 1848, Lord Palmerston, who was then the Foreign Secretary of the British Government, dispatched a circular to the British Representatives abroad, in respect to the claims of holders of foreign bonds, in which he used this language:

"If the question is to be considered simply in its bearing upon International Right, there can be no doubt whatever of the perfect right which the government of every country possesses to take up, as a matter of diplomatic negotiation, any well-founded complaint which any of its subjects may prefer against the government of another country, or any wrong which, from such foreign government, those subjects may have sustained; and if the government of one country is entitled to demand redress for any one individual among its subjects who may have a just but unsatisfied pecuniary claim upon the government of another country, the right to require redress cannot be diminished merely because the extent of the wrong is increased, and because, instead of there being only one individual claiming a comparatively small sum, there are a great number of individuals to whom a very large amount is due."

Many considerations of policy and public morality might easily be adduced, also, to fortify the legal doctrine. It is the policy of all governments to do justice themselves, and to enforce it upon others. This, especially, is the policy of republican governments. They cannot afford an unfavorable comparison with governments of an aristocratical or monarchical character; for, more than these, they rest upon public opinion and moral considerations. Nor can they safely exhibit to their own people examples of disregard or even indifference to honesty or honor. The United States best consult their own interests and their own reputation, when they demand justice from another nation for one of their own citizens. Bolivia, too, will best consult her interests and her reputation by yielding gracefully to the intervention of the United States. Foreigners will the more readily trust her in the future, if they find that, in dealing with her, they have not only the guarantee of her good faith, but also the guarantee of the public law of the world.

DAVID DUDLEY FIELD.

OBLIGATIONS OF GOVERNMENTS.—Grotius.

In his remarkable and excellent work on the "Rights of Peace and War," Grotius said:—" To natural law belongs the rule of abstaining from that which belongs to others; and if we have in our possession anything of another's, the restitution of it, or of any gain which we have made from it; the fulfilling of promises, and the reparation of damage done by fault; and the recognition of certain things as meriting punishment among men. * * * People who violate the laws of nature and nations beat down the bulwark of their own tranquillity for future time. This performance of promises proceeds from the nature of immutable justice. If the promiser has been negligent in inquiring into the matter, or in expressing his intention, and another person has thereby suffered loss, the promiser will be bound to make that loss good; not by the force of his promise, but as having done damage by his fault."

OBLIGATIONS OF GOVERNMENTS. — Puffendorf.

In his learned work "On the Law of Nature and Nations," Puffendorf says :—"A perfect promise is when a man not only determines his will to the performance of such or such a thing for another hereafter, but, likewise, shows that he gives the other a full right of requiring it from him. And as of individuals, in this respect, so also of nations and governments."

OBLIGATIONS OF GOVERNMENTS.—VATTEL.

In his "Law of Nations," page 161, Vattel says:—" We have the right to obtain justice by force, if we cannot obtain it otherwise; or to pursue our right by force of arms. * *
* If there were a people who made open profession of trampling justice under foot,—who despised and violated the rights of others whenever they found an opportunity,— the interests of human society would authorize all other na‧ tions to form a confederacy in order to humble and chastise the delinquents. If, by her constant maxims, and by the whole tenor of her conduct, a nation evidently proves herself to be actuated by that mischievous disposition,—if she regards no right as sacred,—the safety of the human race requires that she should be repressed."

OBLIGATIONS OF GOVERNMENTS.—PHILLIMORE.

In his great work on International Law, volume II, page 8, Phillimore says:—" The right of interference on the part of a State, for the purpose of enforcing the performance of justice to its citizens from a foreign State, stands upon an unquestionable foundation, when the foreign State has become itself the debtor of these citizens. It must, of course, be assumed that such State has, through the medium of its proper and legitimate organs, contracted such debt; whether that organ be the sovereign alone, according to the constitution of Russia, or the Sovereign and Parliament, according to the constitution of England, the debt as contracted with foreign citizens, whether in an individual or a corporate capacity, constitutes an obligation of which the country of the lenders has a right to require and enforce the fulfillment." Again, in volume II, page 12, Phillimore says: —" The obligation of the State debtor is, if possible, yet stronger when the debt has been guaranteed by treaty. For in that case, the foreign may be entitled to a preference over the domestic creditor." (Mr. Colton's claim has been " guaranteed " by at least six formal and official acts of the Bolivian Government, and by an almost countless number of diplomatic promises. It has, indeed, been one vast system of " guaranteeing " ever since the year 1858. H. R. H.) Again, in volume III, page 34, Phillimore says :—" One of the grounds of the war between the United States and Mexico, was the non-payment of debts due from the Government of that country to citizens of the United States."

OBLIGATIONS OF GOVERNMENTS.—WILDMAN.

In his "Institutes of International Law," volume I, pages 187 and 188, Wildman says :—" When a State refuses to repair any injury, or to pay a debt, or to redress any wrong, the State that is injured may seize anything that belongs to the offending State, and detain or confiscate it in satisfaction of such wrong. For this purpose the property of all private persons forms part of the State whereof they are members, whether as native-born citizens or as persons domiciled therein. * * * As every State considers an injury to any one of its citizens as an injury to itself, it is not unjust that they should be liable for the obligations of the State, which is bound to indemnify them for any losses which may ensue."

OBLIGATIONS OF GOVERNMENTS.—MARSHALL.

In the case of Marbury *vs.* Madison, Chief Justice Marshall, one of the ablest and purest jurisconsults of any age or country, said:
"The very essence of civil liberty consists in the right of every individual to claim the protection of the laws whenever he receives an injury. One of the first duties of Government is to afford that protection. In Great Britain the king himself is sued in the respectful form of a petition, and he never fails to comply with the judgment of his court." Again, in the case of Ogden *vs.* Saunders, Judge Marshall said: "So far back as human research carries us, we find the judicial power, as a part of the executive, administering justice by the application of remedies to violated rights, or broken contracts. We find that power applying these remedies on the idea of a preëxisting obligation on every man to do what he has promised on condition to do; that the breach of this obligation is an injury for which the injured party has a just claim to compensation, and that society ought to afford him a remedy for that injury. * * * In a state of nature, individuals may contract, their contracts are obligatory, and force may rightfully be employed to coerce the party who has broken his engagement. Independent nations are individuals in a State of nature. Whence is derived the obligation of their contracts? They admit the existence of no superior legislative power which is to give them validity; yet their validity is acknowledged by all. If one of these contracts be broken, all admit the right of the injured party to demand reparation for the injury, and to enforce that reparation if it be withheld. He may not have the power to enforce it, but the whole civilized world concurs in saying that the power, if possessed, is rightly used. In society, the wrong-doer may be too pow-

erful for the law. He may deride its coercive power; yet his contracts are obligatory; and if society acquire the power of coercion, that power will be applied without previously enacting that his contract is obligatory. The rightfulness of coercion must depend on the preëxisting obligation to do that for which compulsion is used. It is no objection to the principle, that the injured party may be the weaker. * * * Every man retains the right to acquire property, to dispose of that property according to his own judgment, and to pledge himself for a future act. These rights are not given by society, but are brought into it. The right of coercion is necessarily surrendered to government, and this surrender imposes on government the correlative duty of furnishing a remedy."

OBLIGATIONS OF GOVERNMENTS.—KENT.

In the very first chapter of the first volume of his perspicuous and profound Commentaries on American Law, Chancellor Kent says:
"The law of nations, as it is now understood by us and by the European world, is the offspring of modern times. The most refined States among the ancients seem to have had no conception of the moral obligations of justice and humanity between nations; and with them there was no such thing in existence as the science of international law. They regarded strangers and enemies as nearly synonymous, and considered foreign persons and property as lawful prize. * * * Grotious has been justly considered as the father of the law of nations. He arose like a splendid luminary, dispelling darkness and confusion, and imparting light and security to the intercourse of nations. It has been

said that Lord Bacon's works first suggested to Grotius the idea of reducing the law of nations to the certainty and precision of a regular science. Grotious has himself fully explained the reasons which led him to undertake his necessary and most useful and immortal work. * * * His object was to correct all false theories and. pernicious maxims, by showing a community of sentiment among the wise and learned of all nations and ages, in favor of the natural law of morality. He likewise undertook to show that justice was of perpetual obligation, and essential to the well-being of every society, and that the great commonwealth of nations stood in need of law, and the observance of faith, and the practice of justice. * * * There is a natural and a positive law of nations. By the former, every State, in its relations with other States, is bound to conduct itself with justice, good faith and benevolence; and this application of the law of nature has been called the necessary law of nations, because nations are bound by the law of nature to observe it; and it is also termed the internal law of nations, because it is obligatory upon them in point of conscience. We ought not to separate the science of public law from that of ethics, nor encourage the dangerous suggestion that governments are not so strictly bound by the obligations of truth, justice and humanity, in relation to other powers as they are in the management of their own local concerns. States, or bodies politic, are to be considered as moral persons, having a public will, capable and free to do right and wrong, inasmuch as they are col'ections of individuals, each of whom carries with him into the service of the community the same binding law of morality which ought to control his conduct in private life."

OBLIGATIONS OF GOVERNMENTS.—PRESIDENT JACKSON.

In the case of the neglect of the French Chambers to make the proper appropriations for the indemnity agreed to be paid to the United States, by the treaty of July 4, 1831, which was itself a recognition of the principle that authorizes a nation to demand compensation for spoliatfons on the property of its citizens, whatever changes may occur in the government of the country that inflicts the injury, President Andrew Jackson, in his message to Congress, of December, 1834, said (as quoted approvingly by Phillimore, volume III, page 33, and by Lawrence, in his Wheaton, page 508):

" It is a well-settled principle of the International Code that where one nation owes another a liquidated debt which it refuses or neglects to pay, the aggrieved party may seize on the property belonging to the other, its citizens, or subjects, sufficient to pay the debt, without giving just cause of war. * * * If an appropriation shall not be made by the French Chambers at their next session, it may justly be concluded, that the Govenment of France has finally determined to disregard its own solemn undertaking, and refused to pay an acknowledged debt. In that event, every day's delay on our part will be a stain upon our national honor, as well as a denial of justice to our injured citizens."

OBLIGATIONS OF GOVERNMENTS.—WHEATON, LAWRENCE, SEWARD.

In his edition of Wheaton's International Law, page 157, William Beach Lawrence thus quotes from Secretary Seward's dispatch of December 4, 1861, tó the Prime Ministers of Great Britain, France and Spain, in prudent protest against the armed intervention of those powers in the domestic affairs of Mexico ; it being at a time, too, when we ourselves, as a nation, were unfortunately involved in a great civil conflict:

" It is true that the United States have, on their part, claims to urge against Mexico. Upon due consideration, however, the President is of opinion that it would be inexpedient to seek satisfaction of their claims at this time through an act of accession to the convention of Great Britain, France, and Spain. * * * The United States habitually cherish a decided good-will toward Mexico, and a lively interest in its security, prosperity, and welfare. * * * Animated by these sentiments, the United States do not feel inclined to resort to forcible remedies for their claims at the present moment." Again, Wheaton, Lawrence, page 506, says: "Reprisials are negative (as opposed to positive,) when a State refuses to fulfill a perfect obligation which it has contracted."

Again, the same authorities, page 509, say:—" The reclamation made on Mexico by England, France and Spain, in 1861, seemed to pass beyond the ordinary case of reprisals for tortious spoliations and violated contracts."

OBLIGATIONS OF GOVERNMENTS.—WOOLSEY.

In his work on International Law, page 171, Woolsey says: —" A contract is one of the highest acts of human free will ; it is the will binding itself in regard to the future, and surrendering its right to change a certain expressed intention, so that it becomes morally and jurally wrong to act otherwise. * * * National contracts are even more solemn and sacred than private ones, on account of the great interests involved, of the deliberations with which the obligations are assumed, of the permanence and generality of the obligations,—measured by the national life, and including thousands of particular cases,—and of each nation's calling to be a teacher of right to all within and without its borders."

OBLIGATIONS OF GOVERNMENTS.—HALLECK.

In his International Law, page 313, Halleck says: "The justifiable causes of war are injuries received or threatened. There must be a strong probability that the threat may be attempted to be carried into execution, as mere empty words will seldom justify us in declaring war. It is not necessary that the injuries should be material or physical, as a national insult is often as injurious as the robbery of a province. The justifiable objects of a war may, therefore, be divided into three classes or subdivisions. 1st. To secure what belongs or is due to us; 2nd, To provide for our future safety by obtaining reparation for injuries done to us; and 3d, To protect ourselves and property from a threatened injury. * * * If one shows a clear and valid title to a thing in dispute, and has first resorted to the amicable modes of settling the question upon an equitable footing, and has been refused all reasonable offers of adjustment, he may be justifiable in resorting to force for the recovery of what really and truly belongs to him."

SENATOR CAMERON TO MR. HELPER.

HARRISBURG, PENN., *October* 25, 1874.
HINTON R. HELPER, *Esq., New York.*

DEAR SIR: I have received the letter you addressed to me on the 20th instant, on my return from California, and have read the copies of the several papers attached. Please send the originals of these papers to my address in Washington, about the first week of the coming session; and I will endeavor to secure prompt attention on the part of the Committee. Yours truly,

SIMON CAMERON.

MR. HELPER TO SENATOR CAMERON.

NEW YORK, *December* 1, 1874.
HON. SIMON CAMERON,
*Chairman of the Senate Committee on
Foreign Affairs, Washington.*

SIR: Acting in conformity with the suggestion contained in the note which I had the honor to receive from you, under date of the 25th of October last, in reply to mine of the 20th of the same month, I herewith inclose to you the following additional vouchers, in the case of the rightful and oft-admitted claim of Mr. Joseph H. Colton against the Government of Bolivia. * * * Sincerely thanking you for your assurance that you "will endeavor to secure prompt attention on the part of the Committee," and trusting that the attention so given will well accord with the highest principles of individual justice, governmental equity, diplomatic veracity, and international honor.

I am, sir, with great respect, your obedient servant,

H. R. HELPER.

MR. COLTON TO SENATOR CONKLING.

NEW YORK, *December* 7, 1874.

HON. ROSCOE CONKLING, *United States Senator*.

DEAR SIR: Another session of Congress is now open, and I am still suffering the gross and oppressive injustice which the Government of Bolivia, notwithstanding our uninterrupted and friendly diplomatic relations with that Republic, has been permitted to inflict upon me, with impunity, ever since the year 1858. In the seventy-fifth year of my age, I now again earnestly appeal to my own Government for the simple measure of redress which I have hitherto sought in vain. Within the last day or two, my present and permanent attorney in this case, Mr. Helper, has written to Senators Cameron and Hamlin, renewing the offer of his best services in my behalf, whether in or out of Washington; and I sincerely trust that you, and the other members of your honorable Committee, may be pleased to coöperate with him in at last securing my rights,—so far as it is now possible to secure those rights,—from Bolivia without further delay.

As for the large sum of expenses, amounting to over $27,000, legitimately and unavoidably incurred by me, during the last sixteen years, in unavailing efforts to obtain my just dues from the Government of Bolivia, is there no easy and proper way for me to recover those expenses in addition to the amount of principal and interest so frequently admitted by the Government itself to be due and payable to me? I ask this question, not as now making any new demand, but rather as a matter affecting the purer principles of international law and equity, and as the statement of a fact, a very serious fact for me, which ought, I think, to impart much weight to my ctition, already before you, for the prompt intervention of the Government of the United

States for the righting of at least the acknowledged part of this great wrong. Pray be good enough to lay before the honorable Chairman of your Committee, Senator Cameron, the suggestions thus submitted.

I have the honor to be, most respectfully,
Your obedient servant,
JOSEPH H. COLTON.

MR. HELPER TO SENATOR HAMLIN.

NEW YORK, *December* 7, 1874.
HON. HANNIBAL HAMLIN, *United States Senator.*

DEAR SIR: Having already spent at Washington a considerable part of no less than three sessions of Congress, in the sincere but unsuccessful effort to obtain at least an approximation to justice for my foreign-aggrieved client, Mr. Joseph H. Colton, a worthy and exemplary citizen of the United States, who, for the last sixteen years, has been a helpless victim of the atrocious duplicity and dishonesty of the Bolivian Government, I have, in the hope of avoiding the sacrifice of still more time and labor and money, concluded not to go again to the national Capital, on this truth-throttled and equity-butchered business, unless the Foreign Relations Committee of the Senate, before whom all the important papers in the case are now awaiting attention, shall indicate that my presence, as attorney for the aged and infirm claimant, may be necessary. At any time, however, that I may be honored with such an indication from your Committee, I shall be happy to respond to it in person, without a day's delay; and I may here frankly inform you, that I am anxiously desirous to receive an intimation that my verbal testimony and explanation, in an ante-room of the

Capitol, would be welcome in this connection, provided the numerous papers now on file before you are not superabundantly sufficient to warrant the Committee in reporting the simple Resolution solicited. Trusting that, because of the shortness of the present session of Congress, your honorable Committee may at once find it convenient to act wisely and justly on this case, and so let it soon go to the House for right action there; and trusting further, that you will be kind enough to submit this communication to the Hon. Simon Cameron, Chairman of your Committee, whose enlightened attention I thus again earnestly and respectfully invoke in this regard,

I have the honor to be, very truly,
Your obedient servant,
H. R. HELPER.

SENATOR MERRIMON TO MR. HELPER.

WASHINGTON, *December* 9, 1874.
H. R. HELPER, *Esq., New York.*

DEAR SIR: I am just in receipt of your letter of yesterday, and beg to say in reply, that I will cheerfully call the matter of the claim against Bolivia, in favor of Mr. Colton, to the attention of Senators McCreery and Schurz, to-day, and hope they will co-operate with the Committee in coming to a conclusion on the subject without further delay. I hardly think you could hasten action on the case, if you were present, particularly as there is no question at all about the proofs.

Yours, very respectfully,
A. S. MERRIMON.

MR. HELPER TO SENATOR CAMERON.

NEW YORK, *December* 19, 1874.
HON. SIMON CAMERON,
Chairman of the Senate Committee on
Foreign Affairs, Washington.

SIR: If the Colton claim against Bolivia has been regularly referred for examination and report, please place in the hands of the gentleman having the vouchers in charge, the inclosed additional paper, suggestive of the form of a Resolution, which would seem to be proper and requisite in the premises. The Hon. Godlove S. Orth, Chairman of the House Committee on Foreign Affairs, to whom I personally submitted this paper, at Washington, in May last, suggested one or two slight modifications, upon which he assured me he would support the proposed Resolution; but whatever modifications may be determined on, I should prefer to have them made by you, or by your Committee; only begging leave to premise, however, that any view of the case which accepts and treats the bulk of Bolivians as being impressed with any such elevated convictions of truth and honor as are characteristic of ordinarily civilized and enlightened nations, will prove as certainly fatal to justice and all right dealing, as the recently attempted application of Quaker ethics to the savage Modocs proved futile for the purposes of innocence and peace.

I have the honor to be, most respectfully,
Your obedient servant,
H. R. HELPER.

MR. HELPER TO SECRETARY FISH.

NEW YORK, *January* 4, 1875.
HON. HAMILTON FISH, *Secretary of State, Washington.*

SIR: Right heartily do Mr. Colton and I thank you for your letter of last Thursday, informing us that you are now urging the payment of his fully and specifically admitted claim against the Government of Bolivia, and, in connection with that information, transcribing an extract from one of Minister Reynolds' dispatches to you, No. 24, wherein he says President Frias has assured him that the money so long overdue shall certainly be paid some time this winter. Pray pardon us, however, if we express a real apprehension that this last assurance of President Frias, so much like many of his former assurances, is only a new and enticing refrain of a very trite old song,—a Siren Song of Sixteen Summers,—which, because of its incessant and monotonous vibrations against our auditory nerves, has ceased to charm our ears or soothe our souls.

To us who have, during so many long and weary years, been the victims of so much diplomatic duplicity and dishonor on the part of Bolivia, this autumnal pledge of President Frias,—penned to our Minister in November,—looks amazingly like the first measure of a new crop of piecrust promises, which Bolivia is so skilled in making and breaking with equal ease. In fidelity to the general principles of truth and honor, in vindication of the sincerity and efficiency of American diplomacy, and in simple justice to a long and grievously outraged citizen of the United States, you, as our honored Secretary of State, and Congress and President Grant, as our supreme protectors of the lives and properties of the members in general of a great nationality, will, I trust, soon stop forever the criminal dilly-dallying and audacity of Bolivia, in this matter, and compel her, under just penalties, to discharge at once the very obvious duties which she has so long and so wickedly shirked, in contempt of Mr. Colton's rights and interests.

There is neither fitness nor respectability in such a country exhibiting herself, for sixteen years consecutively,—and always without choking or even blushing with chagrin,— upon maps of her own ordering, but for which she has never yet paid. Whether there is either dignity or any other sort of propriety in our acting toward such a country as one worthy of diplomatic or international recognition, is, I think, a question which ought soon to be seriously reconsidered by the Congress of the United States. In my opinion, the abolition of our mission to Bolivia would be a very just and prudent piece of American legislation. Again sincerely thanking you for the information contained in your letter of last week,

I am, sir, most respectfully,
Your obedient servant,
H. R. HELPER.

SENATOR MERRIMON TO MR. HELPER.

UNITED STATES SENATE CHAMBER,
WASHINGTON, *February* 13, 1875.

H. R. HELPER, *Esq., New York*.

DEAR SIR: I have received your letter of the 12th instant, and have just had an interview with Senator Howe in reference to the Resolution to which you refer. He is anxious to call up and pass the Resolution, and will do so the first opportunity. In the regular course of business, it will probably be called within five or six days from this time. I do not think there will be any objection to it; and I trust

it may so well serve the purpose for which it was designed as to secure an early payment of the debt.
Yours, very truly,
A. S. MERRIMON.

MR. HELPER TO SENATOR CAMERON.

NEW YORK, *February* 22, 1875.

HON. SIMON CAMERON,
  Chairman of the Senate Committee on
    Foreign Affairs, Washington.

DEAR SIR: My aged and esteemed friend, Mr. Joseph H. Colton, of this city, chafed by a keen sense of being the victim of sixteen years of diplomatic chicanery and injustice, perpetrated against him by a degraded and vicious nationality with which the United States are maintaining regular international relations, is very anxious about the passage of Senate Bill No. 1156, Report No. 531, in the matter of his claim against the Government of Bolivia. Will you be kind enough to inform me as to the present status and prospect of the Bill? Has it yet passed the Senate? and if not, can you not, with perfect fairness and propriety of action, call it up and pass it without further delay? Or, is it at all likely that I could, in any way, by my presence at Washington, facilitate the passage of the Bill through Congress? If my personal attention is thought to be necessary, I shall be glad to give it immediately. Nevertheless, I should prefer to be spared the additional expense and time and fatigue and risk of having to go again to Washington, whither,—the same as to various other places on no less than three of the continents of the earth,—I have hitherto gone, again and again, in the fruitless and heart-sickening search for justice in this affair.

I have the honor to be, very respectfully,
Your obedient servant,
H. R. HELPER.

SENATOR HOWE TO MR. HELPER.

WASHINGTON, *February* 23, 1875.
H. R. HELPER, *Esq., New York*.

DEAR SIR: It is not probable that you could advance Mr. Colton's Bill if you were here. It will doubtless pass when the Committee on Foreign Relations is called in the Senate, and it cannot pass before. That Committee will probably be called within four days.

Yours, truly,
T. O. HOWE.

SENATOR CAMERON TO MR. HELPER.

UNITED STATES SENATE CHAMBER,
WASHINGTON, *February* 23, 1875.
H. R. HELPER, *Esq., New York*.

DEAR SIR: In regard to the Bill for the relief of Mr. Colton, it is in the condition of many others. The crush is great and the time is short. I *hope* it may be reached, and I *think* you might be able to aid it if you were here.

Yours, truly,
SIMON CAMERON.

SENATOR HAMLIN TO MR. HELPER.

UNITED STATES SENATE CHAMBER,
WASHINGTON, *February* 23, 1875.
H. R. HELPER, *Esq., New York.*
DEAR SIR: I have your note of yesterday. In answer to the question therein asked, "Is my presence at Washington necessary to the passage of Mr. Colton's Bill against Bolivia?" I have to say that, in my opinion, it is not.
Very truly, yours,
A. HAMLIN.

MR. HELPER TO SENATORS HOWE AND HAMLIN.

NEW YORK, *February* 26, 1875.
SENATORS HOWE AND HAMLIN, *Washington*.
GENTLEMEN: Another evidence of disagreement between doctors,—in this case the doctors being doctors of the maladies of States and nations,—appears in the notes which I had the honor to receive, yesterday, from each of you, respectively, on the one hand, and from Senator Cameron, Chairman of your Committee, on the other. It seems that both of you hold the opinion that my presence at Washington would not be likely to advance the passage of Mr. Colton's Bill against Bolivia. Senator Cameron says: "I think you might be able to aid it, if you were here." This difference of opinion leaves me in a quandary. Pray help me out of the dilemma by passing the Bill immediately in the Senate, so it may yet have at least a day or two of chance for passage in the House.
Yours, very truly,
H. R. HELPER.

After many months of very careful consideration of the subject in all its bearings, the honorable Committee of the Senate on Foreign Affairs, to whom, on the 7th of May, 1874, the case had been regularly referred, and whose gifted and distinguished *personnel* was composed of Oliver P. Morton, Frederick T. Frelinghuysen, Thomas C. McCreery, Timothy O. Howe, John P. Stockton, Hannibal Hamlin, Roscoe Conkling, Carl Schurz and Simon Cameron, unanimously made the following Report; and thereupon, in concert of procedure with the House Committee on Foreign Relations, consisting of the very worthy and accomplished Representatives Leonard Meyers, Freeman Clarke, Samuel S. Cox, E. Rockwood Hoar, Marcus L. Ward, William J. Albert, Charles G. Williams, Henry A. Banning, James C. Robinson, and Godlove S. Orth, your honorable body, legislating in the capacity of an illustrious assembly of American Senators and Representatives, and advancing courageously in the exercise of a just and wise statemanship, passed, without one dissenting voice, on the 3rd of March, 1875, the accompanying Act, which follows immediately the following Report:

REPORT OF THE SENATE COMMITTEE ON FOREIGN AFFAIRS.

In the Senate of the United States, January 19, 1875, Mr. Howe submitted the following report:

The Committee on Foreign Relations, to whom was referred the petition of Joseph H. Colton, asking the intervention of the Government of the United States, in aid of his claim upon the Government of Bolivia, together with the accompanying papers, ask leave to submit the following report:

The memorialist represents that in 1858 he contracted with Col. Juan Ondarza and Commandant Juan Mariano

Mujia, duly authorized in that behalf by the Bolivian government, to engrave and publish on copper-plate a map of the Republic of Bolivia. The map was to be put on canvas, fitted up with moldings, rollers, and rings, and to be six feet in length by five feet in height. Of such a map he agreed to print and deliver to that government ten thousand copies. For the work, the Bolivian government agreed to pay $25,-000 in gold. Two thousand dollars of that sum were to be paid on the commencement of the work, and were paid. The balance, of $23,000, was to be paid on the delivery of the maps, or soon afterward. Of the balance no part has been paid.

The contract is said to have been made with the memorialist at his place of business in the city of New York, where the memorialist at that time resided, and has since continued to reside. The memorialist represents that the work was executed at an extremely low price; and he avers that the Bolivian government actually sold 2,000 copies of the same maps at twelve dollars per copy, and 3,000 other copies at five dollars per copy.

The justice of Mr. Colton's claim appears to have been frequently recognized by the Bolivian government in the most solemn manner. Among the papers accompanying the memorial is an original decree, signed by President Morales, of which the following is a translation:

MINISTRY OF FINANCE AND INDUSTRY,
La Paz, Bolivia, February 1, 1872.

In view of the contract made in New York on the 21st of September, 1858, between Joseph H. Colton, of the one part, and Juan Ondarza and Juan Mariano Mujia, of the other part, for the engraving and publishing of ten thousand maps of Bolivia, for the sum of $25,000 in gold; in view, also, of the decree of March 8, 1858, authorizing the making of the said contract; also the laws of August 12, 1861, and October 27, 1864, which order payment of the sum due the claimant; also the financial law of the Republic for the year 1865, which recognizes the debt, including interest, at the rate of 6 per cent. per annum, and difference of exchange, in the sum-total, at that time, of thirty-eight thousand dollars, it is hereby acknowledged and declared that the claim now made by Joseph H. Colton, through his attorney, Hinton Rowan Helper, is just and entitled to preference in payment. In virtue whereof the government of Bolivia, desiring to maintain the national credit, recognizes as now due the claimant, by way of principal, interest, and difference in exchange, the full sum of fifty-one thousand nine hundred and eighty-five dollars in Bolivian currency, or, as otherwise expressible, the sum of forty-one thousand five hundred and eighty-eight dollars and fifty-four cents in gold, to be paid religiously out of the first funds that are obtained by the loan authorized by the congress of 1871.

Take notice of this, and pass it to the Director-General of Accounts for the registry of the sum of forty-one thousand five hundred and eighty-eight dollars and fifty-four cents in gold ($41,588.54 in gold,) to be paid to Joseph H. Colton.

Sign-manual of his Excellency,

PRESIDENT MORALES.

By order of his Excellency:

GARCIA,

Secretary of the Treasury.

On the 1st of June, 1872, the Bolivian Secretary for Foreign Affairs addressed to Mr. Markbreit, the United States Minister Resident at La Paz, a letter, of which the following is a copy:

DEPARTMENT OF GOVERNMENT AND FOREIGN AFFAIRS,

La Paz, Bolivia, June 1, 1872.

SIR: With your pleasing communication of yesterday I have received Mr. Colton's letter to you, from New York, in which he expresses his thanks to the national government for the decree of the first of last February, which ordered payment of the amount due him for ten thousand maps of this Republic, asking at the same time payment by draft in his favor against Messrs. Lumb, Wanklin & Co., negotiators of the Bolivian loan in London.

So soon as we shall have received a full statement in regard to the said loan, the draft asked for will be given, as the national government

is interested that payment of Mr. Colton's claim be made with preference, as soon as possible. With this motive,
    I have the honor to subscribe myself,
        Your most attentive and faithful servant,
            CASIMIRO CORRAL.
Hon. LEOPOLD MARKBREIT,
    United States Minister Resident

Again, on the 17th of October, 1872, the same official addressed to Mr. Markbreit another letter, of which the following is a copy:

LA PAZ, BOLIVIA, *October* 17, 1872.
DISTINGUISHED AND ESTEEMED FRIEND: At this very moment I have received your valued letter of to-day, in which you acknowledge receipt of communications from Mr. Joseph H. Colton.

I am very sorry that the gentleman intends to present a memorial to the Congress of the United States.

Be you persuaded and assured that the government of Bolivia knows how to regard its obligations touching this just and legal claim, after having acknowledged the debt, and pledged its honor to pay it with preference. Consequently, the time is not distant when the sum of the indebtedness can be raised, and for this reason I do not think it necessary that Mr. Colton should resort to the extreme measures which he seems to contemplate.

Having thus answered your esteemed favor of to-day,
    I have the pleasure to subscribe myself,
        Your attentive friend and faithful servant,
            C. CORRAL.
MR. LEOPOLD MARKBREIT, *Etc.*

All these assurances leave no room to doubt that it is the solemn duty of the Bolivian government to make present payment of the sum promised to Mr. Colton, with all arrears of interest thereon. There is as little doubt of the ability of the Republic to make such payment. The Republic of Bolivia embraces a territory equal to 473,300 square miles. It is more than one-fifth the extent of the United States, excluding Alaska. Its white population is stated at 1,742,352; considerably more than the population of Massachusetts. Its public debt is but £3,200,000. Several of the States of this Union owe more than twice as much as Bolivia. The annual revenues of Bolivia are stated at £1,500,000. Two and one-fourth years of its revenue are equal to the payment of its debt. No other American state could extinguish its debt with its revenues in so short a period. Switzerland, Sweden, and Prussia are the only European states which could liquidate by the same means in the same time.

But of the Bolivian debt, £1,500,000, nearly one-half of the whole, is of a domestic character. The balance, £1,700,000, consists of a loan, negotiated in the year 1872 through the agency of the Bolivian Steamship Company, and in aid of a railway around the Falls of the Madeira. If that road shall be constructed, this portion of the Bolivian debt will make the Republic richer instead of poorer; for it will give Bolivian products access to the navigable waters of the Madeira river, and thus furnish them with an outlet through the Amazon upon the Atlantic markets. There is, therefore, no reason for doubting that, with good faith in the administration of its resources, Bolivia might promptly meet every pecuniary obligation resting upon it.

Since the obligation of Bolivia to pay Mr. Colton's claim, and its ability to pay are manifest, the only questions remaining for consideration are whether this Government is called upon to take any steps to influence payment, and if any such steps, what?

The committee entertain no doubt that whenever a foreign government clearly owes an obligation to a citizen of the United States, this Government should notice the obligation, and should not hesitate to assert it. So much, it is apprehended, the Government may do in every such case. To what extent the Government shall go in enforcing such obligations is a different question, and a question which probably cannot be settled by the adoption of any rule suitable for universal application.

The different countries of North and South America are now indebted in the sum of £751,241,197. European countries owe in the aggregate the sum of £3,153,880,865. The question whether that immense mass of indebtedness *must* be paid, or may be repudiated at the pleasure of the several governments owing the debts, is one of great, if not of paramount, importance to all nations. This Government is one of those most heavily indebted, and may therefore mark its sense of sanctity of the obligation resting on itself by intervening to urge the payment of the inconsiderable sum due by Bolivia to one of our own citizens. The committee do not permit themselves to doubt that Bolivia will promptly comply with the respectful request of this Government that the long-deferred claim of Mr. Colton be liquidated. Should this just expectation not be realized, it may be worth while for the Government then to consider whether we can afford longer to maintain a diplomatic representative at the capital of that Republic. The United States first sent a minister to Bolivia in 1848. That mission is maintained at an annual cost of $7,500. We have no direct trade with that Republic. Since 1862, when we commenced the annual publication of our diplomatic correspondence, only six letters have been received from our representatives in Bolivia which have been thought worthy of publication.

The Committee, therefore, report the accompanying Act, and recommend its passage.

CONGRESSIONAL ACTION.

AN ACT For the Relief of Joseph H. Colton.

Be it enacted by the Senate and House of Representatives of the United States of America in Congress assembled, That the President of the United States is hereby requested to call upon the Government of Bolivia to make payment of the money admitted by itself to be due, with interest thereon, according to the Decree of the said Government of Bolivia,. of February first, eighteen hundred and seventy-two, to Joseph H. Colton, for maps engraved for that Government under a contract made in eighteen hundred and fifty-eight.
Approved March 3, 1875.

Department of State,
Washington, *March* 11, 1875.
A true copy.
SEVELLON A. BROWN,
Chief Clerk.

What effect was produced on the Government of Bolivia by the rightful action of the American Congress in your petitioner's behalf, and what astounding tortuosities of behavior have been subsequently resorted to by both Bolivia and Peru in contravention of the course of justice marked out by your honorable body, will be clearly shown in the series of relevant papers comprised within an ample number of the following pages:

MR. HELPER TO MINISTER REYNOLDS.

NEW YORK, *March* 8, 1875.

HON. ROBERT M. REYNOLDS,
United States Minister to Bolivia.

DEAR SIR: Herewith you will receive a copy of a Report, and also a copy of an accompanying Act, which was finally passed on the 3d instant, by the Congress of the United States, in the matter of the claim of Mr. Joseph H. Colton, of this city, against the Government of Bolivia. I need hardly inform you that Mr. Colton and I are very much pleased with both the Report and the Act. We feel now,—and, thank God, we never felt otherwise,—that it is worth something, that it is, in fact, worth all it implies, to be citizens of the Great Republic of the New World. Under the auspicious circumstances of the passage of this Act, I suppose I might, with no inconsiderable degree of propriety, on this subject, refrain from all further correspondence with persons or places more distant than the White House, or the State Department, at Washington. Nevertheless, touching this affair, even as it now stands, I shall be glad to hear from you, as the head of our Legation at La Paz, so soon as you may find it convenient and agreeable to write. Please let me know exactly what Bolivia says and proposes in view of this significant Act of the American Congress, and inform me what I may depend on beyond doubt or uncertainty.

Yours, very truly,
H. R. HELPER.

SECRETARY FISH TO MR. HELPER.

DEPARTMENT OF STATE,
WASHINGTON, *March* 13, 1875.
HINTON R. HELPER, *Esq., New York.*

SIR: Your letter of the 8th instant has been received. In compliance with your request, I transmit herewith a copy of "An Act for the relief of Joseph H. Colton," approved March 3, 1875. A printed copy of the Report of the Committee on Foreign Relations upon Mr. Colton's claim, is also inclosed.

I am, sir, your obedient servant,
HAMILTON FISH.

INCLOSURES.

Copy of "An Act for the relief of Joseph H. Colton."
Copy of Report of the Committee on Foreign Relations.

MR. HELPER TO SENATOR CAMERON.

NEW YORK, *March* 17, 1875.
HON. SIMON CAMERON,
Chairman of the Senate Committee
on Foreign Affairs, Washington.

SIR: Having received from the Hon. Hamilton Fish, Secretary of State, at Washington, a certified copy of the Act of Congress, approved March 3, 1875, requesting the President of the United States to call on the Government of Bolivia to pay the money so fully and so frequently admittee by itself to be due to Joseph H. Colton, of this city, for ten thousand large maps engraved and published especially for it, in the year 1858, I have the pleasure of tendering to you, for your efforts toward the ends of equity in the premises, the sincere thanks of both the claimant and myself. As, however, Bolivia has, for so many years, been accustomed to trifle with the claimant, with all his agents and attorneys, with most of our Ministers Resident at her Capital, and with several of our Secretaries of State, I am apprehensive that she will not scruple to trifle also with our President, and even with Congress itself. It is not in the nature of Bolivia, of her own volition, to do right in any matter whatever. In all her ways she is jesuitical, and perverse, and untrue. Her proclivities and aptitudes are only for evil. For these weighty and lamentable reasons, while again thanking you heartily for the support you gave to the measure of justice in behalf of the grossly and persistently outraged claimant, I have the honor to request that you, as a clear-sighted and right-minded American statesman, will be kind enough to keep your eye on Bolivia until after this vexatious international affair with her shall have been finally settled.

I have the honor to be, very respectfully,
Your obedient servant,
H. R. HELPER.

MR. HELPER TO PRESIDENT GRANT.

NEW YORK, *March* 24, 1875.
To His Excellency Gen. Ulysses S. Grant,
President of the United States.

SIR: In relation to the Act of Congress, approved on the 3d instant, requesting the President of the United States to call on the Government of Bolivia to pay the money so long over-due from itself to Mr. Joseph H. Colton, of this city, both the claimant and I, as his attorney, have the honor to express the hope that your Excellency's request in the premises may be made so felicitously, and yet so promptly and so firmly, as to induce Bolivia's early compliance with both the letter and the spirit of the said Act of Congress. In this connection, your Excellency's attention is also most respectfully solicited to the inclosed copy of a letter, which, on the 17th instant, I addressed to the Hon. Simon Cameron, Chairman of the Senate Committee on Foreign Affairs.

I have the honor to be, most respectfully,
Your Excellency's obedient servant,
H. R. HELPER.

SENATOR FRELINGHUYSEN TO MR. HELPER.

UNITED STATES SENATE CHAMBER,
WASHINGTON, *March* 24, 1875.

MR. HINTON R. HELPER, *New York*.

DEAR SIR: It will give me pleasure, at any time, to promote Mr. Colton's claim; and if it should not be adjusted by the next session of Congress, you had better call my attention to the subject.

With much respect, yours truly,
FRED'K T. FRELINGHUYSEN.

COLONEL CHURCH TO MR. HELPER.

LONDON, ENGLAND, *April* 10, 1875.
HINTON R. HELPER, *Esq., New York.*

DEAR SIR: It has afforded me great pleasure to receive and read the Act of the Congress of the United States which came with your last letter, and which will, I hope, soon enable Mr. Colton to obtain from Bolivia the amount of his claim, which the Government of that country has, for so long a period, unjustly withheld from him. It will certainly be a great gain to the Bolivians themselves, if they shall be taught by the results of your excellent labors in the Congress of the United States, that good faith on the part of governments is the prime essential for a career of national honor and progress. The Bolivian Commissioners on this side of the Atlantic have recently given my Railroad and Navigation Company much trouble by their strange inability to comprehend the simple truth thus adverted to; yet I am hopeful that their Government, spurred by an improved public opinion, is now beginning to understand more adequately the significance and force of a solemn contract, and that such a contract, when made by a government with a foreigner, partakes very much of the nature of a treaty with the government of the particular State of which the foreigner is a citizen or subject.

Sometimes I almost despair of the possibility of having my life sufficiently prolonged to teach men like the Commissioners now here from Bolivia, that water naturally runs down hill. Certain it is that I have not yet succeeded in convincing these gentlemen of this plain fact, so patent to most other people; for, with an obtuseness peculiar to themselves and their countrymen, they still insist, or at least they seem to insist, that the Valley of the Amazon has its drainage across the Andes into the Pacific Ocean. However, I

hope the present year may see us at work again, driving away merrily and successfully in the construction of the Madeira and Mamoré Railway.
Yours, very truly,
GEORGE EARL CHURCH.

Every honest and well-informed American will heartily sympathize with Col. Church, (formerly of Providence, Rhode Island,) in the unequal war which he, too, has had to wage, during many years past, against the oppressive faithlessness and injustice of Bolivia. A true history of the long series of gross wrongs of which he has been the victim at the hands of the Government of that country, would prove but little less curious and incredible than the outlines herein given of the Colton-Bolivia case itself.
H. R. H.

MR. HELPER TO SECRETARY FISH.

NEW YORK, *May* 4, 1875.
HON HAMILTON FISH,
Secretary of State, Washington.
SIR: I have the honor to request that you will be so kind as to inform me whether any action has yet been taken in or through the Department of State, to give proper efficacy to the Act of Congress, of the 3rd of last March, which requested the President to call on the Bolivian Government for the money due to Mr. Joseph H. Colton, of this city, for the National Maps of Bolivia, published in the year 1858. A private note received on the 28th ultimo,

from Minister Reynolds, at La Paz, informs me that he has forwarded to you, as Secretary of State, a somewhat important memorandum of what he has thus far done in this matter; a sort of joint memorandum, signed, (if I err not in my inference,) by both himself and President Frias. Will you please send me a copy of any such memorandum which you may have received? As usual, Bolivia's mere promises to pay the money are as convenient and plentiful as were ever green leaves in the Hercynian Forest. But Mr. Colton and I have, long since, become so impatient and nauseated with such promises that we would now be but too happy to have them ended, once and forever, by the final settlement in good faith of this long-stretched and time-wasting and life-consuming subject of diplomacy.

I am, sir, most respectfully,
Your obedient servant,
H. R. HELPER.

ACTING SECRETARY CADWALADER TO MR. HELPER.

DEPARTMENT OF STATE,
WASHINGTON, *May* 10, 1875.
HINTON R. HELPER, *Esq.*, *New York*.

SIR: Your letter of the 4th instant has been received. In reply I have to state that a copy of the Act of Congress to which it refers, has been sent to Mr. Reynolds, the Minister of the United States to Bolivia, with an instruction upon the subject.

I am, sir, your obedient servant,
JOHN L. CADWALADER.

THE REYNOLDS-FRIAS SETTLEMENT FOR COLTON.

LEGATION OF THE UNITED STATES,
LA PAZ, BOLIVIA, *May* 10, 1875.

Messrs. JOSEPH H. COLTON,
and HINTON R. HELPER, } *New York.*

GENTLEMEN: As the United States Minister Resident at La Paz, I have the honor to inform you that I have this day secured from the Government of Bolivia, five several drafts, as described below, in full payment of principal and interest of the amount due to Joseph H. Colton for maps furnished this Republic in 1858; the aggregate amount being in conformity with the decree dated at La Paz, on the first day of February, 1872. Thus:

FIRST DRAFT, issued under the Subvention Treaty with
Peru, for Customs due at Arica, December 31, 1875,
drawn on the Minister of Finance at Lima, - - $20,000 00
SECOND DRAFT, Ditto, June 30, 1876, - - - - 10.794 27
THIRD DRAFT, Ditto, December 31, 1876, - - - 10.794 27

Total of the Principal - - $41,588 54

FOURTH DRAFT, issued upon the Customs Due at Cobija,
in Bolivia, July 31. 1875, - - - - - $ 5,372 38
FIFTH DRAFT, Ditto, August 31, 1875, - - - - 5,372 39

Total of the Interest, - - $10,744 77

For these five drafts I have given a receipt, to be in full and final settlement, on the condition that you accept them with this understanding. Should you refuse or fail to confirm my acts in this affair, as your agent, I am authorized by President Frias, under the terms stated in the receipt itself, to surrender all of the drafts aforesaid to the Government of Bolivia, when my receipt so given will be cancelled and re-

turned, without prejudice to your claim. While I am well
aware that this settlement will be to both of you a sore disappointment as to the dates of payment of the later installments, yet I respectfully and earnestly recommend you to
accept the whole arrangement as final, as I am fully convinced that his Excellency, President Frias, has made a tender of all that was in his power to do in the matter of times
of maturity of drafts issued; and I have already extended
thanks to him in your behalf for his unremitting attention to
the various stages of this settlement amid the whirl of
attempted revolutions throughout Bolivia. It will be very
gratifying to me, if you can find it convenient to send to
him, through this Legation, a letter of personal thanks for
his action in the premises.

I have the fullest assurances that the drafts on the Customs
at Cobija will be paid promptly on the days they fall due respectively, and also that the Minister for Foreign Affairs of
Peru will accept the drafts drawn upon him, when presented,
and that they will certainly be paid honorably and promptly.
This will leave only the exchange to be paid by Bolivia,
when the amount thereof shall be ascertained and duly certified as having been actually and necessarily deducted in the
process of transmission. In conclusion, allow me to assure
you that this is the most favorable settlement that could be
obtained at this time, and this arises, not from the fact that
President Frias himself did not wish to make a more prompt
payment, but because he finds the national finances so badly
deranged by continual embroilments and revolutions, that
he could not provide the means for a speedier liquidation
This particular claim has received his personal attention, to
the exclusion of other pressing demands upon the treasury;
and he assures me that, for many months past, he has cherished an earnest desire to conclude the case. Hoping soon
to hear of your full concurrence in the action which I have

taken in the premises, and trusting that the several drafts. may be promptly paid at maturity,

I am, gentlemen, yours truly,
ROBERT M. REYNOLDS.

RECEIPT GIVEN BY MINISTER REYNOLDS TO BOLIVIA.

LEGATION OF THE UNITED STATES,
LA PAZ, BOLIVIA, *May* 10, 1875.

I have this day received, from the Supreme Government of Bolivia, on the conditions hereinafter stated, five several drafts, or letters of credit, in full payment of the principal and interest due from the Government of Bolivia to Messrs. Joseph H. Colton and Hinton R. Helper, citizens of the United States of America, conformably to the decree of the Bolivian Government, dated February 1, 1872, for $41,588.54, as follows:

FIRST DRAFT, Issued under the Subvention Treaty with
Peru, for Customs due at Arica, December 31, 1875,
drawn on the Minister of Finance at Lima, - - $20,000.00
SECOND DRAFT, Ditto, June 30, 1876, - - - - 10,794.27
THIRD DRAFT, Ditto, December 31, 1876, - - - 10,794.27

Total of the Principal, - - $41,589.54

FOURTH DRAFT, Issued upon the Customs due at Cobija,
in Bolivia, July 31, 1875, - - - - - - $ 5,372.38
FIFTH DRAFT, Ditto, August 31, 1875, - - - - 5,372.39

Total of the Interest, - - $10,744.77

The exchange due on the foregoing amounts in coin, upon London or New York, is to be paid by the Government of

Bolivia, so soon as the respective drafts shall be respectively negotiated and the respective sums shall be duly certified as having been actually paid; it being distinctly understood and agreed that Messrs. Colton and Helper shall receive in New York the par value of said drafts, in accordance with the decree aforesaid. The condition referred to is as follows:—That, whereas, the Supreme Government of Bolivia has this day tendered the foregoing drafts in full payment of the principal and interest of the claim of Joseph H. Colton, pledging the perfect faith of the Government for the payment and redemption of the said drafts when due, and, whereas, the undersigned, Robert M. Reynolds, as the agent and attorney in fact for Messrs. Colton and Helper, has accepted the said drafts in payment of the claim aforesaid, with interest thereon; now it is fully understood and agreed that, in the event that Messrs. Colton and Helper shall decline to accept the drafts aforesaid, and so refuse to confirm the action of the undersigned as their agent, then, and in that case, the undersigned, Robert M. Reynolds, may surrender to the President of Bolivia all of the drafts aforesaid, and receive as cancelled this receipt without prejudice to the claim of the said Colton and Helper against the Government of Bolivia. On the acceptance of these several drafts by Messrs. Colton and Helper, this receipt is to be final and conclusive for full payment, as before stated; leaving only the current exchange, when ascertained, to be paid by the Bolivian Government, on the redemption of the drafts aforesaid.

ROBERT M. REYNOLDS.

Approved.
FRIAS.

SECRETARY FISH TO MR. HELPER.

DEPARTMENT OF STATE,
WASHINGTON, *June* 25, 1875.
HINTON R. HELPER, *Esquire, New York*.

SIR: I have to inform you that a dispatch, dated on the 15th ultimo, has been received at this Department, from Mr. R. M. Reynolds, the Minister of the United States to Bolivia, representing that he had an offer for the settlement of the claim of Mr. Colton on the Government of that Republic. As he says that he had also apprised you of the terms, it is superfluous to mention them. Mr. Reynolds is of the opinion that they are as favorable to the claimant as could reasonably be expected. This Department having taken the subject into full consideration, is of the same opinion, especially in view of the present condition of that country. As the offer will not be binding on the Government of Bolivia until accepted by the claimant, it is suggested that the question be decided by him without any delay which can be avoided; and it is recommended that that decision be in the affirmative.

I am, sir, your obedient servant,

HAMILTON FISH.

SECRETARY FISH TO MR. HELPER.

DEPARTMENT OF STATE,
WASHINGTON, *June* 30, 1875.
HINTON R. HELPER, *Esq., New York*.

SIR: Your letter of the 28th instant has been received. This Department is gratified to learn from it that the terms of payment offered by the Bolivian government, in the Colton case, are acceptable. Mr. Reynolds will at once be apprised of the decision. It will not, however, be convenient to authorize him to make remittances in the way you suggest. He will, however, be expected to see that they are made as received, pursuant to the terms offered and the exercise of his best discretion, in view of the interests of the claimant.

I am, sir, your obedient servant,
HAMILTON FISH.

ACTING SECRETARY CADWALADER TO MR. HELPER.

DEPARTMENT OF STATE,
WASHINGTON, *July* 3, 1875.

HINTON R. HELPER, *Esq., New York.*

SIR: Your letter of the 1st instant, in which you request to be informed as to whether the information contained in yours of the 28th ultimo, relative to the acceptance of the terms proposed by the Bolivian Government, in the matter of the Colton claim, was communicated to Mr. Reynolds by the mail carried out in the steamer which sailed from New York on the 30th ultimo, has been received. In reply I have to state that your letter of the 28th ultimo, was not received in time to have a copy of it prepared for transmission to Mr. Reynolds by the mail of the steamer above referred to. A copy of it, however, has been made, which, together with an instruction on the subject, will be forwarded to Mr. Reynolds by the steamer which leaves New York for Aspinwall on the 15th instant.

I am, sir, your obedient servant,
JOHN L. CADWALADER.

MR. HELPER TO MINISTER REYNOLDS.

NEW YORK, *August* 30, 1875.

HON. ROBERT M. REYNOLDS,
United States Minister to Bolivia.

DEAR SIR: Your letter of the 15th of July, received by me on the 28th instant, informs me that you cannot obtain duplicates of the drafts on Peru, corresponding with the originals which you now have in hand. This I am very sorry to hear, as, in case of the loss of the originals, in the course of transmission, much delay, and possibly no inconsiderable misunderstanding and difficulty, might occur before new drafts could be duly executed and sent forward. It seems to me that governments ought to be quite as considerate and accommodating as individuals, and that they should be disposed to furnish just as many safeguards in any and every honorable transaction.

Under all the circumstances of the case, it is the wish and request of both Mr. Colton and myself, that you will be kind enough to send to me immediately, properly endorsed to my order, the three Bolivian drafts on Peru, formally accepted by Peru; retaining in your possession exact copies of the same, duly verified by the Secretary of State of Bolivia, by a Bolivian Notary Public, or by some other competent official of that Republic; or, if the verification be not made by any Bolivian functionary, please make it yourself, as Minister, or let it be made by our own Consul, Mr. Guerra, or by the Peruvian Consul. Such verified copies of the drafts might be made out in duplicate, and one set sent to me, a fortnight or so after the original set shall have been addressed to me. The other set of copies might very properly be filed among the archives of our Legation at La Paz. You may, if you please, forward the original drafts to me without delay, and through the ordinary channel, that is to say, through our own Department of State at Washington. Your communications through this channel have been received very regularly, on an average of about forty days from La Paz to New York. One of your letters was fifty-six days on the way, another fifty-five, and many of them from forty to fifty. Only once, during the last twelve months, have I heard from you in so short a time as thirty days.

Hereafter, if any question should arise in your mind as to what may possibly be the best thing to do, under any particular circumstances, please bring to bear on the matter your own best judgment, and then act upon it accordingly, without referring it at all for my decision; for Mr. Colton and I have already had so many proofs of the general soundness of your discretion, that we would much prefer to take the responsibility of relying on it implicitly, rather than to be put to the great inconvenience and annoyance of the delays which will inevitably attend,—as in this very case,—any reference of the subject here for our decision.

Undoubtedly you were quite right in demanding, as a liquidation of the first installment, a draft for exactly $5,372.38 in silver or gold, payable to my order, so that I might receive here precisely that amount; for if a draft comes to hand for less than that sum, rendering it necessary for me to make reclamation for the difference, and if then the amount of difference be sent, less a certain rate of discount thereon; and then again, if I must make a new reclamation for the newer and smaller difference due, and so on, and so on, it is a question whether, by this peculiarly Bolivian method of imperfect payment, there would not be at least a fraction due to Mr. Colton and myself ten thousand years hence, or at doomsday, and even beyond; in the immeasurable eternities of time and space. I hope Bolivia will not, by forever failing to do her duty on the earth, in this matter, render it obligatory on me to become an accusant and litigant against her from *my* place in the Heavens!

I am almost feverishly anxious to be able to go, first to North Carolina, then to Minnesota, and afterward to Oregon, on business which will require several months of my time; but, though the hindrance is very greatly to my disadvantage, I cannot go until this unsettled affair with Bolivia shall be put in better shape. Pray help me to finish with Bolivia at the earliest possible day. How sincerely, indeed, do I wish I had all of Mr. Colton's interests, and my own, this side of Bolivia at this very moment! * * *

Yours, most respectfully,

H. R. HELPER.

ACTING SECRETARY CADWALADER TO MR. HELPER.

DEPARTMENT OF STATE,
WASHINGTON, *October* 25, 1875.

HINTON R. HELPER, *Esq., New York.*

SIR: Your letter of the 16th instant has been received. It asks whether it is your duty to pay to any Department of this government any part of a certain sum which has reached you on account of the claim of Mr. Joseph H. Colton. In reply I have to state that this Department is not aware of any such duty, legal or moral.

I am, sir, your obedient servant,

JOHN L. CADWALADER.

MR. HELPER TO SECRETARY FISH.

NEW YORK, *October* 30, 1875.

HON. HAMILTON FISH, *Secretary of State, Washington.*

SIR: I thank you for your letter of the 25th instant, informing me, in effect, that neither the State Department nor any other branch of the Government of the United States, so far as you know, has any monetary charge against either Mr. Colton or myself for services rendered on account of the long-pending and, for the most part, still-unsettled Map Claim against the Government of Bolivia. This valuable and gratuitous service on your part, as Secretary of State, imposes on both Mr. Colton and myself the obligation to try to be still better citizens of the United States, and to return, at some time, in some way, if possible, a service to the country equivalent to that which, through your good offices, we have received from it; and though, because of the lack of wit or opportunity on our own part, the patriotic purpose here suggested may never be made manifest in action, yet we shall always cherish a most lively sense of both our benefits and duties in this regard.

I have the honor to be, with great respect,
Your obedient servant,
H. R. HELPER.

MR. HELPER TO MINISTER REYNOLDS.

NEW YORK, *April* 14, 1876.
HON. ROBERT M. REYNOLDS,
United States Minister to Bolivia.

DEAR SIR: * * * I do most earnestly hope that you have already obtained, or may soon be able to obtain, the necessary orders from Bolivia, accepted by Peru, for the difference of value between the gold or silver dollars due, and the depreciated paper money offered. This new delay is a very serious disadvantage to me, and the bother of it excites my indignation against both Bolivia and Peru. Mr. Colton also is almost worn out with the grievous disappointments and despoliations of which he has so long and so frequently been the victim in the course of this reclamation. Please bring the case to an equitable conclusion, just so soon as may be possible. I am tied down here, and cannot get away, simply because this claim, through Bolivia's ever-changing and dishonorable conduct, remains unsettled. Pray open to me, at your very earliest convenience, the way to both justice and liberty in this affair.

If the Government of Bolivia should move from La Paz to Chuquisaca, or elsewhere, leaving any of your business in an unsettled condition, I fear very much that you will not be able to settle it at all without yourself moving there also, and giving personal attention to whatever matter may remain unfinished. In all cases of this kind, where an ignorant and base-blooded Catholic nation is the delinquent, correspondence at a distance from the seat of government,—even if the distance be no more than ten miles from the desks of the officials,—will result in nothing better than promises, and promises, and promises, which will be fulfilled only, if ever, at or after the general judgment, ten thousand millions of years hence, more or less. Please do not gratify either Bolivia or Peru with any such correspondence; for that is just what would make these jesuitical nationalities successful and happy in their wicked ways.

Yours, most respectfully,

H. R. HELPER.

MR. HELPER TO MINISTER GIBBS.

NEW YORK, *May* 29, 1876.

HON. RICHARD GIBBS,
 United States Minister to Peru.

SIR: I have a letter from Minister Reynolds, at La Paz,

in Bolivia, under date of the 13th of April, in which he informs me that he protested to President Frias against the action of the Bank at Lima, in Peru, in paying me only $20,000 in paper, worth but little more than fifty cents on the dollar, whereas it should have paid $20,000 in silver or gold, and that the President replied as follows:

"Peru has charged the $20,000 as if the amount had been paid in silver, and we must reclaim the difference immediately."

If there be no misapprehension nor other mistake about this matter, and if indeed, Peru has, in this case, charged Bolivia the $20,000 as so much money paid on her account in silver, whereas, on Bolivia's order in my favor, Peru has paid me only in very badly depreciated bank bills, it may be well enough for you, as the United States Minister at Lima, to know the fact,—and hence this note.

Yours, very respectfully,
H. R. HELPER.

MR. HELPER TO SECRETARY FISH.

NEW YORK, *June* 2, 1876.

HON. HAMILTON FISH,
Secretary of State Washington.

SIR: I have the honor to inform you,—if you will kindly accept the information,—that I received yesterday from Minister Reynolds, at La Paz, in Bolivia, a brief letter, dated at 4 o'clock, P. M., on the 4th ultimo, wherein, among other things, he says:

"Since mailing my letter to you, at 1 o'clock to-day, a revolution broke out, proclaiming General Daza President of Bolivia. On receipt of the news I repaired to the palace of President Frias, whom I wished to see. Finding the palace under guard, and that admission was denied to every one, I then went to the house of General Daza, (himself one of the candidates for the Presidency,) and there learned that he had proclaimed himself President, because a number of his friends had been suddenly and forcibly ejected from office in Cochabamba, and that he, in self-defence, was compelled to act at once, without waiting for the election next Sunday."

The very novel and interesting occurrences thus narrated, with so much simplicity, equanimity and frankness, did not take place in Spain nor in Egypt during the Middle Ages, nor yet in the Moon nor in Dahomey in the nineteenth century, but in Bolivia, a country in regular diplomatic standing, which, for the last seventeen years, has been emblazoning herself before the world on maps ordered by herself, and published especially for her, but for which, as yet, she has paid only in part; that is to say, less than one-half of the amount due, she having again shamelessly defaulted on the largest installment, now long over-due and unpaid in that regard. Hoping, however, that this new revolution may not be attended with any great loss of valuable lives or treasure, and that more permanent conditions of peace, prosperity and progress may soon be established in Bolivia,

I am, sir, most respectfully,
Your obedient servant,
H. R. HELPER.

MR. COLTON TO SECRETARY FISH.

NEW YORK, *June* 6, 1876.

HON. HAMILTON FISH,
Secretary of State, Washington.

SIR: It is with me a matter of profound regret, amounting almost to shame and abasement, that circumstances again impel me to solicit your oft-asked and oft-granted assistance in the very troublesome case of Bolivia's indebtedness to me for the maps which I engraved and published for her in 1858. This time, however, the delinquency of which I complain does not come up directly from Bolivia, but rather from Peru. Bolivia gave me, through my attorney, Mr. Helper, certain installment drafts on Peru. Peru unhesitatingly accepted the drafts ; but, instead of paying in honest money any one of the several sums which were plainly expressed and called for, she is now, to my further great loss and worriment, paying them in badly depreciated paper currency, worth, according to the latest advices from Lima, where all the drafts are payable, but little more than fifty per cent. of the amount due me!

Minister Reynolds, at La Paz, has informed me that President Frias, of Bolivia, assured him that, although Peru paid me in depreciated bank bills, worth only fifty-four cents in the dollar, yet she charged the amount against Bolivia as so many dollars in silver of full value ! Now almost an octogenarian, I feel very keenly the cruel continuance of these Bolivian and Peruvian outrages, already of so many years' duration, against my rights and interests as a man, and as an American citizen. This morning Mr. Helper and I called, in this city, on the Hon. Richard Gibbs, United States Minister to Peru, now here temporarily, on leave of absence, and requested him to use his good offices at Lima in my behalf. This he seemed willing to do in a mere friendly way, but said he could do nothing officially, unless he should receive specific instructions on the subject from our Department of State at Washington. The particular object of this letter is, therefore, to request that you will be kind enough to instruct Minister Gibbs to use such energetic and prudent efforts in Lima as will, if possible, secure to me the honest payment in honest money, and without any new sort of quibble or subterfuge, of the three installments which Peru has agreed to pay to me for and on account of Bolivia.

I am, sir, with great respect,
Your obedient servant,
JOSEPH H. COLTON.

SECRETARY FISH TO MR. COLTON.

DEPARTMENT OF STATE,
WASHINGTON, *June* 8, 1876.
J. H. COLTON, *Esq., New York*.

SIR: Your letter of the 6th instant has been received. It complains of the manner in which Peru is paying the accepted installment-drafts on her, given to you by Bolivia, in settlement of your claim against the latter government, and requests that Mr. Gibbs, the Minister of the United States at Lima, be instructed to obtain, if possible, their payment in money not subject to depreciation. In reply, I have to state that Mr. Gibbs has been authorized to use his good offices, unofficially, in the matter, and to do what he properly can toward securing the object desired.

I am, sir, your obedient servant,
HAMILTON FISH.

MR. HELPER TO MESSRS. PREVOST & CO.

NEW YORK, *September* 4, 1876.
MESSRS. PREVOST & CO., *Lima, Peru*.

GENTLEMEN: I have the pleasure to acknowledge receipt of your letter of the 11th ultimo, inclosing a draft for

£486-10-0 at ninety days, on Messrs. Henry Kendall & Sons, of London. You inform me that "this amount has been paid as the difference due on the $20,000 which we collected for you, in depreciated bank notes, in January last." In the closing paragraph of your letter of the 13th of last February, you said, speaking of the same difference, " The bank further agrees to pay us, for you, on account of Bolivia, the necessary amount wherewith to complete the sum of £1960-10-6, still due you." While Mr. Colton and I are very much disappointed at the disproportion and meagreness of the remittance looked for, and I am unable to understand the discrepancy apparent in the foregoing statements, yet I feel confident that all the faults and defaults in the premises lie entirely between Bolivia and Peru, and not in the least with either yourself or Minister Reynolds.

If you can coöperate successfully with Minister Reynolds in obtaining for Mr. Colton and myself the full amount of difference due in the matter of this particular installment, and also payment in full of the subsequent installments, pray do so with all your might,—as evidently these tasks cannot be otherwise accomplished,—and thereby increase the aggregate of your commission and the mountain of my obligation. Only use invariably your soundest judgment, doing the best you can in every case, and I shall be quite satisfied with the results, so far as you yourselves are concerned. Ministers Reynolds and Gibbs have both given me such favorable accounts of your firm, and I find, besides, that your drafts have such high credit among the leading merchants and bankers of New York, that I feel fully warranted in thus reposing the utmost confidence in your prudence and probity.

Yours, very truly,
H. R. HELPER.

MR. HELPER TO SECRETARY FISH.

NEW YORK, *October* 21, 1876.
HON. HAMILTON FISH,
Secretary of State, Washington.

SIR: Bolivia and Peru are still practising against Mr. Colton and myself a series of Machiavelian infidelities and delays, which we tolerate only because we have no power to prevent them on the one hand, nor to punish them on the other. As yet, the sum of only a little more than two-thirds of the installment due nearly ten months ago, that is to say, on the 31st of December of last year, has been paid; and of the installment due on the 30th of June of this year, now nearly four months over-due, not even so much as one cent has been paid! If, in this precarious condition of things, you can suggest to our Ministers at Lima and at La Paz, the saying or the doing of anything that will facilitate the equitable ending of this eighteen years' subject of diplomacy, pray do so, and receive the gratitude of two gray-haired, temper-tired, patience-exhausted, labor-oppressed and expense-burdened victims.

The estimable wife of our Minister to Bolivia, Mrs. Reynolds, whom I saw in Philadelphia, day before yesterday, requested me to write, as I am now writing, to our honored Secretary of State at Washington, inquiring whether her husband will probably be retained in Bolivia, in an official capacity, or whether he has been, or soon will be, recalled from that Andean nationality. Please favor me with the information thus sought, and I will at once communicate it to Mrs. Reynolds.

I have the honor to be, very respectfully,
Your obedient servant,
H. R. HELPER.

ACTING SECRETARY CADWALADER TO MR. HELPER.

DEPARTMENT OF STATE,
WASHINGTON, *October* 23, 1876.
HINTON R. HELPER, *Esq., New York.*

SIR: Your letter of the 21st instant has been received It complains of the delinquency of Bolivia in failing to comply with its promise in respect to the Colton claim. This delinquency is regretted here, but, for the present at least, there seems to be no remedy therefor. Congress, at its last session, having omitted to provide a salary for a Minister in Bolivia from the 1st of July, 1876, Mr. Reynolds, who then occupied that office, was instructed to take leave of the Government and return home.

I am, sir, your obedient servant,
JOHN L. CADWALADER.

MR. HELPER TO SECRETARY FISH.

NEW YORK, *October* 30, 1876.
HON. HAMILTON FISH,
Secretary of State, Washington.

SIR: Mr. Colton desires me to thank you for the information contained in your letter of the 23d instant, in relation to our Legation at La Paz in Bolivia. As, however, our Mission in Peru seems to be still untouched and in full force, and as one of Peru's accepted Bolivian drafts in his favor, for $10,794.27, due and payable in Lima on the 30th of last June, is now four months over-due and unpaid, he would like to know whether you will not be good enough to urge

upon this last-named power, upon Peru, a closer attention to its obvious duty in the premises?
I have the honor to be, very respectfully,
Your obedient servant,
H. R. HELPER.

SECRETARY FISH TO MR. HELPER.

DEPARTMENT OF STATE,
WASHINGTON, *November* 1, 1876.
H. R. HELPER, *Esq., New York.*

SIR: Your letter of the 30th instant, relative to an overdue acceptance of the Peruvian government, given in part payment of Mr. Colton's claim on Bolivia, has been received. In reply I have to inform you that Mr. Gibbs, the Minister of the United States at Lima, has been authorized to use his unofficial good offices toward obtaining payment of the draft.
I am, sir, your obedient servant,
HAMILTON FISH.

MR. HELPER TO SECRETARY FISH.

NEW YORK, *November* 25, 1876.
HON. HAMILTON FISH,
Secretary of State, Washington.

SIR: It is now more than eighteen years since two of the most able and eminent military engineers of Bolivia, under commission from their Government, arrived in this city, and, entirely of their own seeking and volition, entered into a contract here with Mr. Joseph H. Colton, a citizen of the United States, for ten thousand large and well-mounted national maps, which were duly engraved and printed and delivered, in strict compliance with Mr. Colton's part of the agreement. For these maps, however, only a little more than one-half of the money due to him under the contract has yet been paid; although full payment of the whole amount was to have been made, by the Bolivian Commissioners, on the completion of the work, and has since been promised and promised and promised an almost countless number of times by the Bolivian Government. On the 14th of last August I addressed to the Hon. Robert M. Reynolds, our Minister at La Paz, in Bolivia, a letter on this particular subject; to the following extract from which I have the honor to request your attention, trusting, too, that you may be pleased to cause the same to be filed among the archives of the State Department:

"Pray have the kindness to inform Bolivia, at once, and very distinctly, that it is my intention, as the attorney for Mr. Colton, after having, for so many years, been so repeatedly victimized by her faithless promises and despoiling delinquencies, to file against her a claim for expenses and damages, on or about the first day of March, 1877, provided the whole amount of her long over-due indebtedness, as last agreed upon, for her national maps, shall not be cancelled by or before that date. This, as you will perceive, is giving Bolivia more than six months' notice (certainly, as it seems to me, a very reasonable and generous notice,) of my intention; and if all just and admitted obligations in the premises shall be discharged by that time, then, notwithstanding the great loss to Mr. Colton and myself of so much time and labor and money, we will be satisfied, and no new claim whatever shall be made. Yet, should it become necessary for me to present the claim thus contemplated, I shall do it in such way, on the broad basis of the facts themselves, that all men of sense and justice will, I doubt not, readily see and concede the perfect rightfulness of my action, and the indefensible and glaring wrongfulness of Bolivia's position. May Bolivia be pleased to save me, and may it please Bolivia to save herself, from the new grievance and international trouble thus foreshadowed."

It is really and deeply humiliating to both Mr. Colton and myself to have to ask again, after having already asked and received so often, your own good offices in this affair; but it would seem that international justice and courtesy and usage allow us no other resource; and so, if you, as the American Secretary of State, can do or suggest anything that will avert the dreaded event of still another shameful delinquency by Bolivia, and so save Mr. Colton and myself from the necessity of having again to carry our case before the Congress of the United States, pray do so, and, as heretofore, greatly oblige us both.

I am, sir, most respectfully,
Your obedient servant,
H. R. HELPER.

Approved:
JOSEPH H. COLTON.

MR. HELPER TO SECRETARY FISH.

NEW YORK, *November* 30, 1876.

HON. HAMILTON FISH,
Secretary of State, Washington.

SIR: Since I last had the honor of addressing you, on Saturday last, Mr. Reynolds, our late Minister to Bolivia, has arrived in this city, and, with the remains of his little boy,

Robert, who recently died in Panama, is now on his way West; he having left here, for Illinois, in the evening of day before yesterday. Mr. Reynolds has placed in my hands a new and formally executed promise of payment of the Colton claim against the Government of Bolivia. If each of Bolivia's countless promises in this matter had only brought to Mr. Colton and myself so much as one cent on the dollar, the claim would have been satisfactorily settled long ago. Under cover of this last "solemn pledge," I find a draft drawn by Bolivia on Peru, and accepted by the latter, for the balance due, $19,609.40 in silver, payable at Lima, on the first day of March, 1878. Mr. Colton and I have agreed to abide by the doubtful arrangement thus made; and we shall make no claim for damages, provided this last of numberless promises in the premises shall be fulfilled.

I have the honor to be, most respectfully,
Your obedient servant,
H. R. HELPER.

MR. HELPER TO MESSRS. PREVOST & CO.

NEW YORK, *December* 1, 1876.
MESSRS. PREVOST & CO., *Lima, Peru.*

GENTLEMEN: Our friend, Mr. Reynolds, late United States Minister to Bolivia, arrived in this city last Sunday. He informs me that, in consequence of Peru's delay in not paying at maturity the June draft, for $10,794.27, and the greatly increased rate of premium on silver at the time it was paid, about three months after the money had become due, my client, Mr. Colton, has sustained a loss,—which can now be made good only by Peru,—of between two and three hundred pounds sterling. According to his figures, I should have received about £1,756; whereas the amount which really came to hand was only £1,429-9-9; leaving a balance still due of about £276. Mr. Reynolds informs me further that he has written to both you and the Hon. Secretary of the Treasury of Peru on this subject. Please give the matter your best attention, and insist, in the names of Mr. Colton, Mr. Reynolds and myself, and likewise in the names of Justice and Honor, that the balance thus due by Peru be paid without further delay, and also that the December draft for $10,794.27, be paid promptly at maturity. If Peru pays the December draft in paper money, please send me, immediately afterward, a bill of exchange for pounds sterling, at the rate of the day of payment, or at once turn the paper money into silver, and hold the silver for a few days, or for a fortnight or so, for a more favorable rate, provided the rate of the day of payment is, in your judgment, unfavorable. I should prefer not to have the fluctuating and precarious paper money of Peru held in possession a whole day, nor even a single hour, on my account. Again thanking you for your earnest and discreet labors in behalf of Mr. Colton and myself,

I remain, yours, very truly,

H. R. HELPER.

MR. HELPER TO SECRETARY FISH.

NEW YORK, *February,* 20, 1877.

HON. HAMILTON FISH,

Secretary of State, Washington.

SIR: In November last I sent to Lima, for collection, a draft drawn by the Government of Bolivia on the Government of Peru, and formally accepted by Peru, for $10,794.27 in silver, payable to the order of myself as the attorney for

Mr. Colton, and due at Lima on the 31st of last December. Since the time when the draft became due, I have received three letters from my agents in Lima, Messrs. Prevost & Co., informing me that they are unable to collect the money, and that, although they keep our Minister there, the Hon. Richard Gibbs, duly advised of all their proceedings and experiences in my behalf, yet even his friendly interviews and pleadings with the Peruvian authorities, on this subject, were also proving without any visible or encouraging result. Under these circumstances, moved again by the beseeching voices of both Colton and Justice, I am constrained to request a renewal of your own good offices in this regard. Mr. Colton and I will therefore be under additional obligations to you, if you will be kind enough to instruct Minister Gibbs to press Peru, with respectful earnestness, to perform at once her very palpable duty in the premises.

I have the honor to be, most respectfully,
Your obedient servant,
H. R. HELPER.

SECRETARY FISH TO MR. HELPER.

DEPARTMENT OF STATE,
WASHINGTON, *February* 24, 1877.

H. R. HELPER, *Esquire, New York*.

SIR: Your letter of the 20th instant has been received. In reply I have to state that, in compliance with your request, Mr. Gibbs, the Minister of the United States at Lima, has been instructed to use his personal good offices with the Peruvian Government toward securing the payment of the draft to which you refer.

I am, sir, your obedient servant,
HAMILTON FISH.

MR. HELPER TO MESSRS. PREVOST & CO.

NEW YORK, *February* 27, 1877.
MESSRS. PREVOST & CO., *Lima, Peru*.

GENTLEMEN: Your letter of the 27th ultimo came to hand on the 19th instant. Mr. Colton and I are filled with disappointment and disgust at Peru's continued failure to meet her own formally accepted obligation, due on the 31st of December last; and these unavoidably bitter feelings on our part are very materially intensified by the prospect of our having to pay a still higher rate of commission, in order to obtain the money at all. You say you may yet have to employ the services of a third party, and that, in such event, you will be under the necessity of charging me a commission of five per cent. I earnestly and solemnly protest, and through me Mr. Colton likewise protests, against these ever-recurring and damaging delays and unjust exactions. Such oft-repeated conduct on the part of any Government pretending to honorable consideration among civilized nations, is absolutely shameful, demoralizing and monstrous. Nevertheless, being on the ground, you are doubtless familiar with all the local circumstances of the case; and it is but reasonable to suppose that you know much better than I what had best be done. So, continuing to repose the utmost confidence in your own integrity and judgment, I give you unlimited liberty to act in every respect as may seem to you most proper. Only do the best you can to obtain payment of the over-due installment, and let me hear from you accordingly. Kindly complying with my request, Secretary Fish has communicated with Minister Gibbs on this same subject; and I trust that his friendly and efficient action in the matter may facilitate you in collecting and transmitting the money.

Yours, very truly,

H. R. HELPER.

MR. HELPER TO MESSRS. PREVOST & CO.

NEW YORK, *March* 21, 1877.
MESSRS. PREVOST & CO., *Lima, Peru.*

GENTLEMEN: Your letter of the 13th ultimo, inclosing to my order a draft, of the same date, for £1,832-6-0, at ninety days, on Messrs. Henry Kendall & Sons, of London, has been received. Accept the thanks of both Mr. Colton and myself; although we regret very much that Peru's inexcusable delays and delinquencies made it necessary for you to pay an outsider an extra commission, in order to enable you to obtain the money even so soon, yet so long, after it had become due. Inclosed herewith you will find Bolivia's accepted draft on Peru, dated at La Paz, Bolivia, October 12, 1876, and at Lima, Peru, October 23, 1876, in my favor, as the attorney for Mr. Colton, for $19,609.40 in silver, due on the first day of March, 1878, and by me made payable to your order. Please cause the draft to be paid on the very day of its maturity, or as soon thereafter as you may find it convenient to do so, and transmit the money to me at once, with as little loss by way of exchange and commission as may be incurred.

I trust you may soon succeed in obtaining from Peru the balance due me on the June, '76, installment. In this case, as in others, Peru should be required to pay not only the difference due in silver, as principal, but also the interest. A few evenings ago, I had the pleasure of meeting two of your recently arrived brothers, at the Fifth Avenue Hotel, in this city, and there proposed to place the accompanying draft, for $19,609.40, in their hands for collection; but, intending to sojourn several months in the United States, they seemed to think it might be better for me to mail the obligation direct to you at Lima; and I have thus acted on their suggestion. Yours, very truly,

H. R. HELPER.

ACTING SECRETARY SEWARD TO EX-MINISTER REYNOLDS.

DEPARTMENT OF STATE,
WASHINGTON, *September* 15, 1877.
R. M. REYNOLDS, *Esquire, Camden, Alabama.*

SIR: Your letter of the 9th ultimo has been received. It is accompanied by one of the 11th of May addressed to you by Mr. J. Oblitas, Minister for Foreign Affairs of Bolivia, alleging that there were errors against his government in adjusting the Colton claim, so-called, and asking for their correction. From your remarks on the subject, there is at least an impression that Mr. Oblitas is mistaken. But even if this should be otherwise, it is obvious that the course he has taken is not the proper or regular one to reach his object. As you observe, you are no longer an officer of this government, and cannot be considered as personally accountable in the matter. Payment was made in a draft or drafts to your order; the proceeds of which ultimately reached* the claimant in the city of New York. If he has been overpaid, it is incumbent on that government to apply to him directly for restitution of the surplus claimed, and if this should be refused, there can be no doubt that the courts would give the case an impartial hearing.† This department does not, for the present at least, enter into any correspondence upon the subject with that government.

I am, sir, your obedient servant,

F. W. SEWARD.

**Should have reached*, Mr. Seward should have said. Even as yet, —September, 1879—only a part of the money due and long overdue has reached the claimant.   H. R. H.

†Exactly so. Let Bolivia at once enter suit against Mr. Colton and Mr. Helper, either or both. That is precisely what Mr. C. and Mr. H. desire; and while one of them cordially invites and courts the liti-

EX-MINISTER REYNOLDS TO MR. HELPER.

WASHINGTON, D. C., *September* 24, 1877.
H. R. HELPER, *Esq., Rio de Janeiro, Brazil.*

DEAR SIR: In reply to your letter of the 28th of July, I must say that I know not what system of figuring the Peruvian officials employ in reducing to so small a sum as $1,100 the amount still due to Mr. Colton in the matter of the only partly paid installment which matured on the 30th of June of last year. According to my best recollection of the facts, those officials should have summed the amount up to several hundred dollars more than that. I myself made out a detailed statement of the true difference due, and left a copy of it with Messrs. Prevost & Co., of Lima, to whom it may be well for you to write; the original account having been presented for payment to the Hon. Secretary of the Peruvian Treasury.

I am in receipt of news of the probable death of Henry Meiggs; and if he dies, I fear you will encounter new and serious trouble with Peru; for, dreadful and exhaustive as have been her delays and delinquencies heretofore, there is really much danger that these deadening defects of the nation will be greatly aggravated after Mr. Meiggs shall have passed away. Indeed it is a question whether you may not have to struggle with difficulty after difficulty, and suffer discomfiture after discomfiture, before you will be able to obtain even the comparatively insignificant balance due on the June, '76, installment.

The Hon. J. Oblitas, Secretary of State for Bolivia, has

gation, the other, wishing to provoke it, thus publicly dares and defies it. Any opportunity to apply the rules and mandates of justice to such an incorrigible wrong-doer as Bolivia, away from the foul and fatal dens and caves and crags and fastnesses of the Andes, would be improved with rare promptness and delight.   H. R. H.

recently written me a long letter, alleging that a very material mistake was made against his Government in my settlement with President Frias of the Colton claim against Bolivia, and demanding that, through my agency and influence, Mr. Colton shall pay back to Bolivia the sum of $16,-683.40! Since the Honorable Secretary of State for Bolivia has undoubtedly addressed to me this extraordinary communication, it is, I dare say, quite safe to suppose that the Bolivians will try to persuade or prevent the Peruvians from paying the last installment, for $19,609.40, due at Lima on the first day of March of next year; and, although the draft for the amount has been formally accepted by Peru, yet she will probably be very glad to avail herself of this or any other excuse to retain the money in her own coffers, until it shall be still further explained and demonstrated that Bolivia does in fact owe the money to Mr. Colton.

Apprehensive that the whole affair might again be relegated into the uncertain mazes of diplomacy, I sent the communication from Secretary Oblitas to our own State Department, accompanied by a note from myself, wherein I endeavored to point out the errors and absurdities of Bolivia's demands in this matter, and stated very plainly and emphatically that the last draft on Peru from Bolivia, for $19,609.40, was justly due to Mr. Colton, and also an additional sum for damages for repeated delays and lapses and shortcomings; I having, by your consent, waived and set aside a considerable part of Mr. Colton's just claim, on the score of interest and otherwise, on condition that all the obligations proposed and given by Bolivia should be promptly honored at maturity.

I have also written a letter to Mr. Jose de Guerra, our United States Consul at La Paz, requesting him to call on Secretary Oblitas, and, after assuring his Excellency that he is laboring under an egregious mistake of his own, suggest to him the justice and propriety of his withdrawing his letter of inequitable complaint and demand, as persistence in his course will only lead to another general reopening of the case, to the inevitable injury and ignominy of Bolivia herself. Through Consul Guerra I reminded Secretary Oblitas specifically of the fact that the written agreement signed by President Frias and myself stipulated that you and Mr. Colton should receive the whole amount with interest, in gold, in New York, and that the last draft, the draft in question, was itself really insufficient to cover the balance due, including the expenses of exchange and other necessary and unavoidable charges at Lima.

After all, I may as well frankly admit that you knew these people much better than I did, and that your invariable distrust of them was fell founded; for I never even dreamed that they would or could be guilty of any such dishonest and disgraceful action as they have finally taken against their too confiding and unfortunate creditor, Mr. Colton. Although you yourself have already earned and won the case at least twenty times, yet it seems that all your skill and strength and patience must now again be called into requisition; else both you and your client, if not also the Government of the United States and several of its officials in the foreign service, will be forced to endure a most unjust and humiliating defeat. Of course you will firmly insist that Peru shall honor her acceptance, and pay the draft. That, as I conceive, is the only policy you can now pursue with any reasonable prospect of success.

Truly yours,
R. M. REYNOLDS.

MR. HELPER TO SECRETARY EVARTS.

RIO DE JANEIRO, BRAZIL, *November* 10, 1877.
HON. WILLIAM M. EVARTS,
Secretary of State, Washington.

SIR: During the whole period of my forty-seven years' intercourse with mankind, I have never experienced anything on the dark side of human nature, at all comparable to the unblushing blackness and baseness of Bolivia in her transactions with Mr. Joseph H. Colton, of New York, concerning the ten thousand maps which, at her own particular suggestion and solicitation, he engraved and published for her, so long ago as 1858, and which, greatly to the detriment and reproach of Republican institutions, now exhibit her as one of the independent and self-governing nations of the earth. Yesterday afternoon, I, as the last and present attorney for Mr. Colton, had the honor to receive from our Envoy Extraordinary and Minister Plenipotentiary in Brazil, the Hon. Henry W. Hilliard, to whose care the communications had been addressed, two letters, with memorandums, bearing on this most bitter and baneful business with Bolivia; one of the letters being directly from the Hon. Robert M. Reynolds, our late Minister to Bolivia, and the other, an inclosure, a copy of a dispatch which he had received from our Department of State at Washington, under date of the 15th of September, of the present year. From these letters I learn (and, but for a previous and thorough knowledge of the measureless obliquity and immorality of most of the political and revolutionary characters of Bolivia, would be astounded to learn,) that Mr. Oblitas, the Bolivian Secretary of State, now pretends that Mr. Colton has been overpaid, and, in the name of Bolivia, demands the restitution of $16,683.40!

The unprecedented effrontery, the unparalleled audacity,

of this pretension is simply monstrous. If to-day, Bolivia were to pay into the hands of Mr. Colton four times sixteen thousand dollars, in addition to that part of his just account against her which she has at last reluctantly and grudgingly paid only on compulsion, (only after, as the result of much additional waiting and working, and the incurrence of many additional outlays and obligations, I had obtained from the Congress of the United States a bill requiring her to pay the whole amount due, a requirement, however, with which she is still very far from having complied,) even that aggregate sum, $64,000, would be much less, less by many thousands of dollars, than the amount necessary, in strict equity, to satisfy the rightful demands which he and his several agents and attorneys might now very properly present against her, for the burdensome expenses, losses, labors, journeys, voyages, postponements, duplicities, and wear and tear and worry and waste of life, to which he and they have herein been constantly subjected during the last nineteen years.

The official and unofficial correspondence with Bolivia on this comparatively unimportant subject, the Colton Map Claim, has been of much greater duration, and but little less extensive and exhaustive, than the very elaborate correspondence which our Government at Washington, during the last decade or so of years, carried on with Great Britain in relation to the Alabama Claims; yet the Alabama Claims, amounting to many millions, have been justly and honorably paid in full, whilst the Colton Claim, amounting to only a few tens of thousands, has been paid only in part. Not taking into account either the ordinary or extraordinary expenses and losses incurred in the prolonged prosecution of this claim, not making any charge whatever for the herculean labors of long and frequent letter-writing so unconscionably imposed as a task on the claimant and his attorneys, and never but once reckoning interest on any of the accumulated sums which Bolivia herself, on numerous occasions, in various years, found and acknowledged to be due in this case, there is,—notwithstanding all these and other relinquishments in her favor, by way of final compromise,— there is yet due from her a balance, a last installment, of $19,609.40, for which I hold a draft, dated at La Paz, October 12, 1876, drawn by the Government of Bolivia on the Government of Peru, and formally accepted by Peru, at Lima, October 23, 1876, due and payable to my order on the first day of March, 1878. This draft I, *in propria persona*, or by my agent at Lima, will present on the very day when it falls due, and also on three successive days thereafter, if it be not satisfactorily honored meanwhile.

Then, if the draft still remains unpaid, I shall, through our Legation at Lima, through our Consulate at Callao, or through the office of a local Notary Public, enter solemn protest against both Peru and Bolivia, and will soon afterward make another memorial to the Congress of the United States, wherein, as regards Bolivia herself, separately, I shall, fortified by a knowledge of the simple rights and maintainable interests of Mr. Colton and his agents and attorneys, sue her, in the highest court of the world, for expenses and damages and losses actually sustained on account of her innumerable wiles and circumventions during the last nineteen years, in the sum of at least seventy thousand dollars, and also for a regular yearly allowance, to himself and his agents and attorneys (by way of indemnification for wilful obstructions and hindrances of the course of justice, and for compensation of the enormous and harassing labors, so often required, of explanations and reëxplanations, and of answers to newly invented and wickedly devised issues,) at the rate of six thousand dollars per annum, commencing on the first day of March, 1878, and continuing until the date, in future, of the final settlement of the claim. Only on this basis, or on a basis substantially similar to it, can either Mr. Colton or myself, or other mortal man, afford to be longer and continually trifled with and troubled by this most untrue, untrusty and tricky body-politic, Bolivia, miscalled à Republic.

Of this determination and notification on my part, I have the honor to request, worthy and distinguished Secretary, that you will be kind enough to take due cognizance. At the same time, I most respectfully and earnestly entreat, that with as little delay as may suit your convenience, you will be so good as to instruct our Ministers to Peru and Chili— we having now no Minister in Bolivia,—to lend me their friendly and official aid, at the proper time, in securing from Peru prompt payment of the last installment, now so treacherously and flagitiously disputed by Bolivia, as explained above, for $19,609.40, due at Lima on the first day of March, 1878. That installment, fully and promptly paid, will relieve me, as I very much desire to be relieved, from the necessity of ever again carrying the case into the Congress of the United States; and I sincerely trust that you may be pleased to receive from me this letter as a special petition for the relief thus anxiously craved and sought.

I have the honor to be, most respectfully,
Your obedient servant,
H. R. HELPER.
NEW YORK, December 24, 1877.
Approved: JOSEPH H. COLTON.

SECRETARY EVARTS TO MR. HELPER.

DEPARTMENT OF STATE,
WASHINGTON, *December* 28, 1877.
HINTON ROWAN HELPER, *Esq.,*
No. 39 Rua da Princeza Imperial,
Rio de Janeiro, Brazil.

SIR: Your letter of the 10th ultimo, relative to the

balance claimed by you on account of the Colton claim, so-called, on Bolivia, has been received. In reply, I have to inform you that this Government has now no diplomatic representative in Bolivia. Mr. Gibbs, Minister to Peru however, will be instructed to use his personal good offices, but not his official interposition, toward securing the payment by that Government of the draft of the Government of Bolivia, on account of the claim, which you say has been accepted by the former.

I am, sir, your obedient servant,
WM. M. EVARTS.

MR. COLTON TO MR. HELPER.

NEW YORK, *December* 29, 1877.

H. R. HELPER, *Esq.*, *Lima*, *Peru*.

DEAR SIR: Your letter of the 10th of November, inclosing a communication for the Hon. Wm. M. Evarts, Secretary of State, at Washington, was received here on the 24th instant. The communication for Mr. Evarts was dispatched to him the same day, with a request for an acknowledgment of its receipt, which latter came to hand this morning, and is herewith inclosed. Mr. Frederick W. Seward, Assistant Secretary of State, has also honored me with a note in reply to my request.

In relation to this new and startling rascality on the part of Bolivia, I know not how to speak. Words can give but poor expression to my emotions of disappointment, surprise and disgust; and so I might almost as well remain dumb. Never for one moment had I supposed it possible that even the Bolivians could condescend to become the authors of such a dishonorable contrivance; although I remember that you always entertained a very different opinion of them, declaring them to be a most mongrel and impure race, incapable of constancy to any agreement, written or verbal, and venturing the prediction that they would yet concoct and put in practice some new species of deviltry before final payment of my claim against their government could be obtained; and, sure enough, to my unspeakable bewilderment, as also to the unparalleled opprobrium of their own nationality, they have done just what you said they would do. But I shall not permit myself to believe that such wickedness can prosper. Will Peru play into the hands of Bolivia in these devices of low cunning, and thereby aid the efforts of the latter to thwart and defeat justice? I think not,—at least I hope not; and of one thing I feel quite certain; if they overreach you, they will have to get up very early in the morning. Knowing that you will do everything that an honorable man can do to secure our rights, I shall be anxious to hear from you at every important turn in the case; and, for your sake as well as my own, I fervently trust that both of us may, with justice, soon be relieved from the necessity of a further prosecution of this excessively trying and terrible business.

Very truly, your friend,

J. H. COLTON.

MINISTER OSBORN TO MR. HELPER.

LEGATION OF THE UNITED STATES,
SANTIAGO, CHILI, *January* 19, 1878.

MR. HINTON R. HELPER,

SIR: After a somewhat careful review of the history of the Colton claim against the Government of Bolivia, as explained in your letter and the accompanying documents of yesterday, I am led to the belief that your apprehensions as to the course which Bolivia may take in regard to the payment of the balance due, are substantially groundless. To conclude otherwise would be to arraign that government as wanting not only in honor, but also in a reasonable knowledge of its own interests. In view of the formal intervention of the Congress of the United States in behalf of the claimant, and of the subsequent execution by the Bolivian Government of bills of exchange in satisfaction of the claim, I cannot see how an attempt now, by Bolivia, to prevent the payment of such bills, could be regarded by the intervening power in any other light than that of a want of good faith. When the American Congress requested Bolivia to pay the amount due, it evidently expected that that request would be complied with; and if Bolivia has taken any steps looking to a repudiation of her promises made in pursuance of that request, she will, I am confident, on reflection, see the propriety at once of retracing her measures to that end. Her statesmen are not lacking in sagacity, and they must certainly see that she cannot afford, for the small amount involved, to take the position which she threatens to assume, if your suspicions are correct.

Very respectfully, your obedient servant,

THOMAS A. OSBORN.

PROTEST AGAINST BOTH PERU AND BOLIVIA.

LIMA, PERU, *March* 19, 1878.

WHEREAS I, Hinton Rowan Helper, a citizen of the United States of America, now temporarily in Lima, Peru, am the attorney in fact for Joseph H. Colton, an octogenarian, of New York, who, in September, 1858, nearly twenty years ago, engraved and published for the Republic of Bolivia, ten thousand large maps, on which, in the way of principal and interest and ordinary and extraordinary expenses, there remains, since the first day of this month, with interest thence accumulating, a balance justly due to Mr. Colton of seventy-eight thousand nine hundred and three dollars and eighteen cents in gold, as I am prepared to demonstrate by an equitable and detailed account; and whereas, under a compromise-settlement (the last of many previous compromise-settlements, to every one of which, however, Bolivia has always proved matchlessly disingenuous and unfaithful,) finally-effected, under a special Act of the Congress of the United States of America, between the Government of Bolivia and the Hon. Robert M. Reynolds, the last Minister from the United States to Bolivia, at La Paz, October 12, 1876, when the Government of that Republic issued a draft in the claimant's favor on the Government of Peru, for nineteen thousand six hundred and nine dollars and forty cents in silver, due at Lima on the first day of March, 1878, which said draft was formally and legally accepted by the Government of Peru, at Lima, on the 23d day of October, 1876; and whereas I, in company with my friend and agent here, Mr. Henry S. Prevost, have, together or separately, called at the Treasury Department of Peru almost every day, since and including the first instant, requesting and demanding payment of the said accepted draft, but have been uniformly, yet not most positively or definitely, refused payment, on the ground that Bolivia alleges that a mistake against her has been made in the account, of the magnitude of the whole amount of the said draft, except only the sum of two thousand dollars thereof, while, in truth, the whole amount equitably due to Mr. Colton is, as stated above, $78,903.18; so that, even if the said accepted draft had been, as it should have been, promptly and fully paid on the first instant, Mr. Colton would still,—even in that case,—have suffered a loss by Bolivia of more than sixty thousand dollars in gold; and whereas, on the twelfth day of this month, I addressed to the Hon. Jose Felix Garcia, the Peruvian Secretary of the Treasury, the original of the following copy of a

MEMORANDUM (No. 1.)

LIMA, PERU, *March* 12, 1878.

As attorney for the long-injured and long-suffering claimant, I have the honor to urge upon his Excellency Minister Garcia, that there are at least four weighty and all-sufficient reasons why the Colton draft from Bolivia, accepted by Peru, should be paid immediately:

First. The formal and legal acceptance by Peru of the said draft, on the 23d day of October, 1876, due on the 1st day of March, 1878, is in itself an ample reason why the draft,—already eleven days overdue,—should be paid at once. Otherwise Peru will commit the grave offence of being the first to violate and break her own national law, which requires absolutely the payment of all accepted drafts, where, as in this case, there is no false signature.

Second. The moment the draft was duly accepted, from that very moment it came to be in the condition, so far as Bolivia is concerned, of having been paid; for Peru, the accepter of the draft, assumed complete responsibility for its payment; and that assumption having been satisfactory to the holder, he was thenceforward, by law and custom and reliance, estopped and prevented from taking any further proceedings against Bolivia; as otherwise he would most assuredly have done. More especially and positively is the acceptance binding against Peru, inasmuch as she never issued to the holder of the draft, after having accepted it, any notice whatever,—not even the slightest intimation,— of any intention or purpose on her part not to comply with her written obligation; her officially executed promise, which if not now fulfilled, will prove to have been, to both Mr. Colton and his attorney, a most grievously and partisanly deceptive and misleading document.

Third. This draft is the final result of a settlement no merely between Mr. Colton and Bolivia, but it is, moreover, in a much higher sense, the result of a settlement, under a special Act of Congress, between the Government of the United States of America, through its Minister, Mr. Reynolds, and the Government of Bolivia; and Peru certainly has no right whatever to assume umpireship, nor to constitute herself a judge, between Mr. Colton and Bolivia on the one hand, nor between the United States of America and Bolivia on the other.

Fourth. The present action of Bolivia, in the absence from her capital of a diplomatic representative of the United States, whose Legation in Bolivia has been abolished, is simply an attempt at insidious evasion of payment of an honest debt; a debt which has already been greatly compromised and dwindled away in the interest of Bolivia as against her unfortunate creditor, Mr. Colton, and which debt, besides, since 1858, the year of its creation, has cost him and his several agents and attorneys, by way of actual expenses and abatements, more than fifty thousand dollars in gold, in their constant and laborious yet fruitless efforts to collect it; not one cent of which extraordinary amount of expenses has ever been taken into account, but the whole of which stands to-day as a total loss, over and above the compromise-balance now due, as per accepted draft on Peru for $19,609.40 in silver; and it is not believed that Peru will now, by dishonoring her regularly and solemnly accepted obligation, lend herself as an aider and abettor in this new and most faithless and wrongful proceeding on the part of Bolivia. In brief, there is but one high and just and honorable course for Peru to pursue in the premises, and that is to pay the draft without further delay. Therefore I thus again have the honor to request payment accordingly, and trust that his Excellency, Minister Garcia, will perceive that, by making such payment, he will only be acting in conformity with both the law and the equity of the case.

Most respectfully submitted,
H. R. HELPER.

AND WHEREAS, on the 15th day of the present month, I addressed to my friend, Mr. Prevost, to be read in translation by him to Secretary Garcia (who had expressed some displeasure and dissatisfaction at the receipt of the first memorandum,) the original of the following copy of another

MEMORANDUM (NO. 2.)

LIMA, PERU, *March* 15, 1878.

My friend, Mr. Prevost, who will kindly retain for himself, or return to me, this memorandum, will please assure his Excellency Minister Garcia, that I entertain for him, personally, and for the Peruvians generally, great respect and good will: That I earnestly desire to avoid giving offence, but that, having already considerately waited two weeks for payment of Peru's accepted draft, due on the first instant, if the money be not paid on or before Tuesday of next week, or if, not later than that day, some satisfactory assurance be not given for the honoring of the draft in the course of a few days thereafter, it will then be my duty to make a formal protest against the Peruvian Government, and to adopt the most vigorous and certain measures within my power to secure the earliest possible payment of the amount of the draft, and also, in that case, payment of all the consequential damages and expenses: That there are many facts of law and facts of circumstance which will both justify and require the making of the protest,—if it must be made,— very energetic, pungent and comprehensive; and that I am profoundly apprehensive that a triple trouble, of unexpected magnitude, may result from such a protest; trouble and more delay and expense to Mr. Colton, trouble to Bolivia, (inevitable trouble to her, happen what may,) and last, but not least, trouble to Peru. In the name of amity and justice, therefore, I thus again request and trust that his Excellency Minister Garcia may now be pleased to make prompt and pleasant payment of Peru's accepted and overdue draft, and thereby end at once all solicitude and all danger, concerning discomposing, costly and prejudicial proceedings.

Very respectfully,
H. R. HELPER.

AND WHEREAS, notwithstanding all these considerate endeavors on my part to induce fair and friendly payment by Peru of her own unconditionally accepted draft, now nearly three weeks overdue, Mr. Colton's rights and interests in the matter are still most ungraciously and unrighteously denied and withheld,—Now, therefore, I, the said attorney for the said claimant, in the name and upon the principles of all that is reasonable and equitable and honorable among mankind, do hereby solemnly and earnestly protest, first against the Government of Peru for thus dishonoring its own accepted draft, and thereby, in effect at least, allying itself as an accomplice with Bolivia in the perpetration of another gross and cruel wrong against the claimant; and further I do hereby protest and declare that, if the money thus so obviously and eminently due by accepted draft, be not paid into my hands within seven days from to-day, that is to say, by or before the 26th day of the present month, it is my intention to take, immediately thereafter, such further lawful and vigorous proceedings in the premises, whether by application to the Supreme Court of Peru for a mandamus compelling payment; by a new and urgent appeal to the Congress of the United States, or to the Department of State of the United States; by lawful seizure at or near New York of Peruvian Government guano; or by such other course or action at law or in diplomacy as I may prefer, at my own discretion, and as may seem to me to be most prudent and proper and promisingly expeditious in securing involuntarily from Peru the measure of justice thus volitionally unattainable. In the event of non-payment within the next seven days, as aforesaid, I further declare it to be my intention to hold Peru responsible, in addition to the amount of her accepted draft, for damages in the sum of ten thousand dollars in gold, and also for all legal and other expenses which may, at any time, or under any circumstances, accrue in consequence of her default of payment in this case. Likewise will I hold her responsible,—and this I must do in any event,—for the sum of eleven hundred and odd dollars in silver, with interest thereon, due as the difference in exchange and in the value of the depreciated Peruvian money, between the 30th day of June, 1876, and the date, in October following, of the payment of the Bolivian-Peruvian installment for $10,794.27 in silver, which was due and should have been paid, on the said 30th day of June, 1876, but was not paid until more than three months afterward. So far in particular protestation against Peru.

Moreover, and finally, I now also, in this connection, emphatically protest against Bolivia, because of this last manifestation of a twenty-years' series of glaringly dissembling and discreditable acts on her part, which said acts have proved ruinously injurious to my aged client, and which, besides, while they are, as the public acts of a nation, in direct contravention of the simplest rules of fairness and justice, are, at the same time, indirect incentives to universal chicanery and corruption; and I further protest and declare that, because of this new and distressful device and duplicity, this new treason against law and justice, this barefaced infidelity to the written and rightful conditions of a plain adjustment, this additional and unprovoked injury and outrage against my octogenary client, on the part of Bolivia, it is my determination, at the proper time, and in my own way, at my own option, to hold that so-called Republic responsible for the whole amount of the $78,903.18 in gold, with interest, as mentioned above, which shall be found to be due thereon after deducting therefrom, when paid, the $19,609.40 in silver overdue, as above protested, on Peru's accepted draft; claiming and insisting that, through this last manœuvre of folly and fraud, as aforesaid, Bolivia, always foully fruitful of delays and evasions and affected excuses, has now completely forfeited her right to all the advantages which were generously yielded to her on various occasions of former compromise.

Dwelling and acting on the bases of the several methods of procedure thus indicated, I shall continue to struggle till the very end of my days, if the issue be not sooner settled, to bring at last to a right conclusion, to recover eventually, in all its justness and fulness, the Colton Map Claim against the Government of Bolivia. Therefore, against all whom it may concern; against Peru on the one hand, and against Bolivia on the other; against them both and against each; against them together and against them separately; I do thus earnestly speak; I do thus really intend; I do thus solemnly protest.

HINTON ROWAN HELPER.

CONSUL CLAYTON'S CERTIFICATE.

UNITED STATES CONSULATE,
CALLAO, PERU, *April* 3, 1878.

Personally appeared before me, this day, at this Consulate, Hinton Rowan Helper, a worthy citizen of the United States of America, to me personally known, and known by me to be the person who executed the foregoing Protest, declaring that he had good and sufficient reasons for so doing, and that he did so specifically for the uses and purposes therein mentioned.

In testimony whereof, I have hereunto set my hand and affixed the seal of my office, at Callao, this the third day of April, 1878.

ROBERT T. CLAYTON,
United States Consul.

MR. COLTON'S APPROBATION.

NEW YORK, *May* 18, 1878: The foregoing protest against Peru and Bolivia meets my entire approbation.

JOSEPH H. COLTON.

DETAILED ACCOUNT AGAINST BOLIVIA.

LIMA, PERU, *March* 30, 1878.
THE GOVERNMENT OF BOLIVIA,
To JOSEPH H. COLTON, OF NEW YORK, *Dr.*

For ten thousand large Maps of the Republic of Bolivia, as per contract under date of September 21, 1858,	$25,000.00
For boxing, shipping, marine insurance, freight, and minor charges on the same, from New York to Arica in Peru, as per instructions, - - - - - -	1,300.00
	$26,300.00
Less cash in advance, as per agreement, - - -	2,000.00
	$24,300.00

Amount forwarded, - - -.- - - $24,300.00
For interest from September 21, 1859, to May 7, 1860, 7 months and 16 days, when the Bolivian Congress ordered payment of the amount due, but paid nothing at all; calculating interest at the rate of seven per cent. per annum; that being the legal rate of interest in New York, where the debt was created, and where, at this rate, and sometimes at higher special rates, money had to be borrowed in lieu of the money uncollectably due from Bolivia. (Other parties having claims against Bolivia have in most cases charged as high as twelve per cent. interest per annum, and Bolivia has admitted the charge; that being the regular commercial rate of interest in that country, - - - - - 1,067.75

$25,367.75

For interest to August 12, 1861, 1 year, 3 months and 5 days, when the Bolivian Congress again ordered payment of the amount due, but paid nothing whatever, - - 2,244.31

$27,612.06

For interest to July 22, 1863, 1 year, 11 months and 10 days, when, for the third time, the Bolivian Congress again ordered payment of the amount due, but paid not one cent, - - - - . - - . 3,758.31

$31,370.37

For interest to October 27, 1864, 1 year, 3 months and 5 days, when, for the fourth time, the Bolivian Congress, without even paying so much as a farthing, again ordered payment of the amount due, - - - - 2,575.39

$33,945.76

For interest to February 1, 1872, 7 years, 3 months and 4 days, when, for the fifth time, Bolivia ordered, but ordered in vain, payment of the amount due, . - - 17,253.87

$51,199.63

For interest to October 13, 1875, 3 years, 8 months and 12 days, when, only under the influence of the positive and impressive action in the claimant's behalf by the Congress of the United States, a few months previously, the first money, a first installment, was received from Bolivia; the maps having been published and

Amount forwarded, . - - - - - $51,199.63
delivered nearly eighteen years previously. (Additional interest must, of course, in justice to the claimant, be calculated on at least a part of this sum, between this date, October 13, 1875, and March 1, 1878, as will be explained in the concluding paragraph of this formal account,) - - - - - - - 13,260.60
$64,460.23
For expenses and fees paid various agents and attorneys, for services, journeys, voyages, etc., etc., from September 21, 1859, to January 1, 1874, $26,840; and also for corresponding expenses, fees and compensations to the same and other agents and attorneys, from January 1, 1874, to March 1, 1878, $11,633.64; making as principal alone, a sum total of actual expenses incurred in this most harassing and ruinous business with Bolivia, during a period of nearly twenty years, of $38,473.64; on which, as a matter of course, it is but right to reckon interest; because it was necessary to pay interest on the money so expended through Bolivia's persistent delinquency. Thus: Principal of expenses, from September 21, 1859, to March 1, 1878, $38,473.64; aggregate of interest on the same, $13,322.28; total $51,795.92, - - - - - - - 51,795.92
$116,256.15
Credit by cash from Bolivia, as follows:
October 13, 1875, - - - $ 4,505.76
December 23, 1875, - - - 5,274.88
January 15, 1876, - - - - 110.78
March 9, 1876, - - - - - 10,678.12
July 24, 1876, - - - - - 253.35
August 31, 1876, - - - - 2,353.62
November 14, 1876, - - - 7,091.15
March 12, 1877, - - - - 8,807.85

$39,075.51—Subtract— 39,075.51
$77,180.64

For the sake of brévity of statement, here entirely suspending, if not abating, the accumulation of interest due on the sum of the original indebtedness, amounting, as will have been seen, to $64,460.23, while pay-

Amount forwarded, - - - - - $77,180.64
ments by installments were being made by Bolivia, between October 13, 1875, and March 12, 1877, inclusive, such payments aggregating a sum total, as shown above, of $39,075,51,—although this is another voluntary and extensive suppression of the rights of the creditor in the interest of the debtor,—it now only remains, in order to ascertain the full amount of the balance otherwise yet due from Bolivia to Mr. Colton, (holding, however, in abeyance, for the present, the right to claim damages for scores upon scores of acts of bad faith in the non-fulfillment of specific and solemn promises,) to add to the last foregoing sum of indebtedness the interest due from March 12, 1877, that being the date of the last payment by Bolivia, to March 1, 1878, on $25,384.72, which is the difference between $64,460.23, the sum, with interest, of the original indebtedness, independently of all expenses, up to October 13, 1875, when the first money came to hand, and $39,075.51, the whole amount thus far received from Bolivia. In this way: March 12, 1877, to March 1, 1878, 11 months' and 19 days' interest on $25,384.72, as stated above, $1,722.54, - - - - - - 1,722.54

Balance due to Mr. Colton, March 1, 1878, - - $78,903,18
E. E.   HINTON R. HELPER,
Attorney for Joseph H. Colton.

The historical items in the foregoing account, the annals of wide divergence, and the oddly aberrant and empty doings of the Bolivian Congress, are worthy of very careful consideration, as giving a clear index to the present proceedings of the Bolivian Government; its latest action being in full accord with the grotesquely deceptive and dishonorable course which it pursued toward Mr. Colton, during more than half a generation, before he was finally provoked, in self-defence, and almost in despair, to invoke and obtain the sustaining intervention of the Government of the United States. How far this anomalous Republic, this un-Bolivarlike Bolivia, speaking so repeatedly, year in and year out, in its very highest capacity, through its Congresses, through a long succession of its Presidents, through its Ministers of Government in Cabinet-Council, through its Department of State, and otherwise in ways positive, peculiar and innumerable, and yet never once complying with its engagements, never once having proved true to its word, is now worthy, if worthy at all, of credence in this twentieth year of its unconscionable tergiversations and subterfuges, is a question which I am quite willing to submit, here or elsewhere, now or hereafter, for the consideration of any number of just-minded men.

As regards Peru, whose accepted and overdue draft from Bolivia I hold for collection, I most earnestly and emphatically protest against her assumption of the position of an adjudicator or arbitrator between either Mr. Colton and Bolivia or between the United States and Bolivia. In this affair, as I contend, she cannot justly put herself forward as the champion of Bolivia's rights without becoming at the same time responsible for Mr. Colton's wrongs; and if, in any voluntary or *ex parte* manner, she takes upon herself the task of redressing the alleged grievances of the Government of Bolivia, it is but fair and reasonable that she should be required to satisfy herein the rightful demands of the Government of the United States. What I ask of Peru, and all I ask of her, but what I steadfastly insist upon, is that she shall honor her acceptance. Any new settlement of accounts between Bolivia and Mr. Colton, or between the United States and Bolivia, in this affair, must be made in the United States or in Bolivia, and not in Peru. Immediate payment of the draft would be the performance of Peru's plain and perfect duty in the premises; and this is precisely what is required of her by her own national law, and also by the opinion of her own Attorney-General.

H. R. HELPER.

THE LAW OF ACCEPTANCES.

Extracts from a work entitled "Banking, Currency, and Exchanges," by Arthur Crump, an official in the Bank of England. Also other authorities, on the same subject, cited by Mr. Helper against the Governments of Peru and Bolivia: "Bills of exchange, on being introduced into Great Britain, were discovered to be of greater use than merely as the representatives of so much money, as they could be instrumental in effecting the assignment of a debt, and as such are now recognized by the common law. Not only was the debt transferred, but its value was inhanced, inasmuch as the debtor himself accepted to pay a certain amount, from which engagement he could not afterward depart."

"A bill is not finally discharged until paid by, or on behalf of the accepter. * * * It was held formerly that part payment by the drawer was a partial discharge to the accepter, but it is now decided that payment by the drawer is no plea, but simply converts the holder into a trustee for the drawer, when the holder afterward recovers of the accepter."

"No one can discharge the accepter of a bill, except the holder, or some one authorized by him."

"Payment must be made to the rightful holder, as payment to any other person does not discharge the accepter."

Chief Justice Marshall, in deciding the case of Ogden *versus* Saunders, said: " The liability of the drawer of a bill of exchange stands upon the same principle with every other implied contract. He has received the money or its equivalent, of the person in whose favor the bill was drawn, and promises that it shall be returned by the drawee. If the drawee fail to pay the bill, then the promise of the drawer is broken, and for this breach of contract he is liable. The same principle applies to the indorser. His contract is not written, but his name is evidence of his promise that the bill shall be paid, and of his having received value for it. In effect, he is a new drawer, and has made a new contract."

In his " Rights of a Citizen of the United States," Theophilus Parsons says: "When a bill of exchange is drawn, nobody promises, in words, to pay it. A orders B to pay C. If B, when requested, says he will not do as ordered, the law supposes A, the drawer, to have promised that he would pay if B did not. If B 'accepts,' the law now supposes that B promises C to pay the bill to him. Now B, being the accepter, is held by the law just as a maker of a note is, because he is supposed to have promised in the same way. A, the drawer, is held just as the first indorser of a note is held, because he is supposed to have promised to pay if B did not. If the bill was negotiable, that is, payable to C, or his order, then C may indorse the bill; and although his name is the only one on the back of the bi l, he is treated in law only as second indorser, because the drawer is bound in the same way as a first indorser. And if D then puts his name below C's, he is treated as third indorser, and so on. * * * If a foreign bill be not accepted, or be not paid at maturity, it should at once be protested by a notary public. Inland bills are generally, and promissory notes frequently, protested; but this is not generally required by the law. The holder of a foreign bill, after protest for non-payment, or for non-acceptance, may sue the drawer and indorser, and recover the face of the bill, and, in addition thereto, his damages, which damages, on protest, are generally adjudged in this country by various statutes, which give greater damages as the distance is greater; and an established usage would supply the place of statutes if they were wanting."

MINISTER GIBBS TO MR. HELPER.

LEGATION OF THE UNITED STATES OF AMERICA,
LIMA, PERU, *April* 2, 1878.

H. R. HELPER, *Esq., Lima*.

SIR: I have the honor of acknowledging the receipt of your favors of yesterday and to-day, with inclosures. I have had a prolonged interview with the Minister of Foreign Affairs to-day, in relation to the draft of Bolivia on Peru, in favor of Mr. Colton, accepted by Peru, but remaining unpaid at the request of the Bolivian Government. I have used all the arguments at my command in reference to this affair, and also all my personal influence to persuade the Minister of Foreign affairs to honor Peru's acceptance; but he answered me by stating that the Bolivian Minister had documents showing that an error of importance had been discovered in the claim of Mr. Colton, and on that account they could not pay, but would deposit the money until the affair was cleared up.

Mr. Rospigliosi proposed that I should see the Bolivian Minister, Mr. Flores, which I dec'ined to do, and referred him to you and your agent. Regretting very much that I have not been able to induce the Minister to comply with what appears to me to be simple justice, I think that your only plan now is to protest in due form, through the proper parties, against whom it may concern; and a copy of the protest should be deposited in this Legation.

I am, sir, very respectfully,
Your obedient servant,
RICHARD GIBBS.

MR. HELPER TO SECRETARY EVARTS.

LIMA, PERU, *April* 19, 1878.
HON. WILLIAM M. EVARTS,
Secretary of State, Washington.

SIR: Through the unblushing duplicity and perfidy of two nations, Peru and Bolivia, acting conjointly, I am now the victim here of the most burdensome and unbearable injustice which has ever yet been inflicted on me; my aged friend, Mr. Joseph H. Colton, of New York, being a fellow sufferer with me, in consequence of the iniquitous conduct of this brace of disorderly and disreputable Republics. The last letter which I had the honor of addressing to you upon this subject was written at Rio de Janeiro, in Brazil, on the 10th of November, 1877; and in view of the fact that, for many years previously, it had been necessary for me, and for other agents and attorneys of Mr. Colton, in endeavoring to secure the rights of our client, to write very often and very voluminously to your predecessors in the State Department at Washington, from General Cass to Secretary Fish inclusive, I had hoped, in view also of the terms of final settlement agreed upon, in 1876, between the Government of Bolivia and Mr. Reynolds, our last Minister at La Paz, that no new occasion would ever arise for troubling you further in reference to a simple matter of business, which, but for the woful absence of sound morals in and about Bolivia, would have been privately and properly adjusted nearly twenty years ago.

The inclosed Protest against Peru, duly verified before the United States Consul at Callao, so fully explains the object of this letter that I need not here enter into a lengthy reëxplanation of it. I trust, however, that the protest itself may receive your careful consideration and action. In the hope of being able at once to get this protest before the Peruvian

Government through the United States Legation at Lima, I offered it to the Hon. Richard Gibbs, our Minister here, requesting him to transmit it to the Hon. Secretary of State of Peru; but, according to his opinion, he had no authority nor duty to dispatch the document to this Government, and so returned it to me, referring me to you for instructions to himself in that regard. I therefore respectfully and earnestly request that you will be good enough to instruct Minister Gibbs to deliver or send to this Government the inclosed Protest; and, if international law and the antecedents of the case will justify you in so doing, instruct him, at the same time, to demand immediate payment by Peru of her accepted draft to my order; leaving Mr. Colton and Bolivia, and also the United States and Bolivia, free from constraint to fight out their grievances or their differences on the neutral, or what ought to be neutral, territory of Peru.

Under advice from Minister Gibbs and other Americans in Lima, I have been trying, though as yet unsuccessfully, to institute proceedings in the Supreme Court of Peru, for a mandamus requiring the Government to pay the draft; the Attorney-General of the Republic having already given his opinion very clearly in my favor; yet, strange to say, his opinion, though very unmistakably and strongly condemnatory of the action of Peru in not honoring her own acceptance, does not seem to have produced any perceptible impression on the higher functionaries of his Government. So many are the difficulties which I have to encounter, and so formidable are the obstacles which I have to surmount, in connection with the danger of years and years of overwhelmingly expressive litigation, where no litigation whatever should be required, that I very much fear I may never be able to obtain justice here by any process of law. Three weeks ago I myself, in person, offered my protest in English to this Government, but it refused positively to receive it from me; and, as already stated above, Minister Gibbs says he has no authority, no obligation, no instruction, to deliver it for me. Ever since the 4th instant I have been equally baffled in my efforts to get before the Government here a much shorter protest in Spanish; the laws of Peru requiring all protests against the Government, or any department thereof, to be made out in accordance with various specified formalities; one of the indispensable conditions in this case being that the paper from Bolivia, upon which Peru bases her refusal to pay her accepted draft, shall accompany the protest; and that paper so absolutely necessary as a preliminary step, and which could probably be easily copied within ten minutes, this Government, apparently indifferent to my petition, has thus far failed to furnish; constantly excusing itself on the flimsy and heartless plea of lack of time to make the copy for which, more than two weeks ago, I presented a respectful written application. Pray let your instructions to Minister Gibbs be just as pointed and strong as possible; as otherwise nothing good, nothing reasonable, nothing right, can be accomplished with these people. This letter, with its inclosures, will reach you through the hands of Mr. Colton; but both the letter and the protest have been submitted for the perusal of the Hon. Mr. Gibbs, our Minister in Lima. Your letter to me,—if you will be kind enough to reply to this communication,—may be addressed to me, in care of our Legation here.

I have the honor to be, most respectfully,
Your obedient servant,
H. R. HELPER.

MR. HELPER TO SECRETARY ROSPIGLIOSI.

HOTEL MAURY, LIMA, *April* 22, 1878.
To HIS EXCELLENCY THE HON. J. C. JULIO ROSPIGLIOSI,
Secretary of State for Peru.

SIR: A stranger in Peru, a citizen of the United States of America, I feel that I have a right to make respectful complaint to your Excellency of two weighty wrongs, which I am now suffering because of action in the one case, and because of inaction in the other, by the Peruvian Government toward me. On the first day of last month, I presented to the Hon. Secretary of the Treasury a draft from the Government of Bolivia to my order, as the attorney for Mr. Joseph H. Colton, of New York, for $19,609.40 in silver, which had previously been duly accepted by Peru, to be paid on that day, and which, in both law and justice, and in conformity with the universal rules of correct business, Peru should have then paid, but did not; assigning as a reason that Bolivia had interposed the allegation that a mistake had been made in the settlement of her account with Mr. Colton, through Mr. Reynolds, the last United States Minister at La Paz. That strange and erroneous allegation by Bolivia was in characteristic keeping with her almost twenty-years' equivocations and artifices and delinquencies in this affair. The true balance, the balance in equity, due to Mr. Colton from Bolivia, on the first day of last month, as shown in the inclosed account, to which I beg your Excellency's attention, was $78,903.18 in gold.

Against Peru's refusal to pay her accepted draft, I offered, about three weeks ago, to the Hon. Secretary of the Treasury, my protest in English, executed before the United States Consul at Callao; but the Hon. Secretary declined to receive it from me; stating that it must be made out and presented in accordance with the laws of the country; which same laws, as I am well-informed, also require that all accepted drafts shall be promptly paid on presentation, when due, except only where there is a false signature, as there certainly is not in this case. Going then to a local lawyer, I consulted him on the subject, and he at once, acting for me, made out a request for a copy of the paper from Bolivia on which Peru had refused to pay her accepted draft; requesting, also, a copy of the opinion of Peru's Attorney-General, whose fidelity to the just and enlightened laws of his country led him to report very clearly in my favor. Almost every day, since the 4th instant, a friend and myself have been trying very hard to obtain those papers, as necessary preliminaries for a protest acceptable to the Hon. Secretary of the Treasury; but we have been baffled and delayed until I am greatly depressed with disappointment and discouragement. Under these circumstances, I trust that it is not too much for me to ask of your Excellency the favor of so far waiving mere formalities as either to accept, for the Government of Peru, my protest in English, or to facilitate me in obtaining the papers mentioned above, so that, through my lawyer, I may make out and present one in Spanish.

I have the honor to be, most respectfully,
   Your Excellency's obedient servant,
                                             H. R. HELPER.

MR. HELPER TO MINISTER FLORES.

HOTEL MAURY, LIMA, *April* 23, 1878.
TO HIS EXCELLENCY THE HON. ZOILO FLORES,
   *Envoy Extraordinary and Minister Plenipotentiary
                                     from Bolivia to Peru.*
   SIR: So large a proportion of the comparatively small

number of Bolivians with whom it has been my privilege to become personally acquainted, have been men of truth, justice and honor, that I am very much surprised not to find those excellent traits of individual character more adequately reflected in the public life and career of the nation. When an aged and veracious man, of four score years, who has been in active business, with his own and other countries, ever since he attained his majority, asserts that a single transaction into which he was involuntarily drawn, nearly twenty years ago, by a certain nationality, has, because of the almost countless number of acts of bad faith toward him on the part of that nationality, cost him more loss and trouble, and corroding care and anxiety, than all the other adverse concerns of his life put together, his words constitute a very strong and serious indictment against that nationality; and that is precisely the indictment which Mr. Joseph H. Colton, an octogenarian, of New York, whose attorney I am, now makes against Bolivia. The inclosed Account on the one hand and Protest on the other, to which I have the honor to invite your Excellency's attention, are, for the present at least, sufficiently explanatory of all the matters at issue affecting my client's peculiar misfortunes in this unfortunate affair.

I have the honor to be, most respectfully,
Your Excellency's obedient servant,
H. R. HELPER.

MR. HELPER TO MINISTER FLORES.

HOTEL MAURY, LIMA, *May* 16, 1878.
To HIS EXCELLENCY THE HON. ZOILO FLORES,
*Envoy Extraordinary and Minister Plenipotentiary
from Bolivia to Peru.*
SIR: On my return to Lima, last evening, from Chicla,

the present eastern terminus of the Oroya Railroad, I received your communication of the 13th instant, inclosing the Letter, Account and Protest, which I had the honor to address to your Excellency on the 23d ultimo. Three weeks' retention of these papers by your Excellency would seem to warrant the inference that you *have probably had them translated into Spanish, and have therefore no fur.her need of the originals in English. That a twenty-years' delinquent should deliberately return his creditor's just account unpaid, without apology or explanation, and, at the same time, as an additional act of wrongfulness, upbraid and insult his injured victim, certainly proves the existence of a condition of things in human affairs most lamentably at variance with the wishes and expectations of the more sanguine school of optimists; and although the sending back of such an account, under such circumstances, may serve as a cheap and temporary convenience, yet it is very far indeed from being either an equitable or a courteous method of satisfying an honest debt.

Ever since 1858, the treacherous course which Bolivia has persistently pursued toward her unfortunate creditor Colton, has been marked by a species of Machiavelism and duplicity so inexpressibly vile and shameless as to be absolutely without a precedent or parallel in any other nation of the New World. No sooner has one set of her peculiarly egotistic and destructive revolutionists arranged, in words at least, for a future payment of the claim, than. another set, without knowing or caring to know anything of the essential antecedents of the case, have come into power, only to mystify and frustrate the proceedings of their predecessors. Thus it is that the prominent features of this noteworthy case constitute, on the part of Bolivia, a long and knotty series of scores and hundreds and_thousands of grossly violated promises and agreements, verbal and written, legal and diplomatic, ministerial and congressional; always, too, at the grievous discomfiture and cost and dismay of the hapless Colton and his several agents and attorneys.

Before receiving your Excellency's communication of the 13th instant, I had been led to apprehend that an occasion might probably soon arise, rendering it right and proper for me to submit all the facts of this very remarkable case for the consideration and action of the Peruvian Congress; the matter at issue having already occupied the serious attention of the Congress of the United States of America, and also, many times and oft and farcically, of the Congress of Bolivia. In this particular regard, your Excellency's communication has very effectually settled the important question, which, for a fortnight or more, I have been mentally debating. If I am to be detained here until the first day of July, I shall immediately thereafter prepare, in Spanish, as briefly as possible, a comprehensive history of the Colton claim against Bolivia, and, in the form of a memorial, will lay the same before both houses of the Congress of Peru, on the very first day of its opening; petitioning for such just and decisive action on their part as I shall therein specifically solicit; using a copy of this letter itself as a basis for the document which, in the event contemplated, I shall have the honor of presenting to the most august and authoritative assemblage of Peruvian statesmen.

I have the honor to be, most respectfully,
Your Excellency's obedient servant,
H. R. HELPER.

MR. HELPER TO CONSUL-GENERAL LANFRANCO.

Hotel Maury, Lima, *May* 20, 1878.
Hon. Joaquin P. Lanfranco,
Consul-General for Bolivia in Peru.

Sir: In the first place, let me assure you that, for yourself personally, as also for other very estimable and worthy Bolivians whom I have met, both within their country and without, and whom I like almost as well as I like myself, I entertain entire respect and good will; only I wish to say this,—that, for Bolivia in the aggregate, for Bolivia as a nationality, I have no respect whatever; she having, long ago, by her course and cruel and criminal conduct toward my client Colton and myself, forfeited all claims to even common civility; and further, as an additional preliminary remark, let me state that having myself nothing to do with the delicate dodges of diplomacy, only to despise them, I feel that I can well afford to be straightforward, use plain language, and tell the truth. Since, as a new link in an old and long chain of offense, it has pleased Bolivia to subject me to the great inconvenience and cost of appearing before the Peruvian tribunals and the Peruvian public in quest of an oft-times demonstrated matter of law and equity, which she now basely denies, I am yet determined to make the best possible use of my rather solitary and disadvantageous situation, in the endeavor to properly expose and counteract this latest phase of her flagitious folly and faithlessness; it being already more than five years since I ceased to occupy toward that most pernicious power the humble position of a petitioner for justice, and took upon myself, as I still take, all the responsibility of speaking only from the standpoint of an unyielding demandant of my rights. It was in this mood, after nearly fifteen years of respectful waiting and continuous application, without any other result than such an overflowing flood of flagrantly false assurances as one might expect to hear only from a blatant mob of utterly unveracious and characterless creatures, like the sable sons of Senegambia, or the serpentsellers of Soudan that I carried the case, successfully, into the Congress of the United States, where, if not settled meanwhile, I shall again carry it, on the first Monday of December next; and it is in this same mood, moreover, that I purpose carrying it into the Congress of Peru, about two months hence, provided I am to be detained here until that time. Of this determination on my part, (but in somewhat different phraseology,) I have already given information to his Excellency, the Hon. Zoilo Flores, the Bolivian Envoy Extraordinary and Minister Plenipotentiary in Peru.

I have the honor to be, most respectfully,
Your obedient servant,
H. R. HELPER.

MR. HELPER TO SECRETARY EVARTS.

LIMA, PERU, *May* 20, 1878.

HON. WILLIAM M. EVARTS,
Secretary of State, Washington.

SIR: The suit of Mr. Colton and myself against the Government of Peru, for payment of its accepted draft, over-due here ever since the first day of last March, drawn by the Government of Bolivia on the 12th of October, 1876, to my order, for $19,609.40 in silver, has now reached a condition wherein, under a special decree of President Prado, issued a few days since, it is only required of me, in order to obtain the money, to give a satisfactory bond in the sum of the amount due; but as this government will not accept the alien bond of Mr. Colton and myself, and I can here give no other, the object of this letter is to request that you will be good enough to instruct our Minister here, the Hon. Richard Gibbs, (if he is not already instructed to demand payment of the said accepted draft, without a bond or any other irregular and burdensome condition,) to give his official obligation for me, which I feel confident he may very safely do, in view of the real facts of the case in law and equity, in view also of the action in the matter by the Congress of the United States, and in further view of the weighty consideration that Peru merely desires, by this extra and formal proceeding, to preserve the friendliest possible relations with her near neighbor, Bolivia.

At my particular request, this letter will be transmitted to you by Minister Gibbs himself, who will, I suppose, take occasion to express to you his own opinion of the propriety or impropriety of complying with my wishes; for I really do not know what his judgment is in this regard. If, however, you should not feel fully justified in instructing him to give his official bond, for me to receive the money here, you may, if you please, instruct him to give such bond, and then transmit the money to your order, as Secretary of State at Washington, or to the order of the Hon. John Sherman, Secretary of the Treasury; for, although Mr. Colton and myself, being only "Gringos" and non-residents, cannot readily give an acceptable bond for nineteen thousand six hundred dollars in Peru, yet we shall experience very little trouble in doing so in the United States. As I shall be detained here, on additional expenses and loss of time, anxiously awaiting your reply, I trust that you will be so kind as to favor me, through Minister Gibbs, with as early an answer as may accord with your convenience.

I have the honor to be, most respectfully,
Your obedient servant,
H. R. HELPER.

SECRETARY EVARTS TO MR. COLTON.

DEPARTMENT OF STATE,
WASHINGTON, *May* 25, 1878.

JOSEPH H. COLTON, *Esq., New York.*

SIR: I have received your letter of the 18th instant, with Mr. Helper's letter and proposed protest. The vexatious delay to which the discharge of your claim against Bolivia has been subjected, is cordially sympathized with. Mr. Helper seems to have acquitted himself, as your agent, with great zeal and perseverance. It is regarded as certain, however, that Peru would not be hastened in paying the draft of Bolivia, which she has accepted, if Mr. Helper's protest were to be officially presented to her. That protest contains expressions, in regard not only to herself, but also in regard to her neighbor, at which she would be likely to take such serious offense that she would be apt to return it to Mr. Gibbs, if he were to be authorized to present it. Under these circumstances, there seems to be, at present, no just occasion for the intervention of this Government diplomatically, in any representation to the Government of Peru.

I am, sir, your obedient servant,

WM. M. EVARTS.

SECRETARY EVARTS TO MR. HELPER.

DEPARTMENT OF STATE,
WASHINGTON, *May* 25, 1878.

HINTON R. HELPER, *Esquire, Lima, Peru.*

SIR: I have received your letter of the 19th ultimo, with a protest of yours against the Government of Peru for neglecting to pay a draft upon it of the Government of Bolivia, issued in discharge of the debt of that Republic to Mr. Joseph H. Colton, of New York, which draft had been accepted by the Peruvian Government. You ask that Mr. Gibbs, the Minister of the United States at Lima, may be instructed to present your protest to that Government, and to insist on the payment of the draft In reply I have to express my regret, that, while I heartily sympathize with the inconvenience which Mr. Colton has experienced in obtaining the payment of his debt, I am not prepared to comply with your request. It is understood that Bolivia claims that there was a mistake made in stating the account against her. This led her to request Peru to decline payment ot the draft, which request has been complied with. It seems to me that, under these circumstances, there is, at present, no just occasion, for this Government to make any diplomatic representations to the Government of Peru, in the matter.

I am, sir, your obedient servant,
WM. M. EVARTS.

MR. HELPER TO THE SUPREME JUSTICES OF PERU.

HOTEL MAURY, LIMA, *June* 6, 1878.
To the Honorable the Members of
the Supreme Court of Peru.

LEARNED AND ILLUSTRIOUS GENTLEMEN: Coming before you as a citizen of the United States of America, a stranger in Peru, I beg the privilege of thus appealing to you for prompt deliverance in a very simple matter wherein I am now, and have been for the last three months and more, suffering here serious restraint, injustice and injury. In consequence of the default of the Peruvian Government, in dishonoring its accepted draft, for $19,609.40 in silver, due to my order on the first day of last March. I am, greatly to my disinclination and detriment, detained here on expenses, in suspense, losing valuable time, and prevented from the fulfillment of various important engagements; besides being subjected to the peculiarly painful circumstances of unexpected and indefinite separation from my family and friends far away. Some time after Peru's indefensible default in this affair, while considering the propriety of applying to the Supreme Court, which, however, was not then in session, for an order requiring the Government to honor its acceptance, in conformity with the laws of the Republic, a gentleman, himself one of the officials of Peru, remarked to me, that he regarded the case as being so very clear and binding against the Government, that he thought the Court would probably issue the order immediately, that is to say, on the same day of the submission of the question to the distinguished Justices of your High Tribunal. In any event he seemed to think that not more than ten days, at most, would be allowed to lapse before the desired order would be given.

It is now nearly four weeks since this case, plain and perspicuous as it is, was placed on the docket of the Supreme Court; but I am even yet, with much unavoidable impatience and anxiety, kept waiting for a decision. I had myself indulged the hope and expectation that only a few minutes would suffice for the determination of the question whether, under the obvious and explicit provisions of Peruvian law, and, in fact, of all laws defining the absolute and sacred obligations of acceptances, the Government should not be required to honor at once its regularly and unconditionally accepted draft. In order that my rights and interests may suffer no further damage nor delay in Peru, I now entreat your Honors to consider and act upon the facts here presented, and so, with your usual wisdom and equity, remove from me all the multiform burdens of subjection forced upon me by the Government's unwarrantable delinquency.

I have the honor to be, most respectfully,
Your Honor's obedient servant,
H. R. HELPER.

SECRETARY EVARTS TO MR. HELPER.

DEPARTMENT OF STATE,
WASHINGTON, *June* 17, 1878.

HINTON R. HELPER, *Esq., Lima, Peru.*

SIR: Your letter of the 20th ultimo has been received. It appears that a bond in the amount due, having been required of you by the Peruvian Government, in the suit against it in the case of the accepted draft of the Bolivian Government, the former Government will not accept you and Mr. Colton, your principal, as obligors in the bond. You consequently ask me to instruct Mr. Gibbs, the Minister of the United States at Lima, to give his official bond for you. If, however, I should not deem it expedient to instruct Mr. Gibbs to give his official bond for you, to receive the money there, you then ask that he may be instructed to give such bond and remit the money payable to my order. In reply I regret to state that I have no authority to give Mr. Gibbs the instructions you desire. However unsatisfactorily and embarrassing to your interests the action of the Peruvian Government in this matter may be, it is quite out of my power to relieve you from its inconvenience.

I am, sir, your obedient servant,
WM. M. EVARTS.

MR. HELPER TO JUSTICE OVIEDO.

Hotel Maury, Lima, *June* 21, 1878.
To His Honor, Judge Oviedo,
President of the Supreme Court of Peru.

Learned and Illustrious Sir: May it please your Honor to pardon any seeming impatience on my part. All the reasons and grievances which impelled me to address your Honor, about two weeks ago, touching Peru's unconditionally accepted draft, overdue to my order ever since the first day of last March, still exist, with increased magnitude. I beg therefore for the privilege to be understood as now reiterating those special reasons and grievances, and also the respectful petition founded upon them. My request is a very simple one; and it is quite as lawful and just as it is simple. I only ask that your equitable and honorable tribunal will issue an order, requiring the Government of Peru to honor its own unconditional acceptance; in other words, to maintain good faith with me; to keep its definite promise; to meet its positive engagement; to be true to its written obligation; to fulfil its solemn contract. Such action, and only such action, on the part of the Peruvian Government, will be in harmony with the categorical rules and laws of acceptances which obtain among all the highly enlightened and rightly progressing nations of the earth. Hoping and trusting that your Honor, acting in concert with your erudite and distinguished Associate Justices on the Supreme Bench of Peru, may soon be pleased to relieve me from the condition of aggravated suspense and injury which now oppresses me in Lima,

I have the honor to be, most respectfully,
Your Honors' obedient servant,
H. R. HELPER.

MR. HELPER TO MINISTER FLORES.

Hotel Maury, Lima, *July* 6, 1878.
To His Excellency the Hon. Zoilo Flores,
Envoy Extraordinary and Minister
    Plenipotentiary from Bolivia to Peru.

Sir: Sincerely regretting the existence of the wrongful and vexatious circumstances which impose on me the obligation of addressing your excellency on a subject in the least disagreeable to yourself, I yet have the honor to inclose herewith, for such attention, if any, as your Excellency may be pleased to bestow upon it, a copy of a somewhat lengthy communication which I addressed, yesterday afternoon, to the Hon. Manuel Antonio Barinaga, Secretary of the Peruvian Treasury, in relation to my demand for payment by the Government of Peru of its accepted draft, for $19,609.40 in silver, drawn on it by Bolivia on the 12th of October, 1876, unconditionally accepted at Lima on the 23d of the same month, and here dishonored and overdue to my order ever since the first day of last March.

I have the honor to be, very respectfully,
    Your Excellency's obedient servant,
        H. R. HELPER.

MR. HELPER TO EX-MINISTER BENAVENTE.

Lima, Peru, *July* 7, 1878.
Hon. Juan de la Cruz Benavente,
    Ex-Minister from Bolivia.

Dear Sir: In behalf of the whole sisterhood of American States; those of them especially which are most truly Republican in their forms and practices of government, and which are most enlightened and progressive in whatever contributes to the highest welfare of mankind; in behalf of the purest and broadest principles of truth and justice; and also in behalf of the frank and artless methods of modern diplomacy; I have the honor to protest to you, first, against Bolivia's long series of wrongful actions against my client, Mr. Joseph H. Colton, of New York, and myself, and next, against the discourteous and unministerial conduct, as I understand it, of his Excellency Senor Doctor Don Zoilo Flores, the Envoy Extraordinary and Minister Plenipotentiary from Bolivia to Peru, in refusing, as he has refused, to accept from my messenger the accompanying original letter, which, with the inclosure therein referred to, I addressed to him yesterday; the said inclosure being one which deals directly with the honor and interests of his Excellency's country. You will readily perceive, therefore, how any further communication from me to his Excellency has been made impossible.

Under really extraordinary provocations, I have just prepared, and am about to publish, a Memorial to the Congress of Peru on the subject of the Colton Map Claim against Bolivia; an eminently just, though inimically delayed and most expensive claim, of nearly twenty years' standing, and which, since 1858, has been a matter of very serious concern with several Congresses of Bolivia, one Congress of the United States of America, eight Presidents of Bolivia, seven Ministers of the United States, and numerous other functionaries and attorneys and agents of both countries. The publication in Peru of the simple facts in this case will, I firmly believe, be an irreparable injury to Bolivia. Why, then, should I, a stranger here, an American, by publishing those facts, cause injury to Bolivia? Because Bolivia arbitrarily and willfully and persistently, both at home and abroad, withholds justice from me; and, as a last and only resort this side of my own government, I must now seek my rights wherever and however they may be obtained; and, as it seems to me, my rights herein can henceforth be obtained only through a full and public explanation of all the antecedent proceedings in the case. While I would myself do no wrong, I am unwilling to submit patiently to wrongs perversely done by others. Toward all governments and peoples and individuals, I should, with fair treatment, much prefer to be on a friendly footing, rather than on terms antagonistic.

Is there no way, then, by which I may receive justice without having to adopt harsh, exasperative and disruptive measures? It is morally certain that such a way ought to be found among reasonable and upright men; and if you have any suggestion to make, with a view of avoiding the unseemly exhibition of Bolivia's twenty years' strange and indefensible delinquencies in this affair, it shall, if presented within the next two days, be considered in the very highest spirit of candor and amity and rectitude in which it may be offered. Saluting you as an able and distinguished gentleman, to myself unknown personally, but of whom,—and more particularly of your very estimable wife, Mrs. Benavente,—I have heard my own good wife, formerly Miss Maria Louisa Rodriguez, of Buenos Ayres, often speak in terms of the sincerest praise, she having known you both very well, many years ago, when you were the Envoy Extraordinary and Minister Plenipotentiary from Bolivia to the Argentine Republic,

I have the honor to be, most respectfully,
Your obedient servant,
H. R. HELPER.

MR. HELPER TO MINISTER PALACIOS.

Hotel Maury, Lima, *July* 8, 1878.
To His Excellency the Hon. Fernando Palacios,
Minister of Government for Peru.

Sir: Since you have ceased to be a mere Counsellor at Law, and have become a Councillor of State, leaving me and my suit, against the Government of Peru, in worthy but less able hands, I feel very perceptibly that, in this respect, the Republic's gain is my loss. Nevertheless, although I may no longer consult your Excellency as my Legal Adviser, yet I beg the privilege of appealing to you, and I now appeal to you accordingly, as a Minister of Justice. Your Excellency is already familiar with the facts, the law, and the equity of my demand. The case is very plain and very simple; as much so, indeed, as daylight is distinguishable from darkness. I hold Peru's unconditionally accepted draft, due and overdue to my order ever since the first day of last March, for $19,609.40 in silver, in a matter wherein the whole amount due in exact justice, by Bolivia, the drawer of the draft, on an always recognized but never paid claim, of nearly twenty years' standing, should have been, instead of only $19,609.40 in silver, $78,903.18 in gold.

Most respectfully and earnestly do I request that Peru will now honorably discharge her obligation to me, and no longer countenance Bolivia in the gross and unfeeling wrongs which the Government of that country has herein so long and so repeatedly and so atrociously committed. In connection with this request I have the honor to solicit your careful perusal of the inclosed copy of a communication which I addressed, on the 5th instant, to the Hon. Manuel Antonio Barinaga, Secretary of the Peruvian Treasury. I trust that an official translation of the original of that communication has been made, and that it may very soon be the subject of á right decision in Cabinet Council. Pray, sir, be kind enough to discuss this matter frankly with His Supreme Excellency President Prado and other high officers of State, and let me be informed, at the earliest convenient opportunity, of the result of the joint deliberations of your several Excellencies thereon.

I have the honor to be, very faithfully,
Your Excellency's obedient servant,
H. R. HELPER.

MR. HELPER'S PROPOSED MEMORIAL TO THE CONGRESS OF PERU.

BOLIVIA'S NATIONAL MAPS,

Twenty years (lacking less than one month,) after the date of publication, still awaiting payment;

And

PERU'S UNCONDITIONALLY ACCEPTED DRAFT,

Six months overdue, in this connection, and yet unpaid.

A

MEMORIAL FROM HINTON ROWAN HELPER,

Attorney for Joseph H. Colton, of New York, (who ever since September 21, 1858, has been an extraordinarily harassed and maltreated creditor of Bolivia,) TO THE HONORABLE AND ILLUSTRIOUS CONGRESS OF PERU.

LIMA, PERU, *September 2, 1878.*
To the Honorable the Senators and Representatives
of the Republic of Peru.

GENTLEMEN: Without having the honor of being personally acquainted with a single member of the Honorable and Illustrious Congress of Peru, whether in the Upper or Lower House, I nevertheless come before you, in behalf of my client, Mr. Joseph H. Colton, of New York, and myself, as an humble petitioner for the redress of a special grievance, which now afflicts me in Lima, as the result of a strange lack of good faith due to one of the Peruvian Government's most solemn and sacred written contracts,—an unconditionally accepted draft, for $19,609.40 in silver, drawn by the Government of Bolivia on the 12th of October, 1876, regularly accepted by the Government of Peru on the 23d of the same month, and here overdue to my order ever since the first day of March of the present year.

Although I am a citizen of the United States of America, and am not so fortunate as to be in the least known among you, yet I am quite willing to trust myself and my cause entirely in your hands, believing that, as wise and upright statesmen, uninfluenced by mere personal considerations, you will readily recognize the obvious merits of my prayer, and promptly grant me the simple measure of justice which I now solicit. The face of the draft itself, including the acceptance, (the back of the document showing proper indorsement to my order,) is in these very words, being here freely and fairly translated into English

(Copy.—Translation.)

For $19,609.40
Department of State.
[SEAL.]
LA PAZ, BOLIVIA, *October*, 12, 1876.

On the first day of March, 1878, you will please pay, at sight of this original First of Exchange, to the order of Mr.

R. M. Reynolds, the sum of nineteen thousand six hundred and nine dollars and forty cents, in current money of gold or silver, which, as a last payment, is debited to Mr. J. H. Colton, in settlement of his account against this Government for the Maps of Bolivia. This said sum I have credited in the current account of our subvention with you in regard to your Custom House at Arica, and have so informed you by letter.

J. OBLITAS,
Secretary of State.

MANUEL PENAFIL,
Chief Clerk of the State Department.

To His Excellency the Peruvian Minister of Finance and Commerce, Lima, Peru.

Treasury Department,

[SEAL.]   LIMA, PERU, *October* 23, 1876.

ACCEPTED,
JOSE QUINONES.

NEW YORK, *November* 27, 1876: Pay to the order of Hinton R. Helper.

R. M. REYNOLDS.

NEW YORK, *Mach* 21, 1877: Pay to the order of Messrs. Prevost & Co., of Lima, Peru.

HINTON R. HELPER.

LIMA, PERU, *April* 26, 1878: Pay to the order of Mr. Hinton R. Helper, from whom we received this document for collection on his account, which we have been unable to effect.

PREVOST & CO.

A complete narration of all the antecedent transactions and facts and circumstances which led to the issuance of the foregoing draft by Bolivia, would cover a period of but little less than a score of years, during which time the very ordinary matter of business involved has occupied the attention of eight Presidents of Bolivia, seven Ministers of the United States, several Congresses of Bolivia, one Congress of the United States of America, numerous Secretaries of State and other high officials of each country, and various attorneys, agents and friends, both at home and abroad; and has meanwhile cost the peculiarly injured and unfortunate claimant and his partners and coadjutors, in addition to the immense labor and loss of time, and the serious wear and tear of mind arising from so many unconscionable hindrances and delays, more than twice the amount of money which was originally due. If all the documents and other papers which have passed in the premises, should be published in book form, they would, I feel confident, fill at least four volumes as large, each, as the quarto edition of the Spanish Academy's Vocabulary of the Castilian Tongue, or Webster's Unabridged Dictionary of the English Language. In a word, the case is one which, well considered in all its phases and bearings, should justly excite against Bolivia the profoundest indignation and loathing of all fair-minded men. A scanty but insufficient summary of Bolivia's reckless and reprehensible career in this affair may be given thus:

1. On the 8th of March, 1858, a Cabinet Council of the Republic of Bolivia passed a Supreme Resolution authorizing the publication of the National Map of Bolivia, which was then only in manuscript.

2. On the 21st of September, 1858, Colonel Juan Ondarza and Commandant Juan Mariano Mujia, two distinguished military and topographical engineers of Bolivia, who were the authors of the map in manuscript, duly commissioned by the Government of Bolivia to procure the engraving and publishing of the same, having gone to New York for that particular purpose, there entered into a written agreement with Mr. Joseph H. Colton, by which he was to furnish them ten thousand copies of the map, as per dimensions and materials specified, and to be finished in superior style. With his own part of the said agreement, Mr. Colton scrupulously complied, receiving the fullest expressions of perfect satisfaction from both of the Bolivian Commissioners in New York, and also, afterward, from the Government of Bolivia itself.

3. On the 7th of May, 1860, the money due on the maps not having been paid in conformity with the terms of the agreement, the Bolivian Cabinet ordered full payment to be made,—but paid not one cent.

4. On the 12th of August, 1861, the Congress of Bolivia, by a special Resolution, authorized payment of the amount due,—but paid nothing at all.

5. On the 22d of July, 1863, the Bolivian Congress again ordered payment to be made,—but paid nothing whatever.

6. On the 27th of October, 1864, the Congress of Bolivia once more, by formal and solemn Act, directed payment to be made,—but paid not. so much as the tenth part of a stiver.

7. On the 1st of February, 1872, the Bolivian Cabinet, like the Bolivian Congresses and other Bolivian tribunals, always fruitful of fair promises, but never once proving true to any engagement of honor or veracity in the claimant's behalf, again, upon the "religious" fidelity and character of the nation, ordered, but ordered in vain, payment of the amount due. So much pelf as would purchase the pearly and pigmy pith of one petty pea was not paid.

8. On the 3d of March, 1875, the Congress of the United States of America, to which Mr. Colton, almost in despair, had earnestly appealed for redress, passed an Act calling on the Government of Bolivia to pay the money.

9. On the 10th of May, 1875, less than three months after the passage of the significant Act of the American Congress at Washington, President Frias, of Bolivia, and the Hon. Robert M. Reynolds, the Minister of the United States, at La Paz, agreed upon terms of final settlement. Under the conditions of this agreement, formally executed in duplicate, the debt was to be liquidated in installments. Yet not one of the installments so agreed upon was ever paid in the full amount due, nor at the time due; and, besides, previous to the maturity of the last obligation, a new revolution and a new President in Bolivia threw everything into confusion in that country, as, from the same or similar causes, things there had so often been thrown before.

10. On the 12th of October, 1876. after correspondence and conference with President Daza, and patient and thorough review with the department officials at La Paz, of all the preceding transactions in the matter, a draft on the Government of Peru, for the sum of the several admitted

balances then due, was issued to Minister Reynolds, acting for Mr. Colton, as the draft itself expressly states; and that draft, duly accepted by Peru, on the 23d of the same month, to be paid on the first day of March, 1878, is the identical document which forms the subject of this Memorial.

The following extracts from a printed Memorial addressed by Mr. Colton himself to the Congress of his own country, about four years ago,—and which said Congress gave him a bill against the delinquent, as stated above, requiring payment of the debt,—will further, though imperfectly, expose the shameful position of Bolivia as the author of all these strategical, time-killing, labor-imposing, expense-involving, ruinous and disreputable proceedings:

" President Acha, in the course of a special Message which he sent to the Congress of Bolivia, on the 20th of September, 1864, said:—' The history of this business, the engraving and publishing of the valuable map of Bolivia, by Mr. J. H. Colton, a citizen of the United States, most clearly shows how just the claim is, and how loudly the dignity of the nation calls for its payment. I reiterate my preceding recommendation, and trust that the subject will receive the serious attention of Congress; since, although the Minister of the United States has not given an official character to his request for the satisfaction of this claim, it is none the less the duty of the Republic to preserve its honor, which is now so deeply committed for its payment.'

" President Frias, writing directly to the claimant's attorney, under date of April 17, 1873, said, but said in vain: ' In reply to your letter of the 15th of February, I have the honor to assure you of the earnest desire of the Bolivian Government to satisfy the recognized debt in favor of Mr. Colton; in virtue of which, I dare announce to you that payment will certainly commence to be made during the present year. In case there should not be at La Paz any direct representative of the creditor,·the matter might be placed in the hands of the Minister of the United States.'

" Again, President Frias, addressing the Bolivian Congress under date of the 28th of April, 1873, said, but said with as little effect as if he had been addressing the snow-capped peaks of the higher Andes: — 'Having already spoken of national obligations, I must not omit to speak also of the absolute preference given to Mr. Colton's claim, which comes of compromises strictly national, in virtue of which I have not hesitated to assure him and his attorney, that satisfaction of the debt shall be commenced during the present year; considering this as one of our first duties toward the liquidation of our national obligations.'

" Sorely chafed under the constantly increasing burden of these and countless other hollow and heartless assurances, received year after year, and at all times and seasons, until there was no reasonable prospect that the end of such folly and fraud would ever come, I felt, and still feel, the conviction that patience and forbearance on my part had ceased to be virtues. It was with these feelings, still justly inflamed with the purpose expressed, — and now rather expanded and aggravated than otherwise,—that I was at last moved to write as follows to the American Minister at La Paz:—' In the event that, in a last effort to obtain my rights in this case, it shall become necessary for me to pursue the course upon which I have now determined, I shall take occasion to urge upon the Government of my own country the very serious consideration of the question, whether a nationality that is either too dishonest or too poor to pay for its maps, is, in any respect, worthy of a place among the family of nations? Taking the negative of this question, I shall, with such humble ability as I possess, endeavor to prove that Bolivia, having, for a period of so many years, been either too dishonest or too poor to pay for her maps, is no longer worthy of recognition as a distinct nationality. Well justified and strongly fortified as I feel I shall be in the position thus assumed, I shall argue further that it is derogatory to the dignity of the United States to maintain a Minister, or even a Consul, within the limits of such a self-exhausted and characterless community as Bolivia; and will further give it as my opinion, with reasons in detail, that all honorable nationalities should at once withdraw from that unworthy country every system and grade of international intercourse, and not only permit, but effectually encourage, the speedy and complete absorption of Bolivia by one or more of the contiguous Commonwealths; in other words, that Bolivia must immediately conform her conduct to a higher standard of honesty and truth and dignity, or be forever ignored and blotted out from the family of nations, and her territory and obligations allowed to lapse to one or more of the abler and better conterminous States; to Peru, to Chili, or to the Argentine Republic; or to any two, or to all, of those neighboring nationalities.' * * * 'Lord Clarendon, for reasons more than sufficient, bluntly blotted Bolivia from the diplomatic map of Great Britain in 1853. France, Germany, Russia, and all the other great governing powers of Europe, have likewise long since ceased to regard Bolivia as worthy of notice as a nation.'

"Repeatedly and profoundly provoked to speak the truth against Bolivia, and believing that it would now be only a vice to shield her further from the odium of the accumulated wrongs which she has so long and so perfidiously inflicted on me, I claim to be fully warranted in here solemnly and formally protesting that she does not seem to be affected or influenced by any impulse of honor, incitation to duty, or sense of shame. Congressional acts, legislative orders, governmental decrees, presidential promises, ministerial pledges, diplomatic guarantees, and consular assurances, have again and again been given by her, with a readiness and redundance that might have been honorable, but for their uniform disingenuity and non-fulfilment. Not merely has Bolivia, by profuse and ordinary promises, written and verbal, misled me and all my special attorneys and agents, and hoodwinked every Minister whom the Government of the United States has sent to her since the year 1858, but she has also, during the same time, by numerous public and official declarations, and extraordinary messages, issued under the signatures and seals of her nationality, audaciously trifled with all our illustrious Secretaries of State, from the days of the Hon. Lewis Cass to the Hon. Hamilton Fish, inclusive. * * * I have some little knowledge of the language in which I am writing this Memorial; and it may be that, if put to the test, I might succeed in applying a few appropriate terms to a so-called gentleman who would seek to evade his just obligations to a washerwoman; but never yet have I seen or heard any words of ordinary usage at all adequate to the description of such varied and unending acts of ineffable meanness as Bolivia is guilty of in this map matter."

Here bidding a somewhat formal adieu to Bolivia, and leaving her the heritage of such consolations as she may be able to find in the foregoing and following evidences of her unprecedented tergiversations and circumventions, permit me now, Honorable and Illustrious Senators and Representatives of Peru, permit me to explain to you, more minutely than I have yet had occasion to do, the exact circumstances of Peru's connection with this case, and her present position in it. This task is at once easily and amply performed by submitting to you the following copies of two communications which I have very recently (on the dates given respectively at the beginning of the communications themselves,) had the honor of addressing to his Excellency

Senor Dr. Don Manuel Antonio Barinaga, Secretary of the Peruvian Treasury; and to both of which I here respectfully and earnestly solicit your special attention:

[COPY.]

HOTEL MAURY, LIMA, PERU, *July* 5, 1878.
TO HIS EXCELLENCY,
SEÑOR DR. DON MANUEL ANTONIO BARINAGA,
  Secretary of the Treasury.

SIR: The Archives of the Department of Government over which your Excellency is now presiding will show that, on the first day of last March, I presented to your Excellency's immediate predecessor, the Hon. Jose Felix Garcia, a regularly and legally accepted draft on the Government of Peru, for $19,609.40 in silver, due to my order on that date; the said draft having been drawn on Peru by the Government of Bolivia on the 12th of October, 1876, and unconditionally accepted by Peru on the 23d of the same month of the same year.

The claim for which the amount of this draft was to have been considered a final settement, has been pending ever since the 21st of September, 1858! and in the way of ordinary and extraordinary expenses, through constantly recuring duplicities and subterfuges and stratagems on the part of Bolivia, it has already cost the claimant, and his several attorneys and agents, more than twice the sum of the original indebtedness. It is no exaggeration to say that the civilized world can hard'y furnish another instance of such flagrant injustice and injury and outrage as Bolivia has been, and is yet, guilty, of toward her unfortunate creditor in this case. The amount herein due in equity by Bolivia, on the first day of last March, so far from being only $19,609.40 in silver, was $78,903.18 in gold; yet after she had issued the draft, and long after its acceptance, but many months before it became due, she requested Peru not to pay it; most cunningly and perfidiously alleging that a mistake had been made in the final adjustment.

To this wrong and unlawful request, Peru listened, and is still listening. Meanwhile the question was referred to the Attorney-General of Peru, the Hon. Mr. LaRosa, who gave a very learned and able opinion upon it, stating, in effect, that my demand for payment of the draft was perfectly just, and also in strict accordance with the laws of Peru and all other laws of whatever country, which have ever yet been framed and promulgated on the general subject of acceptances. When my friend, Mr. Henry T. Prevost, and myself called on the Hon. Secretary of the Treasury, Mr. Garcia, a day or two after the opinion of the Law Officer of the Government had been given, he smilingly remarked to us, immediately after our entrance and salutation, "I have good news for you this afternoon; the Attorney-General has reported in your favor, and we have already notified the Bolivian Government that we will pay you the money."

Notwithstanding the admirable clearness and soundness of the Attorney-General's judgment; notwithstanding the fact that Secretary Garcia himself assured us that his private opinion had warmly sustained us, and that he, as an individual, had always entertained the fullest conviction that it was the duty of the Government to pay the draft; and, besides, notwithstanding the prompt and emphatic verdict in my favor of every clearheaded merchant and banker, and of every first-class lawyer, whose views were elicited in this regard; yet, in the face of all these important facts, it was the pleasure of His Supreme Excellency President Prado to issue a decree which prevented me, and still prevents me, from receiving the money.

Thereupon I made application to the Supreme Court of

Peru, for an order which would constrain the Government to observe toward me the unmistakable behests of law and justice. Because of the plainness and simplicity of the question involved, it was believed (by the Hon. Francisco Garcia Calderon, speaking to Mr. Pedro Telmo Larranaga, and also by Mr. Simon Camacho, speaking to me,) that the said Court would probably grant an order for the payment of the draft in from one to ten days. Greatly to my regret, however, although many weeks have elapsed since my suit was placed on the docket of that high tribunal, no action has yet been taken in my behalf. On the contrary, and immeasurably to my surprise, the said tribunal has publicly declared and published, that it has no jurisdiction in this affair.

Under these circumstances, seeing no prospect of obtaining justice from any regularly organized Court in Peru, within a reasonable time, if at all, I now have the honor to inform your Excellency that, in the event of continued delinquency up to the twentieth instant, it is my intention, immediately thereafter, to carry the case, in the form of an explanatory and historical memorial, before the very highest constitutional power in the Republic—the Honorable and Illustrious Congress of Peru.

I am aware that the Peruvian Congress, as a whole, will not assemble in Lima until the 28th instant, but I am not disposed to wait quite so long; having already waited here more than four months. The plan which I have chosen is to print and publish, in Spanish, several hundred copies of my memorial, and to address it to every Senator and Representative respectively, and also to many other distinguished and influential members of the Government, at least one week prior to the time of the general meeting; so that the minds of all of them may be so well imbued with the facts and merits of the case as to be prepared to act upon it at once, in conformity with the plainest principles of law and equity.

Besides, this is a matter which seems to have a special affinity for Congresses: it having, during the last twenty years, been several times in the Congress of Bolivia, and once in the Congress of the United States of America; always too, successfully for the claimant, except only through the utter and unparalleled faithlessness of Bolivia, which has never yet proved true to any of her almost numberless govermental and ministerial and diplomatic and consular engagements concerning it.

It is proper, hovever, that I should frankly inform your Excellency that I have not arrived at this determination without carefully considering both the probable and the possible consequences which may result from such an unusual and independent method of procedure. As a citizen of the United States of America, I understand perfectly well that I owe to the Republic of Peru, as to all other Republics and nationalities, good thoughts, good purposes, and good behavior. These obligations, however, are, or at least ought to be, reciprocal. The Republic can find no justification whatever for withholding from me my rightful dues; in subjecting me to additional burdens and hardships; nor in restraining me, as an unrelieved sufferer from its own shortcomings and defaults, within its territorial limits.

As a plain man, encompassed with the ordinary relations and responsibilities incident to human nature, it is both right and necessary for me to insist on fair-dealing toward myself and others intimately associated with me; and especially so toward a very aged and long-and-much-injured client, Mr. Joseph H. Colton, of New York, whom I here represent. I owe respect and duty to Peru, and Peru owes me money and time and other valuable considerations, which she is now persistently consuming at my expense, and very greatly to my discomfiture and disadvantage. From this unlawful detriment and injury, I am now firmly resolved, in a certain

contingency, as aforementioned, to seek redress from the
Peruvian Congress; believing that therein I shall be so justly
fortunate as to find an exalted and potent tribunal that will
exercise the highest possible jurisdiction in the premises, and,
for its own honor and the honor of the Republic, order
immediate payment of the said accepted and overdue draft.

On one hand, however, it has been intimated to me that,
because of one particular feature of my memorial, as I propose to present it, such action on my part might lead to
serious, if not sanguinary trouble between Peru and Bolivia;
and on the other hand, the opinion has been very clearly
expressed that certain political and Congressional adversaries of His Supreme Excellency President Prado, will
make use of the circumstance to condemn and denounce
his action in the premises, as an undisguised violation of
Peruvian law and of all other laws of a like kind; and that
thereby, in connection with other similar charges, those adversaries will render His Supreme Excellency less easy and
less secure in his superlative office.

It is believed, moreover, that the peculiar and conspicuous publicity of the facts complained of in the memorial, if
properly prepared and presented to Congress, will have an
irresistible tendency to further weaken and destroy all confidence in Peru's most formal and solemn contracts and obligations; for, whether with Governments or with individuals, no contract, no obligation, in the way of business, can
ever be more binding or more sacred than an unconditionally
accepted draft. Exposed to the penalties of national discredit, dishonor and disgrace thus imminent, Peru, through
her own fault, in culpably refusing to avert the yet-surmountable evil, may have to submit to the loss, directly or
indirectly, of scores and even hundreds of times the amount
of the said acceptance. Whether all or any of these opinions
are well founded, your Excellency's superior judgment will

readily determine. Yet, as for myself, I must candidly confess that the several views and apprehensions thus advanced have thrown me into a sort of pause and quandary.

I beg therefore to be especially advised by your Excellency as to any other course, any wiser or better way, which, as a respectful and well-meaning stranger in Peru,—yet, at the same time, as one who feels that he is suffering a grievous and prolonged injustice at the hands of the Peruvian Government itself,—I ought to pursue in this dilemma. Shall I and other innocent and injured persons be required to submit quietly to the spoliation of our rights and interests, our time and labor and money, in order that Peru on the one hand, or Bolivia on the other, or any high functionary in Peru or Bolivia, may enjoy immunity from official assumption and wrong doing? Never can I willingly yield assent to any proposition of this sort; it being incompatible with rational conduct and good morals as affecting my personal manhood; nor will I ever, of my own accord, be held responsible for any international or other difficulties which may ensue as a sequence of my earnest and straightforward endeavors to obtain justice openly denied or withheld. Of all possible responsibilities of that kind, in this particular case, I hereby wash my hands quite clean, and will so keep them.

If I shall be forced to the necessity of appealing to the Peruvian Congress, in the manner herein apprehended, this communication itself will be printed as a part of my memorial. Will it not, beyond all doubt, be much better for the Peruvian Government to perform at once the simple act of good faith and probity to which it is, under written contract, engaged to me, and for which, on expenses, in suspense, and losing time, I have here been waiting in vain for the last four months,—and by so doing, wholly avoid, for itself, for Bolivia, and for me, all the unknown and unwelcome issues thus foreshadowed? I only ask that, by or before the twentieth instant, Peru will, without any anomalous or entangling requirement, in the way of a bond or otherwise, fully and finally honor her acceptance to my order, due and overdue ever since the first day of March. Can unreserved and reliable assurance be given that Peru will comply with this very just and very reasonable request? An affirmative answer to this question from his Supreme Excellency President Prado, or from yourself, would be very gratifying to me.

Entertaining, from general report, the very highest confidence in your Excellency's statesmanlike wisdom and integrity, I shall await, with deep concern, your reply to this communication; a copy of which will be transmitted to his Excellency, the Hon. Zoilo Flores, the Bolivian Minister, to-morrow morning; when also, another copy of the same will be dispatched to the Hon. Richard Gibbs, the American Minister.

I have the honor to be, most respectfully,
Your Excellency's obedient servant,
H. R. HELPER.

[COPY.]

HOTEL MAURY, LIMA, PERU, *July* 10, 1878.
TO HIS EXCELLENCY,
THE HON. MANUEL ANTONIO BARINAGA,
Secretary of the Treasury.

SIR: Influenced by the suggestion of one of my countrymen, I have the honor to assure your Excellency that the gentlemen who spoke to me in terms of disapprobation of the action of his Supreme Excellency President Prado, in the matter of my Bolivia-Peru accepted and overdue draft, were themselves good friends of his Supreme Excellency, and that they gave feeling expression to their regret at what they could but regard as a downright violation of an important part of the Peruvian Code and of the Code of Nations. Those gentlemen plainly expressed to me their apprehension that such arbitrary administration of the laws of the Republic by his Supreme Excellency, would render it all the more difficult for them to defend him, and would only afford his adversaries an additional opportunity to assail him. What was said should, therefore, in fact, be received, not at all as an ill-humored threat, but only as a friendly suggestion or admonition. After four long months of most wearisome delay, I trust that the Peruvian Government will now fairly honor its acceptance, and so end at once all the future troubles apprehended in this connection.

I have the honor to be, most respectfully,
Your Excellency's obedient servant,
H. R. HELPER.

Thus briefly, Illustrious Senators and Representatives of the Peruvian Congress, thus briefly,—in comparison with the reams upon reams of paper which, from first to last, have been consumed in writs of various kinds in this case, —have I the honor to explain to you how it is that Peru herself, through the wiles of the wrongdoer, has had the misfortune to be brought into very positive and indisseverable connection with a most despicable and disgraceful delinquency on the part of Bolivia; a delinquency musty with time, rank with chicanery, and repulsive with turpitude. As yet, it is not accurately known to what extent the political and financial character of Peru may be demoralized by this association with Bolivia; but it is incontrovertible that deep-rooted contamination and lasting corruption, will inevitably follow any sort of alliance or co-partnership or business with that most faithless and disorderly country. Doubtless, therefore, it is now for the honor and interest of Peru to disconnect herself, as completely as possible, from her notorious neighbor, and remain quite separate and unfamiliar so long as that naughty neighbor continues, as at present, in an independent position of proneness and predilection for evil.

The laws of Peru, as of all other enlightened and honorable nationalities, are very explicit in requiring that every unconditionally accepted draft, when due, shall be paid on presentation, save only in cases of false signature. It is perfectly well known and unanimously admitted that, in this case, the signatures are all genuine. Why, then, does Peru detain me in Lima so many months, away from my family and friends, on expenses, in suspense, losing time, and under subjection to other serious disadvantages? Whatever Peru's real sentiment or purpose may be, the effect of her procedure is to aid and abet Bolivia in the nefarious design of cheating my client out of the sum of $19,609.40 in silver, which is itself, however, only a fractional part of the $78,903.18 in gold, which, in equity, has been overdue ever since the first day of last March. Although the rights of my client, in the matter of the accepted draft, are not openly denied, yet they are covertly withheld; and both to him and to me the wrong is quite as indefensible and oppressive in the one case as it would be in the other.

Only the merest shadow of an excuse could be found for Peru, even if, at any time during the seventeen months which elapsed between the acceptance and maturity of the draft, she had given any intimation whatever of her intention, for any reason at all, not to pay it. It is true that she could not justly nor lawfully repudiate such a sacred and unavoidable obligation; but the manifestation on her part of any disposition not to comply with her written agreement, might at least have afforded my client and myself a basis for new proceedings and better easement against Bolivia; and more especially so if the supposed manifestation of noncompliance had been made very soon after the acceptance. But no such action having ever been taken by Peru, (invalid and vain as such action would have been in any event,) no sign of exoneration, nor even color of exculpation, can now be reasonably offered in her behalf. Under an Act of the Congress of the United States of America, the Hon. Robert M. Reynolds, a Minister of the United States, finally closed the account with Bolivia, in 1876; and our diplomatic relations with that shabby and shameless " Republic " were then very properly abolished.

From September 21, 1858, down to the present date, covering a period of twenty years, lacking less than one month, dozens, scores and hundreds, if not thousands, of memorandums, propositions, agreements, accounts, compromises, notes, letters, dispatches, enactments, protests, orders, decrees, and other writngs, of the most diversified nomenclature; epistolary and documentary, official and unofficial; on the one hand respectful, polite and courteous, and on the other solemn, severe and sarcastic; have been called into requisition in this affair; and yet, through the incorrigible depravity of Bolivia, the claim is still unsettled; the obligation exists unadjusted; the debt remains uncancelled. The whole amount of money equitably due on the first day of last March, $78,903.18 in gold, together with expenses and fees for time and services since addable, remains unpaid; and Peru's unconditionally accepted draft, for $19,609.40 in silver, now full six months overdue, is even yet tarnished with the stains of national dishonor.

So far at least as Bolivia is concerned, the magnitude of

the load of dissimulation and shame here accumulated is enough, is far more than enough, to make all the better elements of the nation bow their heads and hide their faces in profound humiliation. The guilt is overwhelming; the ignominy is fixed; the opprobrium is indelible. Prompt payment of Peru's unconditionally accepted draft is required by every principle and rule of equity; it is required alike by the inviolable essence of individual rights and by the ennobling urgings of international and universal rectitude; and it is more specifically required by the laws of Peru herself, and by the statutes of every other civilized and progressive nation. For these and other weighty reasons already presented, I thus again most respectfully and earnestly request an order or resolution for payment accordingly; that is to say, for payment in fact within a stated number of days, not exceeding thirty. Deeming it unnecessary, for the present at least, to further elaborate or amplify arguments in this really very lucid affair, and hereby terminating my humble and justice-soliciting petition to the Honorable and Illustrious Senators and Representatives of the Peruvian Congress,

I am, worthy and distinguished gentlemen,

Your most obedient servant,

HINTON R. HELPER.

MR. HELPER TO MINISTER GIBBS.

HOTEL MAURY, LIMA, PERU, *September* 9, 1878.
HON. RICHARD GIBBS, *United States Minister.*

SIR: After subjecting me to more than six months' unjustifiable delay, great expense and conscienceless incertitude and perplexity, the Peruvian Government has only to-day paid to me its unconditionally accepted draft to my order, for $19,609.40 in silver, drawn on it by Bolivia in October, 1876, and here overdue ever since the first day of last March. Payment has been made, as usual, in badly depreciated bank bills, at a rate apparently equivalent to silver. If the draft had been promptly honored when it became due, as it should have been, on the first day of last March, I would then have received, in paper, $34,512.54; and if to this sum, as principal, interest be added at the regular commercial rate in Peru, twelve per cent. per annum, the rate which I myself have had to pay for a considerable part of my expenses in Lima, it would swell the amount, up to the present date, to $36,675.29.

The amount which I have received to-day, in consequence of adverse fluctuations in the currency, and without interest, is only $29,903.73; from which, not charging anything whatever for my own time or labor, must be deducted my actual expenses for necessary voyages, lawyer's fees, hotel bills, etc., etc., aggregating a sum total, in paper, of $5,214.27; which, subtracted from the amount paid, $29,903.73, leaves only $24,689.46. Strong as is my provocation to indulge in certain comments on these significant figures, dates and data, I will yet forbear; preferring, for the present at least, to let the simple foregoing facts speak for themselves. It is my purpose, however, as the attorney for Mr. Colton, after further consultation with him, to proceed against Bolivia at a convenient time in the future, for reimbursement of the expenses, and indemnification for the losses here and elsewhere so culpably occasioned by her, in this affair, during the last twenty years—lacking now only twelve days!

I have the honor to be, very respectfully,
      Your obedient servant,
         H. R. HELPER.

MR. HELPER TO SECRETARY EVARTS.

NEW YORK, *October* 31, 1878.

HON. WILLIAM M. EVARTS, *Secretary of State, Washington.*

SIR: Long ill-used by the climates and the governments of both Bolivia and Peru, I am now sick in bed, undergoing a regular course of medical treatment, in the hope of a reasonably early restoration to good health. The annexed papers, consisting of a copy of my proposed Memorial to the Congress of Peru, under date of the 2d ultimo, and a copy of a communication which I addressed to the Hon. Richard Gibbs, the American Minister at Lima, on the 9th ultimo, will, for the present at least, sufficiently explain the peculiar points and circumstances under which the Peruvian Government, influenced solely by my own independent and positive proceedings in the premises, has been at last constrained to perform the greater part of a certain national duty, which, eight months ago, it should have been honest enough to perform cheerfully and fully and promptly without constraint. To the two papers thus alluded to and hereto annexed, I have the honor to solicit from you such attention as may be fitly bestowed upon them by the Hon. Secretary of State of the United States.

So soon as my health and time will permit, I shall take occasion to draw up a true account of the balance, or sum total of balances, still due from Bolivia to my much-injured and aged client Mr. Colton, and will thereupon again seek, through the Department of State at Washington, or through the Congress of the United States, a yet nearer approximation to justice in this affair; an old affair, now of more than twenty years' standing, wherein, from first to last, the action of Bolivia has been most shamelessly and perfidiously unfair and dishonorable,

I am, sir, most respectfully, your obedient servant,
HINTON R. HELPER.

Approved: JOSEPH H. COLTON.

SECRETARY EVARTS TO MR. HELPER.

DEPARTM
WASHINGTON, *November* 6, 1878.
HINTON ROWAN HELPER, *Esq., New York.*

SIR: Your letter of the 31st ultimo, relative to the claim of Joseph H. Colton against the government of Bolivia, has been received. It is gratifying to learn from it that the government of Peru has ultimately paid the draft upon it by the government of Bolivia, which it had accepted, but dishonored at its maturity.

I am, sir, your obedient servant,

WM. M. EVARTS.

EX-MINISTER REYNOLDS TO MR. HELPER.

WASHINGTON, D. C., *October* 23, 1878.
H. R. HELPER, *Esq., New York.*

DEAR SIR: You may rest assured that I was more than glad to receive your last letter, and to learn from it that the chief officials of the Peruvian Government, after having been driven to the wall by your proposed Memorial to the Peruvian Congress, at last concluded to honor their acceptance of the Bolivia-Colton draft to your order, and paid it accordingly. What a pity they did not pay it six or seven months earlier, and so save their credit! On your final triumph in this hard-fought contest, where, during most of the time, the odds were so overwhelmingly against you, I sincerely congratulate both you and Mr. Colton. I had begun to entertain very serious doubts as to whether they would not utterly refuse to pay you, and thereby subject you and your client to still another grievance of great burden. What rendered you strong and invulnerable in your position was that you were entirely in the right. I feel doubly indignant that the Bolivian functionaries at La Paz should have voluntarily imposed upon themselves the vile task of accusing me of having deceived and misled them in the account I presented to them of the amount due to Mr. Colton; and I shall, hereafter as heretofore, take pleasure in aiding you, at any time, in your efforts to recover any balance that may be rightfully claimed.

Truly yours,
R. M. REYNOLDS.

MR. COLTON TO MR. HELPER.

NEW YORK, *November* 23, 1878.

HINTON R. HELPER, *Esq.* .

DEAR SIR: In reply to your inquiries of the 16th instant, I have to inform you that it is quite usual for well-meaning and fair-dealing debtors, throughout the State of New York, who find themselves unable to pay off their accumulated obligations at the end of the year, to renew their notes, on the first day of the succeeding January, with interest added to the principal, as principal; so that, by this system of yearly renewal of running obligations, certain careless and slow-paying people pay interest on both principal and interest annually, as is just and proper. Bankers and other financiers almost invariably practice the same or a similar system four times per annum; that is to say, they require a renewal of all obligations into one common sum at the end of every term of three months; and on the common sum so found, as principal, interest is always charged until the expiration of another period of three months, when a new renewal is made; and so on until a final extinction of the debt shall have been effected.

Not, however, on this bankers' basis of quarterly reckonings, a basis of prompt adjustments and new contracts and obligations, but only on the general business basis of yearly accountings, the true balance due to me by the Government of Bolivia, on the first day of last March, as you yourself have shown, would be upward of NINETY THOUSAND DOLLARS; and I see no reason why, in law and equity, Bolivia should not be held to responsibility for the entire sum so stated by you. Yet as I am not disposed to require payment of the largest amount which might rightfully be demanded in this case (a disposition on my part which, even in Peru, you seem to have understood very intelligently and correctly,) I approve, in preference, the smaller account which you have presented on the basis of calculations of principal and interest up to and from such times only as Bolivia herself, during a period of nearly twenty years, publicly and repeatedly acknowledged her indebtedness to me; that is to say, the detailed account wherein you demonstrate that the balance due to me, on the first day of last March, was seventy-eight thousand nine hundred and three dollars and eighteen cents; and for the recovery of this balance, as then due, deducting therefrom the net amount since received, you will, at your convenience, please institute new proceedings against Bolivia, continuing the suit against her until she pays the whole amount, or such part thereof as you may, at your own discretion, be willing to accept as a final compromise.

In justice to myself,—if anything like exact justice herein could only once be attained,—damages to the amount of many thousands of dollars, ought also to be charged against Bolivia and collected from her; but whether it is worth while even to contemplate the possibility of ever obtaining from the marvelously unstable and treacherous government of that country, any equitable consideration of my rights in this regard,—rights resulting from the flagrant and numberless wrongs which that same government has hitherto inflicted on me, at divers times within the last twenty years,— I submit entirely to your own decision.

Yours, very respectfully,
JOSEPH H. COLTON.

MR. HELPER TO MR. COLTON.

St. Louis, Missouri, *January* 21, 1879.

My Dear Mr. Colton: Since I saw you last I have been to Washington three times; first, on my way to see my mother in North Carolina; second, on my way back to New York; and third, on my way from New York to St. Louis. During these several stoppings at Washington I have spoken with Secretary Evarts and others there in regard to the balance of your dues from Bolivia, and am now firmly settled in the conviction that it will be quite useless to take any further mere diplomatic action in the premises until after a man of respectability, education and honor, that is to say, a white man, shall have been elected to the Presidency of that so-called Republic, which is now, as a customary condition, and most unfortunately, dominated by an ignorant and unprincipled hybrid, of hazy and hateful hue, who, if I may write right on, without stopping to disguise or counterfeit or avoid the expression of a fact, is almost as destitute of moral sense as a hedgehog or a hound or a hyena. I am aware that these are plain words,—perhaps some people not knowing better, might consider them as harsh terms,—to use of the head of a nation; but if one has more regard to

truth than to flattery, they are not at all inapplicable to General Daza, the military upstart, the usurping zambo, who, not unlike a negro chieftain of Hayti, or a mulatto despot of Santo Domingo, manages to keep his country constantly in a condition of wild commotion and chaotic repulsiveness and ruin. * * * Yours, very truly,
H. R. HELPER.

MR. HELPER TO MR. COLTON.

St. Louis, Missouri, *February* 27, 1879.
My Dear Mr. Colton : The inclosed copy of a note from Minister Pettis to myself, under date of the 24th instant, was received by me yesterday afternoon. If he remembers to notify you, as I trust he will, of his arrival in New York, on his way to Bolivia, please call on him, two or three times, if necessary, until you meet him face to face, and pleasantly but earnestly urge him to assist yourself and me in obtaining from the Government of Bolivia the balance still due on your old map-claim, of 1858; and explain to him, in part at least,—for it would be quite impossible for any mere mortal to explain in full,—the various shifts and subterfuges and countless other duplicities and dissimulations which Bolivia has herein so persistently practiced against you and all your friends and agents and attorneys, and also against numerous Secretaries of State and Ministers and Consuls of the United States, during the last twenty years ; requesting him at the same time to be good enough to hold himself in readiness to act energetically in the premises so soon as I shall have gathered together and properly re-arranged all the papers in the case for submission to him as the new United States Minister at La Paz.

At any time, after the ill-advised and most violent and

sanguinary fashion of several of the Andean nationalities — no one knows how soon,—the dusky and double-dealing Daza, drivellingly drunk and dissolute, may be dazed by a dagger, or a dart, or a drug, and suddenly disappear forever from the dreadful scenes of his detestable debaucheries and other misdeeds; and if, by rarity of occurrence, he should be succeeded by a ruler of the Aryan race, the distance between you and ultimate justice from Bolivia may be greatly lessened; for, with as much exactness and regularity as clock-work, the few white men who have had any influence at La Paz, since 1858, have invariably tried, in honor and good faith, to satisfy your rightful demands; but the overpowering majority of negroes and Indians and bi-colored hybrids have as invariably turned their backs upon you, chuckled in their sleeves at your helplessness and misfortunes, and unscrupulously used the vilest artifices and the lowest tricks to foil and defeat you and all your agents and attorneys in every effort that has been made to effect a proper redress of your time-worn grievance.

I have now an application before the Foreign Relations Committee of the Senate at Washington for copies of certain original documents and dispatches, which, at my instance, as your attorney, were filed in their Committee room, in the Capitol, in 1873-'74; and so soon as may be convenient after transcripts of those vouchers shall have come into my hands, I shall proceed to make up the whole case anew, and will carry it back into the Congress of the United States, or act otherwise, as I may hereafter elect. So many years of wearisome and perilous and expensive and ill-recompensed labor on a claim so very plain and equitable, has only served to inflame me with a fuller and firmer determination to abate no reasonable effort until a nearer approximation to justice shall be attained in this affair.

Yours faithfully,
H. R. HELPER.

MR. HELPER TO SENATOR HAMLIN.

St. Louis, Missouri, *February* 24, 1879.
Hon. Hannibal Hamlin,
Chairman of the Senate Committee,
on Foreign Affairs, Washington.

Dear Sir: On the 18th of May, 1874, as you may remember, I had the honor of addressing to the illustrious Committee of which you were then a member, and of which you are now Chairman, a communication inclosing a large number of original documents touching the claim of Mr. Joseph H. Colton, of New York, against the Government of Bolivia, and of which communication the following is a copy: * * *

In 1875, both the Senate and the House of Representatives acted favorably in this case, passing a bill directing the President of the United States to call on the Government of Bolivia to pay the money which it itself had so long and so often admitted to be due. After paying, in eight widely separated installments, the greater part of the amount finally and mutually agreed upon by way of additional compromises and diminutions to the still further disadvantage of Mr. Colton, Bolivia has again defaulted, having failed to make full payment of the ninth and last installment; and, in the hope of ultimately obtaining redress for my client, I am now desirous of making a new and complete presentation of the claim to our recently commissioned Minister Resident at La Paz. Yet this task I cannot perform without access to the original papers, or copies of them; and therefore,—coming at once to the object of thus addressing you,—I beg to be informed whether those papers are now on file in your Committee room, or elsewhere in Washington, and also whether I myself, or a delegated friend, or your own clerk, acting on my specification and request,

may be permitted to transcribe the particular decuments necessary for consummating the purpose explained above. Trusting that you will be kind enough to favor me with an early reply,
 I have the honor to be, most respectfully,
 Your obedient servant,
 H. R. HELPER.

SENATOR HAMLIN TO MR. HELPER.

SENATE CHAMBER,
WASHINGTON, *February* 26, 1879.
H. R. HELPER, *Esq., St. Louis, Missouri.*
 DEAR SIR: I have your letter of the 24th instant. The papers to which you refer in your letter are on the files of the Senate; and I have this day obtained authority from the Senate allowing Mr. Colton to withdraw them. You can obtain the papers on application to the Secretary of the Senate.
 Respectfully yours,
 H. HAMLIN.

Finally, Gentlemen of the Senate and House of Representatives of the Congress of the United States of America, your petitioner, moved herein, at this last moment, by the special request of his attorney, Mr. H. R. Helper, has the honor to pray that, for the remainder of the present year, 1879, and during the first eleven months of the succeeding year, 1880; you will be good enough passively to treasure up in your minds all the foregoing facts relating to his just claim for a balance of many thousand dollars still due to him on an old account against the Government of Bolivia, and also for heavy damages equitably due to him from both Bolivia and Peru, in a sum not yet definitely fixed; and so be prepared to act again in his behalf on, or immediately after, the first Monday in December of next year, 1880; provided he shall then specifically solicit such further action from your honorable body; the reasons for thus requesting you to refrain, for a time, from the exercise of your potent legislative functions, being reasons of grave national and international import, affecting especially a contemplated total subversion of the form of government of a jesuitically scheming and grasping and over-ambitious Empire, which is now the most insidious and deleterious adversary of all the Republics of South America; and also affecting very materially certain essential interests and considerations connected with a vast intercontinental railway-enterprise, in which my said attorney and other citizens of the United States are, as he has informed me, about to embark. Thus respectfully and earnestly entreating the attention and action of the dignified and renowned Senators and Representatives of the United States of America in Congress assembled, your petitioner has the honor to subscribe himself,

With sincere and profound esteem,
Your most obedient servant,
JOSEPH H. COLTON, *Claimant.*
By his Attorney,
HINTON R. HELPER.

ST. LOUIS, MISSOURI,
September 23, 1879.

MISCELLANEOUS ODDMENTS.

MISCELLANEOUS ODDMENTS.

MR. HELPER TO MINISTER WHITE.

NEW YORK, *August* 1, 1872.
HON. JULIUS WHITE, *Chicago, Illinois.*

DEAR SIR: Perceiving by the newspapers that you have been appointed Minister Resident of the United States to the Argentine Republic, and regarding it as probable that you will accept the office, and soon be in New York, on your way to Buenos Ayres, I take the liberty to suggest that, even at so early a day as this after your appointment, it may not be too soon for you to begin to consider whether you may not, in your official capacity, be able to promote, in a somewhat special and important manner, the general interests of both countries.

Suppose, for instance, that you should, for a time at least, concentrate your attention and energies upon a single subject, the establishment of semi-monthly steam communication between New York, or some other American port, and one or two of the principal cities of the River Plate? That, I believe, is an object well worth striving for; and if you were to take it up earnestly and succeed in it, it would, I doubt not, ultimately be of immense value to our commercial and manufacturing interests. It would also be generally and justly esteemed a great triumph for yourself. Of course I do not mean to say that you should do anything in a private or business way, but only that, in your official relations with both the American and Argentine governments, you might inform yourself so thoroughly of the actual and prospective condition of things between the two countries as to induce, with the assistance of certain reasonable and necessary subsidies from each, the permanent establishment of safe and speedy steam communication between the United States and the River Plate. At first, and for several years perhaps, the unavoidable expenditures for such a service would probably be very greatly in excess of the receipts; but, all things considered, there need scarcely be entertained an intelligent doubt that the enterprise would pay handsomely in the end.

There is already established a monthly line of American steamers from New York to Rio de Janeiro; and I think it not unlikely that this same line, which, as I hear, is in the hands of financially strong men, might, by fair dealing with the owners, be extended, as a semi-monthly line to Montevideo and Buenos Ayres. In this way, as Americans, we might lay the foundation for far more extensive and profitable business relations with the east coast of South America than we can ever possibly attain under the irregular and meagre arrangements now existing for intercourse with the several countries along that coast. When I occupied the position of American Consul at Buenos Ayres, from 1862 to 1866, I had the honor of earnestly recommending to Secretary Seward the importance of steam communication between the United States and Brazil; and I flatter myself that I may thereby have contributed, in some measure, to the establishment of the line of steamers to Rio de Janeiro.

I am very decidedly of the opinion, moreover, that it is high time for us to begin to seek greater facilities for steam communication, by means of an interoceanic canal through some part of Central America,—say the Isthmus of Darien, the Isthmus of Nicaragua, or the Isthmus of Tehuantepec, —with the various republics which border on the west coast of South America. Having recently crossed the continent of South America, from Buenos Ayers to Lima, I noticed, all along the route, that almost every article of merchandise on sale in the stores, was of British or other European manufacture; and not only so, but the thousand and one things so imported, had, for the most part, been brought to the east or west coast in British bottoms; and in this way the manufacturing, shipping and general commercial interests of Great Britain have already secured such a firm foothold throughout that vast section of the New World, that it will be very difficult, if not impossible, to weaken or displace it. But considering our contiguity to the South Americans, and our natural sympathy with their kindred forms of government, we ought certainly to have a liberal share, if not a lion's share, in the great benefits of ordinary trade and intercourse with so large a number of our enlightened fellowmen, and not apathetically yield such important advantages to far-distant and uncongenial Europeans, whose monarchical views and purposes are always more or less antagonistic to republican institutions.

On the leading subject thus mentioned, if you are interested in it, you may do well to procure, at the Department of State in Washington, a brief but very valuable report on our commercial relations with the Spanish-American States, made by the Hon. Hamilton Fish himself, Secretary of State, in 1870; and also the large volume upon our Commercial Relations in general, for the same year. And, finally, trusting that you will kindly pardon me for writing you this long letter, if you will inform me when you expect to be in New York, I shall hope to have the pleasure of seeing you here, and of conversing with you on matters connected with these suggestions.

I have the honor to be, very respectfully,
     Your obedient servant,
       H. R. HELPER.

MR. HELPER TO SECRETARY THOMPSON.

SOUTH AND CENTRAL AMERICAN TRADE WITH THE UNITED STATES.

(From the *South Pacific Times*, Callao, Peru.)

Our enterprising and progressive neighbors of North America, always having an eye to new avenues of business, seem to have fixed their attention upon both the Atlantic and Pacific coasts of South America with a zeal and thoroughness especially characteristic of the citizens of the Model Republic. The grand and colossal achievements of the United States in agriculture, stock raising, mining, railway construction and other material industries, as also in new inventions and discoveries, in science, in literature, and in the fine arts, are now patent to all the world; and what those States are yet destined to accomplish in manufactures and commerce, will probably soon surprise, and may possibly astonish, their friendly rivals on the other side of the Atlantic. In the intelligence brought by the steamer of last week, not the least significant item is the assurance, all the way from the Palace of the Universal Exhibition in Paris, that "The United States will get a large proportion of the grand prizes and gold medals."

We have recently published several communications advocating closer commercial intercourse between the two continents, and now we place before our readers a lengthy letter on the subject from Mr. Hinton Rowan Helper, an American author and traveler, who became famous, just before the war of the great rebellion in the United States, for the peculiar and forcible combination of anti-negro and anti-slavery views advanced in his work entitled *The Impending Crisis of the South*. Mr. Helper we learn has twice crossed the continent of South America by different routes, and he appears to have been a careful observer of many things. His letter, as will be seen, is addressed to the Hon. Mr. Thompson, a member of the Cabinet of President Hayes; and the points he makes in connection with the navy of his country, and what he says in favor of New Orleans and the proposed ship canal across the Isthmus of Darien, will doubtless be read and pondered with lively interest.

LIMA, PERU, *February* 22, 1878.

HON. RICHARD W. THOMPSON,

Secretary of the Navy, Washington.

SIR: Though far away from home, and yet but little beyond the middle of a long journey by sea and land still before me, so much pleased am I with both the letter and spirit of your Annual Report to the President in December last, which, however, I have only now been able to obtain and read, that I beg the privilege of specifying at least two or three of the passages which have impressed me as being filled with suggestions of the very greatest importance to our future national welfare. Especially do I refer to those passages wherein you hint, and well and wisely hint, at the necessity for a better adjustment of relationship and interaction between our Navy of Force and our Navy of Freight; between our men-of-war and our fleet of unarmed vessels engaged in the merchant service. In this regard, as it seems to me, our one great need at this time is more clippers and crafts for commerce, and fewer frigates for fighting; more useful industry and trade and traffic, and less wasteful indolence and extravagance and ostentation.

Only a few days have elapsed since my arrival here from Brazil and the Argentine Republic, on the east side of South America; I having for the second time, (first in 1871–'72, and now again in 1877–'78,) come overland, across the Continent, most of the way on mule-back, with servant and sumpter-mules, carrying my bed and baggage, and often water and provisions with me. During these two trips over the Pampas and over the Andes, over the Llanos and over the Cordilleras, by different routes, the first through the upper provinces of the Argentine Republic, through Bolivia and Peru, and the second in almost a straight line westwardly from Buenos Ayres, near the River Plate and the Atlantic Ocean, to Valparaiso on the Pacific coast, I have been everywhere kindly received and welcomed, not because I was Mr. Helper, but because I was an American citizen, a plain and simple child of the Great Republic. Yet it always grieved me exceedingly, and was particularly offensive to my sense of the fitness of things, to find almost everything in the way of foreign merchandise, throughout the length and breadth of my routes of travel, of European manufacture.

At different ports along the Atlantic and Pacific coasts, in many cities of the plains, in various towns on the mountain slopes, on the apex of Potosi, and on the tops of other Andean peaks higher than Mount Hood, I have gone into stores and warehouses, and looked around in vain, utterly in vain, for one single article of American manufacture. From the little pin with which the lady fastens her beau-catching ribbons to the grand piano with which she enlivens and enchants the hearts of all her household; from the tiniest thread and tack and tool needed in the mechanic arts, to the largest plows and harrows and other agricultural implements and machines required for use on the farm—all these and other things, the wares and fabrics and light groceries and delicacies in common demand, the drugs and chemicals sold by the apothecary, the fermented and malt and spirituous liquors in the wine saloon, the stationery and fancy goods in the bookstore, the furniture in the parlor, and the utensils in the kitchen, are with very rare exceptions of English, French, German, Spanish or Italian manufacture. And what makes the matter still more unsatisfactory and vexatious to the North American, and more expensive and otherwise disadvantageous to the South American, is that these articles are, as a general rule, inferior, both in material and make, to the corresponding articles of American manufacture. In form, in style, in finish, most articles of American manufacture are really far superior to the corresponding European articles, which are generally ill-proportioned, heavy, and clumsy. Yet the American articles, so much more elegant, so much better adapted to the special uses for which they are intended, might be sold here with fair profits, at even less prices than the purchasers now have to pay for those they obtain from the old country. It is, perhaps, not too much to say that our improvements over the handcraft of the Old World have only been in thoughtful harmony and keeping with our improvements over the antiquated and absurd systems of government and religion which still hamper and oppress all the peoples of the Eastern hemisphere.

Now arises the question, What methods ought we to pursue for the mutual advantage of the inhabitants of both North and South America, in order to introduce successfully, and as soon as possible, our manufactures into this great and constantly increasing field of demand and consumption? That is the important question. How and when shall we begin? We ought to have begun long ago. Duty alike to ourselves and to our neighbors ought to have prompted us to governmental effort in this undertaking at least as early as the middle of the present century. Delay has already largely cost us, and is still more largely costing us, prestige and profit and power. We should go to work at once, and in solemn earnest, determined to succeed, even to the extent of making up in some degree for the long time already lost. Not another day should be allowed to elapse unimproved. From our Navy Department, directly and actively, or indirectly and passively, as it seems to me, should issue the first necessary and practical impulse. Our people, right meaning and trustful, but more or less shortsighted, like other people, and not knowing perfectly well their own interests in all respects, are willing to pay eighteen millions of dollars per annum for the expense of a navy. That is more, much more in my opinion, than we ought to spend for a navy in times of peace. Thirty-eight first-rate war ships for service at sea, and the same number of well constructed cutters for river and harbor service—one of each class for each State and State capital in our Union, and so-named respectively—would, as I think, constitute all the floating force we require in ordinary periods; and the entire cost of such a force, being once provided, ought certainly not to exceed ten millions per annum. Does not this suggestion present an opportunity for judicious retrenchment and reform?—and can you not put it into practice, and thereby save to the country annually eight millions of dollars? And then, because of your having thus lightened the burdens of our patriotic taxpayers in the sum of eight millions a year, may you not, in the further interest of those same taxpayers, (for eventually it will be very greatly in their interest), induce Congress to grant a subsidy of two millions or more a year for the establishment and permanent maintenance of a line, a large line, a long line, of first-class steamers, to run from New Orleans, twice a month or oftener, to all the ports of Mexico and Central and South America, both on the Atlantic and Pacific coasts?

Do that, Mr. Secretary of the Navy, do it at once, do it bravely, do it successfully, and you will thereby readily solve one of the most important problems to which you yourself have alluded in your admirable report. In the interest of the industrious and dextrous labor of our country, you will have found fields of almost illimitable dimensions, and of ever increasing demand, for our surplus products and manufactures ; and in that finding you will have proved yourself, beyond all doubt, the most useful and profitable Secretary of the Navy we have ever yet had.

Under proper guarantees, and with a potent governmental voice in the management of the affairs of the company, a subsidy—considering the old and strong and tenacious hold which Europe already has on the trade of this continent—a subsidy of at least two millions a year should be granted for a term, to start with, of not less than fifteen years, or until a ship canal shall be cut through Nicaragua, or across Tehuantepec, or Darien; but for every million thus spent, from two to five millions ought to be gained, and under an energetic and prudent administration of the business of the company, that much, or more probably would be gained as an accretion to the general wealth of the country. Here, however, it may be proper for me to assure you, as I do with all sincerity and truth, that, so far from being myself pecuniarily interested in any enterprise of this sort, I have never had a business word with any one on the subject. In this respect I really have no more at stake nor in prospect than yourself, or President Hayes, or any other gentleman who is wholly disconnected from mercantile pursuits. It is only because, having two eyes, and having seen so repeatedly and extensively, during my two crossings of this continent, the great requirements and opportunities of American commerce in the southern hemisphere, that I have given myself the liberty of addressing you in this manner.

Another point. You will have observed that I have mentioned New Orleans as the port in the United States from which our ships under governmental patronage should sail to Mexico and Central and South America, and to which they should return with their cargoes of far-south products. All the maps and lands and winds and waters of the New World, not less obviously than animated common sense, are equally emphatic in suggesting New Orleans as the only convenient and proper port, the only natural and auspicious port, for the concentration of our trade with these many vast countries, every one of which lies south of the mouth of the Mississippi river. Besides, for pleasure-seekers and other passengers, and also for the mails and for freight from all these southern climes, New Orleans is, by sea, from twelve to fifteen hundred miles nearer than any one of the great cities of the North. Moreover, by going directly to

New Orleans, and thence by railroad or by steamboat to other places, as may be desirable, both time and pleasant changes of situation will be gained, and the ever-stormy and fatal regions of Cape Hatteras, that howling and harmful headland of horrors, the Carolina haunt of Charybdis and Scylla, will be shunned. Furthermore, the climate of all our Northern cities, as I am well aware from the woeful experience of several personal friends, on various occasions, is much too rigorous, much too perilous, for visitors and other passengers from the tropics in the winter season; especially is it so for those who may have been born and reared within the tropics; and they will prudently, for their lives' sakes, remain away from our country altogether, rather than enter it on the Atlantic coast north of Pamlico sound, between November and March inclusive.

It is alike due to the Great West, the South, the North, and the East—it is preëminently due to the United States as a who'e—that the marvelously favorable geographical position of New Orleans for the concentration in North America of our trade with the Southern hemisphere, should be at once recognized and acted upon with good faith, and with unyielding vigor and perseverance. Being so far behind as we are now in the matter of this commercial and manufacturing outlook, any further failure on our part to avail ourselves of the wonderful facilities which Nature so freely and conspicuously offers us, would only be a most culpable continuance of the stupid and discreditable indifference which we, as a contiguous nation of more than forty millions of inhabitants, have thus far strangely manifested toward South and Central America. The large commercial cities of the North have now, and will always retain, the trade of the greater part of the Northern hemisphere, and much also of the Southern; but our Government should not favor those cities exclusively, and, as if both blind and deaf to the unmistakable indications of nature, neglect all the cities of the West and South; for there is much danger that such favor on the one side, and neglect on the other, carried to excess, might render the country topheavy and unsteady.

The remarkable wisdom and liberality of little England (only a fraction larger than North Carolina, and considerably less than Missouri,) in dividing her commercial favors between London, Liverpool, Bristol, Hull, Southampton, and many of her other ports, in divers sections of her cost—not to. speak of Swansea or Cardiff in Wales, of Dublin or Cork in Ireland, or of Glasgow or Dundee in Scotland—may very well serve as an excellent example, and as a policy of great prudence, eminently fit and profitable for us to follow. That is the way for nationalities to be truly national within themselves, and not sectional. Cincinnati, Indianopolis, Chicago, Saint Louis, Louisville, Minneapolis, Kansas City, Omaha, and many other great and growing cities of the West, can find a cheap outlet and lucrative market for the immense surplus products of their manufactories and slaughter-houses and granaries and. tanneries and brewries, only through the mouth of the Mississippi river, near which, at New Orleans, an extraordinary amount of exchanges and transhipments will always need to be made. The sooner we accept the simple truths of these facts in nature, the sooner we establish a line of first-class ocean steamers to run regularly all along both coasts of Mexico and Central and South America, and the sooner we cut, or aid in cutting, a commodious ship canal through Tehuantepec, or Nicaragua, or across the Isthmus of Darien, the sooner we will become in reality the grand and glorious republic of which our wisest and best statesmen have often dreamed, and dreamed longingly, with their eyes wide open.

Yours, very respectfully,

H. R. HELPER.

MR. HELPER TO SECRETARY THOMPSON.

LIMA, PERU, *July* 10, 1878.
HON. RICHARD W. THOMPSON,
Secretary of the Navy, Washington.

SIR: Unexpectedly long detention in Lima, on a matter of business connected with the Government of Peru, has prevented me from calling on you at Washington, as I had hoped to be able to do before this time, with the object of explaining to you, verbally, the nature of certain very gross abuses in our foreign Naval Service; which abuses have incidentally come to my knowledge, both here and at Rio de Janeiro in Brazil. You will remember my postscript allusion to this subject in a somewhat elaborate communication which, in February last, I had the honor of addressing to you in advocacy of more intimate and extensive commercial relations between the United States and Central and South America. The extravagance and waste, and the evidences of cupidity and corruption, which came under my observation at Rio de Janeiro, whilst I was there, during a period of five months last year, and similar proofs of like prodigalities and peculations in connection with our Naval Station at Callao, which have been casually brought before me at Lima, during a residence of more than five months in Peru this year, constitute the bases of the complaints which I now desire to submit for your patriotic consideration and action. Only I must here inform you, that it would be much more agreeable for me to make my complaints to you in conversation, rather than in writing; as, what I wish to say being entirely unofficial and voluntary on my part, I do not at all relish the idea of having to incur denunciation or ill-will on account of any seeming officiousness as a formal reporter of facts implicating American Naval Officers, of whatever grade, in practices wholly at variance with the conduct of gentlemen.

Restrained by this feeling of reluctance to become an emphatic accuser and protester, I have remained silent until the present time; and it may be that I should have continued uncommunicative until my return to the United States, had it not been for the seasonable incitements hereto, which, as general news in the public journals, have just come to me in the form of a Report from the Committee on Expenditures of the Navy Department, made to the House of Representatives at Washington, only a few weeks since. From that Report, carrying with it the weight of official investigation, and relieving me from a great part of the task which I had felt it proper to impose on myself as a future labor to be performed when convenient and face to face, I make the following extract from an abstract which I have seen in several American newspapers received in Lima by the last mail from Panama:

"The Committee on Naval Expenditures say that extravagance and a disregard of legal restraints have been recognized at almost every step of their inquiry and previous to the beginning of the present administration of the Department. At the outset they were staggered at the immense amounts apparently owing by the several bureaus, reaching the sum of more than $7,000,000; and this, too, notwithstanding the enormous appropriations made annually from 1869 to 1876, both inclusive, aggregating in amount $149,000,000. There is nothing to compensate this vast outlay save a Navy contemptible even in comparison with those of third and fourth rate powers. Notwithstanding the plain terms of law, open purchases have been the chief mode by which the Navy Department has been supplied with materials, not in obedience to actual expediency or necessity, but vastly in excess of its means. This violation of law, without warrant of precedent or authority, has depleted the Treasury to the extent of millions of dollars, and has been the food upon which pampered favorites have fattened, while it has prevented the payment of moneys due a meritorious class of creditors to such an extent that many have been involved in bankruptcy, and all of them subjected to irreparable loss. The amount of open purchases and bureau orders within the last few years aggregate more than $20,000,000. All the advantages of dealing with rivals in the markets have been ignored, fair competition avoided, and both the letter and spirit of the law disregarded."

Taking it for granted that a man ought always to be justified and defended in telling the truth, and that he should invariably dare to tell it whenever he finds any great right or principle violated in consequence of its suppression, yet I confess that, in view of the foregoing Report within reach as a voucher, it is now a much easier matter for me to write exactly what I have seen and learned at Rio de Janeiro and Callao, than it was prior to the time of the publication of the results of the Naval Committee's investigation.

What I wish to mention distinctly, and what I here desire to protest against as a condition of things both disgraceful and ruinous to a world-wide branch of the public service, is the immense quantity of needless and expensive Naval Stores kept in warehouses and hulks at the two stations named, (and doubtless at others also,) and which said stores, to the amount of many hundreds of thousands of dollars, are already, for the most part, so rusty or rotten, so corroded or mouldy, so stale or sour, so wormy or moth-eaten, or otherwise so badly damaged, that they are now almost valueless, and will soon have to be sold for the merest nominal sum, or thrown away altogether, under a summary and sweeping condemnation.

It would be exceedingly inconvenient and tiresome to enumerate even a tenth part of the vast agglomeration of things, bulky and weighty and of all sorts and sizes on the one hand, and small and light and of all shapes and colors on the other, which I saw either entirely spoilt or rapidly spoiling at Rio de Janeiro, where, according to my estimate, the total loss to the Government of the United States, arising alone from the natural waste and destruction of superfluous articles there warehoused at the particular time of which I speak, will amount to nearly if not quite, half a million of dollars. But this is not all, nor is it the worst, if my information be correct. It seems that an enormous excess of stores has hitherto, for many years past, been regularly sent out by a class of special Navy Agents in the United States, who, devoid of honor and patriotism, are interested only in receiving a stipulated commission on the gross amount of all purchases made by them; and that they resort to every conceivable device to ship away as many goods at as high prices as possible, no matter whether or not there exists, or ever will exist, any real or prospective necessity for them!

Under these corrupt and shameful practices, our Navy, such as it is, and with little or nothing to do, has cost us, on an average, during the whole of the two presidential terms of Gen. Grant, nearly nineteen millions of dollars per annum. Just think of it! One hundred and forty-nine millions of dollars in only eight years,—and yet, where is the good, where is the worth, of half the money? Rather than continue to maintain the American Navy after this fashion, it would, I am inclined to believe, be better to abolish it altogether. To say the least, a few millions of dollars annually curtailed from our little-laboring and scarcely-necessary navy, and prudently spent in fostering a first-rate steam commercial service to and from various foreign countries, particularly Central and South America, would, as it appears to me, be a far more judicious expenditure of a portion of our appropriable revenues; and more especially so inasmuch as all the steamers for freight and passengers might, under proper governmental subsidy and supervision, be so constructed as to be easily convertible into formidable war-ships in case of need. Less, therefore, of an idle and profligate Navy, and more of a usefully-busy and honestly-managed Commercial Marine, would seem to be in the line of beneficial reforms which should at once receive our most earnest and steadfast attention.

Yours, very respectfully,
H. R. HELPER.

MR. HELPER TO SECRETARY EVARTS.

LIMA, PERU, July 26, 1878.

HON. WILLIAM M. EVARTS,
Secretary of State, Washington.

SIR: I have already had the honor to inform you, on more than one occasion, that I do not like to be the recipient of favors, from any source whatever, without being permitted to give back something in the nature of an equivalent in return. In the long course of my delicate and difficult dealings with certain distressingly dilatory and delinquent Governments in South America, I have frequently found it necessary, as a means of securing even a shadow of justice, to trouble you, as Secretary of State of the United States, for various points of information in diplomacy, which you have always kindly and frankly imparted, whenever you could do so in clear conformity with the code of international law. Recognizing these official and semi-official favors, and desiring to reciprocate them in some measure, however inadequately, I now have the pleasure of submitting for your enlightened and statesmanlike consideration, the inclosed copy of a communication which, written solely with a view of promoting the public interest, I addressed under date of the 10th instant, to the Hon. Richard W. Thompson, Secretary of the Navy; the said communication, as you will observe, being a sort of sequel to a somewhat similar communication which I dispatched to the same distinguished Secretary, and also, in copy, to yourself, several months since.

I have the honor to be, very respectfully,
Your obedient servant,
H. R. HELPER.

ASSISTANT SECRETARY HUNTER TO MR. HELPER.

DEPARTMENT OF STATE,
WASHINGTON, *April* 19, 1878.
HINTON R. HELPER, *Esq., New York.*

SIR: Your letter of the 26th ultimo, from Lima, Peru, has been received, and the instructive one which you addressed to the Secretary of the Navy, a copy of which you have kindly appended to the former, has been read with much interest.

I am, sir, your obedient servant,
W. HUNTER.

MR. HELPER TO SENATOR MERRIMON.

DAKAR, (near GOREE,) AFRICA.,
June 29, 1877.
HON. AUGUSTUS S. MERRIMON, *Washington, D. C.*

DEAR SIR: On my way from Bordeaux in France, to

Rio de Janerio in Brazil, where I have business with the Government of His Imperial Majesty Dom Pedro II, with whom, after correspondence, I recently had the honor of an interview at the Grand Hotel in Paris, the steamer on which I took passage has stopped here, at Dakar, a French settlement in Senegambia; and this stoppage affords me the pleasant pastime of thus communicating to you my compliments from Negroland; a land, albeit, of barbarous blackness and abomination, from which and to which few emblems or evidences of civilized life have ever yet passed; and these only, at any time, through the persons or agencies of white strangers from other countries, or through their descendants; never once in the past, nor possibly in the future, through the persons or agencies of the repulsively sable and soulless savages who are autochthonous to the soil.

Of the mother country and the honorable ancestry of your eight hundred thousand white constituents in North Carolina, you know a great deal; but of the original habitat and despicable pedigree of your three hundred thousand black supernumeraries in the same State, you, yes, even you, a learned and upright judge in matters of law and equity, and an able and distinguished Senator of the United States, know comparatively but very little. * Every white man who

---

* Since this letter was written, Judge Merrimon, through the whimsical and mysterious maneuvering of political caucuses at Raleigh, has ceased to be a Senator of the United States; but the conspicuously elevated and honorable position which he has already won in the councils of the nation has not ceased to attract and hold fast the heart-felt attention of his compatriots; and it is by no means improbable that his sterling character and ability, as a liberal and enlightened legislator, may soon again be called into requisition. North Carolina would but certainly secure and advance her own best interests by making him her Governor; and the United States at large have not unfrequently chosen, as their highest exemplars, for a term of four years or more, men of far less worth and wisdom to walk and work in the ways of Washington.
H. R. H.

emigrated from Europe to America emigrated voluntarily, impelled in his westward movements by certain well-settled aims and objects which looked to the general betterment of himself and family; he also took with himself, besides the inalienable mastership of his own manhood, a name, a suit of clothes, a knowledge of letters, genius, courage, self-respect, tools, implements, utensils, and skill in all the great arts and industries of civilization.

On the other hand, every negro who went from Africa to America, went there involuntarily, doltishly and doggishly; he went as a reality of opprobrium, penury and wretchedness; he went nameless, shirtless and naked; he went ignorant, indolent and incompetent; he went unapt, undextrous and unaspiring in everything; he went senseless of all energy and enterprise, being apathetic and sluggish in both muscle and mind; he went as a captive and craven creature, absolutely averse to exertion, and was and is an anomalous despiser and shirker of labor of whatever kind, whether material, mental or moral; he went as the embodiment of all that is coarse, gross and vulgar; he went as a slave, a savage, a criminal; he was and is guilty of the revolting and unpardonable crime of loving life better than liberty, and is justly chargeable with the indelible odium of most flagitiously enthralling both himself and his posterity forever to the will and caprice of other men.

Yet this is the man, the vile man of Africa, the Ethiopian of grovelling nature, unsightly skin, and noxious stench, with whom certain very contemptibly foolish and knavish politicians in America would have you and me and other decent people, of Olympian and Heliconian descent, fraternize and coalesce upon terms of equality; as if indeed he is, or ever can be, our equal, or even approximately our equal, any more than lead can ever be the equal of silver, copper the equal of gold, or a half pennyweight fragment of common bottle-green glass the equal of a three-carat diamond of the first water. The bare proposition for miscegenation, or for long continuance together in the same society, under any arrangement or regulation whatever, the mere thought of such a thing, in any conceivable form of accommodation, is repugnant and demoralizing to the last degree. In my humble but mature judgment, there is nothing in the antecedents of the negro, nor in his present or prospective character or condition, which justifies us in regarding him otherwise than as an ill-starred alien among us, an alien of most pestilent and pernicious presence, to be tolerated only so long as a fair and favorable opportunity may offer for getting rid of him effectually and forever; and this very desirable opportunity we ought not merely to wait for, like drones of redundant faith and deficient diligence; but we should rather, like rational and sedulous men, work for it, and so, by honest thought, earnest inquiry, and intelligent action, hasten its coming. When the negro shall have been once entirely ousted from the Southern States, and his place filled by the white man, then the White South, like the White North, the White East, and the White West, will be on the highway to unexampled greatness and glory; and with all our people, of every section, homogeneous in race, and harmonious in sentiment, in purpose, in performance, we shall, for the first time in the history of our republic, begin to realize the bright predictions of national power and grandeur which have always been favorite themes with our most far-sighted and patriotic statesmen.

The exchange of the negro for the white man will be, in comparison of dignity and worth, much like the exchange of the periwinkle for the oyster; of the tomcod for the trout; of the stickleback for the salmon; of the booby for the duck; of the gull for the swan; of the buzzard for the turkey; of the rat for the squirrel; of the goat for the sheep; of the ass for the horse; of the Indian turnip and the toadstool for the Irish potato and the Dutch cauliflower; of the night shade and the nettle for the geranium and the rosebush; of the blackjack and the alder for the whiteoak and the hickory; of the swamp and the pollywog-pond for the upland and the lake; of the molecast and the anthill for the Blue Ridge and the Peak of Teneriffe; of the glowworm and the firedrake for the moon and the sun; of deformity and filth and ugliness for symmetry and cleanliness and beauty; of falsehood and vice and ignominy for truth and virtue and honor; of hatred and strife and misery for love and peace and happiness.

But I must not write to you as if I were in Asheville or in St. Louis, and you in Raleigh or in Washington. Let me remember, with due deference and decorum, that I am in Dakar; Dakar of dynastic dignity; for Dakar has a King, whose name, savoring of Saracenic sound, is Selim; Selim the Sad; for he is certainly the most solemn and sorrowful Selim I ever saw; and this same Selim has eight wives, all, like himself, blacker, if possible, than the ace of spades, or even Erebus itself, and more hideous than the witches of Endor; swarthy consorts, who, though not sweetly smiling nor savorly scented, have nevertheless not been slow in supplying their sympathizing spouse with an abundance, if not a superabundance, of young Selians, Selims and Selimesses, for the succession to his sooty sovereignty.

We arrived here amid the cimmerian moments of one o'clock last night; and so anxious was I for an opportunity to see the Africans in Africa,—a race of barbarous and bloodthirsty blackamoors, for whom, speaking frankly, I have little more liking than I entertain for their submundane congeners, the other imps of darkness,—that, even at that moonless and dismal hour, (though the stars were shining brightly,) I went on shore among the negroes, naked or half-naked native negroes, without any guide or companion, and continued alone among them until seven o'clock this morning, when several of my fellow-passengers from the steamer joined me in the curious sight-seeing and sound-hearing of this indescribably heathenish and mysterious land. The very earth itself and everything it contained, the air and all the visible space and objects surrounding me, seemed to be swayed or spell-bound by some strange or unpropitious influence. In no other part of the world have I ever been affected by such amazingly weird impressions and feelings as those which came over me here, about two o'clock this morning, when, solitary and alone, I found myself standing under the outspreading branches of a gigantic baobab, with prostrate groups of houseless, homeless, slumbering, snoring savages around me, and two vampires, one nearly as large as a crow, and the other about the size of a sparrow-hawk, flitting over my head; while the dark and dreary stillness of the hour was further interrupted by the buzz of myriads of musquitoes and gnats and night-flies about my ears, and the melancholy croak and trill of frogs and screech-owls and various unknown but noisy insects, or other autochthonous creatures, only a few yards distant on either hand.

An hour or so later, that is to say, about three o'clock, I went into the outskirts of the further end of the town, having met, in the course of my perambulations, several darkies, men and women, mutely prowling about, like lost souls, (as they are, in fact, and ever will be,) apparently without aim or interest. To most of these silent strollers, whom, in the blackness of darkness not unlike their own faces, I thus encountered afoot, I issued a sort of imperious and impatient grunt of recognition, and then, without pausing a moment, passed on, with intenser pride than ever before in the consciousness of possessing a Caucasian nose; whilst they, the sauntering vagabonds, first stopped and stared in astonishment, and then made their salaams with grotesquely awkward and comical gestures.

About this same hour, three o'clock in the morning, while it was still very dark, I heard, a few hundred yards from where I was walking, a succession of measured and distinct mechanical sounds, peculiar and striking, such as I had never heard before in all my life; and, stopping for a few minutes to listen more attentively, I soon heard a similar sound, or rather series of sounds, in the opposite direction; very soon another quarter of the town saluted my auditory nerves with a reduplication of the same strange noise; then, within the next three hours, it gradually broke out here and there and everywhere, until the whole town became an ear-piercing racket of monotonous thumping and bumping and banging.

These singularly strange and almost deafening sounds, as I was not slow to ascertain, were occasioned by the negro women and girls, who, with large wooden mortars and pestles, were pounding their millet, a kind of wild rice, which, in combination with much of the straw and chaff, generally more or less damp and mouldy, they reduce to the fineness of ordinary grits or bran, and then make into a sort of coarse bread, which constitutes their principal food. In nine cases in ten this bread, if bread it may be called, is such stuff as a good farmer in Carolina or Missouri would feed to his cattle in midwinter, when, perhaps, it might be inconvenient or impossible to obtain anything better.

Dakar being a French settlement, and therefore amenable to the laws of France, or measurably so at least, (for King Selim, in the presence of a French garrison, reigns only on sufferance, with limited powers, and is allowed a small pension,) it is required here that every darky, outside of his own hut, shall wear at least one garment; and so, for the most part, as a consequence of this Gallic interference with the immemorial costume of Negroland,—*in puris naturalibus,*—the men wear only a pair of tow trowsers, reaching from the navel to the knee, and the women only a calico frock or slip, of corresponding length; all being quite naked from the waist upward, and from the knee downward; neither hats, nor bonnets, nor coats, nor jackets, nor shirts, nor sacques, nor shawls, nor shoes, nor slippers, nor socks, nor stockings, having any wearers or wishers among the swinishly slothful and slovenly satyrs and sluts of Senegambia. As the women, especially the more.elderly ones, were comminuting, in their mortars, their millet and millet-husks,—for in no case had the grain been more than half cleaned, or otherwise properly prepared,—the vigorous and constant strokes which they necessarily made with their pestles, caused their extraordinarily long and flabby breasts to flop up and down in the most jerky and amusing manner; whilst the mammæ of the younger maidens bobbed and quivered about like a multiplicity of little balls or globules of calves-foot jelly on a dish in transit.

With rare exceptions, two women or two girls, always on their feet, were pulverizing, face to face, at every mortar. Both the mortars and the pestles were, in most cases, very rudely and clumsily constructed. The number of huts in the town is probably about two hundred, giving mean shelter to nearly one thousand inhabitants; and when we consider that this millet-mauling is going on for so long a time every day, every morning, in front of every Ethiopic habitation throughout Dakar, if not indeed, throughout the whole of Senegambia and all other sections of nude and needy Negroland, we can form a faint, but only a faint and most inadequate, idea of the immense waste of energy and life among these and other nations of listless noodles and numbskulls who never manifest any predilection or desire for the use of labor-saving machinery. One little mill, of only one-horse power, industriously run and properly managed, would grind more millet than is now crushed by mere matronly and maidenly manipulation in all the two hundred misfashioned mortars of Dakar; it would be ground far better, too, and with much less noise and nonsense.

Besides the time-wasting trituration of the millet, and the sluggish and sloppy carrying of water in gourds on the head, all of which was done by women and girls, I have seen here nothing else performed in the way of labor. So far as I have been able to observe, no man, no "noble lord of creation," has deigned to do anything whatever, except to loll and loiter about, beg, grin, giggle and guffaw.

On the premises of a Frenchman, who kept a store and hotel combined, in the Frank part of the town, (quite separate from the niggerville,) with whom a fellow-passenger and myself had bargained for breakfast, I saw three full-grown darkies, all women, by their united and most vigorous and violent efforts, succeed, within the space of little less than half an hour, in catching and killing one poor little pullet. Their method, not at all of gentle artifice or stratagem, not in the least of quiet insnarement or entrapment, was one of most rousing and rampant attack with sticks and stones. It so happened that I witnessed the whole proceeding; and many a circus has afforded me much less amusement, barring the sincere sympathy I felt for the unfortunate fowl. The first stick, in the hands of a bawling and bouncing and bounding wench, was thrown at the chicken when it was at least twenty yards distant; but the missile missed its mark. Then the other two women, similarly armed and similarly acting, joined in the chase, sometimes throwing sticks, sometimes stones, and meanwhile making such a din of harsh and confused and deafening exclamations as one, in our own country, is but seldom apt to hear outside of a lunatic asylum. I was quite surprised at the length of time that the chicken ran and flew and avoided its three cruel pursuers and the numerous death-designed darts aimed at it; and there was also conspicuously visible, during the prolonged exercise, a most unseemly and outlandish air of wildness and savagery in the leaps and jumps and skips and capers and contortions and outcries of these bareheaded, barebacked, barebreasted, barelegged, barefooted jetty jades, who were certainly a most simple and sorry sort of henhunters on this occasion. It may possibly have been their first experience in this lively phase of domestic life. They took no short nor modest steps, but vaulted like kangaroos or roebucks, lifting up and spreading out their heels, both behind and sideways, and with unique curves and twists, from three to four feet above the ground at every saltation, and exposing their hams and other portions of their posteriors with an unconsciousness and freedom not often seen in America beyond the in-door limits of an infant's nursery. Finally, however, after having been hunted hither and thither, and chased high and low, often indirectly hit and much bruised, amid the fright and squalls and flutter and hubbub of all its companions, the doomed pullet was struck a fatal blow athwart the neck, with a stick forcibly hurled from the hand of one of the three graceless Dianas of Dakar; and about three hours afterward, that is to say, at or near eleven o'clock, (everything in Africa is either done very slowly and imperfectly, and with an obstructive and depressive superabundance of assistants and consumers, or not done at all,) our breakfast, consisting mostly of crackers, cheese, sardines, bread, boiled chicken, and a bottle of Medoc, was ready, and was taken with an excellent appetite, but not without our being subjected meanwhile to an immense amount of molestation and mendicity.

Seating ourselves in the back part our of host's store, where a common pine table, without cloth, had been set for us, and where an open door on either side of the building afforded good ventilation and convenient means of ingress and egress, swarms of the nasty negroes, big and little, old and young; male and female, the larger half-clad, or less than half-clad, and the smaller with only a pack-thread tied around their loins, (for the tiniest string, they contend, is a garment, and so, by this absurd quibble and device, as yet tolerated, they satisfy on the one hand, or defy on the other, the law of France,) began to crowd around us, holding out their hands and soliciting, with the most shameless urgency, a portion of our morning meal. This abrupt and boisterous importunity on their part at once became to us an annoyance barely endurable. The wretches blocked both doorways and extended themselves in crowded lines far out on both sides of the store, excluding from us the air, and almost suffocating us, besides, in another way, with the foul exhalations from their disgustingly filthy and skunkish persons. To have been besieged by five thousand gallinippers on the one hand, and by ten thousand polecats on the other, would hardly have placed us in a more perplexing dilemma.

Before we could take a morsel in peace, it became necessary for us to appeal to the landlord for protection against this loathsome and harassing mob of half-starved beggars. With both hands he quickly and passionately grasped a wide board, a piece of plank from a dry-goods box, about four feet long, and, Frenchmanlike, rushed furiously upon those who were pressing us most closely, banging them over their unbreakable heads and pachydermatous shoulders, and causing many of them to howl and scatter in every direction, like a pack of whipped curs; while others, further off and unhurt, fell down upon the ground in paroxysms of laughter, kicking up their heels and rolling and tumbling and screaming like demons. What a scene! what a spectacle! It was at once, in combination, a bedlam for the eye and a pandemonium for the ear. How very little of good in anything may we ever rationally expect from any set of creatures capable of such a disgraceful exhibition of sportive levity and tomfoolery under the just complainings of bare backs and the rightful cravings of starving stomachs! Of sadly short duration, however, was the relief which my companion and myself enjoyed from this more than ninefold nuisance of noisome and nonsensical negroes.

Scarcely had our worthy host returned to his duties in the store, when we were again almost insufferably beset and encircled by great numbers of the more wary miscreants who had been so fortunate as to escape chastisement. . Again we demanded the immediate and remedial interference of our landlord, who, seizing and uplifting his broad board of dry-goods box, as he had done at first, started full tilt against the enemy, who, however, broke ranks and ran away so rapidly, helter-skelter, as to evade entirely the heavy blows which were rightly intended to be laid upon the loathsome skin and flesh nearest to their good-for-nothing bones. Once more the merchant returned to his counter, and yet once more the swarm of noxious negroes gathered around us, completely filling the doorways again, and, with extended hands and glaring eyes and chattering speech, entreated us for anything and for everything which we might be disposed to give them. Just then how heartily, how earnestly and profoundly, I wished for a full-loaded Gat'ing gun at my right hand, and for a well-charged blunderbus at my left! There was simply no remedy, none whatever; the evil was too complex, too rank, and of too great magnitude. Tired and hungry as we were, we had to worry through our dear-bought breakfast as best we could, amid a buzz and fever of importunities, and a concatenation of ridiculous and favor-currying grins and grimaces, which only served to fortify me in my long-settled convictions, that it is utterly impossible for clean-natured and clear-sighted white men ever to disdain the negro in a manner at all commensurate with his manifold and measureless demerits.

Immediately after breakfast, my friend and myself called on the " King," and, by paying twenty francs for the privilege, we had the " honor " of an introduction to, and shook hands with, " His Majesty" and several of his eight "Queens," and also with many of the " Princes " and " Princesses " of the " Royal Blood," of whom many of the younger ones, in their huts, were as stark naked as minnows or mice or monkeys in midsummer. It is probable that a more indigent and woe-begone set of dynastic darkies can nowhere be found this side of the lower regions. All the toggery upon their persons, and everything in their eight huts, including the eight huts themselves,—in short, all their property of whatever kind,—did not cost, and would not bring at any ordinary sale, public or private, the sum total of two hundred dollars. Think of this trifling amount as representing the combined wealth of every member of the " Royal Family " of Dakar, comprising one " King," eight " Queens," and thirty-four " Princes " and " Princesses," being an average of less than five dollars for each, and it will convey a moderately correct impression of the extreme destitution and distress common among the uncommonly common commoners of these most unimprovably proletarian and plebeian people. Including the glass beads and brass rings and other shabby trinkets around their necks and wrists and ankles, and in their ears, (I have seen as many as fourteen dingy, dirty, greenly-tarnished rings in the ears of a single wench, seven in each ear, leaving scarcely a particle of the lobe remaining undestroyed,) the average intrinsic value of their wearing apparel and all their other possessions, would probably not exceed one dollar per capita ; and certainly, in very many cases, it would not amount to so much as fifty cents.

Soon after leaving Selim's "palace," which, both within and without, is far inferior to the meanest negro-kitchen I ever saw in North Carolina, I went to a large tree, a baobab, near by, in the shade of which two lousy-looking, and assassin-visaged mulatto Marabouts (itinerant Mohammedan missionaries from Morocco,) were lying flat on their stomachs, on the ground, one reading aloud, and the other copying, in the Arabic language, passages from the Koran. These "scripture" passages, freshly written, the proselyters rolled or otherwise compressed into minute billets, and either sold or presented them to the Mumbo-Jumbo darkies, who sewed them up in bits of leather, which were also supplied for the purpose by the Morocco saints, and, with silly awe and stupid wonder, wore them around their necks, or carried them elsewhere about their persons, as amulets and fetiches. It needs no argument to prove the pitiable superstition and the matchless folly of such missionary operations as these; but what shall be said of the success or non-success of the creed-carrying crusaders of our own country, or of the evangelizing efforts of the vast brotherhood of European zealots and enthusiasts, who, under the impulses of a similar delusion, are so uselessly and foolishly, if not culpably, wasting away their energies and lives in behalf of an utterly despicable and execrable and God-forsaken race? A Jesuit missionary, a queer and questionable prig of piety, is permanently sustained in Dakar by the Catholic propagandists of Rome and Paris. For any real or lasting good that he or any of his fellow fanatics, in the capacity of priest, whether Catholic, Protestant, Mohammedan, Brahman, or Buddhist, will ever be able to accomplish among A.. ..n negroes in Africa, he might just as well be sustained in a community of gorillas or baboons.

Such a thing as a decent and comfortable residence in

Negroland, outside of the white section of a white settlement, may be a thing of excogitation, but not of sight or reality. Here, in the ebon quarter of Dakar, one may behold many huts, hovels, and holes, but no houses. All the huts in this niggerville are of about the same size and shape and material. They are built of bamboo, bunglingly bound together and wattled with withes, wiregrass and clay; are in the form of old-fashioned bee-gums, looking, at a distance, very much like haystacks; and are generally from seven to eight feet high, with a diameter of about nine feet at the base. The openings, which serve the purposes of doors, without any other means of closing them than pieces of old bagging, or other strips of coarse cloth, are so low and small that a man of ordinary stature needs to bend down almost to his hands and knees in order to be able to enter within. Both the walls and the roofs of all the huts I examined were more or less open to the weather; and not one of them seemed ever to have been honored with the completeness of even an ignoble finish. The average of the entire cost of the construction of these huts was probably a sum equal to about four dollars of our money; many of them less, and some more. The 'palace" of the "King," the materials of which, as of all other huts, consist of posts or stakes, bamboo, and mud intermixed with grass, could have been built anywhere in the United States (but for the shame and stigma of having it in the country,) for ten or twelve dollars.

Furniture, beds and bedding, the various necessary wares and utensils, and the countless other cozy and convenient things which a Caucasian naturally expects to see in and about a human habitation, are here quite as scarce and invisible as hens' teeth. Only a few straw mats on which they sleep, earthen pots in which they cook, and big gourds in which they carry water, were perceptible as the adjuncts and appendages of their surprisingly squalid and abject abodes.

Nor was the eye gladdened, in a single instance, by the sight of any garden, or field, or lawn, or cultivated vine, or vegetable, or fruit, or flower. They have no horses, nor mules, nor asses,—except themselves; no cows, no hogs, no sheep; but here and there were a few flop-eared goats, whose presence I could account for only on the ground of a probable affinity of scent and satyr-descent between themselves and their owners. As for barn-yard fowls, where, in the first place, there are no barns, and where, in the second place, everything is foul even in the absence of fowls, I saw them not, not one. So far, indeed, are these Yoloff yahoos from all friendly and actual relationship with any species of domestic animal, that I have not been able to find among them even so common a creature as a cat or a dog; though they themselves dwell in kennels, and are doubtless the most doggish dullards and drones anywhere discernible under the disc of the dogstar.

The inveteracy and persistency of begging and teasing among these clattering and cajoling clowns and caitiffs, are positively marvelous. The doctrine of equivalents, the idea of justice and propriety in exchanging one thing for another, would seem never to have once penetrated their murky minds. Like hobbling and hungry hounds, they all know how to receive, but not one of them seems ever to have learned any fundamental principle of the noble art of giving. Equally true is it that, even if any one of them did possess both the knowledge and the disposition to make a present, or to confer a benefaction, he would yet totally lack the ability to do so. Nor is it at all possible ever to satisfy these pagan petitioners; the more one gives them, the more they ask and expect. Numbers of them followed me everywhere I went; and three or four, in particular, exercised a species of low cunning, coupled with a degree of impudence and shamelessness, which I had never before witnessed. Within half a minute or so after I had placed a coin in the open right hand of him on my left, he would dart behind, among the rabble, and reappear at my right elbow, with his left hand open in appeal for another contribution, assuming, meanwhile, a peculiar expression of newness and innocence, as if indeed I had never seen him before, nor he me. When I first discovered that several of these coal-black and baseborn bamboozlers were systematically and repeatedly practicing against me in this manner, I could scarcely believe my onw eyes. Notwithstanding my long familiarity with the naturally deceitful and scurvy nature of the negro,—from the very days of infancy, in fact, when, in North Carolina, near the banks of the South Yadkin, I was nursed in the arms of my father's slaves,—I was yet unprepared to observe at once, with perfect equanimity, these new evidences of his inherent sneakingness and dissimulation. To what an excellent use I could just then have put, if I had only had them, a few first-rate Orsini bombs! Other darkies, less active and less monkey-like in their slyness, audaciously maintained their position on whichever side of me they happened to be, and begged incessantly, quickly transferring from the hand that received into the hand of deposit, and then unblushingly thrusting back the empty hand; the palm being distended with expectation, and the fingers moving with the very ecstacy of eagerness, for an additional gratuity.

One of the worst of these tormentors, a rawboned but youthful rascal, to whom, even after the discovery of his double-dealing in the matter of money-getting by means of money-begging, first on one side and then on the other, I had, winking at his tricks, given at least three half-francs, on as many different occasions within the brief space of a quarter of an hour, began seriously to beg me for my boots, (a new and excellent pair, made over my own lasts, and for which under somewhat exigent circumstances of time and business, I recently paid, in New York, the really exorbitant price of sixteen dollars,) and, during the next two hours, my ears were certainly not free from a repetition of that special and modest request at a longer interval than three minutes at most. Finally, wishing to ascertain whether or not the fellow was gifted, even in the remotest degree, with any sense of equity, I began, with the assistance of an interpreter, to argue the case with him, justifying my refusal to comply with his request, and inquiring of him what he proposed to give me in exchange for my boots. His reply was, in substance, that they were good boots, and he wanted them; that he had no money, nor other thing of value, and could not therefore give me any material consideration for them; that he was engaged soon to be married to a young woman, and had nothing to wear on his feet, (all he wore anywhere was a pair of knee-and-navel reaching tow trowsers,) and that I had a pocket full of money, and could buy for myself another pair! Herein, however, the prayer of the kinky-haired and connubially inclined candidate for happiness unspeakable in this world, proved altogether bootless. Severely obdurate and uncompliant, I kept my boots in continuous service above and below the very insteps which they were made to infold.

All things considered, Ethiopia, in the most free and extensive signification of the word, is a very remarkable part of the world. The continent of Africa comprises a territory whose area covers nearly eleven millions of square miles; being, next to Asia, the largest division of land on our globe. It contains about three millions of square miles more territory than North America, is considerably larger than all Europe and South America combined, and is more than three times larger than Europe by itself. The extreme length of Africa, from north to south, measures a distance of about five thousand miles; while, in its widest part, its breadth is not less than four thousand six hundred miles. Through the Semitic and other semi-Caucasian cities of Egypt, through Caucasian-founded Carthage, and through other white and half-white settlements in northern Africa, civilization has been gently, most of the time too gently, offering itself to the negroes almost ever since the dawn of authentic history; but they have always repulsed it with rudeness, with revilings, with riotous rashness, and with murder. Neither of the two great Americas, nor Australasia, no, nor even Europe itself, has enjoyed such early and various and favorable opportunities for culture and refinement as, especially since the first days of Israelitic and Phœnician expansion, have been extended to Africa, both north and south of the great desert of Sahara. This monster region of sterility, this mighty desert in the midst of an almost immeasurable continent, is, however, as a torrid waste in Africa, of much less superficial extent than the aggregate of our frigid wastes in North America. Yet, in all the essentials which constitute and characterize the greatness and grandeur of nations, little white Rhode Island, the runtiest of our States, despite her comparative youth and inexperience, is this day infinitely superior to the whole vast area of big black Negroland.

Coming down from the earlier ages, when the active and enterprising whites first brought themselves and their institutions in contact with the inert and listless blacks, we find that, in the seventh century preceding the Christian era, as related by Herodotus, the " Father of History," a company of Phœnician navigators, under the patronage of Necho, the Egyptian king of that epoch, made a three-years' voyage round Lybia, Ethiopia, Africa; having sailed out through the Erythræan Sea, the Red Sea, on the East, and returned by way of the Pillars of Hercules, the Strait of Gibraltar, on the West. About two centuries later, as we learn from his Periplus, Hanno, the Carthaginian navigator, (a white man, of Phœnician descent,) who was contemporary with Pericles of Greece and Cincinnatus of Rome, made very important explorations and discoveries along a great part of the west coast of Africa; and from his time, down through the long period of nearly two thousand years, the whites of both northern Africa and southern Europe kept well ajar the doors of civilization to the negroes in Negroland, and encouraged them in every possible manner, but always in vain, to adopt habits of life more in conformity with the laws of common decency and respectability and human progress and welfare. Then, in 1412, twenty odd years before the birth of Columbus, Prince Henry of Portugal, son of King John I, began to incite and promote a series of bold African explorations, which, wisely continued by his successors, finally culminated, in 1487, in the glorious discovery and rounding of the Cape of Good Hope, by Bartholomew Dias. That was five years prior to the discovery of America by Christopher Columbus; and it is by no means improbable that the brilliant success of the Portuguese navigator stimulated very materially, in the breast of the Italio-Spanish discoverer, a spirit of world-wide enterprise and adventure.

In 1618, the African Company of Great Britain established English settlements near the mouth of the Gambia. The Dutch founded Cape Colony in 1650. French settlements on the banks of the Senegal and along the coast between that river and Cape Verde, were made in 1675. Sierra Leone was settled by the English in 1787. Wholly at the expense, and solely under the advice and direction of benevolent-minded white Americans, Liberia was settled by free negroes from the United States in 1820. It thus appears that while the negro's way was paid from Africa by a low class of white men, whose inordinate cupidity, in connection with his atrocious cowardice, led them to capture and treat him as a slave, his way was paid back to Africa by a higher class of white men, who, notwithstanding the generosity and nobleness of their natures, yet lacked the wit and foresight necessary to perceive the utter ultimate uselessness of making any additional effort to lift him alive out of the black and blighting shades of barbarism in which he has been so stupidly sleeping and steeping and slaveing and starving during all the long centuries of the past.

Apparently in wilful or perverse ignorance of these plain facts, however, there are multitudes of otherwise sensible and worthy Caucasians, in the United States and elsewhere, constantly speaking and acting in real or pretended blindness to all that has been thought and said and done and suffered for the negro by the ancient white Phœnicians, Carthaginians, Egyptians, Assyrians, Arabians, Grecians and Romans; and by the modern white Portugues, Spaniards, Italians, Frenchmen, Germans, Britons and Americans; who exclaim in argument, and in extenuation of the darky's despicable duncery and dronishness, that he, poor fellow, has never yet had a fair chance! Fy! Fudge! Fiddlesticks! The negro, forsooth, has never yet had a fair chance? I know very well what would be a proper system of discipline for the mind-deficient or mind-diseased Caucasians who nauseatingly unbridle their tongues to babble and gabble such intolerable nonsense as this. Every time they malapertly separate their lips for the utterance of pro-negro sophistries and misstatements, from one to three fresh-boiled potatoes, about the size of owls' eggs, slightly cooled down to the two hundredth degree of Fahrenheit, ought to be inserted within the molar-touching and distensible vicinage of their uncomely cheeks. That, as I conceive, is what would constitute a most fit and wholesome corrective of the unworthily white apologists for a race of vile-visaged and mean-spirited blockheads, as naturally and unchangeably base and beggarly as they are black.

The simple truth is, that the negro, from the time when he first became known, in the dim ages of the past, down to the present day, has had, from outside influences, far more, and far better opportunities for improvement and progress than any white race on the face of the whole earth. In fact, there has always been, on the part of many of the larger-hearted and purer-minded classes of all the white peoples who have ever come in contact with the negro, a general and continuous combination of misplaced sympathy and action in his behalf; such an organized concentration of earnest effort in his interest, indeed, as has never yet been devised or practiced for the exaltation of any one of the different white families or nations of mankind. Yet everything that has been done for him has been done in vain. He is the same savage to-day that he was thousands upon thousands of years ago, when the infant Moses, famishing for feminine favors, was found fretting among the bulrushes near the banks of the Nile; and if, unfortunately for the world, this thick-lipped and flat-nosed non-proficient, this ink-colored and ogre-like jackanape, this night-born and bane-bringing tomnoddy, should live so long, he will not be a whit better off ten thousand years hence than he was then or is now. Still tolerated in Caucasian communities, he may, as he has already done, contribute very disastrously to the demoralization and degradation of the natures of a certain sort of uncertain white men, bringing them down, in many cases, by means of mulattoism and other mongrel and monstrous misdeeds, almost to his own low level; but left to himself, pushed aside, driven away, as he ought to be, just as if he were a mangy or leprous cur, he will for a time remain in existence, a delinquent, a rapscallion, a reprobate, and will then die and disappear forever; so that he will thenceforth be known only in defunct and fossil form ; and very soon after the extinction of his race the whole earth will joyfully reawaken and find itself born anew to a higher and whiter and better life. Not more foolishly and fruitlessly did the mediæval and self-deluded alchemists of Europe experiment long and laboriously in their endeavors to transmute base materials into precious metals, than the over-credulous negrophilists of America are now struggling, —struggling against the decrees of Heaven itself,—to convert fell and fated blackamoors into men of estimable traits of character.

One of the very worst things about slavery was, that it brought and fostered the two races face to face, and kept them in continuous juxtaposition; a most heterogeneous and sinister condition of things, under which the negroes' negative influence for evil against the whites always preponderated over the whites' positive influence for evil against the blacks ; so that, considered collectively, and taking into account all the facts and consequences, the whites were invariably the greater sufferers. Yet the whole system of slavery, on either side, was one only of evil, and that continually. Most sincerely and profoundly do I thank God that we have so completely emancipated the negroes from ourselves; for, in simple truth, as every well-informed person is aware, the work of freeing the fungous and fœtid fellows was our own work, the work of white men, and not the work of the blacks themselves. That, though, was truly a very important step in the right direction. Yet we shall have earned the honors of a far more brilliant and laudable achievement, when we succeed,—as God grant we may succeed erelong,— in thoroughly and forever emancipating ourselves from the negroes. That indeed is the next and, beyond all question, the most momentous step for us to take ; and it is eminently desirable and proper that we should take it, or at least begin to take it, at the earliest practicable period.

Never does a dog more delight in securing for himself the overruling providence and protection of a white master, than does the negro delight in securing for himself the same boon; in which case both the dog and the negro are, in one sense, to be complimented and envied; while the white master, in at least nine cases in ten, is to be both pitied and blamed. The white man who degrades himself by becoming the master, or employer, or overseer, of the negro, or by any other sort of close relationship with the caitiff, thereby inevitably incurs the imminent risk, to both himself and his posterity, of being, soon or late, involved in all the worst vices and crimes which have ever yet oppressed the human heart, or blackened the pages of history. In one way, or in another, the negro will always victimize us, as a hanger-on, whenever he has it in his power to do so, just as will also the flea, the tick, the jigger, the louse and the chinch. It behooves us all to guard, with especial vigilance, the integrity of our blood, our health, our substance, our peace and our honor. Pestiferous creatures must no longer be gently cared for and nurtured, as if they had an indefeasible right to demand sumptuous maintenance and peculiar privileges at the expense of their betters; nor must things positively deleterious in themselves be quietly suffered to exist at large, as if they were not already teeming and overflowing with the latent agencies of a common fatality.

Henceforth, with the past and the present in full view before us, justice and acumen and common sense, and an enlightened regard for the future general welfare of the world, dictate to us but one policy to be pursued toward the negro, toward the Indian, toward the Chinese, and toward all other races of mankind not white, not wise, not worthy; and that policy has already been well portrayed to us by our prudent forefathers of New England and other conspicuously and gloriously white sections of the United States, in their temporary intercourse with the aboriginal and abandoned and extirpable sons of the soil. As the humble but honored and honorable white instruments of a white and ever-whitening Providence, it is to be hoped that we may not, at any time, be found to be reprehensibly nor remissly unmindful of the high privileges and white duties which so momentously devolve upon us in this regard.

Despite the superficially formed and flippantly expressed judgments of a very considerable part of mankind, we shall all be rewarded, here or hereafter, in exact proportion to the faithfulness and efficiency of our services in any really good words or works which may constitute the most prominent features of our respective careers. In the preëminently good and all-important work of whitening up three Americas, Africa, Asia and Oceanica, let there be no cessation nor intermission whatever; for just as these several grand divisions of our globe shall become more and more white, and more and more like New England and Old England and the continent of Europe, there will be a corresponding expansion of the area of civilization and progress, and in due time the inestimable blessings of peace, plenty, purity and happiness will universally abound with the most exquisite and delightful profusion.

Yours, very truly,
H. R. HELPER.

MR. HELPER TO CONGRESSMAN COX.

St. Louis, *August 25, 1879.*
Hon. S. S. Cox, *New York.*

DEAR SIR: My thanks are especially due to you, and I desire to offer them accordingly, for the varied and sincere pleasure which I have just derived anew from a reperusal of your long and meandering, yet very agreeable and successful, "Search for Winter Sunbeams," through Italy, Spain, Corsica, and Algeria. Of all your books, this is the one which my wife and myself like best; and the place it occupies in our library is immediately between "Seward's Travels Around the World," and "The Old World in its New Face," by Dr. Bellows.

By your "Buckeye Abroad" and your "Search for Winter Sunbeams," you have secured for yourself a firm and exalted position among travellers and authors; by your "Eight Years in Congress," you have clearly established your right to be ranked as a statesman; and by your explanation of the volatile and exquisite mysteries of "Why We Laugh," you have proved yourself a philosopher. So, my good friend, what more do you want in this world? or what higher ambition can you reasonably indulge or expect to gratify? I can conceive of only one other round in the ladder of fame to which you may perhaps prudently aspire; but whether that might not be on the descending scale, rather than on the scale of elevation, admits, I think, of much doubt. So far as my own limited vision enables me to discern the situation, it now only remains for you to become two-fifths crazy, like Oliver Wendell Holmes, and turn poet!

In reality, however, I trust you will attempt nothing of the sort, but stand steadfast just where you are, as a man of plain and strong common sense, as one of the Republic's spiciest and sprightliest Representatives, and as a national legislator of well-proved integrity and ability, who, though possibly unable to boast in fact of a larger share of infallibility of judgment than is claimed by the popishly pious Pecci in the palace of the Vatican, is nevertheless always found on the right side of every measure of government in which is certain to inhere any logical and inevitable outcome of positive importance. On this subject I am quite earnest in my wishes; for, without meaning to flatter you in the least, I have discovered that, touching our foreign relations particularly, you possess a quality and scope of statesmanship that cannot be well spared from the sphere of our Congress at Washington.

Not longer in the future than next year, if not in the latter part of this, it may be proper for me, it may become my duty, to ask the American Congress to ponder and act on the proposition whether, on the one hand, there are not good and sufficient reasons why, regardless of mere personal considerations, and only for considerations of Justice and Honor and State, we should at once reduce the grade of our diplomatic representative in the Empire of Brazil to a fourth-class ministership, or a consul-generalship, and, on the other hand, whether there are not very cogent and solid reasons why we should, without delay, raise the grade of our diplomatic representative in the Argentine Republic to a first-class ambassadorship. It is further possible, and by no means improbable, that I may take occasion to suggest certain needed changes in our diplomatic relations with two or three of the West Coast nationalities of South America; and feeling assured that you will continue to weigh all the facts and arguments and suggestions which may be submitted to you, in the scale or balance of their own merits, I shall, with your permission, presume to reckon on the very efficient aid which you yourself will doubtless be able to render me in this absolutely serious and prosaic work; provided, as I have already surmised, provided you do not meanwhile, in a rash effort to outrival the rhythmical reputation of the Hub-honored Holmes, become two-fifths demented, and turn poet.

Pray, sir, be kind enough to indicate to me what I may depend on in this regard. In accordance with my usual habit, I shall confidently hope for the best; and the best that can be in this case, is that, turning a cold shoulder to the bewitching beckons and blandishments of the Boston bard, you will unswervingly remain true to your own elder self, hereafter as heretofore, and then all will be as right and regular and merry as a happy marriage.

Yours, most respectfully,
H. R. HELPER.

CONGRESSMAN COX TO MR. HELPER.

NEW YORK, *August* 30, 1879.

H. R. HELPER, *Esq., St. Louis*.

DEAR SIR: I am in receipt of your interesting and unique letter of the 25th instant. Waiving all the neat and suave things you have said to me and of me, and crimsoning not a little with that roseate modesty for which the average Congressman is not celebrated either by Boston Muses or journalistic squibs, I presume to respond,—that, perfunctorily, as Chairman of a Committee on Foreign affairs, and otherwise as a citizen and a Member of Congress, I shall be glad to hear and heed any suggestions you may make pertinent to any judicious and necessary reform in our diplomatic relations. I am sure the Committee on Foreign Affairs, in the House, which includes myself, will be disposed to consider, in the fullest spirit of fairness and friendship toward yourself personally, any matter of public importance which you may deem proper or have occasion to lay before it. With kind recollections of pleasant interviews with you in other days,

I am, very truly yours,
S. S. COX.

MR. HELPER TO DR. LIEBER.

NEW YORK, *August* 30, 1872.

DR. FRANCIS LIEBER,

DEAR SIR: Permit me to request of you the favor of informing me where I may be able to purchase, if it be on sale in any bookstore or elsewhere, your poem, written many years ago, on the long-proposed Ship Canal through Central America; a poem which I have never yet had the pleasure of either reading or seeing, but complimentary references to which I saw in a Spanish-printed newspaper at Cochabamba, in Bolivia, when I was there, last January. Yet I may here very frankly acknowledge, that it is the subject itself rather than the literary merits of the poem, however ingeniously and powerfully the theme may have been treated by you in metrical form, which influences me, for the most part, in making this request; it being my earnest desire to obtain all the stimulative facts, arguments and suggestions that can be easily got together in advocacy of the cutting, just so soon as may be practicable, of the huge interoceanic highway for commerce under consideration, whether across the Isthmus of Darien, the Isthmus of Nicaragua, or the Isthmus of Tehuantepec. For the general good and advancement of all parts of the New World especially, the projected canal is very greatly needed; let it be cut.

Yours, truly,

H. R. HELPER.

DR. LIEBER TO MR. HELPER.

NEW YORK, *September* 2, 1872.

HINTON R. HELPER, *Esq.*,

DEAR SIR: Your note of the 30th ultimo brings to my

recollection an old and rather fugitive effusion, too diminutive and unimportant ever to have been published by itself, and therefore not purchasable in separate form. I wrote it nearly a quarter of a century ago, and it was then published in several periodicals; but in this country at least, it seems to have been lying dormant for many years. I feel flattered to hear from you that what I was quite prepared to regard as a fossil, has but recently cropped out in animated form on the surface of Bolivia. The incentive to my writing the poem was a portion of a very prosaic but terse and statesmanlike Message from President Polk to Congress in 1847, during the progress of our war with Mexico; and I will now quote the particular part of his message which aroused the afflatus of my good-natured but feeble Muse.

"The Peace Commissioner from the United States to Mexico was authorized to agree to the establisment of the Rio Grande as the boundary, * * * and to obtain a cession to the United States of the Provinces of New Mexico and Upper California, and the privilege of the right of way across the Isthmus of Tehuantepec. * * * It has been my constant effort to maintain and cultivate the most intimate relations of friendship with all the independent powers of South America; and this policy has been attended with the happiest results. It is true, that the settlement and payment of many just claims of American citizens against these nations have been long delayed. The peculiar position in which they have been placed, and the desire on the part of my predecessors, as well as myself, to grant them the utmost indulgence, have hitherto prevented these claims from being urged in a manner demanded by strict justice. The time has arrived when they ought to be finally adjusted and liquidated, and efforts are now making for that purpose."

In view of the information given in your supplemental communication, in the form of a postscript, I take it for granted that certain striking coincidences apparent in, or connected with, the foregoing extract from President Polk's Message to Congress, in 1847, will not fail to attract your attention. The matter contained in that extract, besides serving its purposes so well in the sterner actualities and realities of our nation, afforded me, at the same time, ample cantering ground for my Pegasus; and it now tallies exactly with the large practical acquaintance which you yourself are manifestly making with South American affairs. Taking pleasure in transcribing for you, from one of my repositories of things personal, the little poem in regard to which you have made inquiry, and which you will find herewith inclosed, I shall be especially happy if you can use it in any manner that will aid in carrying out its author's most ardent aspirations, as they are therein but too imperfectly expressed.

Yours faithfully,
FRANCIS LIEBER.

THE CENTRAL AMERICAN SHIP CANAL.

FROM THE ATLANTIC TO THE PACIFIC.

AN ODE TO THE AMERICAN PEOPLE.

BY FRANCIS LIEBER.

Rend America asunder!
And perfect the Binding Sea
That emboldens Man and tempers—
 Make the ocean free!

Break the bolt which bars the passage;
Then our Mississippi pours
Western wealth still farther westward;
 Let that sea be ours—

Ours by all the hardy whalers,
By the westward Oregon,
By the west-impelled and working
　　Unthralled Saxon son.

When the mighty God of Nature
Made this favored Continent,
He allowed it, yet un-severed,
　　That a race be sent,

Able, mindful of his purpose,
Prone to people, to subdue,
And to bind the lands with iron,
　　Or to force them through.

Long indeed they have been wooing,
The Pacific and his bride;
Now 'tis time for holy wedding—
　　Join them by the tide.

What the prophet-navigator
Seeking straits to far Cathay,
But begun, now consummate it—
　　Make the water-way.

Blessed eyes that shall behold it,
When the pointing boom shall veer,
Leading through the parted Andes,
　　While all nations cheer!

There at Suez, Europe's mattock
Cuts the briny road with skill,
And must Darien bid defiance
　　To the pilot still?

Up, then, at it! Earnest People!
Bravely wrought just now thy blade,
But there's fresher fame in store yet,
　　Glory for the spade!

What we want is nought in envy,
Nought,—for *all* we pioneer;
Let the keels of every nation
    Through the Isthmus steer.

Write the tidings on a pillar
That the Law of Nations, hear!
E'en in war; proclaims this channel
    Free for all and clear.

Shall the globe be always girded
Ere we get to Brahma's priest?
Take the tissues of your Lowells
    Westward to the East.

Ye that vanquish pain and distance,
Ye, en-meshing Time with wire,
Court ye patiently for ever
    Yon Antarctic ire?

Shall the mariner for ever
Double the impeding Capes,
While his longsome and retracing
    Needless course he shapes?

Let the vastness not appall thee;
Greatness is thy destiny;
Let the doubters not recall thee;
    Venture suits the free.

Like a seer I see thee throning
Winland! strong in freedom's health;
Warding peace on both the waters,
    Widest Commonwealth—

Crowned with wreaths that still grow greener,
Guerdon for untiring pain,
For the wise, the stout and steadfast;
    Rive the land in twain!

Cleave America asunder!
This is worthy work for thee;
Hark! the seas roll up imploring
"Make the ocean free!"

MR. HELPER TO CONSUL CAHILL.

St. Louis, *September* 1, 1879.
Hon. John F. Cahill,
Consul for Mexico, St. Louis, Missouri.

Dear Sir: Your brave championship of the Isthmus of Tehuantepec as the best of all the proposed routes for a Ship Canal from the Gulf of Mexico, or from the Caribbean Sea, to the Pacific Ocean, is marked by so much unmistakable sincerity and patriotism, that, to say the least, it justly inspires for your opinions a high degree of respect and confidence. Yet, as a comparatively silent but diligent student, during the last twenty odd years, of this vast and important problem, I may frankly inform you that I have thus far failed to observe the adduction of any fact, or reason, or argument, from any source whatever, which would seem to be incontrovertibly conclusive in favor of Tehuantepec, as against Nicaragua and Darien.

Just twenty-five years ago, that is to say in 1854, I crossed the Isthmus of Nicaragua; since which time I have twice crossed the Isthmus of Darien; and, judging from the general topographical features of those comparatively narrow necks of land, it is, with a sufficiency of money and skill and physical force and industry, perfectly practicable to cut and utilize a ship canal across one or the other, or both. Several of our able and distinguished naval officers, especially Rear Admiral Ammen, Commodore Schufeldt, Commanders Selfridge and Lull, and Lieutenant Collins, who have, from time to time, respectively, been commissioned by our Government to examine those routes, with the object of ascertaining, if possible, which is the better of the two for the purpose indicated, have reported favorably in either case, according to the line of their respective operations; and the sterling character for veracity of these competent officers being well established, there can be no question that all their reports are worthy of credence and acceptance to the fullest extent of their positive statements and recommendations. Nor, if one may form an opinion on the careful surveys and reports of such eminent engineers as Gen. Barnard and Col. Williams, do I doubt in the least the feasibility of a maritime ship canal across the Isthmus of Tehuantepec.

Distance alone, however, distance of width, as it seems to me, is a very serious drawback to both Tehuantepec and Nicaragua, in comparison with Darien. A good ship always dislikes and dreads the land, except when she is strongly attached and made fast to a friendly anchor or hawser. From Gulf to Ocean, across Tehuantepec, the distance is one hundred and seventy-three miles; from the Caribbean to the Pacific, across Nicaragua, the distance is no less than one hundred and eighty-one miles; while from Aspinwall to Panama, across Darien, the distance is only forty-six miles. These simple and undeniable facts certainly constitute a very powerful, if not irresistible, argument in favor of Darien. and more particularly so since the engineering difficulties there apparent in nature's whimsical works, are probably no greater than those which would be encountered in corresponding lengths or breadths of land, or land and sections of zigzag and unserviceable river-bed, along either of the other routes.

Still, though well pleased with the narrowest route, yet I am by no means so fixed in my predilections for Panama as to be proof against conviction of the existence of a better place. Other conditions being equal, or even approximately so, I, as a citizen of the United States, should much prefer the geographical position of Tehuantepec, because of its greater proximity to all of our own eastern and southern and western seaports, as well as because of its being, for us, so much nearer Japan, China, India and Australia, and also because, in comparison with Nicaragua and Darien, it is generally believed to possess very superior climatic and sanitary advantages. What I should now particularly like to see would be the appointment at once, by the Government of the United States, of our own meritorious and far-famed Capt. Eads and two other first-class civil engineers,—no matter whether or not any one of them has ever seen either Annapolis or West Point,—all new men in this business, as a plenipotentiary and decisive commission to examine together the three routes so much discussed, first Darien, then Nicaragua, and then Tehuantepec, and report, at the earliest convenient day, the result of their joint labors and deliberations, stating unequivocally which of the three routes, under all the present and prospective circumstances of the times, commends itself to them, or to any two of them, Capt. Eads himself being one of the two, as being the best, and giving besides, in detail, the reasons which shall have led them to their conclusions. Then, as I feel fully persuaded, it would be entirely safe and proper for our own people, after having obtained all the necessary franchises and privileges, to go to work at once, by themselves exclusively, as an American company, and carefully avoiding all entangling European copartnerships, cut the canal,—a wide and deep and unlocked and unobstructed tide-level canal, if such a canal be fairly feasible,—without thenceforth ever deigning to listen to even so much as one more word on the subject of disputed or rival routes.

If Mexico would but faithfully and efficiently coöperate with us, it is a weighty consideration whether, in a certain contingency, before or during or after the carrying out of any European-Panama project, we might not even go so far as to open at Tehuantepec an independent canal in sharply-defined and never-ending opposition to Darien; provided the latter should, in any manner, so demean and un-Americanize herself as to forfeit the esteem and good will of the two great republics of North America. An intercontinental enterprise of huge dimensions, which I myself now have in hand, but the nature of which I need not here stop to explain, except to say that it is at least three times the magnitude of the proposed interoceanic canal, or, in other words, about thrice the size and grandeur of any one of our transcontinental railroads, will, I trust, be successfully undertaken and consummated, solely under American auspices; by American engineering, and with American capital, prior to the 14th day of October, 1892, which will be the four hundredth anniversary of Columbus's discovery of the New World; and, so far as I am able to perceive, there is no good reason why a judicious and energetic employment of the same mighty influences and forces of our own and sundry neighboring nationalities, may not secure to us, simultaneously, a superb and ever-enduring ship canal across Tehuantepec, or Nicaragua, or Darien. Zealously entertaining these several views, I have the honor to request that you will kindly oblige me with a condensed statement of what you yourself regard as the strongest and most convincing points of your own advocacy of the Tehuantepec route; and I shall also esteem it a special favor if you will be good enough to inform me, if you know, how the masses of the Mexican people themselves are now estimating and measuring this momentous matter.

I am, sir, with great respect, your obedient servant,

H. R. HELPER.

It is with much regret that lack of space here prevents me from printing more than about one-half of an important reply which I have had the honor to receive from Consul Cahill, in answer to the last foregoing letter. Hence, the frequent use of asterisks between the several extracts which constitute the following imperfect compendium of his views, in support of the claims of Tehuantepec.

H. R. H.

CONSUL CAHILL TO MR. HELPER.

CONSULATE OF THE REPUBLIC OF MEXICO,
ST. LOUIS, MISSOURI, *September* 3, 1879.

H. R. HELPER, *Esq.*,

DEAR SIR: I have had the pleasure of receiving and reading, with great interest, your esteemed communication of the 1st instant, in which you do me the honor of qualifying my unwavering advocacy of the Tehuantepec route as being marked by unmistakable sincerity and patriotism. Before entering on the argumentative points of the very important subject concerning which you have addressed me, permit me to say that, independently of the national reputation which your published works have achieved for you among the people of the United States, your name and your labors in Central and South America, within the last few years, have become so intimately and thoroughly identified with all movements tending to the development of the vast resources of our Spanish-speaking neighbors, that, in addressing you, I feel at liberty to do so in the frankest possible manner; particularly as the subject under consideration is one of world-wide interest, and involves many weighty questions, the present judicious decision of which may enable us to avoid much future embarrassment and many grave complications with one or more of the transatlantic powers, under whose auspices it would appear that the grand work of wedding the two great oceans has already, in a measure, been begun.

Especially do you honor me in asking my opinion on this momentous matter, inasmuch as you must be aware that I am myself not an engineer, and have never surveyed nor even traversed either of the three mooted routes for the proposed interoceanic canal, which have, at different periods, during the last three hundred years, attracted the attention of the scientific world, and furnished a theme of profound study and investigation for the ablest engineers of both America and Europe. Yet, notwithstanding the lack of scientific acquirement and personal experience in this projected enterprise, I have, like yourself, for several years past, been a close and painstaking student of all the commercial problems connected with the prosperity of my own country and her natural allies and neighbors, the Republics of Mexico and Central and South America ; and, as the editor of *El Comercio del Valle*, a Spanish and English newspaper, which I founded in this city, nearly four years ago, with the cherished object of bringing into closer and more friendly intercourse the peoples of the United States and those of all Spanish America, the field of my observation and the scope of my experience have, in some degree, compensated for the absence of the scientific knowledge which may, by many, be deemed necessary to give weight and value to opinions on a subject upon which regularly educated engineers are supposed to exercise an almost exclusive right to be heard.

I am myself a firm believer in the infallibility of science, but not in the infallibility of scientific men ; for whose opinions, however, I entertain the highest respect. With you, sir, I fully concur in the belief that, with a sufficiency of money, a ship canal may be cut across either or all three of the isthmuses,—Tehuantepec, Nicaragua, and Darien; but there are other considerations to be regarded, which, in my opinion, are of far greater importance than the mere difference of a few millions of dollars in the comparative cost of these several routes. It is quite probable, though, that these considerations, which I will now explain, have greater weight with me, as an American, than they are likely to have with citizens or subjects of any transatlantic country. In the first place, while admitting he apparent advantage of the Darien route in point of narrowness, it has been, time and again, demonstrated that the serious difficulties to be encountered in the excavations, the large amount of tunnelling necessary to be done, and the very notorious and fatal unhealthfulness of the climate, together with the incalculably great cost, constitute grave, if not insurmountable, obstacles to its selection as the best route. Again, the persistent advocacy of the isthmus of Darien by certain European governments and capitalists, and the recent selection of this route by M. De Lesseps' Congress at Paris, which refused even to consider the claims and merits of the other routes, by way respectively of Tehuantepec and Nicaragua, is but another strenuous effort on the part of our rivals of the Old World, to perpetuate their control over the commerce of South and Central America, at the expense and debarment of the United States.

You, sir, in the able communication which, while at Lima, in Peru, in the early part of last year, you addressed to the Hon. Richard W. Thompson, our Secretary of the Navy, at Washington, have not failed to observe the omnipresence of European influence throughout the southern hemisphere; and the following passage in that letter, which I had the pleasure of reproducing in the columns of my newspaper, many months before I had the honor of making your acquaintance, or knowing that you entertained any intention of ever coming to reside in the valley of the Mississippi, cannot be read too often, nor learned too well, by the people of the United States. * * *

Inasmuch as Darien, in comparison with Tehuantepec, is from one to two thousand miles further from our Atlantic and Gulf seaports, it is correspondingly nearer to the seaports of many of the European countries, whose commercial supremacy and political sway have ever been hostile to the promotion of intimate relations of any kind between the United States and the many independent nationalities which lie to the south of us. It is manifest, therefore, that a ship canal at Darien would militate against the interests of the people of both North and South America. The Nicaragua route does not present, in so forcible a manner, the geographical disadvantages of Darien; but it is too remote from the coasts of the two great republics of North America, and is, besides, a longer and more difficult and expensive route than that by way of the isthmus of Tehuantepec; necessitating the coöperation of the two diminutive republics of Costa Rica and Nicaragua, which have heretofore invariably maintained toward each other an irreconcilable spirit of jealous rivalry in this regard. Holding in view the following extract from a report made in the year 1866, by Rear Admiral Davis, of the United States Navy, it would seem to be a waste of time to devote further consideration to Nicaragua as an eligible route for a ship canal, since we have at Tehuantepec a much safer and healthier and better point for the meeting of the waters of the two mighty oceans. * * *

In considering the important question of severing the two great Americas, and thereby uniting the two great Oceans, by the construction of a ship canal hat will satisfy all the demands of the world's commerce, and become at the same time a fitting and perpetual monument to the superior genius and civilization of the American people, my reasons for preferring Tehuantepec over all the other proposed routes, may be briefly summed up by stating that it is much nearer to all our ports. Moreover, it is shorter than Nicaragua, and not more expensive than Darien. Again, there is another reason, of a sanitary nature, which, when thoroughly investigated, will, in my opinion, at once lead to the adoption of the Tehuantepec route, to the proper exclusion of all other claims and propositions on the part of individuals, localities and nations. * * *

It is perfectly plain that the people whose real interests the cutting of the canal will most affect, either by promotion or depression, are the inhabitants of the United States and Mexico, and more especially the indwellers of the Mississippi Valley; and, as I have endeavored to show, nature points unerringly to the isthmus of Tehuantepec as the most proper place for the interoceanic communication thus sought. There, without obstruction, the Mississippi would flow freely into the pacific; and it is there that already its yellow waters are often seen, endeavoring to cut their own way to the great western ocean, into which, if given passage, they will pour most of the fever-engendering and mortiferous matters which, during the process of gradual dissolution and decay, annually fill so many of our fair cities with disease and death on the one hand, and with financial disaster and ruin on the other. The early cutting of a ship canal across the isthmus of Tehuantepec, no matter how great the cost which may be unavoidably necessary for the full and perfect accomplishment of the object, will, as I conceive, be the only wise solution of a stupendous problem which now largely involves the welfare of the whole commercial world. This vast enterprise, as it seems to me, is one which should receive the immediate attention and aid of the Government of the United States; and it is but reasonable to believe that it would be warmly approved and encouraged by the Republic of Mexico, through whose favored territory the proposed canal would pass. * * *

Yours, very respectfully,
JOHN F. CAHILL.

IMPERIAL BRAZIL

AS THE

Diplomatic Deceiver and Despoiler

OF AN

UNSUSPECTING FAMILY OF

Straightforward and Confiding Democrats,

WHO, IN AUGUST, 1867, WERE SO

Rash and Unrepublican and Reprehensible

AS TO

PUT THEIR FAITH IN PRINCES;

AN
EPISTOLARY AND
DOCUMENTARY HISTORY OF THE DOUBLE-FACED
AND UNDERHANDED INJUSTICE AND INJURY INFLICTED ON
ERNEST FIEDLER, HIS WIDOW, AND CHILDREN,
CITIZENS OF THE REPUBLIC OF THE UNITED STATES OF
AMERICA, BY THE GOVERNMENT OF THE
EMPIRE OF BRAZIL.

A BRIEF OF THE CASE,

BY

HINTON ROWAN HELPER,

Who, as the Attorney for his woefully wronged and outraged Clients, respectfully presents to the Honor observing and Equity-enforcing Congress of his own Country, at Washington, the accompanying Claim for Rightful Reparation and Damages.

ST. LOUIS:
SEPTEMBER 29, 1879.

A MEMORIAL.

FROM

HELEN M. FIEDLER, EXECUTRESS OF THE LAST WILL
AND TESTAMENT OF ERNEST FIEDLER, A CITI-
ZEN OF THE REPUBLIC OF THE UNITED
STATES OF AMERICA, AGAINST
THE GOVERNMENT OF THE
EMPIRE OF BRAZIL.

To the Honorable the Senators and Representatives of the United States of America in Congress Assembled:
GENTLEMEN: Your petitioner, Helen M. Fiedler, of the city of New York, Executress of the last Will and Testament of Ernest Fiedler, formerly of St. Louis, in Missouri, but more latterly of the State of New York, begs leave, through the mediumship of her attorney, Hinton R. Helper, recently of North Carolina, but now of the State of Missouri, to whom she has herein given the fullest and most perfect and irrevocable powers of discretionary action in her behalf, to apprise your honorable body of the details of a series of very gross and grievous wrongs, which, during the last twelve years, she has suffered at the hands of the Brazilian Government, in contumacy, and to solicit from you such early and rightful legislation in the premises as will soon result in reasonable reparation for all the wrongs so inflicted.

The whole case, at least in most of its important facts and bearings, is so fully explained in the following somewhat voluminous correspondence between your petitioner's said attorney and other gentlemen directly and indirectly connected with the reclamation, as prosecutors, defendants, querists, informants, and diplomatists, that she deems it quite unnecessary to reproduce here the broad and valid grounds of her great grievance. The documentary information and evidence herewith submitted for the consideration of your honorable body, will prove conclusively that the bad inheritance, in part, which a good husband and father has thus left to his widow and children, is in no respect whatever attributable to any neglect or other fault of his own; but only to the cruel duplicities and subterfuges of an anachronistic and mislocated empire, which, though in fact so effeminate and frail and fraudful as to be thoroughly despicable, yet blushes not to make supercilious pretensions to the possession of special virtues in its form and administration of government.

So long as your petitioner's husband, who was really upright and worthy in all his relations with mankind, did business only with free and white citizens who were the outgrowth of the democratic and republican institutions or North America, his career was one of gradual and uninterrupted success; but from the very moment when he was, as if by inveiglement, first brought in contact with servile and sable subjects of the Brazilian Empire, who, as agents for the government of that country, commenced to practice against him the vile arts of insincerity and dissimulation and double-dealing, which are invariably characteristic ot all peoples among whom, as in Brazil, monarchy and jesuitry and bi-colored hybridity are locked hand in hand in the enforcement and perpetuation of a complex system of sheer despotism over both body and mind, from that very moment his usual prosperity and vivacity began to forsake him; and, as if by a strangely inexplicable and irresistible spell, becoming more and more entangled within the meshes of evil thus woven around him, he, though comparatively yet young, soon sickened and died.

Almost mysteriously, indeed, as between the baleful blandishments of the Brazilians on the one hand, and their bluff baseness on the other, the husband of your petitioner seemed to be absolutely benumbed and blasted, as if, unawares and instantly, the virus of a most venomous serpent had been injected into his veins without his ability to summon to his relief any remedy whatever, or even hope of recovery. It was, in truth, as if all at once he had been awakened to the worst realities of a horrible dream; for, up to the uniformly happy period of his life thus referred to, just prior to his transactions with the Brazilian Government, he had always firmly refused to believe in the existence of any such depth of human depravity as then, for the first time, revealed itself to him, and against him, through the manœuvres of various wily functionaries fresh from the imperial and pestilential palace at Rio de Janeiro. Innately and scrupulously honest and truthful himself, and always accustomed to deal only with considerate and just-minded men, he was totally unprepared, by either propensity or experience, to cope with the presumptuous prevarication and perfidy of the Brazilian agents, into whose pernicious power he had so unsuspectingly fallen. So appalling and overwhelming was both the bulk and the blackness of the turpitude thus brought to bear against him, that he was as completely stunned by the shock as if his whole system had been suddenly struck with paralysis of the worst sort; and it was under these circumstances, and in this situation, that, as if rendered comatose under a shuddering sensation of soul-sickening surprise, he staggered amid the mazes of a profound stupor, stumbled and fell, and never rose again.

Gentlemen of the American Congress: Your petitioner is perfectly aware that, in the very nature of things, it is impossible for you to restore to her or to her children the natural guardian and protector of a forlorn family, whom Brazil has most basely bereft of a husband on the one hand, and of a father on the oher; but it is within the power of your honorable body to redress, in part at least, the rank injustice of bad faith and financial default of which she and others near and dear to her have been made the victims, and of which she here earnestly complains. So far as it may be possible for the imperial and profligate Brazilians to repair the great wrongs which they have perpetrated against her, she respectfully entreats that you will constrain them to do so; for, in this regard, it is now manifest that, without constraint, without compulsion, they will still wilfully persist in the course of injury and outrage which they have so long pursued against her.

Collaterally with the simple and substantial facts of the chartering by the agents of the Brazilian Government of your petitioner's husband's steamship Circassian, and upon which full and ample facts, of themselves alone, she bases her just claim for compensation and indemnity, she would also specifically invite the attention of your honorable body to certain very strong points of legal and diplomatic similarity between this reclamation and the claim of Mr. Joseph H. Colton, of New York, against the Government of Bolivia, which is herewith printed and bound. The admonitions and mandates of international law in the one case are precisely the same as in the other; and, gentlemen, as you may readily and conveniently perceive for yourselves, by reference to the index at the close of this volume, those same admonitions and mandates have been very carefully collated and clearly cited, by your petitioner's attorney, (who was also Mr. Colton's attorney,) from the standard works of Grotius, Puffendorf, Vattel, Phillimore, Wildman, Marshall, Kent, Wheaton, Woolsey, Halleck, Curtis, Field, Evarts, and other erudite and distinguished publicists.

The whole matter, in whatever form or condition it may be found, now or hereafter, has been intrusted to your petitioner's permanent and plenipotentiary attorney, Mr. Helper, with whom alone any and all questions and considerations and interests concerning it, may be definitely and finally settled. Your petitioner's said attorney will inform your honorable body, as he has already informed herself, of an incalculably significant and responsible dilemma in which he has been placed by several of the more enlightened and progressive subjects of Brazil, who, in their patriotic desire to rescue their country from the blighting influences of monarchy and jesuitry and slavery, and also from the inertia and blackness and abomination of negroism and Indianism and Chineseism and bi-colored hybridism, have secretly and informally, but ardently, urged him to make use of the peculiar, if not providential, position and vantage-ground he now occupies, for assisting them to overthrow the demoralized and nerveless Empire, and to establish in its stead a virtuous and vigorous and advancive Republic; they having promised him, so far as it was competent for them to engage themselves to the fulfillment of such a promise, that, if he will, to the best of his ability, so aid them, by his pen, and otherwise as he himself may elect and find opportunity, he shall, within one year after the subversion of the proslavery and pro-negro and imperial and priestly power, receive from the White Republic twice the amount of his claim against the Black Empire.

This premature and anomalistic proposition your petitioner's attorney has neither accepted nor rejected; but, having in contemplation this very memorial to your honorable body, and confidently counting on the reasonable and right results which justice warrants him in expecting to issue from it, he has simply informed the proponents, (with whom, however, his best wishes are warmly associated,) that he has not yet exhausted all amicable or semi-amicable efforts which the laws and usages of nations provide for cases of this kind; and that, until all such efforts, of which this is the last, shall have been regularly made in good faith, and positively repelled, he has nothing further to remark on this subject. So saying, your humble petitioner again especially and earnestly solicits the intervention of your honorable body for justice to herself and children, as against Brazil, and sincerely hopes that her said attorney, in his constant devotion to her rights and interests, may never have any occasion to burden himself with the weighty and perilous contingencies of the ultimate and revolutionary resource thus apprehended.

HELEN M. FIEDLER, *Claimant.*

By her Attorney,
HINTON R. HELPER.

ST. LOUIS, MISSOURI,
September 29, 1879.

MR. HELPER TO MR. JORDAN.

NEW YORK, *May* 2, 1876.

HON. EDWARD JORDAN.

DEAR SIR: Aware as I am of your perfect familiarity with all the facts and circumstances of the claim of Ernest Fiedler against the Government of Brazil, growing out of the chartering by Domingo de Goicouria, an agent of Brazil for purposes of Immigration, of the steamship Circassian belonging to the claimant, in August, 1867, permit me to request that you will be kind enough to favor me, at your earliest convenience, with a synopsis of the whole case, as it stands to-day.

I make this request because, as you are aware, I have myself been commissioned to proceed in person to Rio de Janeiro, with the object of bringing this matter to a final adjustment; and I wish, therefore, to obtain possession of every fact and argument which may be rightly urged in support of the claim.

With the degree of light which I already have on this subject, I am unable to comprehend any principles of international law or equity upon which Brazil has so long failed to recognize the justice of the claim, and the consequent obligation resting upon herself to indemnify the claimant for the heavy expenses and losses which he and his vessel were subjected to in her service, at her own solicitation.

Yours, very respectfully
H. R. HELPER.

MR. JORDAN TO MR. HELPER.

NEW YORK, *May* 6, 1876.

HINTON ROWAN HELPER, *Esq*.

DEAR SIR: In reply to your letter of the 2d instant, making inquiry in regard to the claim of Helen M. Fiedler, as Executrix of Ernest Fiedler, deceased, against the Government of Brazil, I make the following statement:

In the year 1867, application was made to the said Ernest Fiedler, then the sole owner of the steamship Circassian, by Domingo de Goicouria, who claimed to be an agent of Emigration in the United States for the Brazilian Government, to charter the said steamship for a voyage from New Orleans to Rio de Janeiro, to transport emigrants from the United States to the Empire of Brazil. Before entering into such a transaction, however, Mr. Fiedler desired to be assured of the authority of Mr. Goicouria to act for the Bra-

zilian Government in the premises, and for that purpose
made inquiries on the subject, when he was shown by the
said Goicouria a power of attorney from Quintino de Souza
Bocayuva, fully authorizing the said Goicouria to exercise
all the powers of the said Bocayuva as agent of Emigration
for the Brazilian Government, and learned that the authority
of both the said Bocayuva and the said Goicouria, to charter
vessels for the conveyance of emigrants from the United
States to Brazil, had already been recognized by the Brazilian Government, and had been expressly affirmed by the
head of the Brazilian Legation in the United States, Mr.
Cavalcanti de Albuquerque, when applied to for information
on the subject, and in particular that the steamer Catherine
Whiting had, only a short time previously, completed a voyage under a charter-party executed by the said Goicouria in
all substantial respects similar to the one proposed for the
steamer Circassian, and on which the charter-money had
been paid by the Brazilian authorities. The statement of
the Brazilian Minister was contained in a letter dated March
13, 1867, and was very explicit, as follows:

"The agent of the Brazilian Immigration is Mr. Quin-
"tino de Souza Bocayuva. This gentleman has power to
"charter sailing vessels or steamers to take emigrants from
"the South part of the United States to Brazil. According
"to the contract made between the Imperial Government
"and the United States and Brazil Mail Steamship Company,
"he can have a delegate, and Mr. Domingo de Goicouria is
"the delegate appointed by him. I believe the Brazilian
"Government will approve what is done by the said agent."

On the faith of this assurance, the owners of the steamship Marmion, acting through Mr. Russell Sturgis, to whom
the letter of the Brazilian Minister was addressed, on the
day after its date, to-wit, on the 16th of March, 1867, entered into a charter party with the said Goicouria for the

making of a voyage by the said steamship Marmion, upon terms also substantially similar to those expressed in the charter-party of the Circassian, which voyage was performed; the charter-money provided for was paid by the Government of Brazil, and the said steamship had returned to New York a considerable time prior to the chartering of the Circassian.

Being thus fully satisfied of the authority of Mr. Goicouria, Mr. Fiedler, on the 21st of August, 1867, entered into a charter-party, by which it was provided that the said steamship Circassian, which was then on a voyage from New York to Bremen, should make a voyage from New Orleans to Rio de Janeiro, sailing from New Orleans on the 15th day of November, 1867, unless detained at Bremen or elsewhere by causes beyond the control of the said Fiedler, in which case she should sail within ten days after her arrival at New Orleans. The said charter-party also contained provisions in regard to which the steamship was to be kept, the supplies with which she was to be furnished, and other matters of importance, which it is not necessary here to notice, but which are definitely shown by the charter-party itself, a copy of which is among the papers. The following facts, however, are material to a full understanding of the grounds of the present claim, and of the frivolous objections which have thus far been urged against it. The said Goicouria was to be allowed ten running days for loading and discharging the said vessel, and was to pay the said Fiedler the sum of three hundred and fifty American gold dollars for every day the said vessel was detained beyond the time so allowed. He was to provide the said steamship with passengers in the steerage, not to exceed six hundred in number, and to pay the said Fiedler for the hire of the said vessel the sum of forty-two thousand American gold dollars, or the equivalent thereof in millreis, ten days after the completion of the voyage, and sixty American gold dollars in addition, for each cabin passenger; and the said parties respectively bound themselves each to the other for the performance of all the covenants and agreements of the said charter-party, in the penal sum of the charter-money, $42,000 in gold.

Immediately after the execution of this charter-party, Mr. Fiedler notified the master of the said steamship, Capt. Thomas S. Ellis, by letter addressed to him at Bremen, of the making thereof, and instructed him to purchase there certain necessary stores for the contemplated voyage, and to bring the vessel home to enter upon it, in accordance with the stipulations of the charter-party.

With these instructions the master, Capt. Ellis, complied, purchasing provisions and stores to the amount of about three thousand dollars, and returning to New York with the steamship at the earliest practicable day after the execution of the said charter-party.

The Circassian arrived in New York on the 2d of November, 1867, when it was found that she needed certain important repairs and alterations to fit her for the contemplated voyage; and these were made with the utmost practicable dispatch, and at a cost of over twelve thousand dollars; the greater portion of which, as testified by Captain Ellis himself, was indispensably required by the special service for which the vessel had been chartered. So soon as these necessary repairs and alterations were completed, namely, on the 23rd of November, the steamship sailed for New Orleans, proceeding thither without touching at any other port, and without unavoidable delay, and arrived there on the 6th day of December following; when she was at once put at the disposal of the Agent of the Brazilian Government, pursuant to the specific conditions of the charter-party.

While undergoing repairs in New York, the steamship

received on board a small amount of cargo for New Orleans; but this in no way retarded her departure for that city, nor prevented her from being in readiness to enter upon the service to which she was engaged, until after the expiration of the lay days provided for in the charter-party; but no passengers having been furnished for her, Capt. Ellis, representing the owner, Mr. Fiedler, demanded demurrage, in accordance with the agreement embodied in the charter-party; but as no demurrage was paid, he rightly protested against all concerned.

In this dubious position of affairs, it appears that one Cestuo, another Brazilian, to whom Mr Goicouria (who in the meantime had been displaced,) had committed the interests of the Agency, wished—and actually gave directions accordingly—that Mr. Fiedler should dispatch the Circassian to Rio de Janeiro, anyhow, and then claim the $42,000 charter-money. This, however, the latter, as an honest man, was unwilling to do, as under the circumstances the sending her thither would be manifestly without good results to the Brazilian Government; and he therefore addressed a letter, under date of December 17, 1867, to the Chevalier L. A. P. Fleury, Chargé d' Affaires of Brazil, setting forth the circumstances of the case, and saying, " I now address myself to you, as Chargé d' Affaries of the Imperial Government, to advise me. Shall I send the Circassian to Rio de Janeiro, chartered as stated above, without any or perhaps only a few passengers, and thereby lay the Government under obligations to pay me $42,000 in gold, or will you take the matter in hand and relieve me from my dilemma?" and in regard to the remuneration claimed by him, he added, " The expenses so far incurred, in preparing the vessel for such a long and costly voyage, already amount to about $20,000. Reimbursement of this sum would perhaps be preferable to the incurrence of an obligation to pay

$42,000 in gold, now equal to about $55,000 currency."

In reply to this letter, Mr. Fiedler received one from the Imperial Chargé d' Affaires, dated on the 18th of December, 1867, which, after briefly reciting the facts of the case, concluded as follows:

"I advise you not to allow the steamer to sail, but to consider the charter-party as completely null and void. I shall immediately call the attention of my Government to the subject, and will ask it to take into consideration the sum which you claim as due to yourself, and to indemnify you for the losses sustained."

Accordingly the Chevalier Fleury did, promptly, as appears by a letter of his dated on the 10th of March, 1868, present this matter to his Government; but no action, or at least no decision thereon, seems to have been had until late in the year 1870, as is shown by a letter from the Hon. Henry T. Blow, our Minister to Brazil, whose friendly offices, in support of the claim, had been invoked, and who informed Mr. Fiedler that the Brazilian Government positively asserted that neither Mr. Goicouria nor the party authorizing him, (Mr. Bocayuva,) had any authority whatever from it to act in the manner they did; and that consequently no claim against it could be considered as having arisen out of the acts of either of them. Mr. Blow, however, in the clearness and correctness of his judgment, remarked that this Brazilian allegation did not actually prove that those Brazilian subjects were not authorized Brazilian agents,—just such agents as they themselves represented themselves to be,—and added that, if Mr. Fiedler could prove that any charter or charters made by either of those parties had ever been allowed, and the money paid thereon by the Brazilian Government, he was sure that he could obtain from that Government the amount Mr. Fiedler was willing to accept; at the same time suggesting that such proofs might perhaps be obtained from shipowners in New York, through the Consul who was acting for the Brazilian Government at the time the charter was made.

Not very long after this, Mr. Fiedler departed this life; but his widow and executrix having obtained specific evidence of the very conclusive circumstances hereinbefore detailed, showing the recognition of the authority of Mr. Goicouria, Mrs. Fiedler, in April, 1873, through her attorneys, Jordan and Whitney, of New York, addressed a communication to the Hon. Hamilton Fish, Secretary of State of the United States, giving a statement of the facts relating to this claim, and invoking the aid of the Department of State in obtaining justice and satisfaction from the Government of Brazil; which communication, together with the papers with which it was accompanied, was properly transmitted by the Secretary of State to the Minister of the United States at Rio de Janeiro, with instructions to use his friendly offices in endeavoring to procure a settlement of the claim.

It was not until some time in the early part of the year 1875, that an answer was obtained from the Government of Brazil, and on the 16th of March of that year the Secretary of State of the United States addressed to the attorneys of Mrs. Fiedler a letter inclosing a copy of a Report of the Council of State of Brazil, wherein cunningly framed objections were made to the claim, which I will now proceed to notice.

In the first place, the authors of the Report reiterate the denial of the authority of Bocayuva, as well as of Goicouria, to charter vessels of any kind; and, with a view to justifying this denial, they make a statement of the alleged purpose of the Brazilian Government in its efforts to attract immigration from the United States, and certain correspondence on the subject between that Government, its Legation in the

United States, and Mr. Bocayuva, all of which is altogether irrelevant, inasmuch as there is not the slightest evidence or intimation that any knowledge of these matters was ever communicated to Mr. Fiedler. It is worthy of remark, however, that the very statement made to disprove the authority of Goicouria tends, on the contrary, strongly to establish it; or, at all events, to show that Mr. Fiedler was fully warranted in accepting and acting on the evidence of authority given to him; since it shows, first, that no written instructions were given to Bocayuva; and second, that the Brazilian Government was duly notified of the substitution of Goicouria by Bocayuva, and must, therefore, in the absence of any protest against this act, be held to have ratified it; and, finally, that when Goicouria came to be officially discharged, (and how could he be discharged from a position he never held?) it appears expressly that it was from the duty " to freight steamers for the transportation of emigrants." I submit that this shows very plainly that the Brazilian Government itself understood and admitted not only that Goicouria was the legal substitute of Bocayuva, but also that he, as such substitute, had power to charter steamers.

Yet, as I have remarked, all this is comparatively immaterial, since the acts of the Brazilian Government, known to Mr. Fiedler, at the time he entered into the charter-party, were a sufficient affirmance of the authority of the agent, which authority was furthermore expressly affirmed by the head of the Brazilian Legation in the United States.

The Brazilian Council of State insist that Mr. Fiedler should have demanded the power of attorney, or other proper document, under which the agent was acting. To this the reply is, that he did apply to Mr. Goicouria for the evidence of his authority, and that he was shown a power of attorney conferring upon the substitute all the power of Mr. Bocayuva. He did not apply to the latter for evidence of his authority, for the very good reason that he was not then in this country; but he did go to the Chargé d'Affaires of Brazil, or, what is the same thing, he ascertained that others had applied to him and obtained assurances that Bocayuva had power to charter sailing vessels or steamers; that Bocayuva could have a delegate, and that Mr. Domingo de Goicouria was the delegate appointed by him. Upon this the Imperial Council of State declare first, that here was no affirmance that Mr. Goicouria had the power to take up steamers; to which, in view of the terms of the letter of the Chargé d'Affaires I do not feel called upon to make any reply; and second, that, at any rate the Chargé d'Affaires was not the proper person to supply information on this subject; to which I answer, that I do not think the head of the Brazilian Government can honestly take the same view, especially as the papers quoted by the Report show that the Imperial Legation was actually charged with the supervision of the definite measures, whatever they were, of that Government, on this subject. I cannot permit myself to believe that the illustrious Emperor who has given to the world so many and such striking proofs of his wisdom and justice, will ever attempt to evade responsibility for contracts made with his acknowledged agents on the faith of explicit assurances of the representative of his government as to the extent and fullness of those agents' powers. Should he do so, I conceive that it will be of little avail to attempt to effect by argument either his reason or his conscience.

In the next place, the Report seems to suggest that the charter-party was inoperative for want of certainty as to the time when the steamer was to be in New Orleans, and, in this connection, misrepresents,—unintentionally perhaps,—the simple terms of the charter-party. Those terms were reasonable and explicit, namely, that the steamship, which was then on a voyage to Bremen, should sail from New Orleans on the 15th day of November, 1867, unless detained at Bremen, or elsewhere, by causes beyond the control of Mr. Fiedler, in which case she was to sail within ten days after her arrival at New Orleans. Yet the Imperial Council of State aver, in one place, that "the contract did not fix a "time within which the steamer, which had first to make a "voyage to Bremen, *and then might make others that might* "*suit,* had to present herself in New Orleans;" and, in another, uses the following language: " The steamer, being " chartered on the 21st of August, with liberty first to make a " long voyage to Bremen " (as if she were not then in the actual performance of that voyage,) *"and after that, again* "*to carry a cargo from New York to an intermediate port,* " and thence again to New Orleans." A fair inspection of the charter-party will show that there is nothing at all to be found therein of the kind stated above in the passages in italics, and that the supposed uncertainty in the instrument is by no means in that itself, but only in the account given of it by the Imperial Council of State.

And, lastly, the Council insist that, in any event, the amount to which the claimant is entitled is far less than twenty thousand dollars.

In considering this point, however, it is to be observed that the Report admits that, if the charter-party is to be considered valid, the failure to furnish immigrants for the vessel authorized the owner to consider the charter-party as " concluded," or to make the voyage without passengers, at the expense of the hirer. Now, in truth, this charter-party *was* valid to all intents and purposes, and was binding upon the Brazilian Government, and, as admitted by the Imperial Council of State, Mr. Fiedler had a right, on the failure of the agent of that Government to furnish the immigrants whose transportation was the object of the contemplated voyage, either to make the voyage, nevertheless, at the undiminished expense of the Brazilian Government, such expense being of course the $42,000 charter money agreed upon, or, as the Imperial Council of State themselves say, to "consider the charter-party as concluded." In law and equity Mr. Fiedler certainly had a right to recognize the fact that, by the default of the Brazilian Government, the purposes of the voyage had been defeated; and to consider himself, therefore, as having been prevented by such default from its performance, and for that reason to abandon it, and look to Brazil for indemnity for the losses he sustained in consequence of its being broken up. Especially was this true after the refusal to pay demurrage, and after the advice and promises of the Brazilian Chargé d' Affaires, which latter only recognized and reinforced rights which previously existed. Of the two courses thus open to Mr. Fiedler, it is manifest that the latter was the one the least onerous to Brazil, and, as he believed, the most just; and accordingly that was the one which he adopted.

Under these circumstances, the question was, and is simply, What did Mr. Fiedler lose by reason of the non-fulfillment of the contract by Brazil; or what is the same thing, by the Agent of that Government, and the consequent breaking up of the voyage? With a view to the proper determination of this question, the subject may be considered in various lights; as, for instance, the inquiry may be, What loss did Mr. Fiedler in fact sustain by reason of his entering into the charter-party, taking into account all the actual circumstances attending its execution; the prosecution of the voyage up to the time of its abandonment with the heavy expenses incurred, and the immediate and prolonged consequences resulting from the sudden and unexpected deprivation of employment? If this criterion were taken in all its amplitude, it is manifest, from the proof in the case, that Mr. Fiedler's demand would far exceed the sum total of the charter money; and it is therefore of course not insisted on.

In this connection, it may likewise be proper to notice two or three points made in the Report of the Imperial Council of State in regard to the expenses, that those of the voyage to Bremen, and those of the repairs for damages suffered in that voyage, and "expenses also for, or at, the intermediate port for which the Circassian took cargo" from New York, are in no case properly chargeable against Brazil. In reply, it needs only to be remarked, as to the last point, that the expenses thereupon, as has been shown, were wholly imaginary; and, as to the other points, that there is no claim that any expenses whatever are chargeable to this voyage except such as were incurred especially on its account; that the evidence appears to demonstrate that the sum total of the expenses so incurred amounted to at least twenty thousand dollars; but that those expenses, all told, are by no means the full measure of Mr. Fiedler's loss, or of his rightful claim upon the Brazilian Government.

Again, disregarding all consideration of actual expenses, or consequential losses, the inquiry may be, simply, What profit, over and above the expenses properly chargeable to the voyage, would Mr. Fiedler have realized, had he been permitted to prosecute it to its preconceived termination, and been paid the $42,000 charter-money? It is evident that that much, at the very least, he lost by the breaking up of the voyage. And as the evidence further shows, what is entirely consistent with the probabilities of the case, that the claimant's profits would have been not less than twenty thousand dollars in gold, it is apparent that, in no event, can the amount of his loss be equitably reduced below that sum; which being exactly that which Mr. Fiedler himself originally offered to accept in satisfaction, it is precisely that which, with interest accrued and accruing thereon, his representatives now claim.

There are two other points of the Report which require to be noticed. The first is, the attempt to draw from the letter of Minister Blow a degree of support of the Brazilian Government in rejecting the claim; and this is done by what is, in fact, a gross misstatement of the tenor of Mr. Blow's letter; a misstatement, however, which may possibly be attributable to imperfect translation ; or, if not, it is certainly very far from being creditable to the ingenuousness of the authors of the Report. It consists in the far-fetched representation that Minister Blow was of opinion that the charter-party was invalid, and that he stated that it appeared, from his own convictions, that, under such circumstances, no good claim could be founded on what had been done by either Bocayuva or Goicouria; whereas, in the perspicuous passage misquoted from his letter, Minister Blow was simply stating what was alleged in defence by the Brazilian Government; and the whole tenor of his letter shows conclusively that he believed, not only that that allegation was erroneous, but that Mr. Fiedler, by application in the particular quarter suggested by Minister Blow himself, could obtain proof that it was so.

The other point referred to is likewise a flimsy and futile effort to prove that the present Minister of the United States at Rio de Janeiro, Mr. Partridge, in the memorandum submitted by him to the Brazilian Government in connection with this claim, admitted that the charter-party was in itself insufficient as an obligatory instrument, abandoned the claim as a matter of strict right, and only urged it by way of appeal to the "sense of equity" of the Brazilian Government. Nothing, I apprehend, can be further from the truth than this fabricated account of the position of Minister Partridge. So far from having done anything of the character attributed to him, he evidently regarded the charter-party as a valid and binding instrument, and urged, in good faith and full confidence, upon the Brazilian Government, compensation for its violation. That he did not urge a specific demand for the whole amount of the charter-party, $42,000, but only for a just and reasonable compensation, in no way supports the view expressed in the Report. This was simply because, through the advice of the Brazilian Chargé d' Affaires, the voyage not having been completed, the charter-party, calling for $42,000, did not furnish a perfect guide as to the compensation; and the Minister at once proceeds to state his own opinion as to the proper basis of adjustment; a basis with which I am sure the representatives of Mr. Fiedler would be entirely satisfied.

In conclusion, I will only add, that, in my judgment, there is no valid objection whatever, whether of law or ethics, which can be urged against this claim. The only point open to candid argument is as to the amount which should be awarded, which cannot, in my view, be less than what was first asked by Mr. Fiedler, and is still asked by his representatives.

If I had ever entertained any doubt about this claim upon my own examination of the evidence on which it rests, that doubt would now be completely dispelled by the seeming shifts to which the authors of the Report, signed by the Imperial Councillors, are driven in their efforts to find some plausible objection to it; shifts which, if not explainable by misconception, arising from mistranslation, or other innocent cause, I must say I shall always regard as a prodigious study for the curious.

Yours, respectfully,
EDWARD JORDAN.

THE "CIRCASSIAN" CHARTER-PARTY.

[Copy.]

This Charter-Party, made and concluded in the City of New York, on this the twenty-first day of August, in the year one thousand eight hundred and sixty-seven, between Ernest Fiedler, owner of the steamship Circassian, of New York, of the burden of fifteen hundred tons, or thereabouts, now on her way to Bremen, of the first part, and Domingo de Goicouria, Esquire, Agent for Immigration for the Brazilian Government, of the second part, WITNESSETH, that the said party of the first part, for and in consideration of the covenants and agreements hereinafter mentioned, to be kept and performed by the said party of the second part, does covenant and agree on the freighting and chartering of the said vessel unto the said party of the second part for a voyage from the port of New Orleans, Louisiana, to Rio de Janeiro, Brazil, on the terms following, that is to say:

FIRST:—The said party of the first part does engage that the said vessel, in and during the said voyage, shall be kept tight, staunch, well-fitted, tackled, and provided with every requisite, and with men and provisions necessary for such a voyage.

SECOND:—The said party of the first part, does further engage that the whole of the said vessel (with the exception of the cabin, the deck, and the necessary room for the accommodation of the crew, and of the sails, cable and provisions,) shall be at the sole use and disposal of the said party of the second part during the voyage aforesaid.

THIRD:—The said party of the first part does further engage to take and receive on board the said vessel, during the aforesaid voyage, all such lawful goods and merchandise as the said party of the second part, or his agent, may think proper to ship.

AND the said party of the second part, for and in consideration of the covenants and agreements to be kept and performed by the said party of the first part, does covenant and agree with the said party of the first part, to charter and hire the said vessel as aforesaid, on the terms following, that is to say:

FIRST:—The said party of second part does engage to provide and furnish the said vessel with passengers in the steerage, from six years old and upward, not to exceed six hundred in number; except such children under six years of age, as may belong to the passengers, but not in excess of the provisions of law.

SECOND:—The said party of the second part does further engage to pay to the said party of the first part, or his agent, for the charter or freight of the said vessel during the voyage aforesaid, in the manner following, that is to say: Forty-two thousand American gold dollars, or its equivalent in millreis, ten days after the completion of the voyage. For cabin passengers, sixty American gold dollars per head additional is to be paid; say one hundred and thirty American gold dollars in full for cabin fare; and it is hereby agreed that all passagemoney received at New Orleans shall be paid over to and received by the party of the first part, or his duly authorized agent, and shall be credited on account of the charter-money payable hereby.

It is further agreed between the parties to this instrument, that the said party of the second part shall be allowed, for the loading and discharging of the said vessel, at the respective ports aforesaid, lay days, as follows, that is to say: Ten running days for loading and discharging. The vessel is to sail from New Orleans, Louisiana, on the fifteenth day of November, 1867, weather permitting, unless detained at Bremen, or elsewhere, by causes beyond the control of the said party of the first part, in which case the vessel is to sail within ten days after her arrival at New Orleans; and in case the vessel is longer detained, the said party of the second part agrees to pay to the said party of the first part, demurrage at the rate of three hundred and fifty American gold dollars per day for each and every day so detained, provided such detention shall happen by default of the said party of the second part, or his agent.

It is further understood and agreed, that the passengers and cargo shall be received and landed or delivered alongside and within reach of the vessel's tackles.

It is also further understood and agreed, that this charter shall commence when the vessel is ready to receive passengers or cargo at her place of loading, and notice thereof is given to the party of the second part, or to his agent.

Further, it is also understood and agreed, that the party of the first part shall furnish all necessary provisions for the passengers, and supply them with tin plates, cups, knives and forks; do all cooking needful for them, and put up for them berths in the usual way, and have on board a competent surgeon. It is also understood that the party of the first part, after reserving sufficient of the ship's hold for fuel, stores, provisions, water, etc., shall allow the balance of the space to be used by the passengers for their baggage and implements; and the party of the first part shall have the liberty to tow or assist vessels in distress, and to sail with or without a pilot. The vessel is to be consigned at Rio de Janeiro to B. Cayman, Esquire, Agent of the United States and Brazil Mail Steamship Company, of New York, paying him the customary commission of two and one-half per cent. A commission of ten per cent. is to be paid by the party of the first part, on receipt by him of the charter-money herein specified, to the Immigration Agent for the Brazilian Government in New York; and also, at the same time, a commission of two and one-half per cent. on this charter is payable to O. Koch.

To the true and faithful performance of all the foregoing covenants and agreements, the said parties, each to the other, do hereby bind themselves, their executors, administrators and assigns, and also the said vessel, freight, tackle and appurtenances, each to the other, in the penal sum of the amount of the charter-money.

In witness whereof, the said parties have hereunto interchangeably set their hands and seals, this the twenty-first day of August, 1867.

    ERNEST FIEDLER,   [L. S.]
    DOMINGO DE GOICOURIA, . [L. S.]
    BRAZILIAN IMMIGRATION AGENT.

Sealed and delivered in presence of
  EMIL RUGER, Ship Broker.

We hereby certify that the foregoing is a true and correct copy of the original stamped Charter-Party in our possession.

        RUGER BROTHERS,
          SHIP BROKERS.

CHARGÉ D'AFFAIRES ALBUQUERQUE TO MR. STURGIS.

(Translation.)

       BRAZILIAN LEGATION,
      NEW YORK, *March* 15, 1867.

RUSSELL STURGIS, *Esq*.

SIR: In answer to your letter of yesterday, I have to inform you that the name of the Agent for Brazilian Immigration is Mr. Quintino de Souza Bocayuva. This gentleman has power to charter sailing vessels or steamers to take emigrants from the southern ports of the United States to Brazil. According to the contract made between the Imperial Government and the United States and Brazil Mail Steamship Company, he can have a deputy, and Mr. Domingo de Goicouria is the deputy appointed by him. I believe my Government will approve what is done by the said Agent.

I have the honor to be your obedient servant,

H. CAVALCANTI DE ALBUQUERQUE.

THE CHEVALIER FLEURY TO MR. FIEDLER.

(Translation.)

IMPERIAL LEGATION OF BRAZIL,
NEW YORK, *December* 18, 1867.

ERNEST FIEDLER, *Esq*.

DEAR SIR: I have received your letter of yesterday, inclosing various documents relative to the contract entered into, on the 21st of August last, between you and Domingo Goicouria as Agent for Brazilian Immigration. The charter-party declares that Goicouria chartered the steamship Circassian, of which vessel you are the owner, for the sum of $42,000 in gold, or its equivalent in millreis, to take emigrants to Rio de Janeiro; the said steamship to sail from the port of New Orleans. Being informed that the number of emigrants is very small, I advise you not to allow the steamer to sail, but to consider the charter-party completely null and void. I shall immediately call the attention of my Government to the subject, and will ask it to take into consideration the amount demanded by you, and to indemnify you for the losses you have sustained.

I have the honor to offer you the assurances of my highest consideration.

LOUIS AUGUSTUS DE PADUA FLEURY.

MINISTER BLOW TO MR. FIEDLER.

LEGATION OF THE UNITED STATES,
PETROPOLIS, BRAZIL, *September* 22, 1870.
ERNEST FIEDLER, *Esq., New York.*

DEAR SIR: Your favor of the 20th of July last, was promptly delivered to me, from the mails of the August steamer. I am glad to say that I am the person witn whom you had business relations, many years ago, in St. Louis, and that it will afford me the greatest satisfaction and happiness if I can serve you in the case of the steamship Circassian; not only because I like to discharge my duties to every American citizen, but also for the reason that I can never forget that, when I was young, inexperienced and poor, I had your respect and confidence. I have had to proceed slowly in the business which you have intrusted to me, owing to the fact that it was desirable, if possible, to procure some information absolutely essential to the strengthening of your claim; in this I am now beginning to fear that I shall have to rely mainly on the integrity of the Imperial Government.* I have had an informal interview with the officials in the Foreign office, and am promised some information touching their charters. When I procure this, I will write you at once in regard to the prospect for collecting the whole or any portion of the amount due you.

I am, dear sir,
Very truly, your obedient servant,
HENRY T. BLOW.

* All information and proofs necessary to impart perfect validity to the claim, (in fact, a superabundance of such information and proofs,) had previously been submitted to Brazil's diplomatic representatives in the United States; and a large redundance of equally strong and convincing testimony has since been adduced in the claimant's behalf at Rio de Janeiro; but all in vain, as will but too plainly appear within the compass of the following pages.

H. R. H

MINISTER BLOW TO MR. FIEDLER.

(Private)

LISBON, PORTUGAL, *November* 28, 1870.
ERNEST FIEDLER, *Esq., New York.*

DEAR SIR: It was only during the week of my departure from Rio de Janeiro, that I went into an examination of your claim against Brazil, with Mr. J. T. do Amoral, the Director-General of Accounts, and finally obtained from the Department a verbal decision, which, I am sorry to say, is unfavorable. The Brazilian Government asserts positively that neither General Goicouria nor the party whose substitute or agent he was, had any authority from it to act in the manner they did, in chartering vessels, and that, under the actual condition of affairs, it cannot consider any claim growing out of the acts of either. This declaration, however, does not in reality prove that those parties were not authorized as they represented themselves to be, but only that, so far as the present Director-General of Accounts of the Brazilian Government is advised or knows, they were not under Imperial commission as agents for immigration. If you can prove that any charters made by either Bocayuva or Goicouria were ever recognized, and the money paid by the Brazilian Government, for or on account of those charters, I am sure I can obtain from the Imperial Government the amount you are willing to receive; and I am not sure but that you can obtain such proofs from shipowners in New York, through the hands of the very Consul who was acting for the Brazilian Government at the time the Circassian was chartered.

I am now on my way back to the United States, and expect to be in New York about the last of December, when I will advise you where replies can readily reach me. Meanwhile I inclose to you, herewith, the documents you sent me, as they may, perhaps, in other hands, be useful to you.

I am, sir, very truly, your friend,

HENRY T. BLOW.

AFFIDAVIT OF CAPT. ELLIS.

STATE, COUNTY, AND } SS.
CITY OF NEW YORK. }

Thomas S. Ellis, being first duly sworn, makes oath and says, that he is fifty-four years of age; that he resides at No. 277 Dean Street, in the City of Brooklyn, and is master of the ship Fearless of New York; that in the year 1867, he was master of the steamship Circassian of New York, of which Ernest Fiedler was the sole owner; that, in that year, this affiant made a voyage with the said steamship to Bremen, Europe, and while there, in the month of September, he received notice from the said Fiedler that the said vessel had been chartered to transport emigrants from New Orleans to Rio de Janeiro, with instructions to purchase in Bremen certain supplies for the said contemplated voyage, which purchases the affiant made at a cost of about three thousand dollars; that, at the time the affiant received notice of the said chartering, the Circassian was already advertised to sail from Bremen, for New York, on the 14th day of October, and accordingly, on that day, she sailed for New York, making no stoppage on the voyage, and arrived at the latter port on the second day of November, the earliest practicable day after the chartering of the said steamship, which occurred on the 21st day of August; that, on the arrival of the said steamship at New York, it was found that she needed important alterations and repairs, in order to fit her for a voyage for the transportation of passengers from New Orleans to Rio de Janeiro; that the said alterations and repairs were accordingly made, at a large expense, in making which the utmost dispatch was observed, the workmen employed therein working most of the time day and night; that nearly all the said alterations and repairs had especial reference to fitting the said vessel for the voyage on which she was then destined; as a comparatively small outlay would have put her in condition to make a return trip to Bremen; that while the said work was being done, a small amount of cargo was taken on board for New Orleans, but that the taking thereof occasioned no delay whatever in the sailing of the said steamship for New Orleans, where she arrived on the 6th day of December, without having touched at any intermediate port, and without any unnecessary delay, having left New York on the twenty-fourth day of November; that, on arriving at New Orleans, the affiant notified Messrs. Elliott & McKeever, the persons to whom he was ordered by direction of the Brazilian Agent of Emigration at New York, to report, (the said Elliott being at that time the Brazilian Consul at New Orleans,) and informed them of the readiness of the Circassian to take in emigrants and enter upon the performance of the voyage to Rio de Janeiro; that no objection was made by the said parties, nor by any one on account of the time of the arrival of the said steamship at New Orleans, nor on any other ground; that no objection on the ground of the time of her arrival could have been well-founded, because the Brazilian Agent of Emigration at New York, on the 23d day of November, 1867, directed that the said steamship should report under the said charter-party to Messrs. Elliott and McKeever, and the said steamship sailed from New York the next day, and reached New Orleans on the 6th day of December, as before stated, and was ready to proceed on her voyage to Rio de Janeiro within ten days thereafter; as provided in the said charter-party; that no emigrants were furnished for transportation, though the Circassian remained at New Orleans ready to receive such as should be offered, until after the expiration of the lay days specified in the said charter-party; that after the expiration of the said lay days, this affiant demanded the payment of demurrage, according to the said charter-party, which was refused; wherefore the said affiant protested on account of the said failure to provide passengers and to pay demurrage; and the said steamship was withdrawn pursuant to the advice of the Chargé of the Brazilian Government; that, as soon as it was known that the said voyage would be abandoned, every practicable effort was made to secure employment for the said vessel; but nevertheless, her owner suffered for want of such employment for her, during the ensuing three months, a loss of many thousands of dollars; while this affiant believes that, but for the chartering of the said steamship, as aforesaid, profitable employment could have been obtained for her during all the time she would have been occupied in making the said contemplated voyage, had it been prosecuted to a termination, which would have been about one month from New Orleans to Rio de Janeiro, and from two and a half to three months for the entire voyage out and back to New York; and this affiant says, that the profits of the said Fiedler on the said contemplated voyage to Rio de Janeiro would have been large; that those on the return voyage would also have been considerable, and that his losses occasioned by the failure of the said voyage were undoubtedly very heavy, but he will not undertake to estimate their amount, or the amount of profits he would have realized, had the said voyage been performed, as he has not the means of forming a reliable judgment thereon.

T. S. ELLIS.

UNITED STATES OF AMERICA,
STATE OF NEW YORK, } SS.
COUNTY AND CITY OF NEW YORK.

Be it known, that, on this, the eighteenth day of March, 1876, before me, J. Douglas Brown, a Notary Public, in and for Kings County, in the State of New York, residing in the City of Brooklyn, in the said County of Kings, duly commissioned and sworn, and by law authorized to administer oaths and affirmations, in the said City and County of New York, personally appeared the said T. S. Ellis, of the said City of Brooklyn, and who, being by me duly sworn, did depose and say, that the foregoing statement, subscribed by him, was in all respects true and correct.

In witness whereof, I have hereunto set my hand and affixed my seal of office, at the said City of New York, the day and year last aforesaid.

[L. S.] J. DOUGLAS BROWN,
Notary Public.

AFFIDAVIT OF MR. PERSUHN.

UNITED STATES OF AMERICA,
STATE OF NEW YORK, } SS.
COUNTY AND CITY OF NEW YORK.

Charles P. Persuhn, being first duly sworn, says that he is forty-two years of age; that he resides at number Twenty-nine, West Eighteenth Street, in the City of New York, and is a merchant, engaged in business in the said city; that he was a cousin of the late Ernest Fiedler, and superintended the preparation of the Steamer Circassian for her contemplated voyage from New Orleans to Brazil, in the year eighteen hundred and sixty-seven, and is familiar with the circumstances under which the said steamer was chartered for the said voyage, with her preparations therefor, and with the facts re'·ting to the said vessel up to and after her withdrawal therefrom; that the said steamer was, at the time of the making up of the charter-party for the said voyage, in the actual performance of a voyage to Bremen, Europe, where she arrived on the twenty-seventh day of August, six days after the making of the said charter-party; that the said Ernest Fiedler, before entering into the said charter-party, was shown, by Domingo Goicouria, a power of attorney from Quintino de Souza Bocayuva, fully authorizing the said Goicouria to exercise all the powers of the said Bocayuva as agent of Emigration for the Brazilian Government, and was informed that the authority of both the said Bocayuva and the said Goicouria to charter vessels for the conveyance of emigrants from the United States to Brazil had been recognized by the Brazilian Government, and had been expressly affirmed by the head of the Legation of that Government in the United States,—Mr. Cavalcanti de Albuquerque,—and, in particular, that the said Fiedler, before entering into the said charter-party, learned that the steamer Catherine Whiting had, but a short time previous, completed a voyage under a charter-party in all substantial respects similar to the one proposed for the steamer Circassian, and had been paid the charter-money by the Brazilian authorities; that immediately after the execution of the said charter-party, the said Fiedler notified the master of the said steamer Circassian, by letter to Bremen, of the making thereof, and gave directions for her return, to enter upon the said contemplated voyage; but that, on her return to New York, she was found to need important repairs and alterations in order to fit her for a voyage to Brazil for the purpose contemplated by the said charter-party, and that the same were made with all practicable dispatch, she having reached New York on the second day of November, and sailed from thence for New Orleans on the twenty-fourth day of the same month; that the said repairs cost over twelve thousand dollars; that the said steamer proceeded directly to New Orleans, where she arrived on the sixth day of December next thereafter, without having touched at any intermediate port; that the said steamer took some cargo and passengers from New York to New Orleans, but that her doing so was with the express assent of the Brazilian Agent of Emigration, and in no way retarded her departure from the former port, nor her arrival at the latter one, nor her being ready to receive at New Orleans emigrants under her charter-party, for the voyage to Brazil, the said steamer having been ready at New Orleans to receive such emigrants at the earliest practicable moment after the making of the said charter-party; and that the said steamer remained in readiness in New Orleans to receive such emigrants until she was withdrawn from the projected voyage pursuant to the advice of the Chargé of the Brazilian Government. And the said affiant further says that the net earnings of the steamer Circassian, under the said charter-party, over and above all expenses, chargeable to the said voyage, would, had the said voyage been completed, have been not less than twenty thousand dollars in gold, in addition to which the net earnings upon her return trip to New York would not have been less than five thousand dollars in gold; that as soon as the said Fiedler, on advice of the Brazilian Chargé, had determined to withdraw the said vessel from the said voyage, he made every effort to find profitable employment for her, but failed to do so; but, on the contrary, suffered actual loss of nearly twenty thousand dollars within the next succeeding three months.

And the said affiant further says that, had the said steamer not been placed under the said charter-party for the said

voyage to Brazil, and had she been free, on her return to
New York, from Bremen, to seek employment elsewhere,
she could readily have found profitable employment for all
the time she was engaged in going to and remaining at
New Orleans; and for all the time which would have been
occupied in her contemplated voyage to Brazil; and he says
that the said voyage would have occupied, according to the
usual course, about thirty days from New Orleans to Rio de
Janeiro; and he further says that the actual total loss which
accrued to the said Fiedler, from the failure of the said voyage, was not less than fifty thousand dollars.

       CHARLES P. PERSUHN

UNITED STATES OF AMERICA,
STATE OF NEW YORK, } *SS.*
COUNTY AND CITY OF NEW YORK.

 Be it known, that, on this, the seventeenth day of
March, 1876, before me, Frank Thompson, a Notary Public,
in and for the County and City of New York, in the State of
New York, residing in the said City, duly commissioned and
sworn, and by law authorized to administer oaths and affirmations, personally appeared Charles P. Persuhn of the said
City of New York, and who, being by me duly sworn, did
depose and say, that the foregoing statement, subscribed by
him, was in all respects true and correct.

 In witness whereof, I have hereunto set my hand and
affixed my seal of office, at the said City of New York, the
day and year last aforesaid.

       FRANK THOMPSON,
[L. S.]   Notary Public.

MR. HELPER TO THE CHEVALIER BORGES.

NEW YORK, *June* 5, 1876.
TO HIS EXCELLENCY THE CHEVALIER
    ANTONIO PEDRO DE CARVALHO BORGES,
    Minister Plenipotentiary for Brazil.

DISTINGUISHED SIR: I have the honor to request your Excellency's attention to the following correspondence, touching the just claim of Helen M. Fiedler, of this city, the widow and executrix of Ernest Fiedler, deceased, against the Government of Brazil. * * * The foregoing correspondence with the Hon. Edward Jordan is so self-explanatory, in all respects, that I do not feel called upon to elucidate further any fact or circumstance connected with it; my principal object in now laying it before your Excellency being to inquire, whether the presence of his Imperial Majesty Dom Pedro II in this country, or elsewhere out of Brazil, would be likely to operate, in any way, as a hindrance or delay to my success in securing just consideration and action on the claim by the Imperial Regency *Ad Interim* at Rio de Janeiro? May his Majesty's visit here be prolonged in health and happiness!

If there is no danger of my encountering the somewhat apprehended hindrance or delay, because of the absence of the Emperor, I think I shall soon sail hence for Brazil; but if the danger is imminent, or if there is even serious doubt on the subject, I shall, in such case, prefer to wait until his Majesty's return to his own dominions. I hope, however, to be informed that the functions of good Government in Brazil are in unimpaired and full force, and that there is no known or probable reason why, if I go there as a citizen of the United States, carrying with me a just claim for losses sustained by a fellow-citizen in the service of the Empire, I may not rightly expect such prompt redress in the premises as

will be in consonance with the highest principles of international honor and equity.
I am, sir, with great respect,
Your Excellency's obedient servant,
H. R. HELPER.

MR. HELPER TO THE CHEVALIER BORGES.

NEW YORK, *June* 27, 1876.
TO HIS EXCELLENCY THE CHEVALIER
ANTONIO PEDRO DE CARVALHO BORGES,
Minister Plenipotentiary for Brazil.
DISTINGUISHED SIR: About three weeks ago, that is to say, on the 5th instant, I had the honor to address your Excellency on the subject of the claim of Helen M. Fiedler, executrix of the estate of Ernest Fiedler, deceased, against the Government of Brazil. My communication was somewhat elaborate, covering, in the form of correspondence with Edward Jordan, Esquire, the whole grounds of the case. Yet the particular point upon which I desired your Excellency's reply (which, however, has not yet been received,) was contained on the last page, which I here transcribe as follows: * * * Being thus still in a quandary as to whether or not it would be advisable for me to go to Brazil, with a view of prosecuting the claim in question before the Government of that Empire, in the absence of the Emperor, I should be greatly obliged to your Excellency for such information on the subject as would clearly indicate to me, in this dilemma, the path of prudence and justice.
I have the honor be, most respectfully,
Your Excellency's obedient servant,
H. R. HELPER.

SECRETARY TORREAO DE BARROS TO MR. HELPER.

PHILADELPHIA, *June* 30, 1876.

MR. H. R. HELPER.

SIR: I am directed by his Excellency the Minister from Brazil to acknowledge the receipt of your letter of the 27th instant, and to say that, as a matter of course, the absence of the Emperor from the Empire does not hinder the working of the Brazilian system of government, His Majesty's share and authority being temporarily vested in the hands of his daughter, the Imperial Princess Izabel, as Regent, of which fact it would seem that you are already aware.

With the expression of my regards,

I remain, sir, truly yours,

B. TORREAO DE BARROS.

MR. HELPER TO MINISTER PARTRIDGE.

NEW YORK, *July* 12, 1876.

HON. JAMES R. PARTRIDGE,

United States Minister to Brazil.

SIR: Having in hand an important matter of business with the Government of Brazil, in which I hope to have, when necessary and convenient, the benefit of your ministerial counsel and assistance, I am now contemplating the time when I may, with a fair prospect of exemption from the fatalities of yellow fever and other endemic diseases, go to Rio de Janeiro. Will you please inform me whether, in your opinion, October and November would probably be about as safe as any other season of the year for an American creditor and claimant to sojourn at the capital of Bra-

zil ?—or, if not these particular months, which other two or three months would you recommend nearest beyond them.
I have the honor to be, very respectfully,
Your obedient servant,
H. R. HELPER

MINISTER PARTRIDGE TO MR. HELPER.

UNITED STATES LEGATION IN BRAZIL,
RIO DE JANEIRO, *September* 10, 1876.
H. R. HELPER, *Esq., New York.*
DEAR SIR: In reply to your note of the 12th of July, I have to say that October and November are about the worst months in which one may start from the United States for Brazil. The yellow fever generally prevails here from December to May, inclusive; and this year it did not disappear till August. A good time to come to Brazil is to leave the United States in May, so that one may feel reasonably safe in being here during the months of June and July and August, when, as a rule, the weather is cool and healthy.
Yours respectfully,
JAMES R. PARTRIDGE.

MR. HELPER TO MINISTER PARTRIDGE.

NEW YORK, *March* 23, 1877.
HON. JAMES R. PARTRIDGE,
United States Minister to Brazil.
SIR: I have the honor to request that you will be kind enough, in your official capacity, to take cognizance of the

Fiedler claim against Brazil, as it is set forth in the accompanying paper, without, however, making any fresh mention of the matter to the Brazilian Government until after my arrival at Rio de Janeiro, two or three months hence, or until after you shall have heard from me again on the subject.

I am, sir, very respectfully, your obedient servant

H.˙ R. HELPER.

MR. HELPER TO MR. JORDAN.

WESTMINSTER PALACE HOTEL,
LONDON, ENGLAND, *April* 13, 1877.
EDWARD JORDAN, *Esq., New York.*

DEAR SIR: Since my arrival in this mighty metropolis of the world, on Monday last, I have had interviews with the Hon. Edwards Pierrepont, our American Envoy Extraordinary and Minister Plenipotentiary to the Court of St. James, and also with His Excellency the Baron de Penedo, the Brazilian Ambassador to Great Britain. His Imperial Majesty Dom Pedro II, the peregrinating and pleasure-pursuing potentate of Brazil, who was last week in Vienna, yesterday in Berlin, and this morning in Dresden, is still so rapid, so comet-like and uncertain in his movements, that I am quite at a loss to know where to go to find him. Yet the Baron de Penedo has informed me that His Majesty will undoubtedly be in Paris very soon after the first of May, and that he will then remain there several weeks. I have therefore determined to make a hasty tour through England, Wales, Ireland and Scotland, and then go over to the Continent, wending my way to the French capital, where I shall hold myself in waiting with the hope of securing the honor of an introduction to and interview with His Majesty in the early part of next month. If I succeed in obtaining an interview with the Emperor, I shall, fortified and emboldened by the facts of the case, make a strong effort to impress his mind favorably in regard to the Fiedler claim against his Government; and, in any event, you will probably hear from me again, on this subject, by or about the first of June.

Respectfully and truly yours,

H. R. HELPER.

MR. HELPER TO THE EMPEROR DOM PEDRO II.

HOTEL DU RHONE,
PARIS, FRANCE, *May* 9, 1877.
TO HIS IMPERIAL MAJESTY DOM PEDRO II,
Emperor of Brazil.

SIRE: From Asheville in North Carolina, to Paris in France, by the usual route, is a distance of more than four thousand miles; and this is the distance which I have just travelled, by land and sea, in the hope of being honored by your Majesty with a brief interview in relation to a just claim, (now of nearly ten years' standing,) which I have been employed to prosecute against the Brazilian Government.

I refer to the claim of Ernest Fiedler, of New York, a ship owner and citizen of the United States, of whose time and labor and money the Brazilian Government, by one of its Agents for Immigration, made use of, in 1867, without compensation, and otherwise without fulfilling its part of the contract.

Yet by this last remark I do not mean to charge that your Majesty's Government is, up to the present time, wholly or inexcusably at fault in the premises, inasmuch as the circumstances attending its failure to fulfil its part of the contract, were peculiar, and for itself, no less than for Mr. Fiedler, singularly unfortunate.

All the facts in the case were submitted to your Majesty's Council of State at Rio de Janeiro, several years since; and it is believed that justice would have been done there and then, but for an unaccountably strange mistranslation to the Council, of certain important papers.

Briefly and substantially the facts are these: In August, 1867, Mr. Domingo de Goicouria, under full powers of attorney from Mr. Quintino de Souza Bocayuva, an authorized Agent in the United States for Emigration to Brazil, chartered of Mr. Fiedler, in New York, the steamship Circassian (then on a voyage to Bremen,) to convey from New Orleans to Rio de Janeiro, at a later period in the year, six hundred emigrants, more or less; for which service Mr. Fiedler was to receive the sum of $42,000 in gold, and, in the event of undue detention, demurrage at the rate of $350 per day, after the expiration of ten days allowed in the charter-party for embarking and disembarking the passengers.

On her return from Bremen, the Circassian proceeded to New Orleans, and there, according to contract, waited in readiness for the passengers whom Mr. Goicouria was to send aboard; but none came; or at most but very few; and finally, after correspondence on the subject with the Chevalier Fleury, who at that particular time was the diplomatic representative of Brazil in the United States, Mr. Fiedler was advised, by the Chevalier Fleury, to abandon the voyage, and to make reclamation on Brazil for such amount as would promptly satisfy the demands of justice.

Acting on this weighty advice, Mr. Fiedler, who had incurred great expense in making the necessary alterations in his ship, in purchasing provisions and supplies for so large a number of emigrants, and in other respects, put in a claim, not for the whole amount of $42,000, as legally he might have done, (the failure of contract having been no fault of his, but solely the fault of Mr. Goicouria, the Brazilian Agent,) but for the more equitable sum of only $20,000, which, as I have been solemnly and credibly assured, time and again, is much less than the aggregate of actual expenses and losses which Mr. Fiedler suffered in consequence of Brazil's failure in this case,—unintentional as it may have been,—to fulfil her part of the contract. This amount, therefore, $20,000, with interest at the rate of 6 per cent. per annum, is what is now claimed in satisfaction of Brazil's non-fulfillment of her agreement.

Your Majesty, whose long, wise, honorable and successful reign, will impart strength and lustre to all your dynastic successors on the throne of Brazil, needs not to be reminded that justice is a thing that should always be done, and done quickly, for its own sake, and for the sake of all whom it affects; for probably there is no one in all the world who appreciates more fully than yourself the perfect truth and obligation of this sentiment.

This, then, is a case wherein, through the direct intervention of an Agent of your Majesty's Government, an American citizen has been diverted from his regular pursuits, misled into an imperfectly planned Brazilian enterprise, and, in consequence, greatly injured in his business and property. I have therefore to request, most respectfully and earnestly, that your Majesty will be kind enough to take the matter into due consideration, and, with as little additional delay as possib!e, order, or recommend, that just recompense be made to my client.

With this matter in hand I should have gone directly from the United States to Brazil, but for the fact that the claim having been already once before your Majesty, I feared that the Imperial Regency at Rio de Janeiro might not feel disposed to take the responsibility of settling it finally in your absence, and might, therefore, put me off until your Majesty's return to the Empire ; and I may here say, frankly and truthfully, that I purposely refrained from presenting the case to you while you were in the United States, last year, because, as you were then the illustrious guest of the whole country, I considered that, under such circumstances, it would be both impolite and rude for any citizen of the Republic to approach your Majesty there, at that particular time, on a matter of formal and serious business.

While resting this case broadly on its own merits, and claiming for my client compensation accordingly, it yet so happens that there is another reason,—more than a double reason, as I contend,—why, as it seems to me, Brazil should now do full justice to my injured fellow-citizen, or rather to his widow, for Mr. Fiedler himself is no longer alive. The reason to which I thus allude is, as I perceive it, one of vast and auspicious promise, looking to a much larger development of the material resources of Brazil than has ever yet been realized or even projected; and if Brazil will now but do simple justice to my client, that act of justice on her part will (speaking with all candor,) place me in possession of a fee which, in whole or in part, I shall expend very soon afterward in perfecting plans in her behalf, which, if successfully carried out, will, in time, as I really believe, give her back at least one hundred dollars for every dollar she will pay me.

This large and feasible scheme of development has been locked exclusively in my own breast ever since 1866, when I first conceived it; being then off the coast of Brazil, on my way back to the United States from Buenos Ayres, in the Argentine Republic, where, for a period of nearly five years, I had been performing the duties of an American

Consul; and although the time has not yet arrived for the scheme to be made public, (and may not arrive for one or two years more,) yet I should now esteem it an honor to be permitted to lay it fully before your Majesty in confidence.

Trusting that you may be pleased to favor me with the privilege of an interview with your Majesty, in regard to the two matters of business here mentioned,—one, the smaller, against Brazil, and the other, the larger, in the interest of Brazil,—I have the honor to be, with great respect,
Your Majesty's obedient servant,
H. R. HELPER.

SECRETARY ARANJO TO MR. HELPER.

(Translation.)

LEGATION OF BRAZIL, 17 RUE DE TEHERAN,
PARIS, *May* 11, 1877.

MR. H. R. HELPER,

SIR: His Majesty, the Emperor of Brazil, has received the letter which you addressed to him on the 9th instant.

During his travels His Majesty does not occupy himself specially with affairs pertaining to his Government; and he therefore regrets being unable to take into consideration the reclamation which you have addressed to him, and which may properly be submitted to his Government only at Rio de Janeiro.

In regard to the other affair which you mention, His Majesty fears, from the few indications given by you, that it also enters into the same category with those several matters and questions with which he does not actively concern himself while abroad. If this should not be so, (and you yourself are left to be the sole judge of it,) His Majesty will receive you, in the Grand Hotel, at his customary hour for public receptions,—from 5:30 to 6:30 o'clock,—any evening next week; but under the express condition that, during the interview, no mention whatever shall be made of the claim which forms the principal subject of your letter.

Accept, sir, the assurance of my most distinguished consideration.

ARANJO,
Secretary to the Legation.

MR. HELPER TO SECRETARY ARANJO.

HOTEL DU RHONE,
PARIS, *May* 13, 1877.

SENHOR ARANJO,

SIR: I must thank you for the polite note which you have addressed to me, at the instance of His Majesty, the Emperor of Brazil, informing me (in reply to my letter of last Wednesday,) of certain rules which His Majesty has adopted in regard to matters of governmental business submitted for his consideration during his absence from his Empire.

With this information so clearly before me, I shall, of course, not presume to trouble His Majesty, here nor elsewhere out of Brazil, with any claim on the one hand, or enterprise on the other, which would be, even in the least degree, repugnant to his imperial wishes.

I shall, however, seek an early opportunity to pay to His Majesty my sincere respects, and for this purpose will call at his hotel, during one of the evenings of this week, within the hour of general receptions mentioned in your note.

I have the honor to be, most respectfully, your obedient servant,

H. R. HELPER.

MR. HELPER TO MR. JORDAN.

PARIS, FRANCE, *May* 30, 1877.
EDWARD JORDAN, *Esq., New York.*

DEAR SIR: By perusing the inclosed correspondence which I have recently had here with His Imperial Majesty Dom Pedro II, you will be enabled to perceive the obstacles which have hindered me from taking a " nigh cut " to justice and success with our Fiedler claim against Brazil.

It now concerns me not to be defeated in the more regular and determined course of procedure which I am about to undertake.

When I called on the Emperor, three days after the date of my note to Secretary Aranjo, I found his Majesty, as it became him to be, while dignified, yet perfectly polite, and not unaffable. He expressed great delight with most of the incidents and experiences of his visit to the United States, and himself remarked, with reference to the business which had brought me before him, that the rules which he had established for himself and suite, while abroad, and from which he had not once departed, rendered it necessary for him to refer me and my claim, unconsidered by himself, to his Government at Rio de Janeiro, just as he had done in all similar cases; and that, in this way, while he had given me no preference over others, he had, at the same time, given no one any preference over me. His Majesty seemed to be perfectly candid and impartial about the matter; and, upon the whole, I feel rather pleased and encouraged than otherwise. Yet, as things now stand, I do not expect to accomplish anything before November or December; so if you do not hear from me again until then, you may rightly attribute my silence to the fact of my having nothing to say.

Yours, very truly,
H. R. HELPER.

MR. HELPER TO SECRETARY EVARTS.

PARIS, FRANCE, *June* 4, 1877.
HON. WILLIAM M. EVARTS,
Secretary of State, *Washington.*

SIR: It is not Bolivia this time, but Brazil. I have the honor to request that you will be good enough to give your attention to the just claim of Ernest Fiedler, of New York, against the Government of Brazil, as presented in the annexed paper, and as you will find it already on record in the Department of State, as there presented, several years ago, by Edward Jordan, Esquire, who was formerly Solicitor of the Treasury under Secretary Chase, and who is now engaged in the general practice of law, at New York. Mr. Jordan and I are now prosecuting this claim together; and my only object in writing to you these lines, at this time, is to request that you, as the American Secretary of State, will so far further the ends of equity as to instruct our Envoy Extraordinary and Minister Plenipotentiary at Rio de Janeiro to give me, on my arrival there, the aid of his friendly offices in obtaining from Brazil the simple measure of justice so plainly due to the claimant. * * * I expect to sail from Bordeaux for Rio de Janeiro within the next ten days.

I have the honor to be, most respectfully,
Your obedient servant,
H. R. HELPER.

MR. HELPER TO THE PRINCESS IZABEL.

NO 39 RUA PRINCEZA IMPERIAL,
RIO DE JANEIRO, *July* 21, 1877.
TO HER SERENE HIGHNESS,
THE IMPERIAL PRINCESS IZABEL,
Regent of Brazil.

EXALTED MADAM: I have the honor to solicit the official

attention of your Highness to the following correspondence, which, in Paris, France, little more than two months ago, passed between your august father, the Emperor of Brazil, and myself, in relation to the claim of Ernest Fiedler, of New York, against the Government of Brazil; and to request that you will be kind enough to accept my part o. the correspondence, and to act upon it, in all respects, precisely as if the same had been originally addressed to your Imperial Highness.

My first letter to His Majesty, succinctly explaining the nature of the claim, and giving the reasons which influenced me in going from America to Europe, to seek an interview with him on the subject, was as follows: * * * To which letter from myself to the Emperor, I received, on the 12th of May, from Senhor Aranjo, Secretary of the Brazilian Legation, in Paris, the following reply: * * * On the 13th of May, acknowledging receipt of Senhor Aranjo's letter, I wrote a note of which the following is a copy: * *

As for the important enterprise alluded to in the foregoing letter to the Emperor, which enterprise justice and duty to my client require me constantly to hold as secondary and subordinate to the claim, I will here only remark that the claim itself is quite independent of the enterprise; but the enterprise, resting exclusively with myself, (and I, at this time, not being able to go on with it,) may not be entirely independent of the claim. Even the additional necessary planning of the enterprise, up to a point where it will be prudent to begin to execute it, it being now in a rather intricate and chaotic condition, will yet require the expenditure of much time and labor and money; all of which, in the hope of being ultimately able to achieve a due share of the high honor in prospect, I propose shall be borne only by myself.

The only consideration which I would now ask for the enterprise at the hands of your Highness, is the prompt performance by your Government, without further delay, of a simple act of justice, justice to my client, which, speaking with perfect frankness, will place me in possession of a fee sufficient to enable me, within two years from the time of the final settlement of the claim, to commence, and, with the aid of others, to carry on to completion, what I profoundly and honestly regard as by far the most gigantic and progressive scheme which has ever yet been broached to Brazil.

Your Highness will have perceived that, thus far, I have been studiously careful not to give any clew whatever to the nature of the great enterprise to which allusion is here made. A discreet general will, under grave circumstances of situation and resources, frequently keep his purposes and plans a profound secret from his own army; and governments, as your Highness is well aware, often dispatch men-of-war against an enemy, with special instructions which even the admiral in command is himself neither to open nor know until after he shall have advanced a certain number of miles or hours upon the ocean. Publicity of the enterprise, in its present crude state, would, I fear, result only in cloudiness of discussion, wrangling, confusion and failure; whereas, by steadily and prudently pursuing the plans which I have already roughly outlined, I feel confident that I shall, in due time, be able to secure clearness of vision, regularity of proceeding, good order, and success.

Let me now give to your Highness reasonable proofs of my perfect sincerity and good faith in thus writing concerning the possible issue of this long-contemplated enterprise. Be good enough to name to me one of your most wise and worthy Ministers of State,—a Brazilian of well-known integrity and discernment, before whom I may, in strict confidence, lay the principal points of my scheme; only let him, by your command, be responsible to your Highness, to the Emperor, and to myself, that, except to your Highness, to the Emperor, or to myself, he will not, at any time, make the slightest mention of the nature of the enterprise during the full space of two years from the date of the final settlement of the Fiedler claim; unless meanwhile, I shall have given written notice of earlier readiness for open discussion and action in the premises. Another requisite in the qualifications of the gentleman, whomsoever he may be, is that he shall be possessed of a fair knowledge of the English language; as otherwise, my own linguistic defects being both special and general, I may not have the good fortune to make myself well understood.

Columbus, by his grand ideas and achievements, helped very materially to immortalize the name of Isabella of Spain, and, at the same time, to enliven and promote the general progress of the world. Whether I, in all respects a much humbler man than the great Italio-Spanish navigator and discoverer, shall have the honor, by word or deed, to add anything to the renown of Izabel of Brazil, or to advance essentially certain of the important interests of her vast Empire, depends, perhaps, altogether on the manner in which your Highness may be pleased to take cognizance of the double subject of this communication.

In any event, however, whatever may be the pleasure of your Highness concerning the proposed enterprise, I shall not permit myself to doubt of the just and honorable course which your Government will now pursue in regard to the Fiedler claim; touching which I have with me all the documents and other vouchers necessary to establish its equity and footing within the limits defined in the great code of international law.

I have the honor to be, with great respect,
    Your Highness' obedient servant,
      H. R. HELPER.

MR. HELPER TO SECRETARY ALBUQUERQUE.

No. 39 Rua da Princeza Imperial,
Rio de Janeiro, *July* 21, 1877.
To His Excellency the Hon. Conselheiro
Diogo Velho Cavalcanti de Albuquerque,
Seeretary of State for Brazil.

DISTINGUISHED SIR: Although I have not the honor of any personal acquaintance with your Excellency, yet, not being a stranger to the good reputation which is so generally coupled with your name, I take the liberty of requesting that you will be so obliging as to see that the accompanying communication, addressed to her Serene Highness, the Imperial Princess Izabel, be duly presented to her, for any such consideration or action on her part as may seem to be just and expedient.

I have the honor to be, with great respect,
Your Excellency's obedient servant,
H. R. HELPER.

MR. HELPER TO SECRETARY EVARTS.

No. 39 Rua da Princeza Imperial,
Rio de Janeiro, Brazil, *August* 6, 1877.
Hon. William M. Evarts,
Secretary of State, Washington.

SIR: Six years ago, when I arrived at Chuquisaca, the then capital of Bolivia, where I found the Congress of that country in session, and where President Morales (who was, a few months afterward, shot dead by his nephew,) was residing and giving attention to public affairs, I, having special business with the Bolivian Government, expected to find at that *de facto* capital of the country, a Minister of the United States; as we were then in full and regular diplomatic intercourse with that Republic. It so happened, however, that, although we had in Bolivia a Minister who had been instructed, by Secretary Fish, to assist me in an effort to effect the settlement of a just claim which I had undertaken to collect from the Government of that Andean Power, yet he was quietly and permanently residing at an out-of-the-way sort of place, called Cochabamba, about one hundred and fifty miles distant ; the road or, rather the rough and narrow path to which, leading over sky-reaching spurs of the Andes, and along perilous precipices, whose lower depths seemed to run but a little way this side of the centre of the earth, was passable, barely and hazardously passable, only on mule-back.

After ten days of most wearisome and doubly-dangerous travel, having, meanwhile, as in all other parts of Bolivia, to carry with me, on sumpter mules, my bed, baggage and provisions, I had the honor and pleasure to alight safely at Cochabamba, in the presence of our amiable Minister, Mr. Markbreit, who assured me (and truly, I dare say,) that he had permission, from our own Department of State, to reside continuously at Cochabamba, because it was and is a more genial and pleasant city than either Chuquisaca or La Paz, which are, alternately, for a year or so at a time, the statutorily recognized capitals of Bolivia. I had hoped that that was the last disappointment I should ever have to suffer because of not being able to find, when I had legitimate and important business with him, an American Minister at the capital of the country to which he had been accredited. But a second disappointment, a new disadvantage, of a similar kind, has now befallen me in Brazil. Three weeks ago I arrived here, with the purpose of prosecuting against this Government the Fiedler claim, in relation to which I had the honor of addressing you from Paris, France, on the 4th of June. The Hon. Mr. Partridge, recently here in the capacity of Envoy Extraordinary and Minister Plenipotentiary, had, as I am informed, left Rio de Janeiro for Europe and the United States,—ostensibly on mere leave of absence, but in reality not intending to return to Brazil,—about three weeks before my arrival.

Not only is there here no American Minister, but there is not even a Chargé d' Affaires, nor any other representative of our country invested with diplomatic powers. I am, therefore, unable to proceed regularly with my business, and will, I suppose, have simply to wait, with such poor patience as I can command, under heavy expenses and many other detrimental conditions, such as are common in this country and climate, until a new Minister from the United States shall have arrived at Rio de Janeiro. Yet I indulge the hope that President Hayes and yourself may soon find it consistent with public interests, and promotive of justice and comity in international intercourse, to dispatch to Brazil one of our most able and upright statesmen, an experienced diplomatist, who, by his wise and faithful services, will honor alike the great Republic of his citizenship, and the vast Empire to which he will come as an Envoy. Please also let our new Minister come instructed to use his good offices in assisting me to settle, upon principles of equity, the Fiedler claim; for I am confidentially and credibly assured that Brazil, during the continuance of the present strange and calamitous development of anthropological supremacy hereabout,—constituted as it is of a most heinous and hideous hybridity of Portuguese and negroes on the one hand, and of Indians and mulattoes on the other,—will not, at any time, pay anybody nor anything, unless she be closely and repeatedly urged to the performance of her duty in that respect by one possessing both the right and the ability so to urge her.

Another point: Of late years our Ministers here have resided, all the year round, at Petropolis, which is to, the capital of Brazil, Rio de Janeiro, much the same that Long Branch, during the Presidency of General Grant, was to the capital of the United States, Washington City. This permanent residency of our Ministers at Petropolis—which is not the capital of the country to which they come accredited,—has, as I am well assured, been a source of great inconvenience and disadvantage to every American citizen in Brazil, who has had occasion to require their services; the trip to Petropolis and back to Rio de Janeiro generally consuming three or four days' time, and thirty dollars, more or less, in the way of necessary and unavoidable expenses. I would respectfully suggest therefore, that, henceforth, our Ministers to Brazil be required to reside in or near the capital of the country, Rio de Janeiro, during the time, at least, that the Emperor and the Parliament hold their own persons and sessions here, which, as a general rule, is not less than eight months in the year. During some years the Emperor never goes to Petropolis at all. At no time, in no year, does either he himself or any one of his Ministers ever transact there any public business. All the official business of the Empire whether legislative, judicial, or executive, is transacted only at the capital, Rio de Janeiro.

I have the honor to be, most respectfully,
Your obedient servant,
H. R. HELPER.

MR. HELPER TO MR. JORDAN.

RIO DE JANEIRO, *August* 6, 1877.
EDWARD JORDAN, *Esq., New York.*
DEAR SIR: Without waiting to hear from you in reply to

any of my letters from London and Paris, I may now inform you that I duly presented here, on the 21st ultimo, to Her Serene and Imperial Highness Izabel, the Princess Regent of Brazil, through her Secretary of State, the Hon. Conselheiro Diogo Velho Cavalcanti de Albuquerque, our Fiedler claim against this Government; but thus far, for reasons which I am not well able to explain, I have received no answer to my communication.

Yesterday, however,—I may just as well say it to you as it was said to me,— I was informed by an intimate friend of Baron Cotegipe, the Brazilian Secretary of the Treasury, to whom, as also to his friend, my informant, I brought letters of introduction, that it was thought Brazil ought not to pay, and would not pay, the Fiedler claim,—and for the reasons (equivocal and flimsy as they are,) which have already been given in the Report made to the Emperor, in 1873, by His Majesty's Council of State.

As, however, this information is unofficial and from mere hearsay, I can, of course, take no serious notice of it. Thus, during a period of at least two weeks, that is to say, since the 21st ultimo, I have been, and am still, simply in suspense, awaiting the reply of the Brazilian Secretary of State to my letter; but His Excellency seems to be in no hurry; and Heaven only knows how much longer I may, in this manner, be compelled to practice, seemingly, if not in reality, the virtues of patience and forbearance.

What is now most against me is the fact that we have here, at this time, no American Minister, nor even a Chargé d' Affaires; no representative higher than a Consul-General, Mr. Hinds, who assures me that, so long as Brazil remains in her present unprosperous condition, she will not pay our claim, nor any other claim, however just, unless she be actually forced to do so. From all I have thus far been able to learn, it is probable that little or nothing can be done in the absence of a Minister of the United States at Rio de Janeiro; and if any one has yet been appointed to succeed Mr. Partridge, who, it is said, has resigned absolutely, and will not return to Brazil, I have not seen any notice of the appointment. Mr. Partridge left here, as I am informed, about three weeks before my arrival. The Emperor's continued absenteeism from Brazil,—he is still sojourning in Europe,—is also an unfortunate circumstance for us in the Fiedler case. Yet it is sincerely hoped and expected that His Majesty will return to Rio de Janeiro not later than two months hence. If it be necessary, and I dare say it will be necessary, I shall await his coming. I trust that President Hayes and Secretary Evarts will not permit our mission here to remain vacant much longer. It ought to be filled immediately by a native citizen,—a real American,—who should be a statesman and diplomatist of first-rate character and ability. Can you not do something to hasten the coming of such a Minister?

Yours, very truly,

H. R. HELPER.

MR. HELPER TO SECRETARY ALBUQUERQUE.

RIO DE JANEIRO, *August* 22, 1877.
TO HIS EXCELLENCY THE HON. CONSELHEIRO
    DIOGO VELHO CAVALCANTI DE ALBUQUERQUE,
        Secretary of State for Brazil.

DISTINGUISHED SIR: Full four weeks ago, that is to say, on the 21st ultimo, I, as a citizen of the United States, and as the duly authorized attorney for the claimant, had the honor to address your Excellency on the subject of the Fiedler claim against Brazil; but up to the present time I have not had the honor to receive from your Excellency anything in reply. It is not my fault, though it may be my misfortune, that there is now no American Minister here, through whom I might, in accordance with international usage, in cases of this kind, present my claim to the Brazilian Government. As, however, the case is in reality very plain and very just, I feel warranted in requesting that, under the circumstances of my being here alone on this business, your Excellency will so far dispense with the mere formalities of diplomacy, as to designate an ab.e and upright official, or a number of such officials, representing Brazil, before whom I may appear with my documents, and with whom I may equitably and finally settle the said claim.

In consideration of the fact that this claim against Brazil, founded as it is upon principles of both law and justice, has already been pending nearly ten years, I trust that your Excellency may perceive that now is a proper time to bring it to a right conclusion. Almost the only objection which Brazil has hitherto urged, or can urge, in defence of her non-recognition of the claim, is the allegation (strange, extraordinarily strange as it is, indeed, it being in direct opposition to the statements contained in the letter of the Brazilian Chargé d' Affaires, Senhor H. Cavalcanti Albuquerque,) that Mr. Bocayuva, on the one hand, was not the agent of Brazil, and that Mr. Goicouria, on the other hand, was not Mr. Bocayuva's attorney. Now, putting aside for the time, all the other papers and points in the case, let us see exactly what Senhor Albuquerque, as the diplomatic representative of Brazil in the United States, did say in this regard, when, having been referred to, he was applied to for information touching the positions respectively of the said Bocayuva and the said Goicouria. Here is a true transcript of his letter: * * *

Very difficult indeed would it be for any one to state four importa .t facts (for facts they were and are to Fiedler, and to Fiedler's misleading and misfortune,) more pointedly, or with less verbosity, than they were stated by Chargé Albuquerque in the foregoing letter; and I contend that, according to all just rules and principles of international law, that one letter of itself is quite sufficient to fix upon Brazil complete responsibility for the Fiedler claim. Yet I have with me much other collateral evidence, equally or more strong and conclusive, which I desire to adduce in support of the claim, and will do so as soon as your Excellency may be pleased to inform me before whom, when laid, it will be fully and fairly considered.

Brazil may now prove beyond a doubt, if she can, that neither Bocayuva nor Goicouria was ever, in any manner whatever, connected with either her Government or her government schemes of immigration; furthermore, she may prove conclusively, if she can, that no such man as either the one or the other ever existed; that is to say, she may prove incontestably, if she can, that both Bocayuva and Goicouria were and are mere myths, and not men; yet, nevertheless, there are the absolute and formal assurances of Brazil's diplomatic representative in the United States, to a certain citizen and shipowner of the United States; first, that Bocayuva was the Agent for Brazilian Immigration; second, that Goicouria was his attorney; third, that they had power to charter sailing vessels or steamers; and fourth, that he, Chargé Albuquerque himself, believed the Government of Brazil would affirm their acts accordingly.

If, from failure from whatever cause, to comprehend with precision the laws or instructions of his Government, Chargé Albuquerque, in his official capacity, misrepresented any fact to our citizen, and through that misrepresentation our citizen was (as he was indeed,) seriously injured in his business and property, it behooves Brazil, in the maintenance of her prominence as an honorable and exemplary power among the family of nations, to make good the words of her representative in respect to that citizen; and her recourse, if recourse to her be possible, must be against her own representative, whose inadvertent exaggerations or misstatements involved her in an unpremeditated obligation.

Only a few years ago, (it is a great grief to have to mention it,) one of our own United States Ministers to Brazil exceeded his rightful duties in a matter of diplomacy, wherein Brazil, though yielding under protest to his demand, for the time being, very properly held our Government at Washington responsible for his unauthorized and inequitable proceedings. Within a short while, however,—certainly in much less time than ten years,—after our Government was made acquainted with the facts in the case, it was plainly seen that Brazil was in the right; and so restitution with interest was made of a certain amount of money which our Minister had arbitrarily and illegally exacted. That was simply a case of holding, and rightly holding, the United States responsible for the anomalous conduct of one of their representatives. In like manner, it is but fair, it is but conformable to the highest rules of international law and justice, that Brazil should now be held responsible for the effective action, whether in itself regular or irregular, right or wrong, of her own representative, through whose official assurances a citizen of the United States, in his own country, was misled into a disastrous undertaking.

Trusting that your Excellency may be pleased, without further delay, to appoint a learned and ingenuous official, or two or more such officials, to take into consideration all the facts and precedents pertaining to this claim, and to co-operate with me in soon bringing the case to an honorable and satisfactory adjustment,

I have the honor to be, with great respect,
Your Excellency's obedient servant,
H. R. HELPER.

POSTSCRIPT:—Touching the other matter, the great enterprise projected in Brazil's behalf, which formed a subordinate part of my letter of the 21st ultimo, but which, as your Excellency will have perceived, is not mentioned at all in the foregoing communication, I may here remark, that, of itself, as I understand it, (and I, being the originator and as yet sole custodian of the scheme, ought certainly to understand it reasonably well,) it is not only a thing of excellence, but it is also a thing of dignity; a dignity which I am not in the least disposed to sacrifice by any over-eager or imprudent presentment of its surpassing merits. If, therefore, your Excellency should not hear from me again on this particular subject, my silence may be properly attributed to what I can but regard as the listless indifference of Brazil to one of the most important measures ever yet devised for her general development and aggrandizement. Only this I will say in addition, that I am now holding myself in readiness to make good every word of my first letter in this respect; and that while the enterprise itself is of such a nature that it requires, for its full comprehension, the grasp of an uncommonly masculine mind, yet I should be very glad if her Serene Highness, the Princess Regent, after appointing one of her ablest and best subjects to give me an audience, in accordance with my suggestion, would herself condescend to be present at the interview, so she might prompt any examination, ask any question, or interpose any word or act of approbation or disapprobation, which, in the judgment of her Highness, might be necessary for the protection and advancement of Brazilian interests. If, then, the contents of my first letter have been communicated to the Princess Regent, I would thank your Excellency to communicate to her Highness the contents of this one also; including, of course, the contents or at least the substance of this postscript.

H. R. H.

EX-CONSUL UPTON TO THE BARON CABO DE FRIO.

RIO DE JANEIRO, *August* 23, 1877.
To HIS EXCELLENCY THE BARON CABO DE FRIO,
Assistant Secretary of State.

MY DEAR BARON: It seems that I have somewhat misapprehended the wishes of my friend, Mr. Helper, in not delivering the letter which he addressed, this forenoon, through my hands, to Secretary Albuquerque, and which, as you will remember, I showed to you when I had the honor of calling to deliver it to your Excellency, informing you at the same time that I was aware of its contents, the writer himself having read it to me; but which I did not deliver, because, as I remarked, I supposed it might not be necessary to do so in view of the letter from Secretary Albuquerque, which just then you placed in my hands for Mr. Helper.

Meeting Mr. Helper at the United States Consulate, between two and three o'clock this afternoon, he seemed rather surprised to learn that I had not delivered his letter, remarking that the circumstances under which it was written rendered it but fair and just to his client, and also to himself, that it should take its regular course as he intended when he wrote it, and stating further that he desired to be placed on record in the case in accordance with his communication.

So, still wishing to serve my friend,—as, in fact, I having promised, he expected me to do,—I went back immediately to your Department, to deliver the letter absolutely, but met, only a few yards this side of the door, the Departmental Letter-Receiver and Registrar coming away from his office, who informed me that it was then too late (it being about five minutes after three o'clock,) for him to receive and register the letter to-day. Inclosed with this I will take it back to the Registrar early to-morrow morning, and will then deliver to Mr. Helper the letter from Secretary Albuquerque, which you handed to me for him, he preferring, he said, not to receive it until after the delivery of his own, which, by the space of an hour or more, first came into my hands this forenoon.

I am, my dear Baron, most sincerely,
Your friend and servant,
BENJAMIN UPTON.

SECRETARY ALBUQUERQUE TO MR. HELPER.

(*Unofficial.*)
(Translation.)

RIO DE JANEIRO, *August* 23, 1877.
H. R. HELPER, *Esq.*

DEAR SIR: I have received your letter of the 21st of July, together with your Memorial addressed to Her Highness, the Princess Regent, to whom it has been presented; and, instructed by the same august Princess, I have to inform you that, if you desire to make any explanation in regard to the matter mentioned by you in connection with the Fiedler claim, you may, for that purpose, call upon his Excellency the Baron Cabo de Frio. This functionary, because of his position as Assistant Secretary of State, and also because of his almost perfect familiarity with the English language, is worthy to receive your fullest confidence. Wishing you to accept the assurance of my consideration,

I am, sir, yours respectfully,
DIOGO VELHO CAVALCANTI DE ALBUQUERQUE.

It is a somewhat singular coincidence that the foregoing

note from Secretary Albuquerque, of the 23d of August, in reply to the first one from me, which was written and delivered on the 21st of July, four weeks previously, is of even date with my later letter complaining of His Excellency's having paid no attention to my opening communication. This note was brought and offered to me in the afternoon immediately succeeding the morning on which I had dispatched my letter of complaint to His Excellency; my worthy friend, Ex-Consul Upton, having been the bearer of both letters, as he himself has already particularly explained, in his own communication of the same date, addressed by himself to the Assistant Secretary of State, Baron Cabo de Frio.

H. R. H.

MR. HELPER TO SECRETARY ALBUQUERQUE

RIO DE JANEIRO, *August* 24, 1877.
TO HIS EXCELLENCY THE HON. CONSELHEIRO
   DIOGO VELHO CAVALCANTI DE ALBUQUERQUE,
    Secretary of State for Brazil.

DISTINGUISHED SIR: The letter which your Excellency did me the honor to address to me, under date of yesterday, in reply to my communication of the 21st ultimo, has been received; and although it is almost silent on the subject of the Fiedler claim, the subject of immediate and special interest which has brought me to Brazil, yet I accept, with much pleasure and many thanks, the reference which your Excellency, as Minister of Foreign Affairs for her Imperial Highness the Princess Regent, has been pleased to give me to the Baron Cabo de Frio, on the subordinate subject of my present business in the southern hemisphere. My friend, Mr. Benjamin Upton, formerly United States

Consul at Pará, who already enjoys the honor of acquaintanceship with Baron Cabo de Frio, and who speaks of him in the highest possible terms, as a statesman of rare ability and integrity, has kindly consented to introduce me to him; and will do so, he says, on Monday or Tuesday of next week, provided it will be agreeable to the Baron to receive us on either of those two days; but if not then, on the earliest day afterward which the Baron's pleasure may designate.

I have the honor to be, most respectfully,
Your Excellency's obedient servant,
H. R. HELPER.

MR. HELPER TO SECRETARY EVARTS.

RIO DE JANEIRO, *August* 24, 1877.
HON. WILLIAM M. EVARTS,
Secretary of State, Washington.

SIR: With a perfectly just cause in hand, in behalf of Helen M. Fiedler, executress of the estate of Ernest Fiedler, of New York, an American citizen, deceased, against the Government of Brazil, I am yet absolutely helpless here, and can do nothing in the absence of an American Minister, unless you yourself, as the United States Secretary for Foreign Affairs, will kindly come to the aid of my client and myself. I have requested Edward Jordan, Esquire, of New York, an able and distinguished attorney at law, to send you a copy of his synopsis of the case, as he gave it to me; and, on this same subject, I would also respectfully solicit your attention to the following copy of a letter which I addressed yesterday to the Hon. Diogo Velho Cavalcanti de Albuquerque, the Brazilian Secretary of State, who, as I have been verbally and confidentially assured, to-day, will not consider the case officially, or with any view of settling it, until an American Minister shall have arrived at Rio de Janeiro to assist in re-opening the claim, in regular diplomatic order. You will readily perceive, therefore, what an awkward and vexatious position I am in here, simply because our Legation in Brazil is now,—whether blamably or blamelessly, I will not undertake to say,—destitute of an incumbent. If no American Minister has yet been appointed to come to Brazil, will you not be good enough to instruct our worthy Consul-General here, Joseph M. Hinds, Esquire, to intercede with the Brazilian Government so far as to secure, if possible, in this tenth year of its pendency, an early and honest settlement of the Fiedler claim?

I have the honor to be, most respectfully,
Your obedient servant,
H. R. HELPER.

MR. HELPER TO THE BARON CABO DE FRIO.

RIO DE JANEIRO, *August* 28, 1877.
TO HIS EXCELLENCY THE BARON CABO DE FRIO.

WORTHY BARON: Since I had the honor of an introduction to your Excellency, in the forenoon of to-day, by my friends Consul-General Hinds and Ex-Consul Upton, it has occurred to me that, inasmuch as the stupendous enterprise to which I have thus far merely alluded, and which, as already explained, is not yet sufficiently matured for either execution or publicity, is one that promises to Brazil, in the near future, permanently and increasingly great results, it might, perhaps, all things considered, be fit and proper for both Her Highness the Princess Regent, and her noble Consort the Count d'Eu, to be present (if Their Highnesses will deign to be present,) during the approaching interview between your Excellency and myself, when, with all confidence, I propose to lay before you, systematically and somewhat in detail, an outline of all my plans and purposes in this prodigious endeavor.

I have the honor to request, therefore, that your Excellency will be good enough to ascertain the pleasure of Their Highnesses in this regard; and if they, as the highest representatives of Brazil now within the Empire, will vouchsafe their presence for the occasion, please receive, for yourself and for me, Their Highnesses' commands as to the day and hour when we may wait upon them.

Yet in the event that it may not be convenient or agreeable to Their Highnesses to receive us for an hour's consultation upon the subject of this grand enterprise,—an enterprise which, as I fully believe, is pre-eminently worthy of the profoundest attention of even so great a potentate as the Emperor Dom Pedro II himself, if His Majesty were here,— you will please, speaking only for yourself, name the particular time when I may call on you for the purpose of explaining everything to your Excellency alone, and I will call accordingly.

While I am decidedly of the opinion that the presence at our interview of both of Their Highnesses, the Princess Regent and the Count d'Eu, would be especially protective and promotive of the enterprise itself, and therefore helpful to Brazil, yet, if it would not be convenient for both of them to attend, I doubt not that the merits or demerits of the undertaking might be more clearly established by such pertinent interrogatories and suggestions as either she or he might elect to lodge at different stages of our conference; and for these reasons I trust that one or the other of Their Highnesses, if not both, may, for the once, be pleased to honor and assist us in our well-meaning deliberations and discussions on the subject.

I have the honor to be, most respectfully,
Your Excellency's obedient servant,
H. R. HELPER.

SECRETARY ALBUQUERQUE TO MR. HELPER.

[Translation.]

RIO DE JANEIRO, *September* 4, 1877.

H. R. HELPER, *Esq*.

DEAR SIR: After sending you my letter of the 23d of August, authorizing the Baron Cabo de Frio to hear whatever you might wish to say in relation to the enterprise which you mentioned, I received the communication of the same date, which you addressed to me, respecting the enterprise and the claim of the American citizen Fidler.*

Returning to you the said communication of the 23d of August, the language of which does not permit it to be filed among the archives of this Department while under my charge, it devolves upon me to say, in reference to the claim, that the Imperial Government, considering it unfounded, have declared to the Legation of the United States of America, their conclusion not to pay it; and as to the enterprise, that it is impracticable as you have proposed it in your letters, and in the conversation which you have since had with the Baron Cabo de Frio.

*Let the reader not fail to note the fact that, while Secretary Albuquerque takes exception to a part of the language contained in my letter of the 23d of August, which speaks for itself, as I am quite willing to have it speak, he nevertheless here persumes to designate my honored client, Mr. Fiedler, as a "Fidler"!

H. R. H.

Wishing you to accept the assurance of my consideration.
I am, sir, yours respectfully,
DIOGO VELHO CAVALCANTI DE ALBUQUERQUE.

In the foregoing letter, Secretary Albuquerque is just and polite enough not to assert absolutely that my huge enterprise is in itself impracticable; for in truth, how could he, or the Baron Cabo de Frio, or any one else, who had not then, and has never yet, heard one word in explanation of its real nature, form any reasonable or even intelligible opinion as to whether it was or was not a feasible project? He only says, and for this he and his Government are responsible, that "it is impracticable as you have proposed it in your letter, and in the conversation which you have since had with the Baron Cabo de Frio." Very well; be it so; I must accept the inevitable; and in this case there are special considerations which lead me to accept it without unassuageable grief. The very positive condition, the full acknowledgment and settlement of the Fiedler claim as a condition precedent, only on which I was in any manner disposed to make known the enterprise to Brazil, and to secure to her a prominent and important identification with it, not having been fulfilled by her, I had nothing whatever to say, and said nothing; and so the matter ended, leaving everybody and everything situated essentially as if no step in the premises had ever been proposed or taken. It remains to be seen, however, whether what was thus so ill-looking and impossible for Imperial chicanery and stupidity and weakness, may not, at a period not far in the future, prove altogether fair and feasible for Republican integrity and wisdom and strength.

H. R. H.

MR. HELPER TO SECRETARY ALBUQUERQUE.

RIO DE JANEIRO, *September* 5, 1877
TO HIS EXCELLENCY THE HON. CONSELHEIRO
DIOGO CAVALCANTI DE ALBUQUERQUE,
Secretary of State for Brazil.

DISTINGUISHED SIR. In reply to your Excellency's letter of yesterday, inclosing mine of the 23d ultimo, because of implied disrespect in language, I trust that you will permit me to disclaim, as I do most emphatically, any intention to have been, or to be, otherwise than entirely respectful and candid toward your Excellency.

Born and reared as an humble and unpretending citizen of a Republic, where plainness and distinctness of speech are thought to have special virtues in practical life, and where the simplest and most direct forms of expression are generally used, it is very possible that some of my words may disclose a want of knowledge of the more courtly circumflexions and embellishments which lend grace and fascination to the phrases of the favored subjects of an Empire.

[So far, however, as my own poor judgment enables me to arrive at anything like a correct decision in the premises, it is not my own humble self, but a no less accomplished and celebrated personage than your Excellency, who is incontestably at fault on account of impropriety of language in this correspondence. Indeed, if one so habitually unpresuming as myself may be permitted to speak the truth straightforwardly, it is quite impossible for me to restrain my surprise and dissatisfaction, not to say humiliation and grief, at finding that your Excellency, in your letter of yesterday, the very letter of complaint of language, does not scruple to denounce and libel my deceased client, whose whole life was singularly blameless and exemplary in all respects, as if he had been a hare-brained buffoon, or a harum-scarum vagabond. This strange denunciation of a good man departed, this utterly uncalled-for libel on the irreproachable and honored dead, occurs at the close of the paragraph wherein your Excellency inelegantly and sportively, if not contemptuously and profanely, assumes to speak of my inanimate but worthy countryman Fiedler as "the American citizen Fidler!" How exceedingly vexatious it must inevitably prove to the surviving relatives and friends of the deceased, that, by this unprovoked and gratuitous remark of your Excellency, his name is thus officially and irreparably linked to such an uncommendable and ridiculous occupation, too economically spelled with only one d! Let me assure your Excellency that Mr. Fiedler, a true gentleman of sterling qualities and unblemished character, whose good name it is now alike my duty and my pleasure to defend from the opprobrium of unmerited jeers and epithets, was never, whilst on earth, a " Fidler " at all; but having been an eminently right-minded and fair-dealing denizen of the world, it may, perhaps, for aught I know, not be too much to suppose the possibility of his now being actively and blissfully musical, with voice, or instrument, or both, in a heavenly choir! Never, let me again assure your Excellency, never at any period of his life, was Mr. Fiedler a " Fidler," nor a fiddler; a giggler, nor a jiggler; a higgler, nor a niggler; a riddler, nor a wriggler; a quiddler, nor a piddler; nor was he ever, in any way, either the shadow or the substance of a Jeremy Diddler. On the contrary, in the business world, he was always known as a highly respectable and justly-esteemed ship-owner and merchant; and it is in these honorable and important vocations, and not as a mere " Fidler," that I would now unfeignedly desire and request your Excellency to take cognizance of his career.]

In further reference to the Report made to His Majesty, the Emperor, by a number of his Honorable Councillors of

State, in 1873, on the Fiedler claim, when certainly at least one of the essential papers in the case had been mistranslated, I have with me, as I once stated to His Majesty in Paris, and as I have already twice stated to your Excellency in Rio de Janeiro, various documents, old and new, which prove conclusively both the rightfulness and the tenableness of the claim under the law of nations; else I have myself read to little or no purpose the works of Grotius, Puffendorf, Wheaton, Woolsey, Phillimore, Vattel, and other eminent publicists, whose learned treatises on international law are now fitly reckoned as precious jewels of just rules among a large majority of the more advanced nationalities.

Whenever, whether under Her Serene Highness, the Princess Regent, or under His August Majesty, the Emperor, it may be compatible with the pleasure of the Brazilian Government to permit me to present, for due consideration, all the vouchers I now hold in support of my client's rights, I shall, I doubt not, be able to establish the perfect validity and equity of the Fiedler claim.

Although, much to my disadvantage and regret, I do not find now, on the part of your Excellency's Government, any disposition to grant me the privilege of proving my claim in the absence of a Minister of the United States, yet I indulge the hope that that privilege will not be denied me after such a Minister,—at a somewhat indefinite period in the future,— shall have arrived in Brazil.

I have the honor to be, very respectfully,
Your Excellency's obedient servant,
H. R. HELPER.

After careful reconsideration, the long paragraph embraced within brackets in the foregoing letter was entirely left out, whilst the other portions only were rewritten and dispatched to Minister Albuquerque; the conclusion to which

I came being that this was one of those little semi-diplomatic and semi-personal contests wherein, for a time at least, it was better to suffer a temporary and retrievable defeat rather than to achieve only an indecisive and unavailing victory.

H. R. H.

MR. HELPER TO SECRETARY EVARTS.

RIO DE JANEIRO, *September* 8, 1877.
HON. WILLIAM M. EVARTS,
Secretary of State, Washington.

SIR: As I have sometimes, during the last few years, had occasion to ask and receive the friendly services of the Hon. Secretary of State of the United States, in certain matters of business of only a semi-official nature, between the various citizens of our country and three or four of the Governments of South America, with which those citizens have had dealings, I feel it incumbent on myself, as a duty which I owe to my own Government, to report to the Department over which you now have the honor to preside, any important fact or facts which (especially where, as here at this time, there is no Minister,) may come to my knowledge affecting the welfare or the good reputation of our pre-eminently great and glorious Republic.

Yesterday was enthusiastically celebrated here as the fifty-fifth anniversary of Brazilian independence, Dom Pedro I and his brave compatriots having shaken off the yoke of Portugal on the 7th of September, 1822. Within the radius of a stone's throw, at one of the principal places of assembly and demonstration in this city, I counted no less than ninety-two unfurled and waving flags, representing respectively almost every nation under the sun; but the Star-Spangled Banner, the most beautiful and auspicious of all national ensigns, was not among them.

Remarking the humiliating absence of our flag from these festivities, and inquiring of a number of my American friends as to the probable reason of it, I was informed by some that, for several years past, the diplomatic relations of Brazil with the United States have not, as concerns Brazil herself, been on a very cordial basis; one of our Ministers here, within the last dozen years or so, having, unfortunately for both his country and himself, brought with him to Brazil and carried in Brazil, a haughty head and a high hand. Others, of whom I made inquiry on the same subject, thought it probable that our flag may not have been displayed with the many others, one hundred, less eight, merely because of an oversight, or possibly because of a scarcity of bunting; the supposition being that, after ninety-two had been finished, there may not have been found enough material remaining to make another! Even this slightly comforting supposition, however, would still leave us last and least in the estimation of Brazil.

Another fact, far more inimical to the United States than the occasional failure to display here the non-black and beautiful American colors in juxtaposition with the standards of other nations, is the almost daily publication in the *Jornal do Commercio,* of Rio de Janeiro, the most widely-circulated and influential newspaper in Brazil, of real or fictitious correspondence and other writings, original and selected, the purpose of which is manifestly and provokingly hostile to our country, our people, our republican institutions, our system of government. This paper, the *Jornal do Commercio,* is confidentially and largely in the service of the Imperial Government, and is the only paper which publishes full reports of the speeches made in the Brazilian

Parliament. The animus of these many and constantly-recurring articles in the *Jornal do Commercio* is of a similar kind to that which appeared in all the Anglo-Rebel newspapers (of Great Britain) from 1861 to 1865, when their columns diurnally teemed with the grossest misrepresentations and most doleful prophecies concerning the United States of America, and when we ourselves had been laid under the direful necessity of struggling like Greeks, as against Trojans, to maintain the imposing completeness and excellence of our nationality.

Whatever ground we may have lost here, through the wrong-headedness and wrong-handedness of one or more unworthy Ministers, we ought now to be deeply concerned to regain, as soon as possible, through a succession of other Ministers of unmistakable ability and integrity. A Minister possessed of the qualifications and virtues above mentioned,' should certainly be in Rio de Janeiro at this very time, and all the time, indeed, while the American Legation here continues to be maintained at so heavy an expense to our Government as twelve thousand dollars per annum.

Brazil, though, on her own part, is by no means faultless in her diplomatic relations with us; on the contrary, she is justly chargeable with having taken many strange and devious steps, both in advancing toward us and in retreating from us. In a remarkably disingenuous Report now before me, covering twenty-eight pages of foolscap, which a committee of her high-titled nobility made to the Emperor, some years ago, on the Fiedler claim, I have just counted no less than forty-three distinct and glaring quibbles. In this case I heartily wish I could fitly employ a milder word than quibble, and yet give proper expression to the facts as they exist; but it has been absolutely necessary for me, with a due regard to truth and justice, and with my limited knowledge of the euphemisms of the English language, to use here the word quibble, or duplicity, or jesuitry; and, of these three words, it has seemed to me that quibble is the one which is most fairly and gently descriptive of the shocking shifts and subterfuges of this sycophantic and scandalous script.

It would now be a plain disregard of the higher requirements of international law, as expounded by the most learned publicists, and also a downright injustice to Brazil herself, if she were not held to a rigid responsibility for the satisfaction of this claim. Even yet a very considerable number of Brazilian statesmen in high places need to be taught that there is an important and praiseworthy difference between the straightforward diplomacy of the nineteenth century and the crafty evasions and circumventions of mediæval times.

It is, I trust, but right and reasonable for me to hope and expect that a very able and excellent Minister of the United States will soon be sent hither, pointedly and strongly instructed to assist me, while attending to his comparatively few other duties, in obtaining at last the small measure of justice which Brazil has, for so many years, been permitted to withhold from a bereaved and worthy claimant, my client, Mrs. Fiedler.

I have the honor to be, most respectfully,
Your obedient servant, .
H. R. HELPER.

ACTING-SECRETARY SEWARD TO MR. HELPER.

DEPARTMENT OF STATE,
WASHINGTON, *September* 11, 1877.
H. R. HELPER, *Esq.*,
   Rio de Janeiro, Brazil.
SIR: Your letter from Paris of the 4th of June last, and

that from Rio de Janeiro of the 6th ultimo, relative to the Fiedler claim, so called, on Brazil, have been received. In reply, I have to inform you that the Minister of the United States accredited to that government has been instructed upon the subject.

I am, sir, your obedient servant,
F. W. SEWARD.

MR. JORDAN TO MR. HELPER.

WASHINGTON, *September* 28, 1879.
H. R. HELPER, *Esq., Rio de Janeiro, Brazil.*

DEAR SIR: Your several letters have been received, for which please accept my thanks. I am sorry to learn that the Brazilian authorities have displayed so little readiness to do justice in the matter of the Fiedler claim; and especially am I surprised that those officials appear disposed to question what they have heretofore impliedly, if not expressly, conceded. You will, of course, have noted the fact that the Imperial Council of State do not cast any doubt on the authenticity of Chargé Albuquerque's letter, but only deny that that letter gave any warrant for the action of General Goicouria in chartering the Circassian.

As soon as your communication of the 10th of August reached me, I sent it to Mr. Persuhn, with a request that the letter in question, the letter of Chargé Albuquerque, or a properly authenticated copy thereof, should be furnished for transmission to you. On the 18th instant, I received a reply from him, saying that, owing to the death of Mr. Russell Sturgis, to whom the letter was originally addressed, he had not yet been able to obtain or find the document itself, but suggesting that Mr. Stillman, the attorney for the estate of Mr. Sturgis, might either have it in his possession or know where it could be found. Accordingly, I wrote immediately to Mr. Stillman, who, however, has not yet replied to the note of inquiry which I addressed to him. To-day I have written again to Mr. Persuhn, urging him to omit no intelligent effort to discover the desired document, and I sincerely hope he may find it.

Going to the State Department this afternoon, I took with me the copy of your letter to Secretary Evarts, and learned that the original had already been received. In conversation with the Assistant Secretary, the Secretary himself being absent, I expressed the hope, as an indorsement of your own desire, that an able representative of our Government may soon be appointed to Brazil. * * * Rest assured that I fully sympathize with you, in view of the very difficult task you have in hand; but I feel confident, at the same time, that, if success be attainable, as I still believe it is, you will ultimately succeed.

With the best wishes, yours, very truly,
EDWARD JORDAN.

SECRETARY EVARTS TO MR. HELPER.

DEPARTMENT OF STATE,
WASHINGTON, *October* 9, 1877.

H. R. HELPER, *Esq., Rio de Janeiro, Brazil.*

SIR: Your letter of the 24th of August last, relative to the Fiedler claim, so-called, on the government of Brazil, has been received. In reply, I have to state that Mr. Hilliard, the newly appointed Minister, embarked for his destination some time since, and was subsequently instructed upon the

subject, pursuant to your letter from Paris, the receipt of which was at the same time acknowledged.
I am, sir, your obedient servant,
WILLIAM M. EVARTS.

MR. HELPER TO THE EMPEROR DOM PEDRO II.

RIO DE JANEIRO, *October* 11, 1877.
TO HIS IMPERIAL MAJESTY DOM PEDRO II,
Emperor of Brazil.

SIRE: Sincerely congratulating your Majesty on your safe and happy and profoundly welcome return to your throne, after a long absence in many of the grand and far-distant nationalities of the world, and having now, from a sense of propriety, waited upward of two weeks for a gradual subsidence of the more prolonged and enthusiastic ovations and festivities which your devoted subjects have prepared in joy and honor of your regression, I beg the privilege of recurring once again to the special business which, unable to settle in either the United States or France, has brought me to Brazil. Since I had the honor of some very pleasant correspondence and an interview with your Majesty, in Paris, five months ago, on the subject of the Fiedler claim against Brazil, I have had here, in Rio de Janeiro, on the same subject, with His Excellency the Brazilian Secretary of State, the Hon. Diogo Velho Cavalcanti de Albuquerque, additional correspondence, which, however, to my great regret, has not been perfectly agreeable on both sides.

Permit me now to re-state to your Majesty a few brief facts. Invested with full and ample powers of attorney I hold in my hands, for collection against Brazil, a somewhat ancient claim, the Fiedler claim, already of nearly ten years' standing, which is just, and which, according to the ablest expositions of the principles of international law and equity, as laid down in the works of Vattel, Wheaton, Woolsey, Field, Phillimore, and other eminent publicists, the Government of Brazil is in honor bound to pay. This claim, with the principal and interest combined, up to to-day, amounts to a little less than $32,000.

Although this claim was diplomatically presented to your Majesty's Government many years ago, and an equitable settlement requested, yet, owing either to mistranslation of some of the documents, or to misconception of certain facts of law and precedent in the premises, payment was then denied. It so happens that I am now here just at a time when, incidentally, there is no American Minister in Brazil; and I should like, therefore,—having already been here three months in this unpleasant and disadvantageous situation,—to be favored with the privilege of seeing the case re-opened and reconsidered on the basis of simple justice and the law of nations.

During a period of nearly eleven years, that is to say, from November, 1866, to the present time, I have almost daily and nightly, but not exclusively, busied my brain in Brazil's behalf with a problem which, when properly worked out into its preconceived reality, will, as I honestly believe, be worth to Brazil quite as many millions of dollars as she now owes thousands on the Fiedler claim. At least two years more will be required to complete the plans for proposing publicly, and for beginning prudently and auspiciously, this great enterprise; an enterprise the nature of which I have never yet breathed to a human soul; for, for its own sake, for its own ultimate success, I have not dared to make it known in the immature condition in which it now is, and in which it will probably remain until I myself shall be able to expend.

of my own means, and at my own option, a very considerable amount of money,—many thousands of dollars,—in fairly submitting it for the decisive judgment and energy and action of such men as are gifted with far-reaching wisdom, world-improving aims, and ample resources.

Under all these circumstances, is it too much for me to ask (is it not about the least thing in all the world that I could ask?) that your Majesty may now be pleased to co-operate with me in bringing the Fiedler claim to an early and equitable termination, so that I may soon be free to go on with my labors in the colossal enterprise which will, I doubt not, when completed, infuse into Brazil a vast amount of new life and energy and wealth and greatness?

In this affair, let me, if possible, not fail to be fairly comprehended. The Fiedler claim, as an international cause, is, in itself good and strong and self-sustaining. It stands out distinctly and entirely on its own merits. By the law of nations, and by the laws of equity and honor, Brazil is fully and irreversibly bound to the payment of this claim. The only consideration, over and above my own resources, which I now ask for my gigantic enterprise (notwithstanding the fact that, before it can be properly matured for open consideration and action, it will yet cost me, besides much additional time and labor, an outlay of at least five or six thousand dollars,) is that Brazil will no longer delay the particular act of justice due from her in the Fiedler suit. Only let Brazil expedite equity in the Fiedler reclamation, and all will be well with the enterprise.

My action in proposing, as I proposed at Paris, and as I now again propose at Rio de Janeiro, to explain,—yet to no less important and responsible a personage than your Majesty, or to one of your Majesty's household, or to a special appointee of your Majesty,—in strict confidence for two years from the date of the settlement of the Fiedler claim, the character and magnitude of my enterprise, must be received, if received at all, as simply what it is in fact; namely, an act on my part of voluntary good will and grace toward Brazil; for which the mere hastening by Brazil of justice in the Fiedler affair, can be accepted by me as only a satisfactory offset of corresponding good will and grace on her own part toward myself. An Empire will then have done me a small favor, by doing at last an act of justice without further postponement, in a time-consuming and ire-provoking matter, already of nearly ten years' standing; and I shall be happy in the consciousness of having rendered to that same Empire a most signal and lasting service; a service of infinitely greater value than the amount of the comparatively unimportant claim which I have come to collect. In point of law, Brazil will then owe nothing to Fiedler, nothing to me; and I shall owe nothing to Brazil; only she will, of course, in honor keep faith with me, and I will in honor keep faith with her; fulfilling all my promises to develop, at the appointed time, to the best of my ability, the grand and glorious enterprise, which, many years before I ever heard of even the name of Fiedler, I devised rudimentally in Brazil's behalf.

In no case, in no degree, can I consent that Brazil shall acquire any voice or direction or control in this matter until I shall myself, two years or so after the settlement of the Fiedler claim, be ready, entirely of my own volition, to impart to her, and to surrender to her, a certain power in the premises which, for the final consummation of the enterprise itself, she will then need to exercise with all vigor and prudence. But until the lapse of the time thus mentioned, my own pleasure and judgment in the enterprise must continue, as at present, unquestioned, absolute, supreme.

Proposing, as I now do, in all confidence, to submit to your Majesty, *in writing,* a full explanation of my scheme, I respectfully suggest and request that your Majesty may be pleased to appoint a highly honorable and competent gentleman, a Brazilian statesman, familiar with the English language, who will be wholly responsible to your Majesty, and to the Government of your Majesty, for the strictest observance on his own part of perfect secrecy in this affair. Let him then, in the first place, call for all the papers in the Fiedler claim, and after carefully examining them and finding that they constitute a just and valid claim against Brazil, let him, in the second place, demand of me a written presentation of the details of my enterprise, which, after perusing and approving, he will, I trust, from motives of wisdom and patriotism, and in harmony of consultation and understanding with your Majesty, feel impelled to indorse and justify in a manner somewhat as follows:

Rio de Janeiro, Brazil,
October———, 1877.

Both for reasons of Justice and for reasons of State, I advise that the Fiedler claim against Brazil, as presented to the Imperial Government by Mr. H. R. Helper, be paid in accordance with the several papers, public and private, which, by arrangement with His Imperial Majesty, have been submitted to me for my consideration. This, the within principal private paper has, by me, been thus carefully enveloped and sealed and placed in the custody of His Imperial Majesty, under whose orders I have so done; His Majesty having been previously pleased to peruse and discuss its contents with me, and to give to the same his august approbation. But this particular paper may, or may not, by the consent of Mr. Helper, as already given, and wholly at the option of the Brazilian Government, for the advancement of the Empire, be opened and published two years after the date of the final settlement of the Fiedler claim. I believe that the true interests of Brazil will be subserved by not opening this

paper, and by not publishing anything concerning it, prior to the expiration of the two years above mentioned.
Respectfully submitted.

To the foregoing proposed indorsement I should desire the simple addition of the word CORRECT, and your Majesty's signmanual thereto; and then, in that form, or in such similar form as might be more pleasing to your Majesty, I should feel quite content to let it remain in your Majesty's own keeping; well assured that no one would dare to tamper with the paper contrary to your Majesty's expressed wishes and instructions.

As a step preliminary to the formal proceeding here proposed, I shall, if agreeable to your Majesty, take pleasure in waiting on you at any time that may suit your convenience, and which your Majesty may designate, with a full written outline of my really extraordinary scheme in the interest of Brazil.

I have the honor to be, with perfect respect,
Your Majesty's obedient servant,
H. R. HELPER.

MR. HELPER TO SECRETARY ALBUQUERQUE.

RIO DE JANEIRO, *October* 11, 1877.
TO HIS EXCELLENCY THE HON. CONSELHEIRO
DIOGO VELHO CAVALCANTI DE ALBUQUERQUE,
Secretary of State for Brazil.

DISTINGUISHED SIR: Certain facts and circumstances in connection with what passed between his Imperial Majesty the Emperor of Brazil and myself, at Paris, France, in May

last, would seem to call for the letter which I have herewith addressed to him; and I trust, therefore, that your Excellency may be pleased to submit it to him for any such action as His Majesty's wisdom may dictate in relation to its contents.
I have the honor to be, with great respect,
Your Excellency's obedient servant.
H. R. HELPER.

MR. HELPER TO THE EMPEROR DOM PEDRO II.*

[*As written and held in readiness for submission to His Imperial Majesty's judgment, but never read nor delivered nor sent to him, for the reason that His Imperial Majesty was not pleased to comply with the writer's conditions; conditions which have been specifically stated in several previous communications. Yet it is here but just and right for me to remark further, in reference to His Imperial Majesty Dom Pedro II, that he himself, a white man, a man of pure Aryan descent, is by far the ablest and best Brazilian whom I have ever met in or out of Brazil; and it is my firm belief that if his big-titled but black or bi-colored and bombastic and blundering Ministers and Council of State had only been a little more like their august master, the Fiedler claim would have been amicably and equitably settled many years ago.
H. R. H.]

This communication is to be regarded as strictly private, for the period of two years, in compliance with the conditions proposed in the last preceding letter from Mr. Helper to the Emperor of Brazil.

RIO DE JANEIRO, *October* 12, 1877.
TO HIS IMPERIAL MAJESTY DOM PEDRO II,
Emperor of Brazil.
SIRE: Coming now in this manner, concordantly with my letter of yesterday, to an explanation of the nature of my subordinate and confidential business here, in connection with the Fiedler claim against Brazil, I have the honor

to venture the remark, that, if I am not laboring under the spell of an egregious error of judgment, your Majesty will hardly fail to recognize at once the unequalled magnitude and importance of the enterprise to which I have already alluded, in several previous communications, when I inform you that it looks to nothing less than the construction, within thirteen or fourteen years from to-day, of a double-track railway, of first-class materials and workmanship, from the southwestern part of Canada, or from southern Manitoba, or from the western shores of Hudson Bay, to that particular part of Southern Patagonia bounded or divided by the Strait of Magellan,—right down along or near the longitudinal centres of North and Central and South America, with lateral lines leading to the capitals of all the nationalities through which the main trunk will pass.

At a later period, perhaps, yet probably not later than two or three generations hence, extensions may, for the profit and well-being of all concerned, be made northwestwardly through British America and Alaska to Behring Strait, and southwardly through Tierra del Fuego to Beagle Channel, and possibly beyond, even to Cape Horn.

Animated as she is by the liberal spirit of the most enlightened statesmanship of modern times, Brazil, I am fully persuaded, will look with none the less but rather the more favor on this project, because it aims at the improvement and elevation of other nations as well as herself. Brazil will be benefited and advanced, and in no way injured, by a degree of welfare on the part of her sister States corresponding with her own prosperity; and as with Brazil, in this respect, so also with all the other Commonwealths, a dozen or more, which are to be leagued and linked and locked together in inviolable unity, comity and reciprocity, as the happy recipients, during all the ages to come, of the brilliant honors and advantages which will accrue to them from ownership in, and connection with, the largest and best railroad on the face of the earth; a skillfully constructed railroad, of steel and other superior substances, and of double-track width and facility, which, lying midway between the two great oceans of the world, will grandly and conspicuously utilize and enrich the length, yes, and breadth as well as length, of two continents to a distance, in length alone, of nearly or quite eight thousand miles! If the uniquely outstretching and far-extending intercontinental railway thus contemplated should ever be constructed all the way from Behring Strait to Cape Horn, or from a particular point to a specified locality in proximity to those widely-separated places respectively, following the deflections suggested in the last foregoing paragrah, then the entire length of the road will be not less than ten thousand miles!

Besides the almost incalculable advantages of a material nature which this road, with its great Brazilian branch, will bring to the vast dominions of your Majesty, to Brazil will also belong the honor of having been the place where the idea of building it originated; for my first thought on the subject (whilst writhing under the tortures of a terrible attack of seasickness, during a three days' tempest, sixty miles or so off the coast of Brazil, in the very latitude of Rio de Janeiro, in November, 1866, I being then in course of my first return from the Argentine Republic to the United States,) was only suggestive of a road from Rio de Janeiro to New York; and from that thought, good as it was in itself, but less feasible, has been gradually evolved the immensely larger and better scheme here partly presented.

It is but reasonable to hope and believe that, directly and indirectly, by an adequately elongated straightforwardness of the main stem, and by a judicious deflection of its branches, the railway thus projected is to become a general diffuser of peace, prosperity and plenty throughout most of the larger and better portions of the New World. Yet, in the very nature of things, Brazil in South America, and the United States in North America, will probably be greater gainers by the road (though not, it may be supposed, in proportion to territory,) than any other two countries. It is believed, moreover, that by the general and dextrous use of certain of the latest and best inventions in the art of railroad-building, the vast system of railways here contemplated can be constructed at less cost per mile (on the average, and in comparison of conditions of Nature and quantities and qualities of performance,) than any similar work that has ever yet been done in any part of South America.

This, then, thus briefly, is the most significant part of the outline of the enterprise which, with all due deference, I have the honor to submit for the consideration of your Majesty; and for the consummation of which, including the eastern and western branches of the main road, the enormous sum of three hundred millions of dollars, more or less, will probably be required; every dollar of which amount can, I think, at the proper time, and under proper guarantees of interest,—at a rate not exceeding six per cent. per annum, proportionately divisible in its obligations among all the nations to be benefitted by the road,—be easily raised in the United States.

Only there are certain somewhat voluminous, and as yet incomplete details (such as showing specifically how the several States of South and Central America and Mexico may, respectively in one or two or more ways, for their own advantage, bear a fair ratio of the burden of the undertaking,) concerning which I do not deem it necessary to venture a definite or written opinion at this time. A fitter time, not more than two or three years hence, (nearly eleven years already have I silently studied these problems,) will, I trust, afford me the occasion to present, in a well-digested and practical form, all the details to which I have here and elsewhere referred.

Meanwhile, in order that I may be free and able to work out these details in the best possible manner,—a task by no means simple, nor exempt from either labor or expense,—I only ask that your Majesty will be good enough to do now, or cause to be done, what it is but right that Brazil should do in any event, even though she should be found to be wholly regardless of the gigantic scheme here submitted for her betterment, and for making all American interests mutually convergent and helpful to each other, and that is to command, or at least recommend, speedy justice to my client.

Let the Fiedler claim be paid. It is a just claim, already of nearly ten years' standing, and might certainly, with all propriety, have been paid long before this time. The entire sum due on this claim, with interest, at six per cent. per annum, from the date of Chevalier Fleury's advice to Mr. Fiedler to abandon the voyage, December 18, 1867, up to the 18th instant, October 18, 1877, amounts to only $31,-800; and this, too, to a citizen of the United States, a country which bought from Brazil, last year, coffee and other South American products of the value of nearly $46,000,000; while Brazil bought from the United States, during the same time, North American products of the value of but little more than $7,000,000. So that with a mere fraction, so to speak, of the enormous balance of trade against us, as between the United States and herself, Brazil can easily pay off this obligation.

For Brazil's sake, for the claimant's sake, and, above all, for the sake of justice itself, cause this ten years' claim to be paid within the next two months, (why not within the next two weeks?) and I can then promise at least a fair possibility, radiant with the roseate hues of probability, that your

Majesty may, on a certain Saturday morning, not more than fourteen years hence, take a special train from Rio de Janeiro, and arrive in New York, amid demonstrations of the most hearty welcome, in the afternoon or evening of the following Saturday, if not sooner. Besides, your fare and other general accommodations, all along the route, shall be quite as good as those obtainable in any of the better sort of hotels; and in thus making an overland pleasure excursion from the greatest city in South America to the greatest city in North America, your Majesty will, in 1891, a little earlier or a little later, unlike your Majesty in 1876, avoid a long voyage, seasickness, storms at sea, and all the other discomforts and perils incident to ocean travel.

It is intended that the numerous sections of the unmatched and unmatchable intercontinental railway here proposed, shall be so equally and perfectly finished and interlocked, into a single line of vast longitudinal stretch, as to constitute, in this nineteenth century, and in all the centuries to come, one of the most palpable and imperishable proofs of the superiority of North American and South American and Central American energy, ingenuity, enterprise, integrity, honor and achievement; and while no part of the road itself, the tunnels, the bridges, or the viaducts, no part of the rolling-stock, or other property or appurtenances of the road, must be other than first-class in all respects, yet everything, including the obtaining from Governments of the necessary charters and franchises, must be done with such exact rectitude and economy, that, from the beginning to the end of the work, not so much as one dollar shall be uselessly, extravagantly or corruptly expended.

Another very important condition which it is desirable shall be well understood and established in relation to this road of roads, is that a strip of territory of reasonable width, on both sides of the main stem, shall be declared and forever maintained as neutral ground to all belligerents; that the road itself shall never be interrupted in its regular schedules of daily working, nor used in any manner whatever for facilitating military movements, or for other purposes of war; and that any nation or faction daring to violate this signally beneficent compact of peace and improvement, shall at once become the common enemy of all the other parties to the agreement, and be punished accordingly.

Superior lines of telegraph along the entire length of all the roads here projected, are held in view as collateral improvements which it will be well to construct simultaneously with the roads themselves; so that, in this way, correspondence may be greatly facilitated, business promoted, and the invincibly powerful and widespread family of American nationalities, occupying all the territory between the Artic Regions and Cape Horn, and harmoniously allied with each other in the industrial development and enlightening march of peaceful and prosperous and progressive civilization, may be respectively heard from, in accents of sisterly greeting and fraternal emulation, every morning at the breakfast-table.

Under the existing condition of things, the one great desideratum of Brazil, at this particular time, is the development of her exhaustless internal resources; and these resources she can develop only by enlarging her facilities for internal communication. Whilst heretofore Brazil has laudably and liberally encouraged the growth and extension of her interests without, that is to say, her interests on water, yet it seems to me that she has, meanwhile, given too little attention to her interests within, that is to say, her interests on land. The grand and mighty railway, with its many connections, which I now propose for Brazil, will act upon her much the same as the heart, the seat and center of life, acts upon the human organism; by channels of radiation in every direction, it will vigorously dispense its vitalizing forces to the very extremities of the Empire, and help very obviously and largely to impart prosperity and happiness to millions upon millions of grateful souls. In short, the road will be of immense usefulness and profit to Brazil, a benefit to every other nationality in South America, and an advantage, without exception, to all the States and other Commonwealths of North America. How high the privilege, how great the honor, and how certain and glorious the gain, to be engaged, as Brazil may now engage herself (at the cost of only an act of justice in another matter of comparative insignificance,) in the joint inception and furtherance of a work so vast and so good; a work which, when completed, will conduce to the marvelous and ever-increasing welfare of nearly half the world! In the course of my letter to your Majesty, in Paris, France, five months ago, I said, in allusion to this great railway scheme, that, if successfully carried out, it would, in time, as I believed, give back to Brazil at least one hundred dollars for every dollar which she will pay me on the Fiedler claim. Your majesty or any other just-minded and clear-sighted personage, may now decide whether, if, in that opinion, I had used the ten times greater numeral *thousand*, instead of "hundred," I would not have been much nearer to the prospective and probable facts. Not only will the great Empire of your Majesty, by the consummation of this enterprise, gain very largely in trade and money, but it will also, at the same time, gain immensely in white immigration, which is the only sort of immigration that can henceforth be decently or respectably useful to Brazil or to any other country,—and in general improvements; so that, in this way, the Fiedler affair, which at first might seem to have been a minor misfortune, may at last prove to be one of the greatest possible blessings to Brazil. So may it prove!

  I have the honor to be, most respectfully,
    Your Majesty's obedient servant,
        H. R. HELPER.

MR. HELPER TO MINISTER HILLIARD.

RIO DE JANEIRO, *October* 15, 1877.
HON. HENRY W. HILLIARD,
Envoy Extraordinary and Minister Plenipotentiary of the Republic of the United States of America to the Empire of Brazil.

SIR: Permit me to extend to you my sincere congratulations on the fact of your arrival here, yesterday, in good health, and under other desirable conditions, as Envoy Extraordinary and Minister Plenipotentiary from the Republic of the United States of America to the Empire of Brazil. I trust that your mission here may prove highly honorable and satisfactory to yourself, and conspicuously and lastingly advantageous to both the Republic and the Empire.

More than three months ago, that is to say, on the 10th of July, I arrived at Rio de Janeiro, under power of attorney to settle the claim of Ernest Fiedler, of New York, a citizen of the United States, against the Government of Brazil; and was much disappointed and chagrined to learn that your honorable predecessor in our Legation here, Mr. Partridge, had sailed hence for Europe and the United States, about three weeks previously. Under these circumstances, I indulge the hope that you will kindly excuse me for coming before you, so soon after your arrival in this city, with a matter of international business, which you will find fully explained in the seventeen inclosures herewith, and which, in order to facilitate you in perusing them intelligently, I will now particularize as follows, respectfully requesting your attention to the same *seriatim:*

No. 1. Power of Attorney from Helen M. Fiedler, executrix of the last will and testament of Ernest Fiedler, deceased, to Mr. Hinton Rowan Helper; May 5, 1876.

No. 2. Letter, dated March 15, 1867, from Chargé d'

Affaires Albuquerque, the diplomatic representative of Brazil in the United States, to Mr. Russell Sturgis, giving information, in reply to inquiries on the subject, that Mr. Quintino de Souza Bocayuva was the agent in the United States for Brazilian Immigration; that Mr. Domingo de Goicouria was Mr. Bocayuva's attorney; and that he, Chargé Albuquerque, believed his Government, the Brazilian Government, would approve whatever might be done by the said agent, or by the said attorney. If it be true that a merchant is responsible for the acts of his clerk, that a banker is responsible for the acts of his cashier, or that a government is responsible for the acts of its diplomatic representative; if it be true that there is anything of international value in the writings of Grotius, Puffendorf, Vattel, Phillimore, Wheaton, or Woolsey, or anything worthy of diplomatic regard in the dissertations of any other learned and distinguished publicist, then, whether, in reality, either Bocayuva or Goicouria was, or was not, the agent or subagent of Brazil, whether either or both were alive or dead, or whether, in fact, the one or the other, as man or as myth, ever existed, there can be no ingenuous question at all about Brazil's unevadable responsibility in this case.

No. 3. Charter-Party of the "Circassian;" August 21, 1867.

No. 4. Charter-Party of the "Marmion;" March 16, 1867.

No. 5. Mr. Goicouria to Mr. Fiedler; November 23, 1867.

No. 6. Mr. Fiedler to Chevalier Fleury; December 17, 1867.

No. 7. Chevalier Fleury to Mr. Fiedler; December 18, 1867.

No. 8. Mr. Fiedler to Chevalier Fleury; December 18, 1867.

No. 9. Mr. Fiedler to Minister Magalhaens; February 6, 1868.

No. 10. Minister Magalhaens to Mr. Fiedler; February 8, 1868.

No. 11. Minister Blow to Mr. Fiedler; September 22, 1870.

No. 12. Minister Blow to Mr. Fiedler; November 28, 1870.

No. 13. Report made to his Imperial Majesty Dom Pedro II, by three of his high-titled Councillors of State, namely, the Viscount de Souza Franco, the Marquis de Sapucahy, and the Viscount do Bom Retiro, attested by the Baron Cabo de Frio, formally and solemnly denying Brazil's responsibility in the premises. This aberrant Report covers *twenty-eight pages of foolscap,* and contains *forty-three misstatements of law and fact;* but further, on this particular point, I deem it prudent to say nothing, not daring, as a mere private individual and petitioner, to subject my hot head, in this calorific climate, to any elaborate service in a task wherein such an extraordinary amount of coolness and forbearance are required.

No. 14. Affidavit of Charles P. Persuhn; March 17, 1876.

No. 15. Affidavit of Capt. T. S. Ellis; March 18, 1876.

No. 16. Mr. Helper to the Hon. Edward Jordan; May 2, 1876.

No. 17. Hon Edward Jordan, (formerly Solicitor for the United States Treasury, under Secretary, afterward Chief-Justice, Chase,) to Mr. Helper; May 6, 1876. This brief from Mr. Jordan is a masterly *resumé* of the whole case.

In addition to the papers enumerated above, you will find others of importance bearing upon this claim among the archives of the Legation; and these several papers, as I doubt not you will perceive on examination, constitute a very clear and strong case against the Government of Brazil. The long and devious steps which Brazil has hitherto taken in diplomacy, to delay on the one hand, or to defeat on the other, the ends of equity in this matter, are both glaring and grievous, and are not to be borne hereafter with either silence or patience   As it is now nearly ten years since the claim has been pending, and I am here, as I have been for the last three months, in the absence of an American Minister, on expenses and with nothing else to do but solicit justice to my injured client and fellow-citizen, I trust that you will, in your official capacity, be good enough to co-operate with me in honorably adjusting the reclamation with the least additional postponement possible.

I have the honor to be, very respectfully,
Your obedient servant,
H. R. HELPER.

MINISTER HILLIARD TO MR. HELPER.

UNITED STATES LEGATION,
No. 9 RUA DO MARQUEZ DE ABRANTIS,
RIO DE JANEIRO, *November* 20, 1877.

H. R. HELPER, *Esq*.

SIR: I called at the Department of Foreign Affairs yesterday, and had an interview in regard to the Fiedler claim. If it will be convenient for you to call on me at two o'clock this afternoon, do so, and I will report the result.

I am, sir, very respectfully, yours,
HENRY W. HILLIARD.

MR. HELPER TO MINISTER HILLIARD.

RIO DE JANEIRO, *November* 22, 1877.
HON. HENRY W. HILLIARD,
United States Minister.

SIR: · When I first took in hand the claim of Ernest Fiedler, of New York, a citizen of the United States, against the Government of Brazil, it was my intention to prosecute it in strict conformity with the established rules of artless and honest diplomacy until the 18th day of December, 1877, (if not sooner settled,) on which date the tenth year of the existence of the said claim will have elapsed; and then, finding Brazil still perverse and persistent in her apparent purpose not to pay the amount so obviously due from her in the premises, it is my determination to carry the case into the Congress of the United States, and there petition my own Government for a bill which will secure to my fellow-citizen and client the measure of justice which Brazil has thus far, unheedful of the lucid requirements of the code of international law and equity, dared to withhold.

This determination on my part I have already had the honor of stating to you verbally, on at least three different occasions. Yesterday afternoon you returned to me the seventeen vouchers, covering the case, which I had the honor to transmit to you on the 15th ultimo, informing me, at the same time, that the Government of Brazil refuses positively to pay the claim, and declines even to peruse the papers which plainly prove the validity and rightfulness of the reclamation. Because of this unworthy mood and action on the part of the imperial and delinquent government, I am sorely surprised and disappointed. I had thought and hoped and believed better things of Brazil. Permit me to inquire: Am I now to consider myself debarred from proceeding further with this suit in Brazil? If so, having no other business here, I shall remain only a few days longer in Rio de Janeiro.

As the attorney for the claimant, with full powers, I would be willing to submit the matter to the arbitration of three foreign Ministers, Brazil naming the first, you the second, and they two the third. Or any other fair and simple method of arbitration which the Brazilian Government and yourself might mutually agree upon, would be satisfactory to me, and final to Fiedler. Pray be so kind as to ascertain for me the disposition of Brazil in regard to this proposition; and if she accepts it, you may, if you please, act upon it immediately in my behalf.

I have the honor to be, very respectfully,
Your obedient servant,
H. R. HELPER.

MR. HELPER TO MINISTER HILLIARD.

[Private Note.]

RIO DE JANEIRO, *November* 22, 1877.
HON. HENRY W. HILLIARD, &c., &c., &c.

DEAR SIR: It seems to me that the arbitrary and unjust decision of the matter mentioned in the accompaying communication, is, most likely, only the decision of Secretary of State Albuquerque, or of Baron Cabo de Frio, or of both, and not the decision of the Emperor himself. There ought certainly to be found some simple means of righting a gross wrong like this. My suggestion for easy arbitration in the premises may possibly be accepted; and if so, I shall be quite content to abide by the finding of the arbiters. Might it not be worth your while, as the American

Envoy, to call on the Emperor and explain to him frankly the course which the claimant's attorney is resolved to pursue, if the present decision of His Majesty's Ministers be sustained and adhered to, and the possible, if not probable, consequences to Brazil?

I am, dear sir, yours, very truly,
H. R. HELPER.

MINISTER HILLIARD TO MR. HELPEP

RIO DE JANEIRO, *November* 23, 1877

H. R. HELPER, *Esq*.

DEAR SIR: It would afford me sincere pleasure to act in accordance with your suggestion, in your note of yesterday, looking to the adjustment here of the Fiedler claim by arbitration, if my instructions permitted; but as they do not, I must respectfully decline.

My conversation with Baron Cabo de Frio was informal; but it satisfied me completely that it would be a task at once hopeless and vexatious to attempt to influence the Government of Brazil to change its decision in regard to the Fiedler claim. Of course it would be very agreeable to me personally to have you remain here while I stay; but I may repeat my assurance, that it would now be only a waste of time to press upon this Government the views which you entertain of your client's rights, and in which I fully concur.

Very respectfully and truly yours,
HENRY W. HILLIARD.

NEW PROOFS FROM BRAZIL'S OWN ARCHIVES.

CONSULATE-GENERAL OF THE
UNITED STATES OF AMERICA,
AT RIO DE JANEIRO BRAZIL,
November 29, 1877.

I, Francis M. Cordeiro, Vice-Consul-General of the United States of America, at Rio de Janeiro, (in the absence from Brazil of Consul-General Joseph M. Hinds,) do hereby certify that, at the instance of Mr. Hinton Rowan Helper, I have this day examined the *Diario Official do Imperio do Brazil*, of July 21, 1867, and have therein found, on the first page, fourth column, in Portuguese, as appears verbatim on the fourth page of this certificate, and here translated into English, the two following items, the same, in regular order of publication, being brief memoranda and information of certain official dispatches from the Brazilian Government:

1. "A dispatch to Quintino de Souza Bocayuva, advising him that his action in transporting to New York the one hundred and fifty shipwrecked persons from the brig Derby, bound from Galveston to this port, is approved."

2. "A dispatch to the same, informing him that the Government is duly advised of his having appointed, as his substitute in New York, the merchant Domingo de Goicouria."

I further certify, that, in the *Diario Official do Imperio do Brazil*, of the 27th of September, 1867, on the second page, and in the second column thereof, the following item appears in Portuguese, as copied verbatim on the fourth page of this certificate, and here translated into English, thus:

3. "A dispatch to Domingo de Goicouria, informing him that he is relieved from the obligation which he was under to charter steamers for the transportation of North American immigrants."

In testimony whereof, I have hereunto set my hand and affixed the seal of this Consulate-General, this the 29th day of November, 1877.
[L. S.] FRANCIS M. CORDEIRO,
Vice-Consul-General.

The foregoing Consular certificate, verifying certain stubborn facts explanatory of Brazil's indisputable intercourse with, and authority over, both Bocayuva and Goicouria, as her regularly recognized agents for purposes of immigration, deals only, as will have been observed, with openly published fragments of the Brazilian archives. As a matter of course, however, the unpublished and secret records of the Imperial Government at Rio de Janeiro, if they could be examined, would show much more fully, if not more plainly, the guilty collusion and connection and conduct between the said country and her said agents.
H. R. H.

MR. HELPER TO MINISTER HILLIARD

RIO DE JANEIRO, *November* 29, 1877.
HON. HENRY W. HILLIARD, *United States Minister.*

SIR: Whilst in this capital, from the 10th of July to the 14th of October, in the absence of an American Minister, it came to be convenient for me, from time to time, to lay the papers relating to the Fiedler claim against Brazil, before several estimable citizens of the United States, permanently or temporarily residing in Rio de Janeiro; among whom I may mention Consul-General Hinds, Ex-Consul Upton, Maj. James, Mr. Shannon, Mr. Longstreth, Prof. Hartt, and Dr. Wilson. All these gentlemen, having respectively examined and considered the facts in the case, have unhesitatingly expressed their judgment in favor of the claimant, declaring their conviction that it is clearly the duty of Brazil to pay the money (notably just and moderate as to the amount claimed,) for which the widow Fiedler's attorney has here recently, heretofore and elsewhere, duly presented an account.

The amount thus claimed is, as you are aware, only twenty thousand dollars, (it being less than one-half of the sum which was formally and legally agreed upon for the particular service required,) with interest thereon, at the rate of six per cent. per annum, from the 18th day of December, 1867,—the date of the letter of Chevalier Fleury, Brazil's Chargé d' Affaires in the United States, to Mr. Fiedler, advising him to relinquish the pre-determined and pre-stipulated voyage, for which, during the period of four months, so many and such expensive preparations had been made.

If your views in this case are in harmony with the opinions of the seven sagacious and substantial gentlemen named above,—and, having patiently perused all the papers, your views of the legal and moral merits of the claim can hardly be otherwise than quite correct,—will you not be kind enough to say so specifically, and thus favor my client and myself, and at the same time favor Right as against Wrong, with the value of your own more able and weighty judgment? Such an expression of opinion from you, given in virtue of your comprehensive knowledge of the matter at issue, would, I doubt not, be of fair service to the claimant; and it might, moreover, I dare say, eventually be of signal service in the general cause of international justice and honor.

I am, sir, with sincere regard, yours, very truly,

H. R. HELPER.

MINISTER HILLIARD TO MR. HELPER.

LEGATION OF THE UNITED STATES,
RIO DE JANEIRO, *December* 1, 1877.
HINTON R. HELPER, *Esq*.

DEAR SIR: As I have already said to you, an examination of the papers submitted to me in support of the Fiedler claim against the Government of Brazil, has satisfied me that the claim is at once just and moderate; and it seems to me that it should be recognized and paid in full. I am not, therefore, surprised to learn that our American citizens here, to whom you have shown the papers, concur in this view. Every consideration recommends this claim. Not only is it based on grounds which make it good in law; but even if any technical objection could be raised against its validity, still in equity I do not see how it can be disregarded or set aside.

Mr. Fiedler might well have claimed the full amount named in the contract, when, at the suggestion of the representative of the Brazilian Government, he withdrew his vessel from New Orleans, and did not sail for Rio de Janeiro. In consideration of the circumstances at the time, he generously proposed to receive twenty thousand dollars for his claim, when he might have demanded the paymer. forty-two thousand dollars, as he was ready to perform his contract in every particular.

It seems to me that, in proposing at this time to receive, with interest, twenty thousand dollars in satisfaction of the claim, you show commendable moderation.

As the claim is based on a contract, I can only aid you with my good offices, which I have cheerfully extended to you; and I only regret that you have not met complete success in bringing it to the attention of the Brazilian Government. I am, dear sir, very respectfully yours,

HENRY W. HILLIARD.

Touching the present imperfect and reformable practice in American diplomacy, which looks only to the exercise of "good offices" in matters of contract between our own citizens and foreign governments, see Secretary Fish's letter to Mr. Helper, under date of December 11, 1872, and also the reply of Secretary Fish to Senator Cameron, Chairman of the Senate Committee on Foreign Affairs, dated May 27, 1874.

H. R. H.

MR. HELPER TO A COMMITTEE OF AMERICAN SENATORS.

RIO DE JANEIRO, BRAZIL, *December* 1, 1877.
TO THE HONORABLE THE SENATE COMMITTEE
ON FOREIGN AFFAIRS, *Washington*.

GENTLEMEN: About to undertake a second fatiguing and perilous journey, on mule-back, across the continent of South America, from the Atlantic to the Pacific, I respectfully request that, in the event of my death within the next two years,—only in which event my brother, Mr. Hanson Pinkney Helper, of Davidson College, North Corolina, will forward to you this communication,—you may be pleased to give special attention to the subject explained in the accompanying papers.

It has been frequently remarked, and quite as truthfully as frequently, that every country in Europe which, for any considerable period, has ever yet enjoyed anything like a monopoly of the trade with India, has thereby greatly enriched itself. By the consummation of the gigantic intercontinental railway-scheme proposed in the annexed communication, (addressed to the Emperor of Brazil, but never sent nor shown to him, for the reason that he has manifested no disposition to comply with the only conditions, fair and simple as they were, on which I could prudently explain the matter,) the United States may soon be made the peerlessly powerful and self-protective recipient in perpetuity of the untold and inexhaustible riches of no less than three Indias,—the India of all South America, the India of all Central America, and the India of all Mexico. That is to say, all the separate and distinct countries in the New World south of the United States, and north as well as south, including moreover every State and Territory of the American Union itself, may thus reciprocally, for their own advancement and for our advancement, for their own aggrandizement and for our aggrandizement, be at once and forever rendered plentifully and peacefully and prosperously tributary to the Republic of Republics.

Under the regular and rightful operation of the vast system of railways here projected, we can, in the course of the next fifteen or twenty years, take permanently from Europe, as, by virtue of our geographical position and contiguity, and in consideration of our superior energy and skill, we ought to take, the immense trade and the profits of trade of the greater part of the southern hemisphere. At the same time, and by the same means, we shall become much more generally and genially and thriftily identified with that adjoining but as yet comparatively undeveloped and uninhabited hyperborean region which we find delineated as forming such a marvelously extensive portion of our own continent.

Gentlemen of the Committee : I honestly believe that if you will kindly and actively and successfully carry out this enterprise, in all the breadth and fulness of detail suggested by me, and with such important improvements in plans and principles as you yourselves will doubtless be able to introduce, you will thereby do for your own country, and for all the other countries of the New World, one of the very greatest services upon which you can possibly bring to bear the benign and far-reaching influences of your wisdom and patriotism. For my inception of this grand and prospectively glorious enterprise, I expect no remuneration whatever, other than that which I now find, and shall always find, within the recesses of my own breast; only I profoundly hope and trust that you will cause the work to be done in a manner every way worthy of American statesmanship, American honor, American interests, and, above all, American unity and nationality.

I remain, gentlemen, most respectfully,
Your fellow-citizen abroad,
H. R. HELPER.

A BROTHER'S REQUEST.

RIO DE JANEIRO, BRAZIL, *December* 1, 1877.

In the rather unwelcome contingency (which may Heaven avert!) mentioned in the first paragraph of the accompanying letter addressed to the Senate Committee on Foreign Affairs at Washington, my brother, Mr. Hanson Pinkney Helper, at Davidson College, North Carolina, will please transmit all these papers to the said Committee, meanwhile being very careful himself not to utter even so much as a vowel or a consonant to any one else concerning the new and important project therein partly explained.

Fraternally,
H. R. HELPER.

MR. HELPER TO SECRETARY EVARTS.

HOTEL DE LA PAIX,
BUENOS AYRES, ARGENTINE REPUBLIC,
December 18, 1877.
HON. WM. M. EVARTS, *Secretary of State, Washington.*

SIR: Between the political immorality of the military and revolutionary statesmen of Bolivia on the one hand, and that of the monarchical and conservative statesmen of Brazil on the other, it would seem that there is, after all, but very little difference.

I have the honor to solicit your attention to the following recital of certain facts: To-day completes the tenth year of the existence of the legal and equitable claim of Ernest Fiedler, a citizen of the United States, against the Government of Brazil; the claim having arisen out of the chartering, by an Immigration Agent for Brazil, of the steamship Circassian, belonging to Mr. Fiedler, on the 21st of August, 1867. Hitherto the claimant and his attorney in this case have been humble and patient supplicants for justice; henceforth they will appeal only as indignant and diligent demandants of their rights.

The following copy of a letter addressed to Mr. Fiedler, by Brazil's Chargé d'Affaires in the United States, the Chevalier Fleury, under date of December 18, 1867, has special significance in this connection.

*   *   *   *   *

Brazil now refuses to pay this claim, because, as she alleges, Mr. Bocayuva and Mr. Goicouria, her Agents for Immigration, held from her no authority nor power to charter steamships; and this allegation she has the hardihood to urge in positive conflict with the solemn and specific assurances given by her diplomatic representative in the United States, at the time of the chartering of the Circassian, that the said Agents did hold just such power! Here follows exactly what Brazil's Chargé d'Affaires, Mr. Albuquerque, wrote in reply to inquiries concerning the position of the two gentlemen in New York, who were there and then representing themselves as Imperial Agents for the encouragement and transportation of emigrants from the United States to Brazil.

*   *   *   *   *

In the light of the law of nations, as I understand it, that one letter of itself, from Chargé Albuquerque, fixes upon Brazil full and irrevocable responsibility for the Fiedler claim. The mischief having already been done by her representatives and agents, Brazil must not with impunity be permitted to unsay, at a long subsequent period, what her diplomatist said for her, officially, in 1867; the first saying, the ministerial assurance, for which she must be held to account, having gained the desired credence with our citizen, and caused, in consequence, great damage to his business and property.

Besides, there are other proofs, proofs equally positive, that Mr. Bocayuva and Mr. Goicouria were Brazil's Agents for Immigration, and that their power to charter vessels for the transportation of emigrants has been duly and repeatedly recognized by the Government of that country. In the *Diario Official do Imperio do Brazil*, of July 21, 1867, the two following items appear, the one immediately following the other, as brief memoranda of official acts of the Brazilian Government; it being customary to publish, in like manner, memorandums, respectively and in regular order of occurrence, of all the official acts of the said Government.

*   *   *   *   *   *

These several papers prove conclusively that both Mr. Bocayuva and Mr. Goicouria were in the service of Brazil, as her authorized and lawful Agents for Immigration, and that they, either or both of them, had power, as Chargé Albuquerque himself gave assurance, to charter sailing vessels or steamers for the transportation of emigrants from the United States to Brazil.

Moreover, the steamers Marmion and Catharine Whiting, both chartered by Mr. Goicouria, as the attorney for Mr. Bocayuva, precisely the same as in the case of the Circassian, performed their voyages as agreed upon, and were paid for their services by the Brazilian Government. Notwithstanding these two striking precedents against her, however, and notwithstanding all the other corroborative and incontestable facts in favor of the claimant, Brazil still declines to indemnify him for the damages which she occasioned to his vocation and property by non-compliance with her part of the contract between herself and him; and, in direct contradiction of her Minister's statement, she now shamelessly and brazenly repeats her untruthful declaration, that neither Bocayuva nor Goicouria had any power from her to charter steamers!

There are more than a dozen other important papers which, but for their length, I might here copy in support of this claim; all of which are elucidative of facts which impart to it additional strength and validity. Our present Envoy Extraordinary and Minister Plenipotentiary from the United States to Brazil, the Hon. Henry W. Hilliard, has patiently and carefully examined all the vouchers in the case; and I here transcribe a letter which I had the honor to receive from him in this regard, on the 2d instant, only three days prior to my departure from Rio de Janeiro for Buenos Ayres.

* * * * *

It now only remains for me to request, Mr. Secretary of State, that you will be kind enough to take note of the fact that, if the just and reasonable account, already of full ten years' standing, which I have thus presented against the

Government of Brazil, aggregating with principal and interest, at six per cent. up to to-day, the round sum of $32,000 in gold, be not paid by or before the end of seven months more, that is to say, by or before the 18th day of July, 1878, I shall immediately thereafter, if not impeded in my movements by any unforeseen obstacles, publish a pamphlet embodying all the principal facts in the case, and will send the same by mail or otherwise, to every American Senator and Representative; and soon afterward, on the first day of the meeting of Congress, I shall ask that pre-eminently honorable and distinguished national council for a bill of indemnity against Brazil.

If, therefore, worthy Secretary of State, you can yet give to our Minister in Brazil any additional instructions which may lead to an early and amicable adjustment of the claim, I entreat you to do so; for I am really very loath to say or do anything that might have a tendency to disturb, even in the slightest degree, the harmony or well-being of any of our international relations. Yet I certainly cannot willingly or quietly submit to an act of gross injustice, defiantly and persistently perpetrated against either my client or myself.

It may be that, if you could feel justified in instructing our Minister at Rio de Janeiro to say to the Brazilian Government, that the Fiedler claim appears to be one well founded under the law of nations, and that it might perhaps be better for Brazil not to provoke the discussion and criticisms which are almost certain to follow the introduction of the case into the Congress of the United States, she might possibly come forward meanwhile and do justice in the matter, and thereby help to avoid and prevent everything so unseemly as bickering and wrangling in public assemblies. Earnestly, ardently do I hope for the result thus supposed possible. I have the honor to be,

Very respectfully, your obedient servant,
H. R. HELPER.

MR. HELPER TO SECRETARY EVARTS.

HOTEL DE LA AMERICA DEL SUR,
SANTIAGO, CHILI, *January* 19, 1878.
HON. WM. M. EVARTS, *Secretary of State, Washington.*

SIR: One or two more words at least do I desire to say, in the form of addenda, to the communication which I had the honor to address to you from Buenos Ayres, in the Argentine Republic, on the 18th ultimo, in relation to the claim of Ernest Fiedler, of New York, against the Government of Brazil. All the more am I surprised that Brazil has latterly, as formerly, treated the claimant and his attorney so unfairly in this matter, because, after more than eleven years of silent and special consideration, I have myself almost matured in mind an exceedingly important enterprise in her behalf, which I feel soberly confident will some day be worth to her, in spite of her present unworthiness, millions upon millions of dollars; an enterprise, indeed, which was inceptive with me long anterior to the time when I first heard of the name of Fiedler.

Reasonably proud of being the originator of this grand enterprise, and disposed, through mere enthusiasm and good will, to show Brazil that I was not one of the more ordinary sort of claimants, who have something to ask, but nothing to give, I proposed to present to her, without money and without price, on the simple condition of the immediate payment of the Fiedler claim, (which law and justice require her to pay anyhow,) a full written explanation of the scheme; only stipulating that, for its own sake, she should make no rumor nor publication of its nature until such time as I myself should be ready for general and public action in regard to it.

Not only, however, has Brazil manifested no desire whatever to do justice to my client, but she has meanwhile displayed an amazing amount of indifference toward my priceless project, which, as I calmly and conscientiously believe, is of incalculable importance to her future welfare. Singular as the circumstance may appear, and strange as may eventually be the turn or sequel in the affairs of a far-off nation, this unparalleled enterprise is yet of a kind that will probably not fail of fair appreciation before a Committee of enlightened American statesmen; and when I go (if I must go,) to the Senate Committee on Foreign Affairs at Washington, with my Fiedler claim against Brazil, I shall also take with me, and collaterally lay before that able and distinguished Committee, a full explanation of the feasible and invaluable project here alluded to ; so that they may, if they will honor me with their attention for an hour or so, become possessed of ample data for judging impartially of Brazil's ideas of justice toward citizens of the United States on the one hand, and of her capacity for wisdom affecting herself on the other. For any loss of respect, or other disadvantage, which, in this connection, Brazil may possibly suffer from an unbiased exposition of certain of her real and leading characteristics of demerit, no one but herself will be to blame.

In friendly conversation with Baron Cabo de Frio, one of Brazil's active and prominent statesmen, on this subject, he ventured the remark, in extenuation of his Government's inaction and apparent unconcern in the premises, that there was "no form nor precedent," for the guidance of the Empire in any case of this kind! It would seem, therefore, that certain established "forms" and "precedents," however antiquated and clumsy, are necessary conditions, conditions precedent, to the improvement of Empires. Though, so far as I am aware, none of the great discoveries, or helpful inventions, or wonderful works of utility, which have most largely advanced the interests of mankind, have ever yet been made by simple adherence to the common and ordinary proceedings of primitive and plodding people.

If, in the course of the further unfolding and advancemen of this enterprise, facts should be brought to light which will prove more conclusively than ever before, the existence of a greater oneness and nearness and sympathy and practicability between Republics and their citizens, than has ever been found existing between Empires and their subjects, and if, moreover, it shall be made to appear that the true principles of republican government, when wisely aad justly administered, are always and everywhere more pliable and favorable to the conditions of general development and progress, and to the realization of all new and worthy thoughts and purposes,—in that case even Brazil herself, measurably disenthralled and enlightened, and relieved from the dull routine and deadweight of monarchical preconceptions and practices, may erelong, it is hoped, also become a participant in the material enrichments and other great gains which such superior political knowledge will impart.

I have the honor to be, with great respect,
Your obedient servant.
H. R. HELPER.

ASSISTANT SECRETARY SEWARD TO MR. HELPER.

DEPARTMENT OF STATE,
WASHINGTON, *March* 8, 1878.
H. R. HELPER, *Esq., New York.*

SIR: Your letter of the 19th of January last, from Santiago, Chili, has been received and placed on file.

I am sir, your obedient servant,
F. W. SEWARD.

SECRETARY EVARTS TO MR. HELPER.

DEPARTMENT OF STATE,
WASHINGTON, *April* 13, 1878.

H. R. HELPER, *Esq., New York.*

SIR: Your letter from Buenos Ayres, on the 18th of December last, relative to the Fiedler claim, so-called, upon Brazil, has been received. In reply I have to inform you that another instruction upon the subject has been addressed to Mr. Hilliard, the Minister of the United States at Rio de Janeiro.

I am, sir, your obedient servant,
WILLIAM M. EVARTS.

MR. HELPER TO MINISTER HILLIARD.

NEW YORK, *November* 15, 1878.
HON. HENRY W. HILLIARD,
United States Minister to Brazil.

SIR: Since I last had the honor of hearing from you by letter, ill-health and other detrimental conditions have prevented me from paying prompt attention to my correspondence. Now, however, thanks to Heaven, I am rapidly convalescing, and am again ready for business. The inclosed printed pamphlet, on the subject of my Colton claim against the Governments of both Bolivia and Peru, will explain to you (if you will honor me by perusing it,) many of the reasons of my comparatively long silence in regard to my Fiedler claim against the Government of Brazil.

Among many papers awaiting me on my return from the West Coast of South America, I found one, in the form of a letter, from the Hon. William M. Evarts, Secretary of State;

of which letter, under date of the 13th of last April, the following transcript is a full and correct copy. * * * What I wish to know now, honorable sir, is whether the new instruction from Secretary Evarts, of which he makes mention in the foregoing letter, has yet produced, or is likely soon to produce, the desired effect on the Brazilian Government. Pray inform me at your earliest convenience; for if Brazil still maintains her attitude of indifference on the one hand, and of opposition on the other, to my client's just demands, the duty will erelong devolve on me of openly and strenuously seeking redress through the Congress of the United States. I feel confident that it will be best for Brazil not to provoke a fight on this question; but if fight I must, fight I will; and, being forced to it, I shall fight hard and persistently, and will never desist, while living, until the wrong of which I here complain shall have been righted.

I have the honor to be, very truly, your obedient servant,.

H. R. HELPER.

MR. HELPER TO SECRETARY EVARTS.

NEW YORK, *November* 27, 1878.
HON. WILLIAM M. EVARTS, *Secretary of State, Washington.*

SIR: Among much correspondence which had accumulated here for me, during my recent protracted sojourn in South America, I found myself honored, immediately after my return, with a letter from yourself, under date of April 13, 1878, wherein you kindly impart to me the following information: * * * Desiring to know what effect, if any, the new instruction mentioned above may have produced on the Brazilian Government, I beg leave to request of you the favor of sending to me, if you can do so compatibly with the

28

rules of your Department, a copy of Minister Hilliard's reply to your own dispatch. What I am particularly anxious to ascertain in this connection, is whether or not Brazil now manifests any disposition to act honorably and equitably toward my client, Mrs. Fiedler, whose just claim, of nearly eleven years' standing, against the Government of that country, still remains unsettled. It would be very gratifying to me to hear that the matter is in such shape,—if, in reality, it is in such shape,—as not to need or require any reference or appeal to the Congress of the United States.

I have the honor to be, most respectfully,
Your obedient servant,
H. R. HELPER.

ASSISTANT SECRETARY SEWARD TO MR. HELPER.

DEPARTMENT OF STATE,
WASHINGTON, *December 2*, 1878.

H. R. HELPER, *Esq., New York*.

SIR: Your letter of the 27th instant, relative to the Fiedler claim, so-called, on Brazil, has been received. In reply I have to state that Mr. Hilliard, the Minister of the United States at Rio de Janeiro, duly acknowledged the receipt of the new instruction upon the subject, which this Department in its letter to you, of the 13th of April last, said would be addressed to him. The subsequent dispatches received from him, however, do not appear to refer to the matter.

I am, sir, your obedient servant,
F. W. SEWARD.

MR. HELPER TO MINISTER HILLIARD.

NEW YORK, *December* 4, 1878.
HON. HENRY W. HILLIARD,
United States Minister to Brazil.
DEAR SIR: The two inclosed copies of letters, one from me to the Department of State at Washington, on the subject of the Fiedler claim against Brazil, and the other from the said Department of State in reply to me on the same subject, are each self-explanatory; and I respectfully request that you will be so kind as to favor me with the asked-for and desired information. Can it be possible that the Government of the real Empire of Brazil is no better than the Government of the so-called Republic of Bolivia? and will it eventually be necessary for me to pursue against the former the same severe course, in the Congress of the United States, which I was so repeatedly and profoundly provoked to pursue against the latter?
, Yours, most respectfully and truly,
H. R. HELPER.

MR. HELPER TO MR. PERSUHN.

ST. LOUIS, MO., *March* 4, 1879.
CHARLES P PERSUHN, *Esq., New York.*
DEAR SIR: On Saturday last I received from one of my friends at Rio de Janeiro, a letter, and also a marked copy of the *Jornal do Commercio*, of that city, under date of the 28th of January, of the present year, informing me of still another adverse decision by His Majesty Dom Pedro Segundo's Imperial Ministry, in the matter of the very just and very perspicuous claim of Mrs. Helen M. Fiedler, of New

York, against the Government of Brazil. From near the top of the second column of the second page of the semi-official newspaper mentioned above, I have clipped the particular item marked for my consideration; aud this item I herewith inclose to you, requesting that, after exhibiting it to Mrs. Fiedler and her children, you will be kind *enough to return it to me, or hold it subject to my order. The following is a free and fair translation into English of this new piece of Portuguese-American perverseness:

"CLAIM REJECTED."

" On the 21st instant the Minister of Agriculture answered the Minister of Foreign Affairs, in regard to the claim of the heirs of Ernest Fiedler, a citizen of the United States of America, for charter-service, not performed, of the steamship Circassian. The Minister of Agriculture sustains the declarations accompanying the advices of the 19th of December, 1874, and the 16th of January, 1875, by which that claim was then disallowed; not passing unobserved the significant, circumstance that the parties interested remained in absolute silence for three years after the last answer of the Imperial Government, which would seem to give evidence on their own part of their conviction of the ultimate failure of success in further prosecuting this claim."

The untruthfulness and the cool effrontery and injustice of this special Repbrt from the Brazilian Ministry,—in crafty keeping with their equally fallacious Report of the 26th of November, 1873,—are exceedingly barefaced and provoking; but I do not now, nor can I ever, accept, as a finality, their disingenuous action against my wronged and widowed client. Please assure Mrs. Fiedler that I shall continue to press the Brazilian Government for the recognition of her obvious rights and interests in this affair, and that so soon as official notification of this last Imperial and insolent verdict against her shall have come into my hands, I shall, in her behalf, institute proceedings on an entirely new and less deferential basis.

Yours, very truly,
H. R. HELPER.

MR. HELPER TO MR. JORDAN.

ST. LOUIS, Mo., *March* 4, 1879.
EDWARD JORDAN, *Esq.*, *New York*.

DEAR SIR: The unwelcome news which you will read in the following copy of a letter which I have just addressed to Mr. Persuhn, in New York, containing a translation of the substance of another unfavorable and unjust judgment recently pronounced at Rio de Janeiro, in the case of our client, Mrs. Fiedler, will again rightly arouse your contempt and indignation against the odious obliquity of Imperial Brazil. But the end is not yet. We must wait and work, and never allow ourselves to become weary in well-doing.

Yours truly,
H. R. HELPER.

MR. HELPER TO SECRETARY EVARTS.

ST. LOUIS, Mo, *April* 23, 1879.
HON. WILLIAM M. EVARTS, *Secretary of State, Washington*.

SIR: On the 27th of November last, while in the city of New York, I had the honor to request you to inform me what action, if any, the Brazilian authorities at Rio de Janerio had taken upon any issue or sequence of the new instruction which you informed me, in your letter of the 13th of April, 1878, had been given to Minister Hilliard on the subject of the Fiedler claim against the Government of Brazil; and on the 2d of December following, you replied, in substance, that, upon that particular subject, nothing had been heard from Minister Hilliard beyond the mere acknowledgment of his acceptance of the new instruction. Nearly five months having elapsed since the date of my last inquiry in regard to the condition of this claim at the capital of the Emperor Dom Pedro II, I would now thank you for information of any further proceedings which, meanwhile, may have been had there, in the case, and of which you yourself, as Secretary of State, may have been advised.

I have the honor to be, most respectfully,
Your obedient servant,
H. R. HELPER.

ASSISTANT SECRETARY HUNTER TO MR. HELPER

DEPARTMENT OF STATE,
WASHINGTON, *April* 30, 1879.

H. R. HELPER, *Esq., St. Louis, Missouri.*

SIR: I have to acknowledge the receipt of your letter of the 23d instant, and to say in reply, that a dispatch has just been received from the Chargé d' Affaires *ad interim*, of the United States in Brazil, announcing the rejection of the ,'' Fiedler claim," on the presentation made thereof by Mr. Hilliard.

I am, sir, your obedient servant,
W. HUNTER.

MR. HELPER TO SECRETARY EVARTS.

ST LOUIS, MISSOURI, *May* 22, 1879.
HON. WILLIAM M. EVARTS, *Secretary of State, Washington.*

SIR: Acknowledging with sincere thankfulness the full and prompt services which you have always rendered on request, in the matter of the Fiedler claim against Brazil,— a claim which Second Assistant Secretary Hunter, in a letter under date of the 30th ultimo, informs me the Government of that Empire has again rejected,—I have now the honor to suggest that there remains, as it seems to me, just one other little favor which you may, if you will, do me in this affair; and that is to send me a copy of the dispatch Mr. Partridge, the Minister of the United States at Rio de Janeiro, addressed to the Department over which you now preside, at the time he transmitted the elaborately and artfully adverse Report made to the Emperor Dom Pedro II, under date of November 26, 1873, by a committee of Brazilian notabilities, namely, the Marquis de Sapucahy, the Viscount de Souza Franco, the Viscount de Bom Retiro, and the Baron Cabo de Frio; who were, it seems, by direction of their sovereign, constituted into an Imperial Council of State for the express purpose of considering the circumstances and validity of this reclamation.

I do not know the date of Minister Partridge's dispatch, a copy of which is now desired, but suppose it was written in the month of December, 1873, or in January, February, or March, 1874. Just now I am busily occupied in making up the case, in regular order, for an appeal in the claimant's behalf to the Congress of the United States; and am of the opinion that a copy of the dispatch thus requested, if incorporated as a part of my memorial; would probably contribute, in some degree, to the ends of justice in this case.

I have the honor to be, most respectfully,
Your obedient servant,
H. R. HELPER.

MR. HELPER TO SECRETARY EVARTS.

St. Louis, Mo., *June* 10, 1879.
Hon. William M. Evarts, *Secretary of State, Washington*.

Sir: On the 22d ultimo I had the honor to write you a communication, requesting a copy of a dispatch which Minister Partridge, at Rio de Janeiro, addressed to the State Department, at Washington, late in 1873, or early in 1874, when he transmitted an elaborately adverse decision of the Brazilian Government against the Fiedler claim. Not having heard from you in reply, I fear my letter may not have reached you; or, possibly, you may not have deemed it perfectly proper to furnish me a copy of the desired dispatch. Be this as it may, I inclose herewith a transcript of my communication of the 22d ultimo; and trust that I may yet receive from you a copy of Mr. Partridge's dispatch, unless there be a good reason (to me unknown,) for withholding it.

I myself have never seen Mr. Partridge, nor have I ever had any correspondence with him on this particular subject; but when I was at Rio de Janeiro, on this business, in 1877, at a time when, to our national discredit, and to the disadvantage of individuals, we had, during a period of many months, no Minister nor open Legation there, I learned incidentally, but certainly, that Mr. Partridge, by whom, as Minister, all the facts of the claim had been well considered, had written a dispatch to Secretary Fish, transmitting Brazil's denial of justice in the case, but himself fully and strongly sustaining the rightfulness of the claimant's demand. As a matter of course, I, as the claimant's attorney, now busy in making up the case for the consideration and action of our Congress at Washington, should be very glad to obtain a copy of that dispatch; but, in the end, it may perhaps be as well for Mrs. Fiedler and myself to request a Committee of Congress to call for the document. What Minister

Partridge said on this subject,—he, by virtue of his familiarity with all the facts, having been well qualified to express an opinion as to both the law and the equity of the case,— was substantially what any other clear-headed and right-minded man would have said under the same or similar circumstances; and I had supposed it not improbable that his views, so formed and formulated, might facilitate other honest men herein and hereafter in arriving at corresponding conclusions of justice.

I have the honor to be, most respectfully,
Your obedient servant,
H. R. HELPER.

SECRETARY EVARTS TO MR. HELPER.

DEPARTMENT OF STATE,
WASHINGTON, *June* 18, 1879.

H. R. HELPER, *Esq., St. Louis, Missouri*.

SIR: Your letter of the 22d ultimo was duly received. I have caused an examination to be made of the records in the Fiedler claim against Brazil, with a view to ascertaining whether it would be practicable to depart from the long-established rule of the Department, which requires that copies of the diplomatic notes on file should not be communicated to private parties, except under special circumstances; but I do not perceive any sufficient reason to depart therefrom in your case to the extent of furnishing you with a copy of Mr. Partridge's dispatch communicating to the Depaitment the Report of the Brazilian Council of State, made under date of November 26, 1873.

Regretting my inability to favor you in this matter,
I am, sir, your obedient servant,
WILLIAM M. EVARTS.

MR. HELPER TO CHANCELLOR ELIOT.

St. Louis, *July* 11, 1879.
Dr. William G. Eliot,
Chancellor of Washington University,
St. Louis, Missouri.

Dear Sir: Whilst you and your able corps of coadjutors of Washington University and its associate institutions of learning are accomplishing so much in the development of the intellectual, ethic and artistic interests of this broad, blooming, busy, bright, and beautiful city, I, working in a less elevated sphere, have projected an enterprise which looks confidently to the unparalleled growth and grandeur of its material greatness. For the further nurturing and final consummation of this enterprise, however, the early and earnest coöperation with me of three gentlemen, who are more or less familiar with the best methods of constructing and managing railroads, is now desirable.

An almost total stranger in St. Louis, and having come here especially for the purpose of promoting and carrying out, so far as it may be possible for me to do so, the important scheme alluded to above, I take the liberty to request of you the names of three gentlemen, such as I have thus indicated the wish to meet; gentlemen only of integrity, foresight and energy, whose largeness of mind and liberality of views will enable them to judge fairly and act wisely in regard to a project of uncommon magnitude, which involves very strong probabilities of both private gain and public advantage; a project in the inception and furtherance of which I have already, as an individual, spent much time and labor and money, and am willing and prepared to spend more.

It is only the names, as requested, and not a letter of introduction, that I seek by this note; for I am quite disposed to rely exclusively on my business itself, when explained, to introduce me fitly to the three gentlemen with whose address you may be pleased to favor me, and whose character and qualifications will, I trust, prove worthy of your best thoughts and designation in this connection.

One who, like yourself, as a constant friend and assistant, has stood steadily and manfully by St. Louis during a period of forty-five years, seeing her, in the youth and flush and pride and pomp of her prospective aggrandizement, gradually yet rapidly increase, from a town of only five thousand inhabitants, to a metropolis with a population of more than half a million, and who is well acquainted with a large number of her estimable citizens in every honorable vocation, can, I dare say, easily give me the names of just three superior local railroad men; and by doing me personally the little service thus solicited, you will also, it is hoped and believed, be doing an additional service to the Empire City of the Mississippi Valley.

Yours, most respectfully,
H. R. HELPER.

CHANCELLOR ELIOT TO MR. HELPER.

WASHINGTON UNIVERSITY, ST. LOUIS, *July* 12, 1879.
H. R. HELPER, *Esq*.

DEAR SIR: In compliance with your request I give, in the inclosed list, the names of several gentlemen, who are, in every respect, well qualified to aid you in any enterprise undertaken for the public good. If needful, many others can be found; but I confidently hope that those now named will cheerfully consent to coöperate with you in your great work, and am sure that no better selection could possibly be made. Wishing to you and them all manner of success, and thanking you for the opportunity of rendering this service, I have the honor to remain, very respectfully, yours,

W. G. ELIOT.

MR. HELPER TO BANK PRESIDENT BURNHAM.

ST. LOUIS, *July* 18, 1879.

CYRUS B. BURNHAM, *Esq.*,
President of the Bank of Commerce, St. Louis, Mo.

DEAR SIR: Of the money which you now hold in deposit to my credit, I desire to place in the hands of a local committee of three gentlemen of sterling integrity and clear-headedness, an obligation for the sum of five thousand dollars, payable to their joint order, or to the order of their chairman, on the first day of December of next year, 1880, to be then expended by them in obtaining, severally, five of the best attainable essays in English, three in prose and two in poetry, in advocacy of the early construction of a longitudinal midland double-track steel railway through North and Central and South America, from a point on or near the western shore of Hudson Bay to such part of the northern bank of the Strait of Magellan, as may be measurably equidistant between the Atlantic and the Pacific Oceans.

To this end,—and I trust that the object is one which you and all eminently worthy and progressive Americans may be pleased to approve and promote,—I have to request that you will, to-day or to-morrow, issue to my order, payable, as already mentioned, on the first day of December of next year, 1880, a certificate of deposit, a note, or such other form of indebtedness binding on your admirably and excellently managed bank as you yourself may deem most

convenient and proper, and which it is my purpose to use only in the manner indicated above, as will soon be more minutely and elaborately explained in a printed volume, the manuscript of which will be ready for publication a few weeks hence. Yet, until the time of the actual forthcoming of the book from the press, I indulge the hope that you will so far befriend both the enterprise and its projector as to say nothing whatever on the subject, to any person whomsoever, excepting only, at your own option, to your discreet and estimable Cashier, Mr. Van Blarcom.
Yours, most respectfully,
H. R. HELPER.

BANK PRESIDENT BURNHAM TO MR. HELPER.

BANK OF COMMERCE, ST. LOUIS, *July* 19, 1879.
H. R. HELPER, *Esq*.
DEAR SIR: As requested in your letter of yesterday, I herewith inclose to your order a certificate of deposit in this bank for five thousand dollars, payable on the first day of December, 1880; which certificate can be used for the purpose and in the manner designed by you. The enterprise outlined in your letter is of such magnificent conception, and also of such grand proportions, that it cannot, when once your plans shall be made public, fail to attract the attention and critical examination of all thoughtful and practical Americans; and I trust that the feasibility of your projected improvements may be demonstrated by substantial completion within a reasonable period of time.
I am, very respectfully, yours,
C. B. BURNHAM.

MR. HELPER TO THREE ST. LOUISANS.

St. Louis, Missouri, *July* 25, 1879.
Hon. Thomas Allen,
Carlos S. Greeley, *Esq.*, and
Dr. William T. Harris.

Gentlemen: The occasion of my presuming to address to you this communication is what I have myself long regarded as a perfectly practicable enterprise, of unequalled magnitude and transcendent importance, to which, through your own able and honorable selves, as a committee o three men, I now desire to enlist at once the attention and active coöperation of the multitudinous peoples of three Americas. The object thus aimed at is nothing less than the earliest possible construction of a longitudinal midland double-track steel railway, from a point high north in North America, running more or less southwardly through Mexico and Central America, to a point far south in South America; looking ultimately to such necessary and gradual extensions at either end from time to time, as will eventually place Behring Strait and Cape Horn, and all the intermediate localities, in uninterrupted and continuous overland communication by steam and by telegraph.

My views on this subject will appear somewhat elaborately in a book, not wholly devoted to this scheme, however, which I intend to publish in the course of the next two or three months; and in order to prove conclusively my own earnestness and confidence in the matter, I herewith inclose a certificate of deposit for five thousand dollars in the Bank of Commerce of St. Louis, payable to your joint order, or to the order of any two of you, on the first day of December of next year, 1880; the said money to be then expended by you in obtaining five of the most convincing and meritorious essays which may be offered meanwhile, three in prose and two in poetry, in truthful and vigorous and effective advocacy of the undertaking.

Your particular names have been cordially and emphatically recommended as representing three gentlemen whose
unquestioned probity, public spirit, mental capacity, and
financial responsibility, are all that could be reasonably
wished or expected in such a council of safety and critical
judgment and award as I am now seeking, and I am therefore emboldened to express the sincere hope and request,
that you may all be pleased to give your consent to act together as a potent and permanent committee in this connection. Should you all consent accordingly, please consider
yourselves as at once constituted into such a committee, for
the purpose specifically mentioned above, and retaining to
yourselves the certificate of deposit, already indorsed to your
order, advise me of your acceptance of the trust, and also
of your readiness to receive and adjudge whatever manuscripts may be submitted for your perusal and approbation.
Also be kind enough to designate immediately one of yourselves as the chairman of your committee, giving his exact
postal address, and stating that all essays and communications bearing upon this project, and being prepaid, should
be sent to him by express or by mail, wholly at the expense
and risk of the sender.

For the proper information and guidance of all concerned, I propose to publish, as an essential part of my book
itself, so far as it treats of The Three Americas Intercontinental Railway, both this communication and your reply, in
orderly juxtaposition. In making the certificate of deposit
payable to your joint order, or to the order of any two of
you, I have very plainly indicated my wish that, in the absence, at any time, from whatever cause, of any one of you,
the other two shall constitute a competent and legal quorum
whose proceedings shall be as absolutely valid and final as if
all three of you had acted in concert; and whether any one
of your committee shall ever be absent or not, when the

other two shall meet, it is my sense of right and propriety that the expressed opinions and predilections of the majority of two out of three shall always be recognized as the governing voice, and govern accordingly. I trust, however, that the peerless enterprise itself may never suffer for the lack of the triple wisdom and power which all three of you, acting harmoniously together, will be able to bring to it in any particular situation or contingency.

It is my desire, and I make it a condition accordingly, that all the writings, of whatever nature, without a single exception, which may be offered for prizes in this literary and patriotic contest, shall be conveyed into your hands not later than the first day of October of next year, 1880; and you may now, if you like, completely release yourselves in advance from the labor of examining any composition, under any circumstances, which may reach you after that date. Two months subsequently, that is to say, on the first day of December following, you will please make publication of the names of the successful competitors, and on that very same day, or just as soon thereafter as you may find it convenient to do so, you will please pay them, by means of certified checks on the Bank of Commerce of this city, in sums respectively, without interest, as follows:

For the first best treatise in prose,	$1,300
" second " " "	1,200
" third " " "	1,000
" first best effort in poetry,	1,000
" next " "	500
Total,	$5,000

Other conditions which I make absolutely, and to which I would here respectfully and especially invite the attention of all the competitors for any one of the proffered prizes, are these: No essay in prose must contain more than one hundred pages of closely-written cap-paper, nor less than sixty-six; and neither of the two poems provided for must contain more than five hundred lines, nor less than three hundred and thirty-three. All the writings in the hands of your committee, to whose authors prizes shall be awarded, are at once to become the sole and exclusive property of myself individually, and will be immediately published altogether in one volume, with any such additions, abridgments, or emendations, as I myself may deem it prudent to make. All essays which fail to receive prizes may be reclaimed by their respective authors on transmitting to the chairman of your committee the small amount of money that will defray the usual expenses of expressage or postage. It might be best for the various competitors respectively, to do this at the very time of submitting their writings for the examination and adjudgment of your committee. This is a point which they themselves will settle, each for himself, at his own option. Every author should keep a press copy, or other copy, of his composition; and such extra copy may, at any time, be demanded by your committee.

The several prizes thus offered, may be striven for and achieved by emulous citizens anywhere resident within the universal Republic of Letters, which, like one of the grandest and most precious parts that compose it, the Republic of the United States of America, is, in all things, characterized by fairness and justice and liberality. It is only required that all the papers which may be submitted for examination and award, shall be so written or translated as to appear legibly in the English language.

Doubting not that your committee will be honored with many very interesting and valuable contributions in competition, neither do I permit myself to doubt in the least that you will constantly exercise such diligence and discretion as will result in the strictest and fullest justice, alike to the special object in view, and to the various contestants for prizes. It may be well supposed that the writers who will succeed in winning both reputation and remuneration in this respect, are probably those who will detach themselves most completely from every species of flippancy and frivolity, from everything like superficiality and insincerity, and dive down deep into irrefragable and imperishable facts and arguments, and who will then, on the one hand at least, on the side of poesy, elevate themselves to the loftiest heights of sublime ideas and ennobling sentiments and expressions, whereby they may rightfully and triumphantly captivate the head, fascinate the heart, and enrapture the soul.

It is hoped that such an intense earnestness and enthusiasm may be awakened throughout all the countries from Alaska to Patagonia, inclusive, as will lead to the granting of all the requisite governmental guarantees and privileges and charters, by or before the 14th of October, 1882; so that the vast enterprise may be actually begun not later than that day; and that at least one hundred and fifty thousand strong-armed and cheerful-hearted laborers may soon afterward be given work on the various sections of the line, and, by fair wages and just treatment, induced to continue their wealth-creating and civilizing exertions, without any unusual interruption, until the whole undertaking, in its longest and broadest and best conceptions, shall be substantially and gloriously finished for all future ages. Seven years at most ought to suffice for the completion of this grandest and best of all the grand and good highways of the New World. The lapse of that period will find us facing the 14th of October, 1889. Three years later will take us to the four hundredth anniversary of the discovery of America. Let us be prepared to mark and honor that anniversary, — a veritable index to one of the most conspicuous and momentous epochs in human affairs, — let us welcome and signalize that superlative anniversary in St. Louis, by holding here, at that time, the largest and most splendid and imposing World's Fair that has ever been held on the earth; an exhibition at which shall be especially and fully represented the people, the products, the fauna, the flora, and the minerals, of every American nation between the Arctic and Antarctic seas and the Atlantic and Pacific oceans.

That St. Louis, already the largest and most prosperous and progressive city in the great Valley of the Mississippi, the very heart and center of the continent of North America, for railroading and steamboating, and for travel and trade and manufactures and business of almost every kind, and probably destined, within the next hundred years, to outnumber in inhabitants the combined populations of New York and Philadelphia, — that this wonderfully thrifty and expanding metropolis, so unmistakably betokening for itself a surpassing and transcendent future, is now, and will continue to be, the fittest possible place for such a matchlessly magnificent exhibition as I have here suggested, may be further and more fully inferred from the following pointed opinions expressed, on different occasions, by half a dozen uncommonly foreseeing and discerning men of great national renown. Nor, in the light of the astonishing acquisitions and tendencies of to-day, is it at all unreasonable to believe that the year 1979, will find St. Louis a far more numerously inhabited city than either London or Paris, if, indeed, it shall not then, or soon afterward, be even more populous and thrifty and progressive than both of those leading European capitals considered as one.

On the 4th of February, 1870, my old friend Horace Greeley, one of the ablest and truest and best men I have ever known, writing from the office of his *Tribune,* in New York, to L. U. Reavis, Esq., at St. Louis, said:—"I have twice seen St. Louis in the middle of winter. Nature made her the focus of a vast region, embodying a vast area of the most fertile soil on the globe. Man will soon accomplish her destiny by rendering her the seat of an immense industry, the home of a far-reaching, ever-expanding commerce. Her gait is not so rapid as that of some of her Western sisters; but she advances steadily and surely to her predestined station of first inland city on the globe."

In the course of a letter written at Boston, under date of July 24, 1863, and addressed to Dr. William G. Eliot, Chancellor of Washington University in St. Louis, Edward Everett, whose name is eminently worthy to be held in love and veneration by every American citizen, said:—" The future is, of course, veiled in darkness; but when I consider your central position and your means of communication in every direction, nothing seems to me more probable than that, by the end of this century, St. Louis will be the metropolis of the Union."

Replying, under date of July 16, 1875, to a letter from L. U. Reavis, Esq.,—himself an indefatigable and excellent worker in the interest of a great and growing city, a gentleman with whom I regret that I have not yet had an opportunity to become acquainted,—Gen. William T. Sherman said: "I have every faith in the future of St Louis, and have in fact shown my sincerity by making it my home, and the future home of my family."

Charles Sumner, to whom the vigorous and unlimited growth of the West was always a matter of wonder and admiration, wrote as follows:—" St. Louis alone would be an all-sufficient theme; for who can doubt that this prosperous metropolis is destined to be one of the mighty centers of our mighty Republic?"

In his usual frank and glowing style, James Parton, the distinguished author, speaks thus:—" Fair St. Louis, the future Capital of the United States, and of the civilization of the Western Continent."

While delivering a speech in St. Louis, a few years since, Gen. Benjamin F. Butler said: * * * "I also remember that.I am now in the city of St. Louis, destined erelong to be the great city on the continent; the greatest central point between the East and the West, at once destined to be the entrepot and depot of all the internal commerce of the greatest and most prosperous country the world has ever seen. * * * The next quarter of a century shall see a larger population west of the Mississippi than the last quarter of a century saw east of the Mississippi; and the city of St. Louis, from its central location, and through the vigor, the energy, the industry and the enterprise of its inhabitants, shall become the very first city of the United States of America, now and hereafter destined to be the great republican nation of the world." *

Not one of the foregoing opinions, — four of which, significantly enough, are from far-sighted and far-famed New Englanders, — had ever come to my knowledge prior to my arrival in St. Louis, for the first time, only a few months since. My attraction to the city was solely by its geographical position. A mere glance at the map was sufficient to convince me that it was the most central and convenient point in the United States from which I could operate, under a combination of really propitious circumstances, in the

* On the 12th of September, 1879, while briefly sojourning at the Planters' House in St. Louis, on his way to Lawrence, Kansas, there to deliver an address on the occasion of the Twenty-fifth Anniversary of the Old Settlers' Celebration of the Founding of the State, the veteran Pennsylvania journalist, John W. Forney, proprietor of the Philadelphia *Progress*, in the course of an interview with a reporter of the St. Louis *Globe-Democrat*, said: "I look with amazement upon the growth and prosperity of this immense capital, and am overwhelmed by the hospitality of my old friends."

initiation and furtherance of my gigantic scheme. For a very brief period the city of Mexico, as a sort of imperfectly-discerned yet friendly rival to St. Louis, laid passable claims to my attention in this regard; but the instability of the government of the Mexican Republic, and the comparatively inadequate resources, in both men and means, there existing for the organization of ample physical and financial forces for the prosecution and accomplishment of any great civil or secular undertaking, induced me, with scarcely one serious thought to the contrary, to give St. Louis the preference. Yet, if the unrivalled intercontinental railway here proposed, . shall be built according to the general plans and specifications outlined in my book, it may be conceded as certain that the city of Mexico, and the whole Republic of Mexico, as also all the chief cities and republics through which the road will pass, will, with peace and good government firmly established and maintained among them, soon assume proportions of population, prosperity and progress hitherto but barely contemplated even by their most sanguine supporters.

Well constructed and wisely managed, and fully protected by national and international compacts, from the dangers of undue interference by revolutionary factions, this road of roads, this great northern and southern backbone, from which eastern and western ribs will eventually radiate by scores and by hundreds, conveying an exuberance of new life and energy and hope and blessing to tens of millions of happy human beings, ought, in time, to be worth at least three thousand millions of dollars to North America, the same amount to South America, and fifteen hundred millions, more or less, to Mexico and Central America. Of these vast valuations and earnings, St. Louis and other portions of Missouri ought to be the recipients, from first to last, of one hundred millions or more; but these mere pecuniary estimates are meditative of only a material part of the advantages which may be fairly expected to flow from the colossal enterprise after it shall have been perfected. Every intellectual, moral, social, civil, political and industrial interest of mankind will be advanced; and, as an inevitable and delightful result of the æsthetic culture which will prevail, the most simple and unaffected amenities, elegancies, refinements and purities of life will everywhere increase and abound.

Such, gentlemen, are some of the herculean, yet wholesome and pleasurable, tasks to the completion of which your valuable services are now craved and solicited. Whether, by the methods here mentioned, it is in your power to contribute in any degree to the general well-being of St. Louis, of Missouri, of the United States, and of the three Americas at large, I must now leave entirely to your own judgment and decision; only yet stopping long enough to repeat once more my respectful request, that you, all three of you, will kindly consent to use and expend the five thousand dollars herewith inclosed, in the manner explained above. Though you and I may plant and sow, and others, reaping the harvests with gladness and hilarity, may enjoy the fruits of our labors, yet who knows but that, in this very way, certain of our special duties may be best performed? Next will come an opportunity for the beneficiaries themselves, or for one or more of them, if so disposed, to do something of the kind, something of far greater importance, perhaps; and by constant and judicious action upon the principle thus recognized, our world, in the very nature of things,—a world in itself not half so bad as many pessimists proclaim it,—can never cease to grow brighter and better and more felicitously inhabitable for all diligent and right-doing people.

I am, gentlemen, with sincere regard,
    Yours, very truly,
      H. R. HELPER.

Before bringing this volume to a final termination, I cannot refrain from expressing my perfect satisfaction at finding myself the subject of such unbounded respect and confidence on the part of the three able and distinguished gentlemen who have so fully and frankly consented to act as a Committee to further the foregoing plan for constructing, within the next ten years, a vast New World Longitudinal Railway. Already the question is beginning to present itself to me, whether the enterprise may not soon come to be much more indebted to its Committee, than to its projector, for its successful commencement and consummation. Yet this particularly pleasing impression is only coincident and concordant with the remembrance of the fact that the Chairman of the Committee is very generally and justly recognized as the father of the railroad system of Missouri, and the foremost railway monitor of the Mississippi valley.

Nor is it alone in their confiding and unconditional acceptance of the proffered commission, that these eminently competent and estimable gentlemen have so highly honored me. Although they were plainly informed, nearly three months ago, that my publication, the work in hand, would not occupy itself exclusively with an elucidation of the stupendous international and intercontinental highway here proposed, yet not one of them has ever been so presuming or inquisitive as to ask me the nature of any of the collateral contents of the book. This evidence of their absolute freedom from the spirit of intolerance, shows very clearly their delicate and refined sense of the sacredness of individual rights and private judgment, and also their sublime regard for the inviolability of liberty in literature.

Only to the railway scheme itself are they in any manner compromised; and, as a matter of course, they will always be quite as free as any one else to criticise and condemn any portion of my book, which may not commend itself to their approbation. So also with Ex-Secretary Fish and Secretary Evarts, Senators Hamlin and Howe, Representatives Cox and Myers, Ministers Hilliard and Osborn, and many other' gentlemen, in office and out of office, whose names and communications will be found herein. No one of them individually is in the least responsible for anything for which he himself does not assume responsibility; and precisely so with the excellent Three Americas Railway Committee. Severally and jointly have the members of that Committee agreed and promised to promote the enterprise to the extent specifically stated by them in their own letter. To nothing else have they agreed; upon nothing else have they been consulted; and for nothing else herein (except by their own pleasure and permission,) are they to be held to any account whatever. That they will faithfully and efficiently perform the special labors which they have thus politely and patriotically taken upon themselves, no one will be justified in entertaining the remotest misgiving; they all being fine models, physically, mentally, and morally, of that pure type of Anglo-American stock, whose keen-visioned optics are gifted with the fortunate faculty of always being able to perceive something better in the future than anything that ever existed in the past; and whose rigid fidelity to all honorable engagements is to them, as it should be to everybody, a religion of the sweetest consolation.

H. R. H.

St. Louis, *October* 14, 1879.

DR. HARRIS TO MR. HELPER.

St. Louis, *July* 28, 1879.

H. R. Helper, *Esq*.

Dear Sir: I have the honor to acknowledge the receipt

of your communication, under date of the 25th instant, in which you invite me to serve as one of a committee of three appointed to award five liberal prizes offered by you for a corresponding number of the best essays on the subject of constructing an International Railway connecting North and South America, and extending from this country to the southern extremity of the continent.

I take pleasure in accepting the trust offered me, not, however, from any peculiar sense of fitness for the work, but because of the fact that I recognize the importance of the undertaking, and have full confidence in your ability to arouse public attention to the great issue now before the people of this Republic; namely, to prepare for the great wave of migration now gathering strength, which must spread out laterally to the North and South, after it has peopled our own wilderness to the West. Hitherto we have had sufficient room for expansion, without approaching the borders of other nations. The special function of America, in the history of civilization, seems to make it the theatre for the recomposition of European society, and the means of safety from revolutions occasioned by changes of vocation rendered necessary by the constant invention of labor-saving machinery. Our new territories are therefore a matter of great interest to the thickly-settled Eastern sections of this country; but, at the same time, they are of far more interest to the stability and progress of European nations. The periodic waves of migration from Europe, will necessarily increase in size. Closer commercial relations not only follow in the wake of migration, but must, to some extent, precede it, so as to mark out its path and render it possible. In all this, the Railroad is the most important instrumentality. It permits migration to carry with it and preserve the traditions of metropolitan or urban life, when out on the frontier, and thus prevents too abrupt transitions from the old to the new.

I look upon your enterprise as well-timed and of central importance to society, whether commercially or philanthropically regarded.

Yours respectfully,
WM. T. HARRIS.

THREE ST. LOUISANS TO MR. HELPER.

ST. LOUIS, Mo., *September* 25, 1879.
H. R. HELPER, *Esq.*

DEAR SIR: Having returned to St. Louis, from our respective summer resorts, we have the pleasure to acknowledge receipt of your communication of the 25th of July, inclosing to our joint order, or to the order of any two of us, a certificate of deposit for five thousand dollars in the Bank of Commerce, of this city, payable on the first day of December of next year, and which you request us to expend, in a manner minutely explained by you, for the purpose of procuring five persuasive and convincing essays in advocacy of the early construction of a double-track longitudinal steel railway through North and Central and South America.

You have further paid us the compliment of nominating us a Three Americas Railway Committee, with full powers, to the end proposed, and have requested us to name one of ourselves as the Chairman of our Committee, to whom all competitive manuscripts may be sent for perusal and adjudgment.

We have maturely considered the substantial and business-like contents and bearing of your communication; and, holding in view the gigantic and important objects sought to be accomplished, we scarcely feel ourselves at liberty to refuse to perform the service which you have so politely requested us to render in this connection; and we, therefore, in behalf of the grand enterprise itself, unreservedly accept the commission which you have given us; and hoping thereby to be able to contribute to the general good and advancement of our own and the adjoining continent, we shall cheerfully and gratuitously perform all the duties, as we understand them, which this acceptance implies. All writings which may be submitted to us, in competition for prizes, as provided for by you, should be prepaid, by mail, or by express, and addressed to our Chairman, as follows:

HON. THOMAS ALLEN,
President of the Iron Mountain and Southern Railway,
No. 1 North Fifth Street,
St. Louis,
Missouri.

It now only remains for us to give expression to our ardent hopes, braced by a high degree of confidence, that your dearest aims and expectations in this regard may be realized, in all their magnitude and grandeur, within the time specifically mentioned by you; namely, the 14th of October, 1892, which, as you yourself have reminded us, will be the four hundredth anniversary of the discovery of America.

Yours, very respectfully,
WM. T. HARRIS,
CARLOS S. GREELEY,
THOMAS ALLEN.

THE END.

INDEX TO NAMES AND SUBJECTS.

Acceptances, the Laws of, 217.
Account against Bolivia, 212.
Acha, Jose Maria de, 37.
Act of Congress against Bolivia, 154, 160.
Affidavits of Ellis and Persuhn, 363, 366.
Africa and the Africans, 291-315.
Albuquerque, D. V. C. de, 386, 391, 397, 398, 402, 404, 418.
Albuquerque, H. C. de, 359.
Allen, Thomas, 462, 476.
Aranjo, Secretary, 379, 380.
Barinaga, Manuel Antonio, 250, 256.
Baron Cabo de Frio, 396, 397, 400.
Barros, B. Torreao de, 372.
Bell, Walton P., 91.
Benavente, Juan de Cruz, 236.
Blow, Henry T., 361, 362, 363.
Blyth, Henry A., 116.
Bocayuva, Quintino de Souza, 359, 434.
Bolivia's Indebtedness to Mr. Colton, 21-271.
Bolivia's Secretary of State, 67, 81, 108.
Bolivia, Protest against, 204-271.
Borges, Antonio Pedro de Carvalho, 370, 371.
Brazil's Delinquencies in the Fiedler Claim, 334-476.
Brown, J. Douglas, 366.
Brown, Sevellon A., 160.
Burnham, Cyrus B., 460, 461.
Butler, Benjamin F., 469.
Cadwalader, John L., 167, 173, 176, 185.
Cahill, John F., 324, 328.
Caldwell, John W., 84, 92.
Cameron, Simon, 106, 125, 144, 148, 151, 152, 162.
Campero, Narciso, 102.
Canal, Ship, across Central America, 319-333.
Cartter, David K., 84, 123.
Certificate of Vice-Consul Cordeiro, 434.
Charter-Party of the "Circassian," 357.

Church, George Earl, 165, 166.
Circassian, the Steamer, 357.
Clayton, Robert T., 212.
Colton, Joseph H., 20, 23, 26, 29, 50, 58, 72, 80, 90, 100, 145, 154, 160, 168, 180, 182, 201, 202, 264, 266, 267, 271.
Committee on Foreign Affairs, Senate, 123, 154.
Committee, Three Americas Railway, 462, 475, 476.
Congressional Action in favor of Mr. Colton, 154, 160.
Conkling, Roscoe, 145.
Cordeiro, Francis M., 434, 435.
Corral, Casimiro, 34, 38, 44, 54, 65, 74, 157.
Cox, Samuel S., 315, 318.
Croxton, John T., 65, 75, 84, 103, 113.
Crump, Arthur, 217.
Curtis, George Ticknor, 129.
Dakar and Dakar's Negroes, 291–315.
Darien, Isthmus of, and other Isthmuses, 319–333.
Davidson, James Wood, 108.
Decree of the Bolivian Government, 49, 155.
Dom Pedro II, Emperor, 375, 413, 419.
Draft from Bolivia on Peru, 241.
Eads, James B., 326.
Eliot, Wm. G., 458, 459.
Ellis, Thomas S., 363.
Emperor Dom Pedro II, 375, 413, 419.
Evarts, William M., 128, 198, 201, 220. 229, 231, 234, 262, 263, 290, 382, 386, 399, 407, 411, 441, 445, 448, 449, 455, 456, 457.
Everett, Edward, 468.
Fiedler, Ernest, against Brazil, 334–476.
Field, David Dudley, 132.
Field, Dudley, 117.
Fish, Hamilton, 34, 76, 95, 97, 99, 102, 104, 105, 111, 125, 149, 162, 166, 172, 177, 179, 182, 184, 185, 186, 188, 190, 191.
Fleury, Louis Augustus de Podua, 360.
Flores, Zoilo, 224, 236.
Forney, John W., 469.
Frelinghuysen, Frederick T., 164.
Frias, Tomas, 73, 79, 80, 168, 171.
Frio, Baron Cabo de, 396, 397, 400.
Frisbie, Oscar, 120.
Gibbs, Richard, 178, 219, 260.
Goicouria, Domingo de, 359, 360, 434.

Governments, Obligations of, 135–143.
Greeley, Carlos S., 462, 476.
Greeley, Horace, 467.
Grotius, Hugo, 135.
Hale, Charles, 94, 96.
Hall, Allen A., 84, 92.
Halleck, Henry W., 143.
Hamlin, Hannibal, 146, 153, 269, 270.
Harris, William T., 462, 473, 476.
Hilliard, Henry W., 427, 430, 431, 432, 433, 435, 437, 448, 451.
Howe, Timothy O., 152, 153.
Hunter, William, 291, 454.
Intervention by Congress in Mr. Colton's behalf, 154, 160.
Izabel, the Princess, 382, 397.
Jackson, Andrew, 141.
Jordan, Edward, 342, 343, 374, 381, 389, 411, 453.
Judges of the Supreme Court of Peru, 232, 235.
Kent, James, 139.
Lanfranco, Joaquin P., 228.
Lawrence, William Beach, 141.
Lieber, Francis, 319, 321.
Markbreit, Leopold, 48, 50, 53, 54, 55, 58, 59, 61, 64, 84, 114.
Marshall, John, 138, 217.
Memorials to Congress, 21, 29, 80, 240, 270, 337.
Merrimon, Augustus S., 147, 150, 291, 292.
Miscellaneous Oddments, 274–333.
Morales, Augustin, 50, 386.
Mujia, Juan Mariano, 39, 40.
Myers, Leonard, 101.
Naval Stores and Extravagancies Abroad, 286–290.
Newcomb, Charles S., 122.
Obligations of Governments. 135–143.
Oblitas, J., 195, 196, 242.
Olmsted, Frederick Law, 117.
Ona, Jose Felix, 40.
Ondarza, Juan, 40, 44.
Onderdonk, H. G., 118.
Osborn, Thomas A., 203.
Oviedo, Chief-Justice, 235.
Palacios, Fernando, 239.
Parsons, Theophilus, 218.
Parton, James, 468.

Partridge, James R., 372, 373.
Penafil, Manuel, 242.
Persuhn, Charles P., 366, 451.
Peruvian Delinquencies, 204–271.
Phillimore, Robert Joseph, 136.
Poem on the Ship Canal, by Dr. Lieber, 321.
Prevost & Co., of Lima, 182, 189, 192, 193, 243.
Protest against Peru and Bolivia, 204.
Puffendorf, Samuel, 135.
Quinones, Jose, 242.
Railway, The Three Americas Longitudinal, 9-20, 378-476.
Receipt given to the Bolivian Government, 170, 171.
Request, A Brother's, 440.
Reynolds, Robert M., 161, 168, 170, 174, 177, 194, 195, 242, 263.
Rospigliosi, J. C. Julio, 223.
Ruger Brothers, 359.
Senate Committee on Foreign Affairs, 80, 123, 154, 438.
Settlement (?) of the Colton Claim, 49, 168.
Seward, Frederick W., 194, 410, 447, 450.
Seward, William H., 141.
Sherman, William T., 468.
Ship Canal across Central America, 319-333.
Smith, John Cotton, 84, 119.
South America, 9-20.
St. Louis, Present and Future, 467-470.
St. Louisans, Three, 462, 475.
Sumner, Charles, 468.
Supreme Court of Peru, 232, 235.
Tehuantepec, Isthmus of, 324, 333.
Terraza, Melchor, 78.
Three Americas Longitudinal Railway, 9-20, 378-476.
Thompson, Frank, 369.
Thompson, Richard W., 278, 286.
Trade with Spanish America, 278-285.
Upton, Benjamin, 396.
Vargas, Lorenzo, 44.
Vattel, Emmerich, 136.
Wheaton, Henry, 141.
White, Julius, 275.
Wildman, Richard, 137.
Woolsey, Theodore D., 126, 142.

www.ingramcontent.com/pod-product-compliance
Lightning Source LLC
Chambersburg PA
CBHW051854300426
44117CB00006B/392